indexes
of the
doorway papers

Ah! Just the reference
I needed . . .
          yesterday, alas!

VOLUME X: The Doorway Papers

indexes
of the
doorway papers

ARTHUR C. CUSTANCE

Academie
Books Grand Rapids,
Michigan
Zondervan Publishing House

INDEXES
The Doorway Papers, Volume Ten

ACADEMIE BOOKS are published by Zondervan
Publishing House, 1415 Lake Drive, S.E.,
Grand Rapids, Michigan 49506

Library of Congress Cataloging in Publication Data (Revised)

Custance, Arthur C.
    The doorway papers.

   Includes bibliographical references.
    CONTENTS: v. 1. Noah's three sons.–v. 2. Genesis and early man.–[etc.]–v. 10. Indexes.
    1. Bible–Theology–Collected works. I. Title.
BS543.A1C87   230   75-311880
ISBN 0-310-38651-9

Contents

Acknowledgments

Preface

Serial Listing of the Doorway Papers 11

Alphabetical Listing of the Doorway Papers 15

Diagrams, Figures, Maps, and Tables 19

Brief Bibliographies of Special Interest 21

Subject Index 25

Index of Names 185

Scripture Index 223

Index to Hebrew and Greek Words 251

Acknowledgments

Friends helped us substantially with the work of preparing these Indexes.

Mrs. Greta Vandenbelt, who for a number of months set aside a regular weekly period, ordered and arranged the biblical references pulled together from the nine volumes in which they occur. Mrs. Ruth Lochrie undertook, in a busy life, the typing of the whole of the Names and Scripture Indexes. It is no fun typing numbers by the thousands!

Throughout the whole process, which in terms of total effort occupied months on end, Evelyn M. White as usual sustained a wonderful enthusiasm in seeing the Indexes through to the end.

To these people I would like to say, Thank you, indeed.

Preface

ANYONE WHO undertakes to prepare an Index of Subjects, Names, etc., for a work of some complexity and size, whether the work is his own or someone else's, is giving a kind of testimony. He thereby declares, by his very selectivity, his own particular interests and disinterests. He underscores his own priorities by the amount of space allocated to certain subjects. He reveals his own prejudices by what he fails to list. And he marks out the range of his own ignorance. Thus each individual will make a different index of the same work, placing the same subject matters under headings which may well puzzle other readers.

A Subject Index of data, of things, of discoveries or inventions, of techniques or artifacts, is usually rather straightforward and unequivocal. It is the indexing of ideas that really taxes one's powers of discrimination and involves one in a very exhausting decision-making process. To do this for the Doorway Papers was about the most tiresome work my secretary and I have ever undertaken. . . .

How does one catalogue an idea? We tried to ask ourselves the question: Under what headings is it likely that we or anyone else would look in order to find the page and volume in which the particular idea is explored? And most of the time it seemed necessary to use four or five alternative headings. The result was what seemed to us a substantial element of repetition. This is likely to be a source of annoyance to the user who happens not to be interested in this particular idea. But what can one do?

We have to comfort ourselves with the fact that anyone seriously looking for some particular piece of information has a pretty good idea of what he is after. As a result, he will presumably search on "either side," as it were, of the precise information he is looking for, hoping thus to spot relevant cues that will lead to the subject obliquely.

It will now and then seem that a very important subject has barely been mentioned. The reason is, usually, that the subject is important enough to have a whole part of one of the volumes devoted to it—the Medieval World View, for example. All one then needs is to know where the treatment of it begins, and this can often be done by a single reference.

When it is considered that the whole series involved nearly three thousand pages of text in the nine volumes (of which this Index forms the tenth), a total of one and a half million words of researched and documented material, and that this material required approximately forty thousand entries in the Index, then the possibilities of error will be seen to be enormous!

But we have, with the help of friends, checked as far as possible every single reference back to its original source. One may therefore have reasonable confidence in the dependability of the Index—though there are bound to be some errors!

We began this series of studies over thirty-five years ago, and as far as possible it has been updated continuously ever since, until the time that the copy had to be surrendered to the publisher. For all its inevitable weaknesses and shortcomings, it is at least a unified "world view," being the attempt of a single individual to draw together into a kind of organic unity with the Christian faith the results of research in many of the major areas of knowledge at the present time.

With this word of explanation, we commit our labors to the Lord who in His own wonderful way made possible so much of the material involved.

—ARTHUR C. CUSTANCE
"The Terraces"
Butternut Bay Service Road
Brockville, Ontario
Canada

Serial Listing
of the Doorway Papers

Volume I NOAH'S THREE SONS
Part
Page
I   The Part Played by Shem, Ham, and Japheth
        in Subsequent World History 15
II   A Study of the Names in Genesis 10 52
III   Why Noah Cursed Canaan Instead of Ham: A New
        Approach to an Old Problem 142
IV   The Technology of Hamitic People 154
V   A Christian World View: The Framework of History   218

Volume II GENESIS AND EARLY MAN
I   Fossil Remains of Early Man and the Record
        of Genesis 12
II   Primitive Cultures: A Second Look at the Problem
        of their Historical Origin 60
III   Establishing a Paleolithic I.Q. 144
IV   The Supposed Evolution of the Human Skull 194
V   The Fallacy of Anthropological Reconstructions 226
VI   Who Taught Adam to Speak? 250
VII   Light From Other Forms of Cultural Behavior
        on Some Incidents in Scripture 274

Volume III MAN IN ADAM AND IN CHRIST

I	The Fall Was Down	10
II	Nature as Part of the Kingdom of God	52
III	The Terms "Image" and "Likeness" as Used in Genesis 1:26	100
IV	The Development of Personality: The Old and the New	136
V	The Place of Handicaps in Human Achievement	196
VI	The Subconscious and Forgiveness of Sins	238
VII	The Compelling Logic of the Plan of Salvation: A Study of the Difference Between "Sin" and "Sins"	284
VIII	The Two Species of Homo Sapiens	316

Volume IV EVOLUTION OR CREATION?

I	The Preparation of the Earth for Man	13
II	Primitive Monotheism and the Origin of Polytheism	110
III	Convergence and the Origin of Man	140
IV	The Survival of the Unfit	172
V	Is Man an Animal?	208

Volume V THE VIRGIN BIRTH AND THE INCARNATION

I	Longevity in Antiquity and Its Bearing on Chronology	12
II	The Nature of the Forbidden Fruit	76
III	If Adam Had Not Died	116
IV	The Virgin Birth and the Incarnation	172
V	The Trinity in the Old Testament	216
VI	A Fresh Look at the Meaning of the Word "Soul"	260
VII	How Did Jesus Die?	294
VIII	The Resurrection of Jesus Christ	334
IX	The Unique Relationship Between the First and the Last Adam	368

Volume VI TIME AND ETERNITY
and Other Biblical Studies

I   Time and Eternity: Creation and the Theory
of Relativity 10
II   Three Trees and Israel's History 52
III   Between the Lines: An Analysis of Genesis 1:1, 2 77
IV   The Omnipotence of God in the Affairs of Men 121
V   The Confusion of Languages 176
VI   Cain's Wife and the Penalty of Incest 220

Volume VII HIDDEN THINGS
OF GOD'S REVELATION

I   The Silences of God 13
II   The Necessity of the Four Gospels: Contradiction
as an Essential Part of Revelation 67
III   Some Striking Fulfillments of Prophecy 109
IV   Some Remarkable Biblical Confirmations
From Archaeology 147
V   The Genealogies of the Bible: A Neglected Subject .. 217
VI   A Translation of Genesis 1:1 to 2:4 With Notes 273

Volume VIII SCIENCE AND FAITH
I   The Universe: Designed for Man? 13
II   Scientific Determinism and Divine Intervention 48
III   The Medieval Synthesis and the Modern
Fragmentation of Thought 101
IV   The Fitness of Living Things and the Significance
of Dauermodifications 219

Volume IX THE FLOOD: LOCAL OR GLOBAL?
and Other Studies

I   The Extent of the Flood 13
II   Flood Traditions of the World 67
III   The Problem of Evil: Some Little-considered
Physical Aspects 109
IV   What's in a Name? 167
V   The Meaning of Sweat as Part of the Curse 195
VI   The Place of Art in Worship 223
VII   One Man's Answers to Prayer 257
VIII Christian Scholarship: A Protest and a Plea 289

Alphabetical Listing
of the Doorway Papers

	Volume	Page
Between the Lines: An Analysis of Genesis 1:1, 2	VI	77
Cain's Wife and the Penalty of Incest	VI	220
Christian Scholarship: A Protest and a Plea	IX	289
Christian World View: The Framework of History, A	I	218
Compelling Logic of the Plan of Salvation: A Study of the Difference Between "Sin" and "Sins," The	III	284
Confusion of Languages, The	VI	176
Convergence and the Origin of Man	IV	140
Development of Personality: The Old and the New, The	III	136
Establishing a Paleolithic I.Q.	II	144
Extent of the Flood, The	IX	13
Fallacy of Anthropological Reconstructions, The	II	226
Fall Was Down, The	III	10
Fitness of Living Things and the Significance of Dauermodifications, The	VIII	219
Flood Traditions of the World	IX	67
Fossil Remains of Early Man and the Record of Genesis	II	12
Fresh Look at the Meaning of the Word "Soul," A	V	260
Genealogies of the Bible: A Neglected Subject, The	VII	217

	Volume	Page
How Did Jesus Die?	**V**	294
If Adam Had Not Died	**V**	116
Is Man an Animal?	**IV**	208
Light From Other Forms of Cultural Behavior on Some Incidents in Scripture	**II**	274
Longevity in Antiquity and Its Bearing on Chronology	**V**	12
Meaning of Sweat as Part of the Curse, The ..	**IX**	195
Medieval Synthesis and Modern Fragmentation of Thought, The	**VIII**	101
Nature of the Forbidden Fruit, The	**V**	76
Nature as Part of the Kingdom of God	**III**	52
Necessity of the Four Gospels: Contradiction as an Essential Part of Revelation, The	**VII**	67
Omnipotence of God in the Affairs of Men, The	**VI**	121
One Man's Answers to Prayer	**IX**	257
Part Played by Shem, Ham, and Japheth in Subsequent World History, The	**I**	15
Place of Art in Worship, The	**IX**	223
Place of Handicaps in Human Achievement, The	**III**	196
Preparation of the Earth for Man, The	**IV**	13
Primitive Cultures: A Second Look at the Problem of Their Historical Origin	**II**	60
Primitive Monotheism and the Origin of Polytheism	**IV**	110
Problem of Evil: Some Little-considered Physical Aspects, The	**IX**	109
Resurrection of Jesus Christ, The	**V**	334
Scientific Determinism and Divine Intervention	**VIII**	48
Silences of God, The	**VII**	13
Some Remarkable Biblical Confirmations From Archaeology	**VII**	147
Some Striking Fulfillments of Prophecy	**VII**	109
Study of the Names in Genesis 10, A	**I**	52
Subconscious and Forgiveness of Sins, The ...	**III**	238
Supposed Evolution of the Human Skull, The .	**II**	194
Survival of the Unfit, The	**IV**	172
Technology of Hamitic People, The	**I**	154

	Volume	Page
Terms "Image" and "Likeness" as Used in Genesis 1:26, The	III	100
Three Trees and Israel's History	VI	52
Time and Eternity: Creation and the Theory of Relativity	VI	10
Translation of Genesis 1:1 to 2:4 With Notes, A	VII	273
Trinity in the Old Testament, The	V	216
Two Species of Homo Sapiens, The	III	316
Unique Relationship Between the First and the Last Adam, The	V	368
Universe: Designed for Man?, The	VIII	13
Virgin Birth and the Incarnation, The	V	172
What's in a Name?	IX	167
Who Taught Adam to Speak?	II	250
Why Noah Cursed Canaan Instead of Ham: A New Approach to an Old Problem	I	142

Diagrams, Figures, Maps, and Tables

Vol. I NOAH'S THREE SONS

Table of Noah's descendants according to Genesis 10 56
Probable routes of migration as the earth was first
    peopled after Babel 73
Major centers of primary high civilizations in the Old
    World and Central America 98
General locations of major fossil finds of early man 127
Igloo and snow goggles (Eskimo) 157
Plank construction of Polynesian canoes 157
A modern "reed house" of notable design 177
Fifteenth-century Chinese toothbrush 177
Native South American rubber bulb enema 177
Parthian battery (about 3rd cent. B.C.?) 177
Minoan plumbing components 195
Native African loom 195
Chinese rocket launchers (multiple) 195
Sumerian drinking straws 200
Ancient Chinese cast-iron stove 200
Giant cast-iron figure (about A.D. 953) 200

Vol. II GENESIS AND EARLY MAN

Chart contrasting two alternative interpretations of man's
    cultural rise (evolutionary and biblical) 82–83
Head of Eskimo and of Gainsborough's *Blue Boy*
    contrasted for pattern of bone development 203

Various skull shapes contrasted (Gorilla, Modern man,
Pithecanthropus, Rhodesian man, and Sinanthropus) 209
View of three skulls from above (Gorilla, Pithecanthropus,
and Modern man) 209
Convergence, witnessed in predator skull forms 214
Maurice Tillet, so-called modern "Neanderthal" 218
Comparison of infant high-vault skulls, with adult
depressed skulls 218
"Mr. and Mrs. Hesperopithecus" 226
Neanderthals, reconstructed a second time 230
Neanderthal skull, reconstructed as primitive-type man
and dressed in modern clothes 233
T. Huxley's falsified diagrams of four primates 233
Four stages of reconstruction of a Neanderthal skull,
and a comparative photograph of a delegate
to a modern international conference 237
Two series of skulls (dog and primate) showing fallacy
of Weidenreich's reasoning 239
Illustration of what should not be extrapolated when data
is lacking 242
Animal phylogenetic "tree" that is only a bunch of twigs .. 244
Vertebrate "family tree" showing gaps 246

Vol. III MAN IN ADAM AND IN CHRIST

A series of diagrams to illustrate the difference between
structure and *content* in "personality":
unredeemed and redeemed 155, 172, 173, 174

Vol. IV EVOLUTION OR CREATION?

Imperial mammoth, similar to those found suddenly
frozen in Siberia 99
"Animal cemetery": evidence of sudden mass destruction
and indiscriminate burial 101
Divergence vs. convergence, diagrammatically illustrated .. 141
Marsupial and placental jerboas, illustrating convergence
of structure 158
Marsupial and placental wolf head-form, illustrating
convergence 158
Marsupial and placental moles, illustrating convergence ... 158
Head of Eskimo compared with head of Gainsborough's
Blue Boy 163

Primate skull forms (Gorilla, Modern man,
Pithecanthropus, Rhodesian man, and Sinanthropus) 165
Three skulls viewed from above (Gorilla,
Pithecanthropus, and Modern man) 165
Neanderthal skull, reconstructed as primitive-type man
and dressed as modern man 169
Posture (on all fours) of apes and man contrasted 218
T. Huxley's "doctored" drawings of four primate skeletons
posed erect 232
True posture of man and ape, erect 232
Human and ape foot compared 232
Human and ape foot, plantar view, showing difference
in bone and ligament 234
Basal aspect of skull of dog, chimpanzee, and man,
showing position of foramen magnum 237
Entrant angle of spinal column in skull of man, ape, and dog 237
Curvature of spinal column of man vs. ape 238
Scattergram showing relative growth rates from birth
to maturity of man vs. ten other animal species 286

Vol. V   THE VIRGIN BIRTH AND THE INCARNATION

Chart correlating age of Patriarchs at birth of firstborn
and age of death 43
Diagram showing population growth as viewed by
evolutionists and according to Scripture 46
Weismann's view of the continuity of the germ plasm 86
Continuity of germ plasm illustrated (Custance) 88
Early woodcut of "Adam and Eve" seal 97
Tree of knowledge (from early seal) 98
Weismann's view of the continuity of the germ plasm 185
Two contrasting views of continuity of the "Seed" (Michie) 186
Diagram of continuity of the "Seed" (Custance) 187
Diagram of continuity of the "Seed" (Hardy) 187
Early Babylonian pictorial representation of deity (as
a trinity?) 283
Diagram of "time" factors in Christ's entombment 356

Vol. VI   TIME AND ETERNITY

Display of biblical passages showing the extent of the
omnipotence of God in human affairs 146, 147
Genealogical tree of Medici family, indicating the general
effect of inbreeding on life-span in man 223

Vol. VII   HIDDEN THINGS OF GOD'S REVELATION

Photograph of Maria Lani 86
Three portraits of Maria Lani (Goerg, Braque, Matisse) ... 88
Portrait of Maria Lani by Rouault 89
Drawing of head of Lorenzo the Magnificent as
   sculpted by Michelangelo 93
Medallion of Lorenzo the Magnificent 94
"Golden Gate" of Jerusalem, now "shut" 108
Map of island off ancient Tyrus 122
Map of island off Tyrus joined to mainland by
   Alexander's causeway 127
Fishermen drying their nets on fallen columns of Tyre 128
Topography of the site of ancient Jerusalem 130
Aerial view showing site of Zion 131
Successive boundaries of fortified Jerusalem 133
Growth of environs of modern Jerusalem   138
Bust of Hatshepsut 183
Mesopotamian sites showing "Flood" strata 202
Decline in longevity of post-Flood patriarchs 236
Genealogical tree from Adam to Christ 248–251

Vol. VIII   SCIENCE AND FAITH

Representation of "expanding universe" 29
A half-column from the Psalter of Pfister's Bamberg
   Bible of 1460 100

Vol. IX   THE FLOOD: LOCAL OR GLOBAL?

Diagrammatic illustration of the settling of the Ark
   and the subsequent recession of the waters 23
Map of general topography of the "Cradle of Man" 27
Two alternative views of population growth from the first
   appearance of man to the present 56

Brief Bibliographies of Special Interest

	Volume	Page	(Footnote)
On Aegean area prehistory	I	197	(104)
On Chinese civilization and Sumerian ..	II	104f.	(95)
See also possible language connections	VI	186	(22)
On demon possession	III	167	(45)
On diet and bone malformation	II	185	(73)
On Flood Geology and the search			
for the Ark	IX	62f., 99f.	
On the Japhetic Family of Nations	I	80	(27)
Jesus in the Old Testament and			
Old Testament Theophanies	V	249f.	
Mutations: reversibility and self-			
correcting of	VIII	60	(12)
Niagara Falls: recession of, and datings .	II	32	(38)
Plants, and "soul-life"	III	69	(35)
		335	(43)
Primitive monotheism	IV	138	
Science and social responsibility, and the			
method not appropriate to Sociology .	VIII	139	(76)
Surgery among primitive people, etc. ...	I	178	(48)
On sweating	IX	218f.	
Tool-using by animals	II	14	(4)
	IV	264	(127)

Subject Index

A

Abacus, **I** 204
  vs. computer, **III** 61
Abbeville Skull, **III** 199
Abel, ancient meaning of the name,
  VII 208f.
Abnormal(s)
  personality, **III** 157
  among primitives, **I** 313
Abnormal behavior, **III** 21
  definition of, **III** 157f.
  search for "universals" in, **III**
   158
  significance of, **III** 141
"Abolition of man," **IX** 188
Abraham
  battle with the kings (Gen. 14),
   VII 161ff.
  in Egypt, **VII** 153ff.
  and his princess, **VII** 150-176
  Sarah as his "sister," **VII** 154ff.,
   239f.
  three wives, **I** 15, 260; **VII** 98f.
Abstraction
  vs. concreteness, **I** 266, 287 (fn.
   106), 273 (fn. 65), 275, 313; **VI**
   214
  necessary for generalization, **I**
   275
  purely human faculty, **IV** 317

Abstract thought
  absent among primitives, **II** 258
  applied to religion equals theology, **I** 14, 37, 48, 252, 263f.,
   303-319; **II** 138
  applied to technology equals science, **I** 32, 37, 38, 48, 70f., 252,
   263f., 287 (fn. 106), 303-319;
   II 139; **VIII** 31
  involves falsehood, **I** 272
Accident
  man as an, **I** 223, 335; **III** 268
  primitive view of, **VIII** 106
Acclimatization in man, **IV** 260
Accountability, **III** 268. *See also*
  Morals.
  age of, **III** 55, 97, 295, 297f.
  of animals, **III** 97; **VI** 229 (and
   fn.); **IX** 17
Accuracy vs. intelligibility, **III** 322
Acetylcholine, **III** 308
Acoustics of Central American native structures, **I** 185
Acquired characters. *See also*
  Dauermodifications.
  brief history of the doctrine, **VIII**
   219, 220, 230
  Darwin and, **V** 184; **VIII** 220f.
  death as an, **V** 87, 152, 189

25

hopefully to be inherited, **VIII** 131
inheritance of, **I** 357 (fn.); **II** 211; **V** 83, 183f.; **VIII** 220
in man, **VIII** 243f.
mortality in man as an, **V** 87, 151f., 189
original sin as an, **III** 289f.; **IV** 210f.; **V** 188
Acromegaly, **II** 219
Action vs. motive, **VI** 149f., 166f.
Acts vs. ways, **VI** 165
Adam, **II** 254, 267f.; **IV** 133
acquired mortality, **I** 234; **IV** 327; **V** 87, 152, 189; **VIII** 50
bisexual, as created, **V** 18, 155, 180, 397f.
bisexual, traditions regarding, **V** 155f.
body of, **V** 117f.
Christ and, **IV** 21
creation of, **III** 90; **V** 146, 179
descendants of, in his image, **III** 109
Eve separated from, **I** 234f.; **V** 87, 146f., 155ff., 173, 202, 370, 381
father of all dying, **V** 157
father of immortal children? **V** 180
if he had not died? **V** 115-169, 398f.
if he had not sinned? **V** 159; **VIII** 62
image of God in, **III** 102ff.; **V** 146
immortality of, **I** 234f., 237; **III** 290, 302; **V** 82, 116ff., 125, 179, 182; **VIII** 50
influence on whole race, **III** 180
innocence of, **V** 164
Michelangelo and, **VI** 33
naming of animals, **II** 269; **V** 146f.; **IX** 183, 186
naming of Eve, **IX** 186
navel of, **VI** 33
redeemableness of, **IV** 20f.
soul of, **III** 144; **V** 194

temptation of, **III** 308; **V** 148, 381
total potential of, **III** 171f., 187; **V** 206; **IX** 188f.
true father of all men, **V** 202
truly alone in the world, **V** 146; **VI** 235
two faces of, **V** 180
unfallen Adam and Satan, **VIII** 89
unique constitution of, **V** 368f.
who taught him to speak? **II** 249-271
Adam, the First and the Last, **V** 118, 152, 154, 368; **VI** 203; **VII** 316
as Body of Fallen Man and Body of Christ, the Church, **III** 181ff., 316f., 338, 344; **V** 394f.
character of, **V** 384-393
creation of the First linked to sacrifice of the Last, **I** 237f.; **V** 117, 154, 192
destiny planned for First, achieved by Last, **V** 163f.; **VIII** 96f.; **IX** 116
First, made human nature sinful; Last, made human nature pure, **III** 180
genealogies, purpose of, **VII** 218, 220-223, 260, 337
immortality of, **V** 87, 89, 139, 398ff.
implications if body was evolved, **V** 368f.; **IX** 295, 296
moment of birth of each, **III** 144; **V** 193f., 199
nature of their physical bodies, **IV** 325f.; **V** 163, 370-383
of one blood, **I** 61; **V** 139
both true sons of God, **III** 109
sweating, **IX** 216, 217
unique relationship between, **V** 367-400
whole potential of man contained in both, **III** 172, 187; **V** 206; **IX** 188f.

Adam, the Second
   birth and death of, the cause of
      creation, **I** 233
   free of original sin, **III** 302
   necessity of virgin birth, **III** 302;
      V 192
   a true son of the First, **V** 199
Adhonai, pagan corruptions of? **V**
   255
Adapa myth, **V** 96
Adaptation, **III** 71; **IV** 73
   accounting for, **I** 362f.
   anticipatory or preadaptation
      VIII 246. *See further under*
      Preadaptations.
Adoption, **II** 289, 318; **VII** 172
   according to Roman law, **II** 289
   effect on previously barren, **VII**
      172
   by father, of own son, **II** 278f.,
      329ff.
   German law and, **II** 289
   Jewish laws regarding, **II** 289,
      329; **III** 231
   legal requirements for, **VII** 264
   of slaves, **II** 289
   teaching a trade for, **VII** 265
Adrenal gland, **II** 219
Adrenalin, **III** 308; **IX** 201
Adultery, the woman taken in, **III**
   281; **IX** 189
Advent of Messiah
   coming Prince of Daniel (tim-
      ing), **VII** 34f., 36
   Jewish expectation of, **VII** 35
   widespread hope in Roman
      world, **VII** 30
Aerial warfare, immorality of, **VIII**
   140 (fn. 76)
Africa(n)
   alchemy, **VI** 202; **VII** 200
   early high culture of, **II** 121f.
   Flood traditions in, scarce, **IX** 84
   high jump, **III** 201; **IX** 152
   home of iron-making, **I** 201
   hunting techniques, **I** 169

   looms, **I** 195
   languages of, **VI** 185
   metallurgy, **I** 201; **II** 312f.; **VI**
      201; **VII** 198, 226f.
   myth on death, **V** 94
   native view of White Man, **II** 112
Age, an; word for in Hebrew, **VI** 102;
   VII 295
Age of accountability. *See under* Accountability.
Age of Faith, **VIII** 191. *See also under*
   Medieval world.
Age of universe, psychological importance of, **VI** 28
Age
   average, of Stone Age man, **V**
      58f.
   at death not recorded after
      Joshua, **VII** 233, 237, 239
   effect of, on morphology, **IV** 167f.
Aged, the; in primitive society, **II**
   112, 154, 170, 173.
Aggression
   among apes rare, **IV** 189f.
   animal vs. human, **I** 243; **II** 155f;
      III 14f., 16, 23, 25f., 27f., 342;
      IV 322
   defined, **III** 114f.
   human, pathological? **III** 115
   as a misused term, **III** 66
   nature of human, **III** 16f., 114
Aggressive instinct in man? **III** 24,
   25f.
Aging
   begins very early, **V** 133
   cell mutations and, **V** 131
   effect of radiation upon, **V** 131
   factors governing, **V** 23f.
   and mutations, **V** 13f.
   pathology of, **V** 22
   process of, absent in some forms
      of life, **V** 132
   rate of closure of sutures and, **V**
      57
   research into, **V** 12
   wear and tear theory of, **V** 131

Agriculture. *See also under* Domestication.
  artificial insemination in plant breeding, **I** 332
  cultivation, early appearance of in New World, **II** 116
  fertilizers, use of, **I** 168
  irrigation, **I** 165; **II** 117
  how to make a cow give milk, **I** 325
  multiculture by American Indians, **I** 168
  plant "breeding" (manioc and pineapple), **I** 167
  terraced, **II** 121
  tools of, **I** 205
Ahab, King
  attitude toward his sin, **III** 31, 184; **V** 388
  curse on his family, **VII** 255f.
Ainu, **II** 46, 291, 298; **III** 138; **IV** 126
  beliefs regarding conception, **II** 291
  methods of fishing with dogs, **I** 168
  possible racial origin? **II** 114
Air conditioning in early China, **I** 333
Aircraft, early Chinese contributions to, **I** 40, 41, 205, 211
Alchemy, **I** 209, 210
  origin of the word, **VI** 202; **VII** 200
  originated by Sumerians, **I** 190
Alcohol
  content of, in bread, **V** 109
  effect of, on conception, **V** 104f.
  effect of, on nursing infant, **V** 105f.
  effect of, on the body, **V** 102
  effect of, on time sense, **VI** 21
  as medicine, **V** 110
  moral effect of, **III** 35
  as a protoplasmic poison, **V** 107
  as a toxic agent, **III** 293

Alcoholism, inheritable? **V** 104ff.
Aleuts, morphological changes with time and, **VIII** 244
Alexander's conquests, effects of, **VII** 25, 26
Algebra, **I** 189, 191, 327
Algonkins, **IV** 126
Alii, Hawaiian chiefs, **VI** 224
All, meaning "all kinds of," **IX** 21f.
Allegory, story of Eden not an, **V** 367
Alms accepted from the unconverted, **VIII** 198
Alorese, **IV** 294
  aggressiveness of, **III** 148
  mother love missing among, **III** 148
Alphabet
  not developed in certain languages, **I** 273
  vs. ideograms, **I** 286
  invention of, **I** 305, 316
  necessary for abstract thought, **I** 284
  script, early use of, **VII** 184
"Altar to the unknown God," **VII** 20
Altitude, high
  influence of, on personality, **III** 147
  speech slowed by, **VI** 23
Altruism among animals? **IV** 194ff., 275
Amarna Tablets **VI** 61; **VII** 169, 186
America
  civilization of Central, **I** 253
  melting pot of cultures, **I** 310
American Indians. *See also* Aymara, Aztecs, North American Indians, Peruvians.
  agricultural practices of, **I** 168
  corn cultivation, **I** 168
  dental care, **I** 186
  domestication of animals, **I** 40, 166f., 304f.

domestication of plants, **I** 166f.
drugs developed by, **I** 166f.
face masks, **III** 334
ingenuity of, **I** 156, 158, 162ff., 334f.
insecticides, **I** 163
inventiveness of, **I** 36, 162-164, 166f.
languages of, **I** 273; **VI** 183
mathematics of, **I** 183, 328
medicines of, **I** 166f., 329 (fn. 221), 330, 331
pottery of, **I** 181; **II** 151
tribes of, **IV** 126, 129
view of the White Man, **II** 110f.
weaving, **I** 179f.
Amino acids, early "creation" of, **VIII** 73, 83, 135
Amoeba, **II** 252
amoeboid psyche? **III** 328f.
dismembered and reassembled, **VIII** 75
life, characteristic of, **IV** 51; **V** 385
mindedness in, **III** 257
true immortality of, **V** 124f.
variety of responses in, **III** 260f.
Amphibians
vs. reptiles, **IV** 70
salt water, a barrier to, **IX** 41
Amphioxus, **IV** 42
Amraphel, possible identity of, **VII** 166
Anaesthetics, **I** 176
use of, in childbirth, **IX** 138, 139
Anatomy, of man vs. ape, **IV** 215f., 217f.
Ancasmarca Indians (Peru), Flood tradition of, **IX** 71
Ancestors, our contemporary, **II** 154-178
Ancestor worship, **IV** 123f., 126, 131
Ancient modern skulls, **II** 194f., 199
And, Subtle meaning of, **VIII** 60

Andaman Islanders, **II** 105 (fn. 96); **III** 108; **IV** 129
Flood tradition of, **IX** 32f., 76
meaning of name for *man*, **VII** 201 (fn.)
physical paternity and, **III** 139
Anencephalic children, **VIII** 68
Angel(s), **III** 55
fallen, **VI** 127
given wings, why? **VI** 31
have souls? **V** 289
love of God not self-evident to, **I** 234
vs. man and animals, **I** 226ff., 230
not redeemable, **I** 226, 231; **IV** 212
not subject to death, **V** 117
their understanding of God, **I** 230
their worship of God, **I** 230
"Angel of the Lord," **V** 227, 237ff.
Angels on the head of a pin, **VIII** 112
Animal(s)
accomplishments, compared with those of man, **IV** 208, 316ff.
accountability of, **III** 97; **VI** 229 (fn. 12); **IX** 17
aggression among, **III** 23, 25, 114; **IV** 172ff.
aggression of, in captivity, **III** 24; **IV** 190
altruism among? **IV** 194ff., 275
vs. angel and man, **I** 226ff., 242f.
and the ark: supernaturally guided to, **IX** 38
in the ark: problem of multiplication of, **IX** 42
and art, **IV** 317
behavior, learned: transmission, **IV** 293
behavior of, vs. man's, **III** 25; **IV** 263, 281f.; **VIII** 68
beauty vs. ugliness of, **IV** 66; **VI** 28f.

birth rate of, influenced by population size, **IV** 192, 201, 255f.
bodies, high efficiency of, **IX** 133f., 205
brain sizes of, **IV** 223f., 228
breeding among, vs. in man, **IV** 302f.
in captivity, long-lived, **IX** 125
caring for one another, **IV** 194ff., 314
catastrophe: sensitivity of, to imminent, **IX** 72, 90
cemeteries, significance of, **IV** 94ff.; **IX** 59f.
cleaning habits of, **IV** 196f.
communications between, **IV** 276
communication vs. language, **II** 252ff.
as companions for Adam? **IX** 184
and convergence, **II** 17, 208, 212, 215; **IV** 140ff., 146
counting? **IV** 317f.
crippled, **IV** 203f.
crowding, reaction to, **IV** 184f.
cruelty of, apparent only? **IX** 125f.
culture among? **IV** 208
dead bodies, scarcity of, **IV** 100, 186f.
death, attitude towards, **III** 64, 67f.; **VIII** 219
decerebrated, **V** 195, 212f. *See also under* Decorticate.
decorticated. *See under* Birds, Cats, Dogs, Rabbits
defenselessness of, **IV** 201f., 247
defense of territory, **IV** 190ff.
defenses of, **IV** 156f., 201f., 247, 249
dental caries in prehistoric, **IX** 113
diet and effect of, **IX** 123
dietary wisdom of, **III** 62; **IV** 293, 308ff.

diet of, and capacity for travel, **IX** 41, 206
disease and healing in, **IV** 312f.
diseases in, before man, **IX** 113 (fn.)
domesticated by Indians, **I** 40, 166f.
domestication of, **I** 304f.; **II** 88, 97; **III** 120; **IX** 35f., 49ff.
domestication sometimes harmful, **IX** 125
domestication upsets instincts, **III** 63, 65f.
educability, short period of, **IV** 271, 274, 284f.
emotion of, vs. human emotion, **II** 255
erect posture not easily maintained, **IV** 233
as experimental substitutes for humans, **III** 254; **IX** 201
extinctions of, **I** 359; **IV** 92ff., 253
the Fall, its consequences upon, **VI** 229
feeding habits of, harmonious, **IV** 352
feet of, vs. man's, **IV** 218, 232, 234f.
fighting among, causes of, **III** 24
food discrimination among, **III** 63f.
food gathering techniques of, **IV** 264
gazelle rescued by lioness, **III** 73
glosso-labial limitations of, **II** 257, 262; **IV** 269
as God's agents, **VI** 132; **IX** 17
growth rates of, vs. man's, **IV** 285ff.
heat regulation in, **IV** 152
heaven, as they would see it! **IX** 241
herbivores become carnivores, **IV** 256; **IX** 122
herbivorous in Eden only, **VII** 314

herd leaders, **II** 255; **IV** 301
hibernation of, **III** 121; **IV** 257f.
inbreeding, effect of, **II** 28; **VII** 237
instincts. *See under* Instincts.
interfertility of gibbon, chimpanzee and orangutan, **V** 394
"Kingdom" without a king, **IX** 122
kinds of, taken into ark, **IX** 35ff.
languages of, **IV** 269ff., 276. *See also under* Glosso-labial, Language, Speech.
"leaders," **II** 255; **IV** 301
life spans of, **V** 133, 166f.
lioness rescuing gazelle, **III** 73
locomotion of, **IV** 147
man as an? **IV** 208ff.
man's fear of, and their response to, **IX** 208
mating season and climate, **IV** 253f., 303
maturing rate of, **IV** 219, 284ff.
memory of, contingent, **III** 259; **IV** 317
migration, factors in, **IV** 189; **IX** 41f.
mind of, vs. man's, **IV** 229f., 273
moral accountability of, **I** 226; **VI** 229 (fn. 12)
moral responsibility of, **IX** 16f.
moral responsiveness of, **IX** 162f.
music among, **IV** 316f.
mutual aid among, **III** 23, 24; **IV** 195f.
naming of, by Adam, **II** 269; **V** 147; **IX** 183, 186
natural population control, **IV** 182, 184ff., 191
neck, vs. man's, **IV** 219, 236, 287
number of, in the ark, **IX** 36f.
numbers held in check by man, **III** 214
pain not anticipated by, **III** 67; **IX** 126
painting among, **IV** 317

panther chased by a deer, **III** 65
placentals, **IV** 44
population stability of, **III** 63; **IV** 182, 185ff., 191, 255
pouched, **IV** 44
preached to, **III** 82
not redeemable, **I** 226, 231; **IV** 212
response of, to commands, **IV** 271
reproduction of, vs, in man, **IV** 303f.
Satan's control of, limited, **III** 96, 111
savagery among, **IV** 197f.
senescence not found among, **V** 136
sickness and, **IV** 314
size of, **IV** 200ff; **V** 132
skin of, and wounds, **I** 342; **IV** 312f.
social life of, **III** 23, 88; **IV** 184, 196f., 220, 282
societies of, without "culture," **IV** 292f.
society is biological, **IV** 281
soul of, **V** 262, 270; **VII** 307
species of, missing in Egyptian sculpture, **VII** 158
speech of, **II** 255 (fn.), 257, 262; **IV** 266ff. *See also under* Speech.
spirit in, **V** 197, 266, 272
sweating of, **I** 342f.; **III** 120; **IV** 259, 260; **IX** 197, 201
teaching speech to, **II** 262; **IV** 269-276
territories of, **I** 341f.; **III** 71; **IV** 250ff.; **IX** 40f.
"thought," contingent, **IV** 271, 273f., 275, 317
time, sense of, **VI** 24
tool-using among, **II** 14; **III** 107; **IV** 263f.
use of fire by, **IV** 266; **VIII** 40
variability, limits of, **I** 346 (fn.)

vocalization of, **IV** 244. *See also under* Vocalization.

wisdom of, in conflict, **IV** 247

wisdom of, in defeat, **III** 68

wisdom of, in food selection, **III** 62f.

wisdom of, in sickness, **III** 62

wisdom of, when trapped, **III** 62

Animal numbers. *See under* Population density.

Animation

as a literary device, **VI** 112ff.

in the Psalms, **II** 171; **III** 85

Animism, **II** 170; **III** 79f., 334; **IV** 110, 127

Annihilation of man, **IX** 188. *See also under* Nirvana.

Ant(s)

society, **III** 60, 118; **IV** 249, 263, 292

used for suturing, **I** 178

Antarctic flora and fauna, **IV** 102

Antidiluvian king lists, **VII** 203f.

Anthropology. *See also under* Fossil Man, Man. *See Vols II and IV.*

cultural, **II** 276ff.

and Fossil Man. See Vol. **II.**

missing links: uncertainties regarding, **VIII** 136

and missionaries, **II** 63

primitive cultures: changing opinions regarding, **II** 63-80

reconstructions by, fallacy of, **II** 226-248

responsibility of Christian writers and, **II** 60

use of imagination in, **II** 16, 242, 245

Antichrist, **II** 309f., 311

Cain as type of, **VII** 227

Antiquity of man, **I** scientific" vs. biblical view, **IX** 44f.

Antrim and Down Counties (Ireland), displaced peasants in, **II** 183, 221; **IV** 167

Anxiety, sweating due to, **IX** 197f.

Ape(s), and tailless monkeys generally, **II** 13, 18, 19, 29, 212, 238, 240

absence of speech in, **IV** 269-276

aggression among rare, **IV** 189f.

descended from man! **IV** 166f.

diet essentially vegetarian, **IV** 256

erectness of, very poorly developed, **IV** 233

feet of, **IV** 232f.

hairiness of, vs. man **II** 18, 19

jaw structure of, **IV** 162, 243f.

manlike convergence in, **IV** 159

social position of males, **IV** 291

Ape-man, the creation of an, **VIII** 81

Aphasia, **II** 259

Aphids, winged vs. wingless, **III** 63; **IV** 189

Apocrine glands, **IX** 201

Appendix in man, **VII** 314

evidence of dietary change, **IX** 124, 206

Appetite

effect of the Fall upon, **IV** 312

loss of, and fear, **III** 65

loss of, and pain, **III** 67

and "need," out of register in man, **IX** 133

Arab(s)

blood revenge among, **V** 375

carriers of culture, **I** 37f., 306f.

genealogies as passports among, **VII** 218

mathematics of, **I** 307

practical, not philosophical, **I** 307f.

religion of, **I** 276

specificity of language, **VI** 216

uninventiveness of, **I** 37

Arabia, non-Semitic inhabitants of, **I** 20

Arabic language, numerous words for *camel*, **VI** 216

Aramaic, use of, in New Testament, **VII** 73
Arapesh, **IV** 294
  absence of masculine tempera-
    ment, **III** 148
Ararat, description of, **IX** 99ff.
Archaeology, **VII** 145-214
  of Abraham's time, **VII** 150-176
  and the Bible, **II** 76; **VII** 145-214
  confirmations precise, **VII** 194
  evidence for pre-Flood times, **VII** 195-209
  of Joseph's time, **VII** 177-193
  some dramatic recent discover-
    ies, **VII** 194
Archeopteryx, **IV** 48; **VI** 28
Architecture. *See also* Building techniques.
  acoustics of Ball Court of
    Chichen Itza, **I** 185
  arch, **I** 202
  barrel vault, **I** 202
  dome, **I** 200
  earthquake-proof buildings, **I**
    185
  igloos, construction of, and
    "home comforts" of, **I** 157,
    159; **II** 160
  perfection of early, **I** 194
  primitive, **I** 322f.
  reed houses, **I** 193
  pyramids, **I** 194, 323f.
  suspension bridges, **I** 182, 211f.
  and worship, **IX** 227ff.
Archtypes, concept of, **IV** 93
Arctic
  body temperature in the, **IX** 197
  clothing, Eskimo design, **I** 158
Aristotelian vs. Chinese logic, **I** 289
Ark, Noah's, **II** 35, 102, 134
  animals probably taken on
    board, **IX** 35f.
  bibliography on the search for,
    IX 103f.
  crew of, **IX** 36, 37
  dimensions of, **IX** 37

  draft of, **IX** 22
  landing site of, **IX** 28, 33, 75, 91
  mathematical skill required for,
    V 50f.
  no helmsman or steering, **IX** 29
  not a *ship*, **IX** 82, 93
  number of animals taken on
    board, **IX** 36f.
  problems with animals as cargo,
    IX 42
  reported historical sightings of,
    IX 101ff.
  search for, **IX** 99-105
  time taken to build, **IX** 35
  varied forms of, **IX** 70, 78
  wood from, **IX** 105
Ark of the covenant, **V** 316
Armies of God, **III** 218
Armies, private, **VII** 160, 162
"Arriving" vs. "travelling," **VIII**
  14, 127
Arrow(s). *See also under* Bow and
  Arrow.
  "rifled" heads, **I** 184 (and fn.)
  rocket, from China, **I** 195
Art
  among animals, **IV** 317
  appearance vs. character, **VII** 92
  apprehension of truth and, **VII**
    85f.
  beauty of faces in Medieval
    sculpture, **VIII** 114f.
  carvings, **I** 196; **II** 158
  of children, **VII** 90
  early appearance of, **II** 97
  and inspiration, **IX** 251f.
  and mathematics, **III** 54
  objectives of styles in, **VIII** 113
  perfection of early, **II** 89, 97
  pictures of the Lord, **IX** 239, 241,
    243
  place of, in worship, **IX** 222ff.,
    234f.
  and portraiture, **VII** 77f., 85ff.,
    87f., 92, 94
  and psychiatry, **III** 164f.; **IX** 167

as therapy for mental illness, **IX** 167

worship and, **IX** 221-253

Art(s)

loss of, **II** 37, 113, 118

loss of literary, **II** 124

loss of nautical, **II** 124

loss of pottery, **II** 118f.

of making fire, lost, **II** 119f.; **IV** 266

Arthritis in early man, **V** 24. *See also under* Osteoarthritis.

Artificial respiration, **III** 90, 144

Artificial Selection, **IV** 21, 78, *See also under* Selection.

Artist, temperament of the, **III** 154f.

Arunta, **II** 305

Aryan(s), **II** 78; **VI** 180f.

destroyers of Indus Valley Culture, **II** 114

language and race, **VII** 32

language linked to Semitic, **VI** 180f., 186f.

origin of, **VI** 195f.

philosophy of, **I** 31, 70, 295, 296

'Asah, meaning of word, **VII** 283, 297, 313

Asbestos clothing, **I** 322

Ascension of Christ, **VII** 47

circumstances surrounding, **V** 344

Asexual cells, immortality of, **V** 128

Asexual reproduction, **V** 17

Asia, "cradle of species," **II** 41, 55f.

Asiatic languages compared, **VI** 188ff.

"As-if-ism" in scientific understanding, **VIII** 72, 170

Ass

Balaam's, **III** 96, 233; **VI** 132

and ox, plowing with, **III** 347

Asses in early Egypt, **VII** 158

Astronomy

American Indian, **I** 183

Chinese, **VIII** 154

Sumerian vs. Greek, **I** 191

Atheism

demanded by science? **VIII** 93

grounds for, **VIII** 57

of modern society, **III** 274ff.

Athens, **VII** 21f.

Atlantic Charter, significance of, **III** 41

Atmosphere

composition of, **V** 26

of the earth, **IV** 27f.

nature of the earliest, **IV** 40f.

preparation of, for life, **IV** 39

Atoms, consciousness of? **III** 321, 323

Atonement, meaning of the word, **III** 305, 306. *See also* Day of Atonement.

Attributes of God, personified, **IV** 117

Australia, fauna in the ark? **IX** 42

Australian aborigines, **II** 291; **III** 117; **IV** 126, 129, 292, 294; **VII** 201

complexity of social behavior, **II** 287; **III** 208

ingenuity and inventiveness of, **I** 258 (fn. 42)

Neanderthal morphology of, **II** 52

witch doctors, genuine medical practitioners, **I** 173

Australopithecines, **II** 13, 213; **IV** 45, 223, 236

africanus and robustus, **II** 201

cranial capacity of, **II** 213

use of tools by, **IV** 264f.

Autonomic nervous system, **IX** 199

Awls, **I** 163

Aymara Indians

dehydrated (freeze-dried) potatoes, **I** 326

numerous words for *potato*, **VI** 215f.

Aztecs, attitude toward death, **V** 349

B

Babel, Tower of, **II** 35, 80, 137; **VI** 176ff.; **IX** 45
  built by Hamites, **VI** 211
  modern parallel, **IX** 155
  and technical jargon, **II** 137
  traditions of, **IX** 29
Baboons, **III** 107; **IV** 264
  becoming carnivorous, **IV** 256; **IX** 122
Babylonia(ns)
  gods of, **IV** 114, 116f.
  king lists, **V** 51f.; **VII** 203f.
  mathematics, **I** 291; **V** 55
  medical practices, **I** 192
  myths of creation, **VI** 113
  religion of, **I** 276
  symbols of deity, **V** 252f.
  traditions of the Fall, **V** 94f.
  uninventiveness of, **I** 36
  World View of, **III** 78ff.
Bacteria
  capable of "learning," **VIII** 234
  essential to life, **IX** 161
  and viruses, as agents of disease, **IX** 160
Bahu, personification of chaos, **VI** 93
Bakairi tribe, language of, **II** 258
Ball(s)
  rubber, solid and hollow, **I** 178f.
  -and-socket joint, **I** 335
"Ballooning" of the skull, **II** 206, 224
Balloons, early history of, **I** 21
Banking houses, Sumerian, **I** 192
Banyoro, **II** 289
Baptism
  of infants, **III** 307; **V** 279
  formula for, **V** 223, 226
Bara, meaning of word in Hebrew,

VII 282, 298. *See also under* Create.
Barbarism
  vs. civilization, **III** 22
  increase of, in modern wars, **III** 26
Barking vs. howling of dogs, **II** 266
Barnyards, witness to man's supervision of the animal world, **IX** 123
Barrel vault, **I** 202
Barrenness of women, **II** 283f., 318ff.; **VII** 171f.
  effect of adopting a child on, **VII** 172
  penalties of, in society, **II** 295, 304
Bar-sinister, **VII** 257
Barzillu
  cuneiform word for iron, **VII** 199, 227
  origin of the word, **VI** 202
Basques, **VI** 183f.
Bathrooms in antiquity, **I** 333; **II** 95f.
Batik (Indonesian), **I** 181
Bats, **IV** 276f.
Battery
  electric, **I** 177, 196
  theory of operation, **VIII** 169
Be, become, etc., in Hebrew, **VI** 89f.; **VII** 273ff., 284f.
Beads from the Indus Valley, **II** 95
Beard, purpose of? **IV** 174
Bears, **II** 260
  wisdom of, when trapped, **III** 62
"Beautiful Gate" of Acts 3:2, **IX** 229
Beauty
  characteristic of God's handiwork, **VIII** 43

not necessary to survival, **IV** 66, 205
prehistoric animals have no, **IV** 66, **VI** 28f.
and skin color, **IX** 239, 241
Beauty contests in early China, **I** 327
Becoming vs. *being* in Hebrew usage. *See under* Be.
Bedouin, **I** 158, 165
Bees, "language" of, **IV** 276
Beetles, water; bifocal eyes of, **IV** 155
Beginning, In the,
in the Greek, **VI** 83
in the Hebrew, **VI** 180; **VII** 280
Behavior. *See also under* Abnormal Behavior.
of children, asocial, criminal, **III** 30f.
conscious vs. instinctive, **VIII** 68, 137
cultural, varied, **II** 274-331
group, **III** 345
human, basis of, **III** 158f.; **IV** 263, 281f.
human vs. animal, **III** 25; **IV** 263, 281f., 293, 298, 302
instinctive vs. learned, **III** 60
mindless, **VIII** 66
normal, synonymous with sinful, **III** 158f.
and reductionism, **III** 255
social, endangering survival, **III** 117; **IV** 295f.
suicidal nature of human, **III** 163, 296; **IV** 321
Behaviorism, **VIII** 137
Behaviorists, **III** 140f.
Beheading, **VII** 179; **V** 379
Being vs. *becoming* in Hebrew usage, **VI** 89f. *See also under* Be.
Being vs. doing, **VIII** 186
Belief
place of will in, **II** 225
system of, needed by man, **III** 83

Bella Coola Indians, **II** 298
Bering Straits, **VIII** 244
Bessemer process of steelmaking, **I** 214
Bethuel, possible imbecility of, **VII** 245
Betrothal, forms of, **II** 300
Bias
dangers of, **VII** 99
detrimental effects of, upon science, **II** 67; **IV** 148
effect of sin on, **III** 40
necessity of, in science, **IV** 143
theological advantages of, **VIII** 124 (fn. 37)
Bible. *See also under* New Covenant, Old Testament, Scriptures.
archaeology and confirmation of the, **II** 76; **VII** 145-214
historical from the first, **VII** 195, 204, 205, 209
its definition of understanding, **III** 90f., 111
more, not less, detailed in earliest portions, **VII** 194f., 206
myths in? **VII** 195, 204, 205
organic unity of, **VI** 53f.
translatableness of, **IX** 243
Bifacial photography, **V** 180f.
Bifocal eyes in insects, **IV** 155
Big Bang theory, **VIII** 26, 28
and creation of the elements, **VIII** 21
and creation of the universe, **VIII** 19f.
diagrammatic representation of, **VIII** 29
Big Business, evolution and, **IV** 86, 178
Biochemical predestination, **IV** 31, **VIII** 82f.
Biochemical "wisdom," **VIII** 234
Biology. *See also under* Life sciences.
absence of strict predictability in, **VIII** 92

Bird(s)
   banding of, in early China, **I** 335
   convergence observed in, **IV** 153
   decorticated, experiments with, **VIII** 67
   erect posture of, **IV** 243, 277
   and the Flood, **IX** 38ff.
   God's omnipotence and, **IV** 132
   mutual aid among, **IV** 195f.
   navigation, their role in, **IX** 39f., 71, 74f.
   parental devotion of, **III** 68, **IX** 126
   population density of, **IV** 185f.
   and speech, **II** 263; **IV** 277
   temperature regulation in, **IX** 203
   tool-using among, **II** 14; **III** 107; **IV** 264
   vision of, "four-dimensional," **VII** 90f.
   wheeling of, in flight, **III** 69f., 336; **IV** 196

Birth(s)
   of Cain and Abel, **II** 309ff.
   consciousness prior to? **V** 198
   death begins at, **V** 132, 182
   multiplied, **II** 284; **IX** 137f.
   pains in childbirth, **IX** 138f.

Birth of Jesus Christ. *See also* Incarnation, Virgin birth. *See Vol. V.*
   Joseph's and Mary's points of view, **VII** 102f.
   key to the universe, **I** 233f.
   moment of, **V** 282ff., 359; **VII** 36
   timing of, **VII** 20, 34

Birth rate, balanced in animals, **IV** 192
Birth rate vs. death rate, **IX** 137f.
Bisexual(ity)
   of Adam as created, **V** 18, 155, 180, 370, 397ff.
   personality of the, **V** 155f.

Black Death. *See under* Black Plague.
Black Plague, **VIII** 13, 119

Black races, unique contribution of, **VII** 230f.
Blacksmith
   from Africa, **I** 201
   origin of the word, **II** 312; **VII** 198, 226
   significance of the word, **VI** 201
Blasphemy, Jesus accused of, **VII** 40
Blessing
   of David by Saul, **I** 147; **VII** 232
   of Japheth by Noah, **I** 25ff.; 337f.
   of Jesus' mother, **I** 147f.; **VII** 232
   of Shem by Noah, **I** 25ff., 337f.
Blind and deaf, modern examples of; taught to speak, **II** 263f.
Blindness
   and achievement, **III** 206
   Paul, partial? **III** 228
Block and tackle, **I** 160f.
Blood
   cleansing power of, **III** 278
   mankind of one, **IV** 254
   relation of soul to, **V** 273
   separation into coagulum and serum, **V** 309
   source of corruption in death, **V** 108
   specificity of, **IV** 154
   symbolized by wine, **V** 108
   and water, **V** 309f.
Blood circulation
   peripheral, in man, **III** 120
   recognition of, in early China, **I** 294, 330
Blood revenge in Arab society, **V** 375
Bloody sweat, **V** 310f.; **IX** 216ff.
"Blotting out"
   of a name, **VII** 257
   of painful memory, **III** 240f.
   of sins, **III** 240, 277, 279, 280
Blue Boy, **II** 202, 203, (fig. 5); **IV** 163
Boat(s)
   ark not a, **IX** 29, 82, 93
   Chinese symbol for, **IX** 106

development of, in early times, **I** 203

exceptional materials used for, **I** 185

first ironclad, **I** 203

watertight compartment construction, **I** 203, 326

Body
brain size relative to weight of, **IV** 228

cells, mortal, **V** 140

conscious existence requires a, **III** 249, 254

a corpse, without spirit, **V** 273

as a dichotomy. *See under* Dichotomy.

and the disease of sin, **III** 298, 299

environmental factors which modify the, **II** 183, 189, 221f.

of fallen man, still not "animal," **IV** 327

glorified, nature of, **VI** 37

human, low efficiency of, **IV** 297, 311; **IX** 204

Jesus' resurrected b., nature of, **V** 338f.

importance of, to Jesus Christ, **I** 238f.; **V** 161

importance of, to man, **V** 161

light as a natural covering for, **V** 103

maintenance of temperature of, **III** 119; **IX** 196

odor and identity, **II** 285, 306, 330

proportions of, influenced by environment, **VIII** 245

redemption of, **V** 205, 274

resurrection of, **V** 297; **VI** 35f.

salvation of both body and spirit, **III** 303f.

specially prepared for Lord's incarnation, **V** 381

and spirit interactionism. *See under* Dichotomy.

structure of man's, permits worship, **IV** 245f.

temperament affected by chemistry of, **III** 147, 166

temperament and physique of, **III** 145

temperature control of, in Eden, **V** 150

the will and its power to influence the body, **IX** 182

Body of Adam. *See* Body of man.
vs. Body of Christ, **III** 181f.; **IV** 326f.; **V** 117ff., 370ff.

human race as, **V** 384f.

"Leviathan" of Hobbes as, **III** 184f., 341

as an "organism," **III** 183

Body of Christ. *See also under* Church.
as the Body of a Second Adam, **III** 316

always "complete" in the world, **III** 187, 346

as the Church, **V** 384f., 389

never "fails" (Temple), **III** 178

as a habitation of God, **III** 176

nature of, **V** 206ff.

as an "organism," **III** 183

as a structure, **III** 174f.

as a Temple, **III** 191

Body of Man, specifically "human," **IV** 249ff., 323ff.

Body of Sin, **III** 183, 344

Bolas for hunting, **I** 170

Bombs; incendiary, gas, and smoke, **I** 208f.

Bone(s)
if broken, may form a functional joint, **VIII** 77

cells of, under cytoplasmic control, **VIII** 227

diseases of, in early man, **V** 24

influence of endocrine glands on structure of, **II** 185, 220

remarkable properties of, **I** 354 (fn. 275)

"Book of the Dead," **IX** 85
"Book of Life," **VII** 258
"Book of Light," **VI** 107
"Books" of Revelation, **III** 242f., 278
Books. *See under* Publishing.
Bookstores, in ancient Rome, **VII** 27f.
Boomerangs, **I** 171
art of manufacture, **II** 119
Boredom, causes of modern, **VIII** 146, 174, 175, 180
Borough, origin of the word, **II** 286; **VII** 225
Boskop Skull, **III** 49; **IV** 225; **V** 58
Bounty, Mutiny on the, **II** 123
Bow and arrow, **I** 204
crossbow, **I** 204
lost art of making, **II** 118f.
Mongol design of, **I** 209
repeating, **I** 205
Bower birds, **IV** 317
Brace and bit, **I** 202
Brain. *See also under* Mind.
canine, supposed evolution of, **II** 239
cells, constant turnover of, **II** 253
cells, number of, **III** 249
cells, reorganize themselves, **III** 332; **IV** 227
complexity of cell structure of, **III** 249f.
as a computer, **III** 254f.
and conceptual thought, **VIII** 44
consciousness resident in cortex of? **III** 329; in frontal lobes? **IV** 227
cortex of, percentage used, **IV** 297
as "cotton wadding" or batting, **III** 248, 329; **IV** 226
death of, ill-defined, **V** 121f.
defective circuitry in? **III** 20
embryonic b. cell, a single, develops normal b. tissue *in vitro,* **VIII** 77

energy levels of, measured, **VIII** 87, 143
enlargement of, **II** 238f.
faradic stimulation of, **III** 242ff.
and hand interaction, **IV** 242
human, complexity of, **IV** 221-230
harmless sequential operations on, **III** 252
as mechanism, **III** 249
metabolic heat of, **III** 320
metabolism and erectness, **IV** 245
vs. mind, **I** 289; **III** 240ff., 256ff., 320; **IV** 229f., 277f.; **VIII** 87
overcomplexity of? **IV** 296f.
phylogenetic development of? **II** 14
"preparations" of, maintain normal EEG, **VIII** 76
reduced to electrochemistry, **III** 123, 240; **VIII** 187
seat of memory? **III** 249
size. *See under* Cranial capacity.
and speech, **II** 262f.
surface complexity of, **IV** 228f.
surgery and memory, **III** 244
theories of localization in, **IV** 226
unnecessary for memory, **III** 248-250
uniqueness of human, **I** 344
Brain cell(s)
and memory, **III** 256
number of, **III** 249f.
number of, dying per 24 hours, **III** 250
Brain size. *See also under* Cranial capacity.
of animals, **IV** 223f., 228
comparative, **IV** 223, 228
vs. complexity, **IV** 221ff.
effect of domestication on, **IV** 226
learning ability and, **IV** 224, 228
relative to body weight, **IV** 228
Brain waves of identical twins, **III** 265

Bread, alcohol content of, **V** 109

Breakwater design for harbors, **I** 336f.

Breast feeding. *See also under* Nursing, Suckling of infants.
effect of alcohol on, **V** 105f.
extended period of, **IX** 173
by males, **V** 155; **VII** 172

Breeding
artificial, **III** 121
experiments with man, **IV** 306
limited seasons of, among animals, **IV** 303
psychological barriers to animal, **IV** 253

Bricks
purpose of straw in, **VII** 211
types of clay used for, **VII** 211

Bride price, **II** 279, 293, 322, 324; **VII** 245
service rendered for, **II** 295f.

Bridges, suspension, **I** 182, 211f.

Bridgewater Treatises, **VIII** 149

British monarchs, lengths of reign, **V** 56

Broca center and language, **IV** 226

Bronze
Chinese, **I** 322
hatchets of, **II** 94
Sumerian, **I** 188f.
Yoruba, **VI** 200

Brother
extended use of title, **VII** 162
as potential father, **VII** 156

"Brotherhood of man"
proven by the universality of sin, **III** 183ff.
recognized in Genesis 10, **I** 62f., 66f.

Brother–sister
marriages between, **VI** 222-224; **VII** 239f.
special relationships, **II** 279f., 281, 292, 293, 315, 317, 328f., **VII** 157, 242ff.

Brow. *See under* Forehead.

Brow ridges, **II** 201f., 204, 205, 219; **IV** 162ff.

Buddhism, **I** 282f.; **VII** 32f.

Building techniques and materials, **I** 39
barrel vault construction, **I** 202
cantilever principle, **I** 202
carpenter's tools, **I** 163, 185f., 192, 202
cement, **I** 202
igloo construction, **I** 157; **II** 160
gums and resins, **I** 164
list of techniques developed in early times, **I** 139
megalithic structures, **I** 185
mud-dried bricks, **I** 193; **VII** 210ff.
plywood (Sumerian), **I** 202
reeds, **I** 177, 193
stone, **I** 185
wood and wood fibers, **I** 162, 163

Bumblebee, cannot fly! **IV** 199

Buprestes beetle, **III** 58ff.

Burg, origin of the word, **II** 86; **VII** 225

Burial
association of bones, misleading sometimes, **II** 34ff.
depth of, misleading, **II** 34

Bushmen, **IV** 129

Business accounting, early development of, **I** 192

Busyness, deceptiveness of, **III** 132f.

Butterflies, **II** 215

C

C

C$_{14}$, **II** 33, 100f., 132; **IX** 44
Caesarian operation, **I** 199, 330
Cain, wife of, **VI** 219-240
Calamites, effect of natural, **VIII** 13
Calculator, mental; in exceptional individuals, **III** 246
Calendar
  "invention" of, **I** 183
  length of month at time of Flood, **IX** 22, 25
California Indians, **IV** 129
Calvary. *See under* Cross, Crucifixion, Jesus Christ.
Calvinism, **V** 288
Camels
  Arab words for, **VI** 216
  in early Egypt, **VII** 158
Camera obscura, **I** 328
Camera vs. the eye, **VII** 85f.
Canaan
  cursing of, **I** 144-150, **II** 313; **VII** 230.
  skin color of, **I** 151ff.
Canaanite, early high civilization of, **I** 91f.
Canada geese, **III** 202
Canal system and locks, **I** 326
Cancer
  cells immortal, **V** 16
  cured by faith, **VIII** 207
Candles, wax, **I** 333
Canine
  brain, evolution of? **II** 239
  teeth, pronounced in feral children, **II** 200
Cannibalism, **IV** 294
Canoe construction, Polynesian, **I** 157, 164
Canopy theory and the Flood, **V** 26

Canstadt Race, **II** 52
Canterbury Cathedral, **IX** 228
Capital punishment in Roman times, **V** 379
Capta vs. data, **IV** 143; **VII** 205; **VIII** 206
Carbon
  chains and life, **I** 349; **IV** 28
  essential to life, **IV** 28
  for life: temperature critical to, **I** 349; **IV** 28f.; **VIII** 38
  properties of, **VIII** 36f., 38, 43
Carbon dioxide
  and plant life, **IV** 28
  in relation to revolving earth, **IX** 142
  time sense altered by, **VI** 23
Carbon 14, **II** 33, 100f., 132; **IX** 44
Cards, playing, **I** 334
  used as paper money, **I** 334
Carib (Orinoco) Flood tradition, **IX** 90
Caribou, counting ability of, **IV** 390
Carnivorous plants, **VIII** 70
Carnivorous world, A fallen world? **VII** 314
Carpenter's tools, development of, **I** 202
Carrel's chicken tissue experiments, **V** 124
Cartesian dualism. *See under* Dualism.
Cartography, **I** 190
Carthage, trading post of Tyre, **VII** 123
Cartoons in early Egypt, **I** 201
Casseopeia, **VII** 84
Cast iron,
  largest statue in the world, **I** 200

Roman attitude toward, **I** 214

Caste system in India, **I** 296

Casualties,
in ancient wars, **VII** 160
civilian vs. military in modern war, **VIII** 182

Cat(s), **III** 66
conditioning of, **IV** 293
counting kittens, **IV** 318f.
vs. dogs, instincts of, **VIII** 69
experiments with decerebrate, **VII** 67
meat diet makes c. less gentle, **III** 165; **IX** 123

Catastrophe,
animals sensitive to pending, **IX** 72, 90
and reconstitution, **IV** 92-106

Catastrophism, **II** 61; **IV** 15, 92-106
and Genesis 1:1-2, **IV** 107f.; **VI** 75-118

Cathedrals, Medieval,
building of, **IX** 228, 253
as an expression of community life, **VIII** 114

Cattle in early Egypt, **VII** 158

Caucasoid (white race), original homeland, **II** 46

Cebus monkeys, **IX** 202. *See also under* Monkeys.

Cell(s). *See also under* Brain cells, Heart.
active cooperation between, **III** 331f.; **IV** 198
aging of, **V** 131
aggregates of, complex, **V** 386f.
asexual, immortal, **V** 128
consciousness in a single c.? **III** 181, 326, 333; **V** 385
Darwinian struggle between! **IV** 199
development of, modified by environment, **IV** 88
differentiation, initiation of, **V** 139; **VIII** 75, 78
division, initiation of, **V** 183

experiments with enucleated, **VIII** 229
mind resident in every c.? **III** 251f.
"mindedness" of, **VIII** 65, 75, 80, 86
mortality of body c., **V** 140
numbers of, in the brain, **III** 249
purposeful activity of, **III** 333
reorganization and reassembly of, **III** 332; **VIII** 74, 76, 80
somatic, mortal, **V** 140

Celtic uninventiveness, **I** 36

Cemeteries, animal, **IV** 94ff.; **IX** 59f.

Central America(n). *See also* Aymara, Aztec, North American Indians, Peruvians.
acoustics of buildings, **I** 185
belief in a Supreme Being, **IV** 128
calendars, **I** 328
civilization of, **II** 113f., 116
clothing made from paper, **I** 332
dental repair, **I** 186
earthquake-proof buildings, **I** 185
mathematics, **I** 183, 328
paper-making and printing, **I** 182, 183, 330f.
rainmaking, **I** 334f.
sailing boats made of bulrushes, **I** 185
surgery, **I** 183f.
textiles and weaving, **I** 184
tools, **I** 185

Central heating
with coal, by Mongols in antiquity, **I** 333
with naphtha gas, in early China, **I** 203
one penalty of, **VIII** 178f.

Cereals, first appearance of, **IV** 66

"Cerebral Rubicon," **II** 14; **IV** 224

"Certainty" in science, impossible? **VII** 25

Chain of Being, The Great, **IV** 213; **V** 396; **VIII** 84, 134, 141

Chains, **I** 186, 211

Chairs
    rocking, **I** 199
    sedan, **I** 201

Chaldean length of year, **V** 56

Chance
    as an agency of miracle, **VIII** 37
    as an element in Greek philosophy, **VIII** 126
    importance of, in modern philosophy, **I** 223; **VIII** 106
    a poor explanation, **III** 62

Change, current popularity of, **II** 149

Changu Daru culture, **I** 197; **II** 95, 96; **V** 65

Chaos
    goddess of, **VII** 289
    original creation not a, **VI** 80ff.

Character. *See also under* Christian character, Christian growth.
    development of, dependent on balance of three basic needs, **I** 249
    "likeness," biblical term for c., **III** 128ff.
    portrayal of, in art, **VII** 92
    reflected in personal name, **II** 298, **IX** 186

Chastening, **III** 217f., 280; **VI** 163f.

Chedorlaomer, breakdown of the name, **VII** 163

Chemical reactions and temperature, **III** 76

Chemistry of the body and temperament. *See under* Temperament.

Chemistry, origin of the word? **VI** 202

Chicadees, **IV** 204

Chichen Itza, **I** 185

Chicken(s)
    communication between unborn, **IV** 276
    dietary wisdom of, **IV** 310
    experiments with tissue of, **V** 124

Childbirth
    anaesthetics and, **IX** 138, 139
    and multiple conception, **IX** 137
    without pain, **IX** 210
    pain during, **IX** 137
    surprising modern ignorance regarding, **III** 138

Childhood
    of animals vs. man, **IV** 284, 287, 290
    innocence of? **III** 30f.
    long dependency of, **IV** 288

Child raising. *See under* Children.

Children
    accountability of, **III** 297f.
    adoption of, **II** 278, 289ff.; **VII** 264
    art of, **VII** 90
    behavior of young, asocial or criminal, **III** 30f.
    cruelty of, **III** 343
    decerebrate or anencephalic, **V** 213; **VIII** 67f.
    education of, in primitive societies, **II** 169f., 279, 292f.
    a gift of God? **V** 196f.; **VIII** 71, 79f.
    go-carts for, **I** 186
    growth and development of, relatively slow, **IV** 274, 285
    and the kingdom of God, **III** 97
    and language learning, **II** 261; **IV** 270ff.
    learning ability compared with that of animals, **IV** 270, 271, 274, 284f.
    legitimized by marriage, **II** 278
    and mother love. *See under* Mother.
    naming of things, and personality development, **II** 267; **IX** 174f.
    person vs. personality, **V** 197f.
    place of, in different societies, **II** 304; **VII** 171f.

required for fulfillment of marriage contract, **II** 284, 288
Chimpanzees **II** 13, 182, 212; **III** 107, 118; **IV** 314f.
  becoming meat-eaters, **IX** 122
  counting ability of, very limited, **IV** 317
  facial expression of, **IV** 270, 271 (fn.), 273
  needles; as used by c. vs. man, **IV** 314
  paintings by, **IV** 317
  teaching language: Gua, **IV** 269; Sarah, **IV** 274; Vicki, **IV** 270; Washoe, **IV** 272
  tool-making by? **III** 107
Chin
  factors influencing form of, **IV** 164
  human vs. ape, **II** 207; **IV** 243f.
China (Chinese), **I** 204-214, 282-289
  absence of science in, **I** 32, 286f.
  absence of true philosophy in, **I** 31ff., 282
  astronomy, **VIII** 154
  cast iron stoves in early, **I** 200
  civilization of, **I** 284; **II** 104 (fn. 95)
  Confucianism, **I** 32, 257, 283
  early encyclopedias of, **I** 187
  as "Far Cathay," **I** 104, 107
  Flood tradition, **IX** 75, 85
  foot binding of girls in, **IV** 85; **VIII** 223
  gods of, **I** 121f.; **IV** 120ff.
  ideograms not conducive to abstractions, **I** 286
  Indo-European languages contrasted with, **I** 288
  ingenuity of, **I** 285
  language of, **I** 273, 288; **VI** 184
  logic, use of, **I** 289
  materialism in, **IV** 121
  mathematics, **I** 183, 327, 328
  monotheism of early, **IV** 121ff.

nonphilosophical, **I** 33, 282, 285
nonreligious character of, **I** 257, 284
nontheologically inclined, **I** 285
Oracle bones of, **IV** 121
origin of people of, **I** 104, 105ff., 107
practical nature of, **I** 32f., 278
racial mixture in, **I** 312
related to Hittites? **I** 104
religion of, **I** 282ff., 284; **IV** 120ff.
sleeve design in clothing, **I** 213
Sumerian links with? **I** 106; **VI** 186, 210
symbol for boat, **IX** 106
technology in early, **VII** 31. *See* Chinese technology.
tradition of former creation, **VI** 112
wisdom of, **I** 30f., 257, 278
writing limited by ideograms, **I** 286
Chinese and Mongol technology, **I** 205-214, 318f.; **VII** 31
  air conditioning, **I** 333
  aircraft, **I** 205, 211
  asbestos, **I** 322
  balloons, **I** 211
  beauty contests, **I** 327
  bird-banding, **I** 335
  bow and arrow, **I** 209
  bronze, **I** 322
  canals and locks, **I** 326
  central heating, **I** 333
  chain pump, **I** 205
  chains, **I** 211f.
  cire perdu casting, **I** 214
  clocks, **I** 205, 321
  compass, **I** 205
  deep well drilling, **I** 205ff., 212f.
  dentistry, **I** 177, 334
  encyclopedias, **I** 187
  explosives, **I** 205
  ephedrine, **I** 212
  finger printing, **I** 205, 335
  flamethrowers, **I** 208f.

gas warfare, **I** 209
gimbal suspension systems, **I** 205
gliders, **I** 205, 211
gloves, **I** 213
graticules for mapmaking, **I** 206
gunpowder, **I** 205
hairpins, **I** 327
harness, **I** 205
helicopters, **I** 205
ink, **I** 212, 317
kites, **I** 211
medical practices, **I** 294 (fn. 128), 330
metallurgy, **I** 210, 214, 321
naphtha gas, **I** 205, 213
paper-making, **I** 205, 212, 322f.
paper money, **I** 205
parachutes, **I** 211
playing cards, **I** 334
porcelain, **I** 205
printing, **I** 205, 212, 332f.
repeating "magazine" crossbow, **I** 205
rotary quern, **I** 205
shipbuilding, **I** 326
silkworm domestication, **I** 205, 207
sleeves, **I** 213
stirrups, **I** 205
suspension bridges, **I** 211
toilet facilities, **I** 333
vaccines, **I** 330
wheelbarrows, **I** 205
Chipmunks
territorial confidence of, **IV** 191
tree-planting activities of, **III** 52
Chlorophyll and hemoglobin, **IV** 154
Cholinesterase, **III** 309
Choukoutien Man, **II** 42, 51, 115, 223; **IV** 289
Christ. *See also under* Jesus Christ.
God-made man, **I** 229f.
key to the universe, **I** 218, 225-239
physically immortal, **I** 236f.

symbols used for, **VII** 103; **IX** 243f.

Christendom, emergence of, **III** 81

Christian(s). *See also under* Saint.
as another species of Homo sapiens, **III** 110, 315-350
chastening of, **III** 217f., 280
culture viewed as "worldliness," **I** 245
fellowship with God, broken by sin, **III** 276, 279
forgiveness vs. cleansing, **III** 298, 305
and governments, when to be obeyed or disobeyed, **IX** 143ff., 147f.
indwelt by Jesus Christ, **III** 168f.; **V** 206, 208, 364f.
life goal of, **III** 197
maturing, nature of the process, **III** 132f., 189f.
new name of, **IX** 188
new nature vs. old nature in, **III** 127f., 178
other-worldliness of, **III** 133
personality of, structure/vessel and content/filling, **III** 178ff.
and prayer, **IX** 256-286
and pride of grace, **III** 216. *See also under* and spiritual pride.
problem of the suffering of the, **VII** 58f., 60
responsibility for growth, limits of, **III** 189f.
rod of God as a comfort to the, **III** 213-224
as the salt of civilization, **II** 141; **III** 184
sinless? **III** 177f., 189f.; **V** 365
and spiritual pride, **III** 197, 219, 222; **IX** 275, 286
as stones in the Temple of the Body of Christ, **III** 191f.
and suffering, benefit of, **IX** 111f.
the two wills of, **III** 38

value of social restraints to, **III** 215

what is changed and what is not in, **III** 170f.

and the world, **III** 347f.

World View of, and of the naturalist, **IV** 23-33

Christian character
defined, **III** 131
filling, biblical word for, **III** 176f.
fruits vs. works, **III** 131f., 192f.; **VI** 163f.
how produced, **III** 190f.; **VI** 159f.

Christian faith, the. *See also* Christian theology, Theology.
and integration of thought, **VIII** 197
as key to new knowledge, **VIII** 199, 212
logic in, **V** 174; **VIII** 201, 202
organic unity of, **VIII** 200; **IX** 303
premises, importance of, in, **VIII** 202
premises of, vs. of science, **VIII** 200
vs. religious faith, **VI** 56
as a system, **V** 77, 79

Christian growth
and new vs. old nature, **III** 127f., 178
our part in, **III** 189ff.
principles of, **III** 189ff., 216ff., 313ff.
secret of, **III** 128ff., 189f.

Christian scholarship. *See also under* Scholarship.
defined, **IX** 292
moral responsibility of, **IX** 290
a plea for, **IX** 302-306
a protest, **IX** 289-301
specific responsibilities of, **IX** 293

Christian theology
evolutionary philosophy fatal to, **V** 79

premises of, very special, **VIII** 215

Christian World View
building of a, for today, **VIII** 192-216
as a "map," **III** 82

Christmas cards
dangers inherent in, **V** 210
of different cultures, **IX** 240

Chromidrosis, **V** 310f.; **IX** 217

Chromosomal sex vs. gender, **V** 389f.

Chromosomes, sex **V** 91

Chronology. *See also* Dating.
biblical, **IX** 44
data of Genesis and, **V** 28
extended by gaps? **VII** 259
gaps in biblical, accounted for, **VI** 45ff.
of Jewish kings, **V** 355f.
of Josephus, **V** 33f.
longevity in antiquity and its bearing on, **V** 12-74
of Minoan civilization, **II** 32
of the Pharaohs of the oppression, **VII** 181
reductions in dating, recent, **II** 31f.
Ussher and, **VII** 222
variants of biblical, **V** 33f.

Chukchee (Siberia), **II** 294, 296, 298; **III** 118, 137; **IX** 171
meaning of word for *man*, **VII** 201 (fn. 80)
naming of children, **III** 137
Shaman, **V** 311

Church, the. *See also under* Body of Christ.
as a "Body," **III** 348f.; **V** 384f., 389
as His Body, never failing (Temple), **III** 178
an important aspect of its message, **VIII** 193
a neglected task of, **VIII** 216

preparation for the coming of, **VII** 34

as a psychic unity, **III** 346

as a recreated human species, **III** 316

its responsibilities, **I** 46

Cigarettes, **I** 203

Circular reasoning, **II** 250 (fn. 2). *See also under* Reasoning.

to account for geological gaps, **IV** 62

in antropology, **II** 163

in evolutionary theory, **II** 26 (fn. 32), 163, 250 (fn. 2); **IV** 62, 175

Circulation of the blood, early Chinese recognition of, **I** 294, 330

Circumcision, **V** 85; **VIII** 221f.

Cire perdu casting technique, **I** 214

City, the, **VII** 206, 207, 224f.

concept, not Indo-European, **I** 193; **II** 86f.

cuneiform determinative after the word, **VII** 206, 225

earliest concept of, **VI** 199f.

early term for, **I** 108; **VI** 198f.; **VII** 206f., 224f.

the first, **VII** 206f; 225; **IX** 47

founding traditions of, **VII** 207f.

size of early, **II** 187

walled, **II** 121

words for, **I** 108; **VII** 206f., 224f.

City of God (Augustine), **III** 81, 84

Civilization

vs. barbarism, **III** 22

basic centers of, in antiquity, **I** 98

begins high, in Cradle of Man, **II** 86f.

Chinese, early, **II** 104

Christians as the "salt" of, **II** 141; **III** 184

civilizing process defined (Raglan), **II** 149

Cradle of, **II** 95, 102; **V** 61f.

vs. culture, **I** 102, 176, 244f.

cycles of, **I** 311

dependent upon the few inventive people, **I** 160

detrimental effect of, on primitives, **II** 140

effects of, on religious faith, **IV** 133

factors facilitating the development of, **II** 152f.

high, dependent on three dimensions, **I** 45, 48, 252, 263

and man's innate wickedness, **III** 18f., 34

missionaries as agents of, **II** 140

necessary constraints of, **I** 244f.; **III** 341

necessity of, **III** 46

vs. primitive society, **III** 27f.

rapid early development of, causes, **II** 136ff.; **V** 13

as restraints on behavior, **III** 19

size and posture of man and, **VIII** 41

sudden appearance of high, **I** 188, 194; **V** 14

Sumerian, **II** 92, **V** 64f.

uniformity of, at the beginning in the Middle East, **V** 62

war almost inevitable in a high, **IX** 153f.

Civil vs. religious authority, **IX** 148

Cladoselache, **IV** 42

Class distinctions

breakdown of, **VIII** 175f.

not fatal to Christian ideals, **VIII** 116

"Classification," man's propensity for, **IV** 315ff.; **VIII** 113

Classification systems, **III** 56

Cleaning habits of animals, **IV** 196f.

Cleansing from sin, **III** 306f.

Climate

change of, at the time of the Flood, **V** 25

and culture, **II** 136; **IX** 141f.

and disease, **I** 350; **IV** 29; **VIII** 39; **IX** 142

effect on life span, **V** 23
effect on morphology **IV** 159;
VIII 234. *See also under* Temperature.
fluctuations of, beneficial, **IX** 141
influence of, on history, **IX** 51
Climatic change, evidence of drastic, **IV** 102, 105
Climatius, **IV** 42
Clocks, **I** 205, 213, 321 (fn. 196)
Cloning, **VIII** 161
Clothing
Arctic, **I** 158f.; **II** 159
asbestos, **I** 322
buckskin, **I** 164
Chinese sleeves, **I** 213
design features of, **I** 164
diaphanous, in Egypt, **VII** 153
gloves (Crete), **I** 201
man's vs. animal's attitude toward, **IV** 219, 296
paper (Aztec), **I** 332
rubber shoes and ponchos, **I** 179
and sweating, **IX** 213ff.
tailored, **I** 158; **II** 159; **IV** 243
Coal
early use of, for heating, **I** 333
rapid formation of, **II** 32
Coalfields in Antarctic, **IV** 102
Cocaine, **I** 176
Code of Hammurabi, **II** 319; **VII** 264
Coelacanth, **III** 324; **IV** 43; **VI** 28
Coffee, discovery of, **I** 199
Cognition vs. recognition **III** 259f.
Cold, man's defence against, **IV** 258
Cold sweating, **IX** 198
Cold-bloodedness, **IV** 43, 69, 93, 155
Collective consciousness, **III** 183, 263
"Collective unconscious," **III** 142, 160; **V** 387
Color
as basis of racial classification, **I** 72

Fuegan surprise at Darwin's skin, **I** 148
"overlap," as paradigm of soul, **V** 269, 279, 281
Colored races as Hamites, **I** 12f., 14, 53, 102; **VII** 233
"Comfort zone," **IX** 196
Common grace, as a preservative of society, **IX** 163
Communal ownership, **IV** 290
Communication
among animals, **IV** 276
disruptiveness of modern methods of, **VIII** 177
grammar important in, **IV** 274
vs. language, **II** 253
mathematics as universal, **IV** 316
Communion service, use of wine in, **IX** 226
Compass, magnetic, **I** 205
Competition
does not produce species, **IV** 187ff.
intraspecific? **IV** 183ff., 186
not necessarily evil, **IX** 155
Computers
and brains, **III** 254f.; **VIII** 143
and consciousness, **VIII** 143
Concentration camps, **III** 18, 210
Conception. *See under* Fertilization.
effect of alcohol on, **V** 104f.
example of suprising modern ignorance about, **III** 138
original sin introduced at? **III** 292
Conceptual thought, unique to man, **IV** 278; **VIII** 44
Concrete, early use of, **I** 202
Concupiscence, **III** 308
Confinement, influence on animal behavior, **III** 65, 72
Confucianism, **I** 30-33, 257, 283f.
Confusion of languages, **VI** 175-218; **VII** 196
at Babel, **VI** 176ff.

as a judgment and a blessing, **VI** 217f.
of modern times, **VI** 217f.
and technical jargon, **II** 137; **IX** 155
Conjunctive vs. disjunctive in Hebrew, **VI** 87; **VII** 284
Conscience
bad c. as a sickness, **III** 275f.
purging of, **III** 279
Consciousness
biological origins of, **III** 257f.
of cells, individually, **III** 181f., 326, 333; **V** 385
computers and, **VIII** 143
c. of consciousness, **VIII** 42, 92
in the cortex? **III** 329; **IV** 227
cosmic **V** 395
of a crowd, **III** 263, 337f.
as epiphenomenon of matter, **III** 317; **VIII** 142
first emergence of, **III** 324
and frontal lobes, **IV** 227
group, **III** 263f., 336
Huxley's "glorious paradox" and origin of, **VIII** 137
in all matter, **III** 258, 324
matter as "congealed," **III** 317
vs. mechanism, **VIII** 68
as mere electrochemistry? **III** 320
vs. mindedness, **III** 321, 330
in organisms without a brain, **III** 251
origin of, **III** 257f., 259, 324; **VIII** 85, 136, 142
and panpsychism, **VIII** 141
in plant life? **III** 334
prior to birth? **V** 198
protoplasmic? **III** 329
quantification of, **VIII** 87, 143
and reactivity, **V** 276
in the resurrection, **III** 326
vs. self-consciousness, **III** 105f., 182f., 259; **VIII** 42, 92
spinal, **III** 329

and telepathy, **III** 263f.
in unicellular animals, **III** 257
unified into a single sense, **III** 182f., 260, 263f., 335
Conservatism
cultural cost of, **II** 205f.
preserved by education, **II** 173
primitive culture and **I** 300; **II** 126, 150f.; **IV** 300
sometimes a technological advantage, **II** 269
of Stone Age cultures, **II** 102
and survival, **II** 169f., 178; **IV** 300; **VI** 230
Constantinople, fall of, **III** 82; **VIII** 117, 119
Construct form, use of in Hebrew, **VI** 80f.
Contentment, conditions for, **III** 207
"Content" of personality, **III** 152f., 171
filling, N. T. term for, **III** 171
Continental drift, **VII** 302
Continuity, principle of, in biology, **VIII** 84f., 142
Continuity of the germ plasm, **V** 86, 184ff.
Continuity of woman's seed, **V** 157
Contraceptives, native use of, **I** 329
Contradiction(s)
in art? **VII** 85ff.
truth communicated by, **VII** 77ff.
Contradiction(s) in Scripture, **V** 224, 228f.; **VII** 67-104
by design, **VII** 77f.
due to errors in transcription, **VII** 70f.;
essential to revelation, **VII** 104; **IX** 78
in the Gospels, reconciliation of, **VII** 95
more apparent than real, **VII** 72
nature of, **VII** 70-83
of numbers, **VII** 70f.

resulting from translation, **VII** 73

samples of, in the Gospels, **VII** 106

types of, **VII** 68

unity of Scripture preserved by apparent, **VII** 253

Control vs. understanding, **VIII** 169

Controversy, value of, **IX** 149f.

Convergence, **II** 17, 208, 212, 215; **IV** 140-170
of cranial form, **II** 184
and digestive fluids, **IV** 155
vs. divergence, **IV** 141
evolutionary theory and, **IV** 140ff.
and eye formation, **IV** 155f.
fact of, **IV** 146-159
and homology, **VIII** 78, 235
implications of, **IV** 160-170
between man and apes, **IV** 166
meaning of, **IV** 140-145
and the origin of man, **IV** 140-170
pervasiveness of, in nature, **IV** 140f., 149f., 152f.
of skull form, **IV** 160f.
of tooth form, **II** 213ff.

Conversion, **III** 344. *See also under* New birth, Rebirth.
as change of personality, **III** 150, 164, 170ff.
Christian, **III** 168
miracle, place of in c. in early Church, **VII** 53
nature of true, **III** 170-180
"non-Christian," **III** 164, 167f.

Conviction(s)
basis of action, **VIII** 184
healthful influence of, **VIII** 176
penalty of loss of, **VIII** 213
value of, **VIII** 212

Cooperation in nature, **III** 70

Copper
early beads of, **II** 92
early use of, **II** 98

Corals, **III** 73f.

Corinthian society, corruptness of, **VII** 55

Cormorants used for fishing, **I** 169

Corn cultivation by Indians, **I** 168

Cornelius, prayers and alms of, **III** 125

Coronary disease and heart rupture, **V** 309

Corpuscular theory of light, **VIII** 31f.

Correspondence, freedom of, in Greco-Roman world, **VII** 28

Cosmetics
eye salves, **I** 203
hairpins, **I** 327
jewelry, **I** 196
mirrors, glass, **I** 204

"Cosmic consciousness," **V** 395

Cosmic radiation, **VI** 233f.
and the Flood, **V** 25

Cosmogeny, pagan, **VI** 113. *See also under* Cosmology.

"Cosmological principle," **III** 53

Cosmology(s)
four views of, **IV** 17
short life of, **VIII** 26

Cosmos. *See also under* Universe.
into chaos, **VII** 284
"pregnant with man," **VII** 47; **VIII** 45
root meaning of the word, **VI** 84

Cotylosaurus, **IV** 43

Council of Carthage, **III** 291

Council of Trent, **VIII** 121

Counting
by animals, **IV** 317f.
under hypnosis, **III** 246

Courtesy, what it is, **VIII** 190

Cousin relationships, **II** 281ff., 301
cross-cousins, **VII** 156, 241
parallel cousins, **VII** 156, 241

Couvade, **III** 138

Covenant relationship with Israel, **VII** 16, 35, 36, 38, 41, 46, 47, 50, 60, 63

Coveting, seriousness of, **V** 388

Cradle of Civilization, **II** 95, 102; **V** 61f.

Cradle of Culture, **II** 81

Cradle of Man, **II** 40-57
  civilization begins high in, **II** 86ff.
  in Iranian Highland Plateau, **I** 119f., 129f., 130; **II** 28, 35, 40ff., 55; **IX** 45f., 49

Cranesbill plant and pod structure, **IV** 78f.

Cranial capacity, **III** 49; **IV** 223ff.
  of Australopithecines, **II** 13, 212f.
  of Boskop Man, **IV** 225
  of Cro-Magnon Man, **IV** 225
  of early man, **IV** 225; **V** 58
  false estimates of, **II** 21
  of fossil and modern man, **II** 15, 21
  and intelligence, **II** 164, 180, 205f.; **IV** 177
  list of capacities, **II** 181; **IV** 223, 225
  of Neanderthal Man, **II** 230, 232; **IV** 225
  of Pithecanthropus, **II** 236; **IV** 223
  of Sinanthropus, **IV** 225
  of Solo Man, **IV** 225
  of Wadjak Man, **IV** 225

Cranial deformation
  deliberate, **II** 183
  due to dietary habits, **II** 183; **IV** 160f.
  modifications of, **IV** 160

Cranium. *See under* Skull.

Crankshaft, **I** 206

Create, meaning of word in Hebrew, **VI** 83, 115; **VII** 282f.

Creating vs. making, **III** 104f.

Creation
  activity of God, **IV** 13, 15, 50, 85
  of Adam, **III** 90; **V** 146, 179
  Aggasiz's view of, **IV** 90f.
  Big Bang theory and, **VIII** 19f.
  Darwin not opposed to, at first, **IV** 90
  and divergence, **IV** 81-91
  effect of the Fall upon, limited, **VIII** 8
  evidence of throughout geological ages, **I** 359
  ex nihilo, **IV** 19, 88; **VIII** 23f., 135
  forethought in, **VI** 30
  of forms that anticipated man, **V** 127
  God's use of mechanism in, **I** 361
  with a "history," **IV** 33, 108; **VI** 31f.
  idea of, scientifically acceptable, **VIII** 23ff.
  an inconceivable concept, **VIII** 24, 135, 185
  instantaneous, **IV** 32; **VI** 32
  of life, **I** 367. *See also under* Life— origin of.
  vs. making, **III** 104f.
  of man, **I** 240ff.
  of man, purpose of, **III** 274; **IV** 20, 322ff.
  of man, to display God's love, **V** 78
  of matter (Eddington, Gamow), **VIII** 20f.
  moment of, **VI** 20; **VIII** 19
  "perfectly conceivable," **VIII** 24
  with potential for variation, **IV** 88
  for redemption, **IV** 21, 325
  rejected by science? **IV** 35f.
  stages of, orderly, planned with man in mind, **IV** 64ff.
  starting point of, not chaos, **VIII** 95
  successive forms of, evidence for, **I** 357; **IV** 87, 89

theory of relativity and, **VI** 9ff., 27-37

time factor in, **VI** 25, 27f.; **VIII** 247

with time, not *in* time, **VI** 19; **VIII** 111

why not a separate creation for Eve, **V** 203

Creation account, naming of things in the, **IX** 183

Creationism (theological), **VIII** 80

Creative activity

growing evidence of, **IV** 48-63

of Jesus Christ, a succession of, **I** 367f.

special periods of, **IV** 65f.

Creativity, a criterion of humanness, **III** 106f.

Creator, the, **VIII** 16ff., 28ff., 55

"absentee," **VIII** 55

aesthetic sense of, **IV** 205

immensity of work of, **VIII** 28ff.

Jesus Christ as, **I** 367; **V** 218

power of, **VIII** 16-27

primitive view of, **IV** 129

science automatically eliminates evidence of, **IV** 36; **VIII** 55f., 62ff.

universe as the handiwork of, **VIII** 28-34

as "watchmaker," **VIII** 8

wisdom of, as a designer, **VIII** 35-45

Credulity of science, **IV** 69; **VIII** 8

Cree, Flood tradition of, **IX** 32

Creeds, **V** 286

Criminality

and extrovertism, **III** 345

genetic basis of? **III** 30, 146

social environment, effect of on, **III** 31f.

Crippled animals, fate of, **IV** 203ff.

"Critical point" concept of culture, **IV** 320

Crocodiles, **III** 70; **VIII** 236

Cro-Magnon Man, **II** 50; **IV** 225; **V** 58, 67

and language, **IV** 267

Cross, the. *See also under* Crucifixion.

the cause of Jesus' death? **V** 297-301

not an early Christian symbol, **V** 347

extremely prolonged form of capital punishment, **V** 302ff.

superscription of, **VII** 79

"time" spent on, by the Lord, **VI** 49

Crossbow, repeating, **I** 208

Cross-cousin relationship, **II** 281, 301, 324

Crossopterygians, **IV** 42

Crowd behavior, **III** 20, 42f., 183, 345

mass hysteria and, **III** 35

shared "soul" of, **III** 142, 336

Crowding

of animals, **IV** 184ff., 251

does not lead to evolution, **IV** 186f.

effects of, **IV** 185; **VIII** 234

Crowd psychology, **V** 387

Crow Indians, **II** 302

Crown of thorns, **V** 293

Crucifixion

after beheading, **VII** 179

demanded for Christ in ignorance, **VII** 38

examples of, **V** 303f.

of Jesus Christ, **III** 43f.; **V** 294-331

as a judgment upon man, **III** 186

a "key" to the universe, **I** 218, 231

part played by Shem, Ham and Japheth in, **I** 22; **VII** 98, 234

as a stage for the Lord's death, **V** 302, 326, 371

as a special form of cursing, **V** 319

time as experienced during, **V** 313f.

a very slow death, **V** 302ff.

Cruelty
among animals? **IX** 125f.
of children, **III** 343
in nature, **III** 64, 65, 296; **IX** 126, 210

Crystal Palace foretold, **VII** 114

Cubit length of, **IX** 37

Cultural
behavior, illuminates incidents in Scripture, **II** 273-331
conservatism, **II** 105
degeneration, evidences of, **II** 104-125; **IX** 50f.
degeneration, some causes of, **II** 125-141
devolution, **II** 35ff., 61f., 106, 122f.; **IV** 110f.
evolution: fallacies of, **II** 250ff.
  : initially unreasonably slow, **II** 102
  : natural selection in, **II** 108
evolutionary sequences, fallacy of, **II** 71-75
evolutionism: circular reasoning in, **II** 26
  : fallacies in, **II** 26, 65
  : abandonment of, **II** 68ff.
factors influencing personality development, **III** 145, 147ff.
vs. instinctive behavior, **III** 60; **IV** 263, 282
involution, **II** 106
patterns and rationale of, **II** 276-307
relativism, **III** 108
and religious "evolution" do not run parallel, **II** 109
"universals," **III** 157; **V** 334f.

Cultural anthropology, **II** 275-331.
See also under Primitive tribes.

"Cultural Rubicon," **IV** 263

Cultural uniformity
in the early world, **I** 128; **II** 188

vs. physical diversity, **I** 126, 128; **II** 43, 175, 222; **IV** 67; **VI** 230
among primitives, **II** 106
very early parallelisms, **II** 33

Culture(s)
African, evidence of early high, **II** 121
America a melting pot of, **I** 310
among animals? **IV** 208
the beginning of high c. is rapid, **II** 81-103
vs. civilization, **I** 176, 244f.
and climate, **II** 136; **IX** 141
complexification of, harmful, **IV** 295f.
conditions favoring development of, **III** 207, 208
conduct of natural man artificially restrained by, **III** 158
conservatism of, in small populations, **VI** 230
Cradle of, **II** 81
"critical point" concept of, **IV** 320
degeneration of, **II** 35f., 61f., 106, 122f.; **IV** 110f.
effect of migration on, **I** 122, 221f.; **II** 36ff., 69, 112, 123, 125, 221f.; **IV** 167
evolutionary theory and, **II** 65, 68f., 102, 250f.
higher, falls lower, **II** 71, 124
hostile to spiritual truth, **IV** 133
influence of, on cranial form, **IV** 162f.
influence of, on personality devopment, **III** 147ff.
isolation inhibits development of, **II** 119
and language, **I** 254, 269ff.; **II** 137; **IV** 266f.
as learned behavior, **IV** 263, 292
longevity accelerates growth of, **II** 136; **V** 68
man uniquely a maker of, **III** 117, 122; **IV** 126, 263-280, 283

and marriage patterns, **II** 277ff.,
280f., 294f., 299, 302ff., 318ff.;
VII 154ff.
missionaries as carriers of culture, **II** 140
moral limitations of, **III** 18
not genetically determined, **II**
130
opens the way for good to be
done, **III** 18, 22, 42, 46, 97
population size, effect on, **II** 137
vs. religion, **IV** 133
as restraint of human wickedness, **I** 244f.; **III** 18, 42, 45,
158
slavery important to the spread
of, **VII** 27
social behavior's complexity endangers the survival of, **III**
117; **IV** 295f.
vs. society, **IV** 292
stability of, **V** 49
stereoscopic vision, opposable
thumbs and, **IV** 242
sudden appearance of high, **V**
61f.
three-dimensional nature of, **I**
45, 251
tool-making and, **II** 14; **IV** 263
uniquely human? **IV** 263f., 283
universal categories of. *See under*
Universals, cultural.
variability of, and population
size, **I** 126, 128; **II** 43, 175,
222; **IV** 67; **VI** 230
viewed as a "life" process in three
dimensions, **I** 48
war favored by high, **III** 19
zones of, **II** 104f.
Cuneiform
complexity of, **VI** 210f.
determinatives for a place name,
VII 206, 225
difficulties in translation, **VI** 105

flood traditions in c. literature,
IX 76, 78
ideographs relating to original
homeland, **IX** 46
literature, **IV** 113
sign for city, **II** 87; **VII** 206, 225
signs, **VII** 151, 225
tablets, **II** 94f.
Curse
the crucifixion as a special kind
of, **V** 319
of Eden, **IX** 115
of Ham, circumstances of, **I** 25ff.,
144ff.
Cursing
of Canaan by Noah, **I** 25f., 114-
152
of son instead of father, **I** 26,
146ff.; **VII** 231
Cush, two areas so named, **I** 76f.;
VII 197f.; **IX** 47
Cuttlefish, sudden extinction of, **IV**
103
Cyanide poison, extraction of, from
manioc, **I** 172
Cycles of history, **I** 311
the theory of, **II** 83
Cyclic theory of the universe, **VIII**
27
Cylinder of Nabonidus, **VII** 152
Cylinder seals, **II** 94
Cynicism, **VII** 20f.
and apathy, **VIII** 176
Cynics, **VII** 28
Cynognathus, **IV** 44
Cytoplasm
function of, **VIII** 227
importance of, **V** 113f., 189
plasmagenes in, **VIII** 224
of the sperm, **VIII** 229
Cytoplasmic genes **VIII** 228, 229.
See also under Plasmagenes.
Cytoplasmic inheritance, **II** 211;
VIII 224, 226,228ff.

D

Daisy and gorilla quote, **III** 118; **IV** 320

Damnatio Memoriae, **VII** 257

Dancing figure from Mohenjo Daru, **II** 96

Dandelions, Huxley's experiments with, **VIII** 233

Daniel's sixty-nine weeks of years, **VII** 36

Dark Ages, not entirely dark, **VIII** 116

Darkness
and light alternating, **I** 349; **IV** 28; **IX** 142
three hours of, on Calvary, **V** 314; **VI** 26
time sense affected by, **VI** 24
word for in Hebrew, **VII** 288

Darwin and Galileo, parallels between, **VIII** 159

Darwinism. *See also under* Evolution.
evangelistic fervor of proponents, **VIII** 159 (fn.)
timeliness of, **VIII** 133

Data vs. capta, **IV** 143; **VII** 205; **VIII** 206

Dating. *See also under* C₁₄.
by dendrochronology, **II** 132
of the Exodus? **VII** 182, 188
methods of, **II** 33, 132
Niagara River escarpment and, **II** 32, 132f.
reductions in, **II** 31f., 101, 133
by stratigraphy vs. morphology, **II** 194
of the Table of Nations, **I** 75f.
by varve counting, **II** 132.

Dauermodification(s). **II** 211; **IV** 88; **VIII** 9, 219-249
definition of, **VIII** 224, 226, 229

evidence of, in nature, **VIII** 232-237
in man, **VIII** 238-249
nature of, **VIII** 226-231
origin of the term, **VIII** 226
in plants, **VIII** 233
temporary effect of, **VIII** 230
transient nature of, **VIII** 323
ubiquity of, **VIII** 237

David, City of, **VII** 132

"Dawn Man" (Eoanthropus), **III** 57

Day, meaning of, in Genesis, **IV** 108; **VI** 101f., 115; **VII** 294f.

Day of Atonement, **V** 316

Dead, the raising of, **III** 144 (fn.); **IV** 108; **V** 123, 351f.; **VI** 34; **VII** 42f.; **VIII** 87

Deaf-mutism, **II** 263, 266, 300; **IV** 306, 307 (and fn.); **VI** 231; **VII** 235

Dead Sea, geography of the area, **VII** 174f.

Death, physical, **V** 12. *See also under* Jesus Christ (death of), Dying, Natural death.
an acquired characteristic, **V** 87, 152, 189
by an act of will, **V** 379
an advantage to life? **V** 17, 128
age of individual at death, recorded, **VII** 233, 237, 239
animals not living in fear of, **III** 67; **VIII** 219
begins at birth, **V** 133, 182
biological, mechanisms of, **V** 131
as a blessing: African tradition, **IX** 115
cause of, **III** 287
cause of, still a mystery, **V** 119

definition of, difficult, **V** 119ff., 350

eclipses time, **VI** 42

entered through man, not woman, **V** 190

fear of, **III** 64

and hypothermy, **V** 122

introduced by poison of the forbidden fruit, **IX** 114

isolation, absolute, equals death, **III** 274, 276

of Jesus Christ, **I** 231ff.; **V** 294ff., 337

loss of appetite as sign of impending death, **IX** 126

as a merciful provision, **IX** 114

mind persists through, **III** 254, 256f.

natural for animals? **IV** 100, 186f.; **V** 136

"natural," of man, a legal fiction, **V** 17, 178

not due to "old age," **V** 135

not inevitable for man? **V** 134

not natural to plants, **V** 15

occurs upon departure of the spirit, **V** 273

of "old age" in childhood (progeria), **V** 22

origin of, **V** 94

as a penalty for man, **III** 289; **V** 18; **IX** 113

process, not event, **V** 121ff., 138, 146

programmed for some species? **V** 136f.

and reproduction, **V** 136, 137

senescence not equated with, **V** 140, 141, 177

significance of three days and nights before certification of, **V** 123, 348f.

spawning related to death, **V** 136

vs. spiritual, **IV** 321

time eclipsed in, **VI** 42

transfiguration alternative to, **V** 18, 151, 163f., 399

Decapitation. *See under* Decerebrates.

Deception through magnification or speed, **VIII** 69

Decerebrates
animals, **V** 212f.; **VIII** 67ff., 136, 137
humans, **V** 195, 197

Decerebration and memory loss, **III** 252, 256

Decortication. *See under* Decerebrates.

Dedication
capacity for, in youth, **VIII** 212
importance and value of, **I** 220ff.; **VIII** 175f.

Deeds vs. motives **VI** 149ff., 166f., 201f., 247ff.

Deer, **III** 65

Defences of animals, **IV** 156, 201f., 247, 249

Degeneration
causes of, **II** 126-141
of culture, **II** 35f., 61f., 106, 119, 122f.; **IV** 110f.
evolutionary, **III** 50, 159
of facial form, **II** 208
and isolation, **II** 45, 113; **IV** 168
not evolution but d. of high culture, **II** 81-103
physical, **II** 45, 113, 216, 221f.; **III** 49
physical and mental, **III** 47-50
structural, **IV** 166f.

Dehydrated foods, **I** 326

Deity
Babylonian symbol for, **V** 252
Chinese symbol for, **IV** 121ff.
pagan names of, **V** 254f.

Delphic oracle, **VII** 23

Deluge. *See under* Flood.

Demon(s), **VII** 227
origin of, **VI** 127
"physical" strength of, **III** 228

Demon possession
   and epilepsy, **III** 227
   and lunacy, **III** 166
   reality of, **III** 166
Dendrochronology, **II** 132
Denominationalism, "benefits" of, **IX** 157
Dental anatomy and relationships, **II** 21
Dental caries
   in animals before man, **IX** 113
   in early man, **V** 24
Dentistry
   gold capping by early Mongols, **I** 334
   repairs and fillings, (Middle Americans), **I** 186
   toothbrush, early Chinese, **I** 177
   toothpaste, **I** 186 (fn.)
Dentition. *See also under* Teeth.
   and diet, **IV** 169
   and fossil remains, **II** 21
"Denying" what is "ignored," **VIII** 127, 205, 214
Deoxyribonucleic acid, **III** 253. *See also under* DNA.
Departmentalization in university life, **VIII** 168ff.
Dependency
   of childhood in man vs. animals, **II** 128; **IV** 284, 287f., 290
   of man in sickness, **IV** 314
Depravity of man. *See under* Total depravity.
Depression, the Great, **IX** 258f., 279
De Principiis, **VI** 109
Description mistaken for explanation, **III** 63, 326
Desert(s)
   of Arabia, man-made? **IX** 119f.
   in Central Asia, man-made? **IX** 119
   effect of, on animals, **IX** 122
   growth of, observable, **IX** 117
   in the New World, caused by man? **IX** 118

   technology of d. people, **I** 162f., 165
Desertification, since man? **IX** 116f.
Desert rat and jeroba, **VII** 157
Design. *See also under* Perfection of design.
   earth as evidence of, **VIII** 38f.
   economy of, in biology, **IV** 221
   economy of, in nature, **IV** 84f.
   evidence of, denied, **VIII** 148
   evidence of, in DNA, **VIII** 49f.
   faults in, of eye, hand, **VIII** 148
   "faulty," if supervision is necessary? **VIII** 55f.
   hand as evidence of **I** 354f.; **IV** 37, 73, 241
   homologies as evidence of, **II** 247; **IV** 122
   in nature, definition of perfection of, **IX** 148
Destiny
   and origin, relation between, **IV** 211, 329; **VIII** 14f., 81, 188f.
   purpose ultimately related to destiny, **I** 225f.
"Detail" response (Rorschach Test), **III** 151f.
Determinism, **VIII** 48ff., 86, 92
   different types of, **VIII** 129
   essential to scientific philosophy, **VIII** 86f., 91f., 206f.
   mechanistic, an incomplete view of reality, **VIII** 214f.
Devil. *See under* Satan.
Devolution vs. evolution, **II** 45, 70
Devoutness, inadequacy of, **III** 125
Dialectic method, **VII** 24
Diamond drills. *See under* Drills.
Diapedesis, **V** 312
Dichotomy of man, **I** 266f.; **III** 303; **V** 259-291; **VIII** 81
Diet(s)
   and body odor, **II** 285, 306f.
   and cooperative feeding among animals, **IV** 252
   and disease, **II** 221

effect of, on animal form and behavior, **VIII** 235
effect of, on life span, **V** 23
effect of deficiencies in, **II** 38
effect of eating meat, **V** 24
freezing vs. cooking, **II** 202
herbivorous d. slows traveling speed of animals, **IX** 41
herbivorous vs. carnivorous, **IV** 256f.
influence of, on cranial development, **II** 183f., 211; **IV** 162f.
influence of, on dental form, **II** 200; **IV** 169
influence of, on jaw structure, **II** 183ff., 213
influence of, on personality, **III** 165
of man, originally herbivorous, **VII** 314; **IX** 124, 206
of man, now omnivorous, **IV** 256
morphology influenced by, **IV** 157, 159; **VIII** 234
and sweating, **IX** 206f.
upset by domestication, **IV** 308
vitamin deficiencies in, **III** 62
wisdom of animals regarding, **III** 62f.; **IV** 293, 308ff.
Diffusionist school, **II** 117
Diffusion of gases, **I** 349; **III** 75
Digestive systems of animals and plants, **IV** 155
Dimetrodon, **IV** 43, 152
temperature regulation in, **IX** 203
Dipnoi (lung fish), **IV** 42
Disagreement, how to resolve a, **III** 11
Discipline
of the saints, **III** 217
value of self-imposed, **IX** 151f.
Discovery vs. invention, **I** 286f.; **VIII** 105 (fn. 2)
Disease(s)
in antiquity, comparative scarcity of, **III** 48f.

arthritis in early man, **V** 24
bacteria and viruses as agents of, **IX** 160
of bone in early man, **V** 24
and dietary deficiencies, **II** 221
healing and, in man, **IV** 312f.
as a hindrance to achievement, **III** 202ff.
and human sympathy, **IX** 113
man-made? **IV** 312
morphology affected by, **II** 216; **IV** 168
in Neanderthal Man, **IV** 168, 239
older than man? **IX** 113 (fn.), 158
and posture, **IV** 239f.
seasonal temperature variations and, **I** 350; **IV** 29; **VIII** 39; **IX** 142
steady increase of, throughout history, **IX** 159
of White Man, and decimation of native people, **II** 114, 140
"Disney" cartoons in early Egypt, **I** 201
Dispersion of man, **I** 139ff. *See also* Migration—routes of early man.
after Babel, **II** 35ff.
cultural cost of, **II** 36ff.
interaction between d. and language development, **I** 272f.
traditions of, **IX** 29
Disraeli foretold? **VII** 114
Distractions and achievement, **III** 205
Diurnal rhythm of light and darkness, **IX** 142
Divergence, **II** 215
and creation, **IV** 81-91
vs. convergence, **IV** 140f.
and relationship, **II** 20
Diversification of species
in a new environment, **II** 43
time taken for d. of physical type as opposed to culture, **I** 126, 128; **II** 44, 175, 222; **IV** 67; **VI** 230

Divine intervention. *See also under* Miracle.
vs. miracle, **VIII** 87
and natural law, **VIII** 58
in nature, **IV** 19f.; **VIII** 48-98
redemptive in intent, **VIII** 63
scientific determinism and, **VIII** 47-98
specific occasions for, **VIII** 84, 86, 87
when unnecessary, **VIII** 58
Divine nature in man, **III** 186
Divinity "shapes our ends," **VIII** 223
Divorce, grounds for, among primitives, **II** 294
Djapatischa, as Japeth, **IV** 195
DNA
character of, as evidence of design, **VIII** 49f.
differences in identical organisms, **VIII** 78
the Fall has disturbed man's, **VIII** 50
as a "language," **VIII** 49
life the secret of, **VIII** 59
and protein manufacture, **VIII** 70
species coded in, **VIII** 50
Dobuans
attitude toward death, **V** 349
method of fishing, **I** 169
Doctors, native. *See under* Medicine.
Dog(s), **II** 238-240, 266
barking vs. howling, **II** 266
brain of, supposed evolution, **II** 239
breeding of pure lines (an analogy), **V** 203f.
vs. cats, instincts of, **VIII** 69
decorticate, experiments with, **VIII** 67
"dogginess" experimentally destroyed, **VIII** 68

domestication of, **IX** 202
experiments in memory of, **III** 248, 256
helping blind mate, **IV** 195
stereovision in, **VII** 91
a story of a, **III** 200
story of an Eskimo and his huskies, **IV** 300
use of, in fishing, **I** 168
varieties of, **IV** 77
Dogma, in modern science, **II** 75; **IV** 25, 170, 179
Dogmatism
causes of, **VIII** 117
effects of, when unwarranted, **VIII** 128
in evolutionary writing (Simpson), **IV** 172
replaces hard evidence, **VIII** 159
spiritual vs. materialistic, **VIII** 102
Doing vs. being, **VIII** 186
Domestication, **I** 40
by American Indians of animals and plants, **I** 40, 166ff.
of animals, **I** 166f., 304; **II** 86, 88, 97; **III** 120
of animals, first occurrence of, **II** 88; **IX** 35f., 49f.
effect of, on brain size, **IV** 226
effect of, on dietary wisdom, **IV** 308
of grains, **I** 193
of the horse, **I** 193, 205
for improved breeding, has limits, **I** 346 (fn. 262)
instincts confused by, **III** 63, 65f.; **IV** 198; **VIII** 68f.
of mountain ass, **I** 193
not always advantageous to animals, **IV** 198; **IX** 125
of the ostrich! **I** 304
of plants, first occurence of, **I** 166f.; **II** 86, 88; **IX** 149f.

Dominion of man over the earth, nature of, **VIII** 62f.; **IX** 115
Donkey. See under *Ass.*
Doppler effect, **VIII** 16
Doubt
  encouraged by Greek philosophy, **VII** 26
  essential to discovery of truth, **VIII** 24
  principle of, in science, **VII** 24
Dove, as a symbol, **VI** 66
Drainpipes, ancient, **I** 195; **II** 96f.
Dreams
  sharing of, **VII** 177f.
  time sense affected by, **VI** 21, 24
Drills
  deep well drilling in ancient China, **I** 205ff., 212f.
  diamond, **I** 192
Drinking straws, Sumerian, **I** 200, 202
Drosophila melanogaster and simulans, **VIII** 78
Drugs. *See also under* Medicine, Pharmacology.
  anaesthetics, **I** 176
  developed by American Indians, **I** 166f.
  ephedrine (Chinese development), **I** 212
  extraordinary range of, used by Sonoran Desert Indians, **I** 162f.
  from plants, used in fishing, **I** 169, 170
  psychedelic, **I** 174f.
  time sense affected by, **VI** 21, 23
Druid Flood tradition, **IX** 31
Dualism, **VIII** 84. *See also under* Mind.
  Cartesian, **III** 318
  mind/matter, **III** 262
  vs. monism, **I** 266f.; **III** 319
Ducks, adopting puppies, **III** 66
Duckbilled Platypus, **IV** 44
Dwarfs, **IV** 24
  limitations of, examined, **VIII** 41
Dying. *See also under* Death.
  Greek words for, in N.T., **V** 320
  of Jesus Christ vs. ordinary man, **V** 325
  as a process, not an event, **V** 381

E

E = Mc², **III** 54
Earth
  atmosphere of, **IV** 27f.
  center of the universe? **IV** 32
  chemical constitution of, unique, **VIII** 35f.
  cursed because of man, **IX** 115
  distance from the sun, **I** 349; **IV** 28; **VIII** 38
  evidence of design, **VIII** 38
  fitness of, for man, **I** 348ff.; **VIII** 35f., 38
  fitness of, unique, **IV** 27ff.
  Hebrew word for, **IX** 15, 18
  life on earth, dependent on reversal of three laws, **III** 75f.
  man's dominion over the, **VIII** 62f.; **IX** 115
  moon, importance of to the, **I** 352; **IV** 30f.
  preparation of, for life, **IV** 39; **VIII** 35f., 38
  preparation of, for man, **I** 359; **IV** 13-108; **VI** 30f.

proportion of land to water, **VIII** 39

rate of revolution, **I** 349; **IV** 28; **VIII** 39

seasonal variations of, **I** 350; **IV** 28f.

size of, **I** 348; **IV** 27f.; **VIII** 39

size of, determined by man's erectness, **VIII** 41

as a stage, **IV** 38-47

temperature of, **I** 349f.; **IV** 29

tilt of axis, **IV** 105f.; **VIII** 39

uniqueness of, **I** 227f.

unique surface of, **I** 350f.; **IV** 29ff.

"Economic Man," concept of; a fallacy, **VIII** 175

Ectodermal displasiacs, **IX** 196

Edaphic influence defined, **VIII** 234

Eden

boundaries of, to be extended, **V** 168; **VII** 316; **IX** 115

events in, **V** 116ff., 143-151, 367ff.

a garden paradise, **VIII** 96, 249

in Iranian Highland Plateau, **IX** 46, 47

to be "kept," i.e., guarded, **VIII** 62, **IX** 115

reality of, **V** 82, 367

rivers of, identified, **IX** 47f.

site of, not in Mesopotamia, **IX** 46

in an unfallen world, **VIII** 89, 249

Edenic world, nature of, **VIII** 96f., 249

Educability of primitive man, **II** 108, 164f.

Education

advantages and disadvantages of writing, **II** 169f.

biblical emphasis upon, **VIII** 194

of children by uncles, **II** 279, 292f.

Christian abdication of, **III** 83

effect of conservatism on, **II** 173

ends, being lost sight of, **VIII** 190

of Ezra, **VIII** 195

hopes for, **III** 12, 162, 273

lack of, cause of sin? **III** 12, 162, 273

limitations of, **III** 33f.

Medieval objectives of, **VIII** 109

moral limitations of, **III** 18, 20

of Moses, **VIII** 194

of Paul, **VIII** 195f.

practices in primitive societies, **II** 169f.

for "preservation," not "progress," **II** 173

in Roman times, **VII** 27

shifting goals of, **VIII** 122

short period of, in animals, **IV** 271, 274, 284f.

value of, dubious, **III** 39

Edward VI, Prayer Book of, **V** 287

Efficiency

of aircraft engines, **IX** 204

of animals, **IX** 205

in biochemistry. *See under* Protein manufacture.

of human bodies, **IV** 297, 311; **IX** 204

of machines, **IV** 311f.

of steam engines, **IX** 204

Egypt(ian)

absence of animals in sculpture, **VII** 158

absence of theology among, **I** 292

absence of true science among, **I** 315

algebra, **I** 189, 327

asses in early, **VII** 158

camels in early, **VII** 158

cartoons, **I** 201

cattle in early, **VII** 158

diaphanous clothing, **VII** 153

Flood tradition, an anomaly, **IX** 30f., 84

geometry, **I** 189

hens in early, **VII** 158

horses in, **VII** 159

idols, **IV** 117

Joseph in, runner before his chariot, **VII** 180

language, (links with Semitic and Sumerian) **VI** 186

life in early, **VII** 158ff.

mathematics, **I** 34, 189, 293

medicine, **I** 34, 293f.

metallurgy, **I** 196

non philosophical, **I** 33f., 291, 294

philosophical texts, so-called, **I** 33f., 291, 294ff.; **II** 172

practical, **I** 33f.

proliferation of words, **I** 273

pyramids, **I** 194f., 324; **II** 89; **V** 63

religion, **IV** 116

Sarah in, **VII** 154

sheep in early, **VII** 158

story of man and his wife, **VII** 157

story of two brothers, **VII** 154

titles of court officials, **VII** 179

wisdom of, **I** 278

Elam, **V** 65

originally Semitic, **I** 113

El Damieh, collapse of river bank at, **VII** 191

Election, God's sovereignty and, **VI** 155ff.

Electric battery, principle of operation, **VIII** 169 (fn.)

early invention of, **I** 177, 196

Electric shock

an animal defense weapon, **IV** 155

use of, in medicine, **III** 253

Electro-chemistry

brain reduced to, **III** 123, 240; **VIII** 87

consciousness, merely? **III** 320, 324

mind reduced to, **III** 123, 251, 269f.

Electron microscope, **VIII** 133

Electrons, nature of? **VIII** 22

Electroplating, **I** 196

"Elegy Written in a Country Churchyard," **VII** 114

Elements

all playing a role, **VIII** 38

relative proportions of, in the universe, **VIII** 36

Elephant(s)

population growth control among, **IV** 255f.

pygmy, **VIII** 241

Elijah's prayer regarding rain, **IX** 20, 21

Elimination of the "unfit," **VIII** 225

Ellasar, meaning of the word? **VII** 163

Eloquence, importance of, **III** 219, 221,223

Embryo

falsified drawings of, **II** 241

psychological "regression" and embryonic recall? **V** 198, 278

Embryology, **V** 19, 76-113, 172-212. *See also under* Recapitulation.

and the Bible, **IV** 46

and evolution, **IV** 82, 147

fetal development, **V** 183, 196, 198

natural laws governing body development, **V** 196

Emotion(s)

cries of, as language? **IV** 272

human and animal, **II** 255

and language, **IV** 272

in plants? **III** 334f.

price of rapid shifts of, in TV viewing, **VII** 177

relation of, to instincts, **II** 257

relation of, to the body and the spirit, **III** 271f.

Emotional sweating, **IX** 197f., 207ff., 209

Empires, omnipotence of God in, **VI** 30ff.

Encephalitis lethargica, **III** 202

Encyclopedias, Chinese, **I** 187
End(s) *See also under* Means.
  the chief, for man, **VIII** 184ff.
  criteria in evaluation of a life,
    VIII 187
  demand the exercise of faith;
    means, the exercise of intelli-
    gence, **VIII** 188, 191
  education losing sight of, **VIII**
    190
  loss of, **VIII** 14, 172, 183
  vs. means, **VIII** 14, 94, 184ff.
  vs. means in adult education,
    VIII 190
  origin and destiny closely related
    to, **VIII** 185
  universities abrogate interest in,
    VIII 213
Endocrine glands, influence of; on
  bone structure, **II** 185, 220. *See
  also under* Hormones.
Enemas, **I** 176f., 199
Energy
  cost of erectness in man, **IV** 240f.
  cost of memory? **III** 253
  cost of thought, **VIII** 87, 143
  matter as 'congealed' e., **VIII** 22,
    53
  sources available to early man, **II**
    127, 168f.
English public school system, **III** 38
Enlightened selfishness, **III** 19
Enoch, Book of, **V** 98
Enoch, name of first city, **VI** 198f.;
  VII 205f.; **IX** 47
Ensoulment and reincarnation, **IX**
  171
Entertainment, Roman and modern
  parallels, **VIII** 176f.
Entropy, **IV** 151
  and heat death, **III** 196; **VIII** 20
  law of, reversed? **III** 76
Environment
  direct influence of, on organisms,
    VII 221, 227

  factors in, modifying morphol-
    ogy, **VIII** 234, 244
  influence of: on cell development,
    IV 88
    : on human morphology, **VIII**
      238ff., 245
    : on physical development, **IV**
      66, 83f.
    : on physique, **II** 189f.
    : on plants, **VIII** 231
    : on skull form, **II** 200f.
    : on structure, **IV** 144, 157f.
    : on temperament, **III** 147
  nuclear genes resistant to, **VIII**
    231
  plasmagenes responsive to, **II**
    211; **VIII** 231
  social behavior influenced by, **III**
    12, 20, 162, 274
  speciation not produced by new,
    IV 66f.
Eolithic implements, **IV** 265
Ephedrine, **I** 212
Epicureanism, **VII** 19
Epilepsy, **III** 243
  and demon possession, **III** 226f.
  as Paul's thorn? **III** 226
  Welsh word for, **III** 226
"Equality of man" in Genesis 10, **I**
  62
Erasure of memory, **III** 240f., 248ff.,
  253
Ereck, **VI** 199
Erectness in man, **IV** 231-246. *See
  also under* Posture.
  and brain metabolism, **IV** 245
  culture determined by, **IV** 242f.,
    245
  energy cost of, **IV** 240f.
  height limitations of, **VIII** 40
  of Neanderthal Man, **I** 134; **IV**
    168 (fn. 71), 238f.
  posture, and disease, **IV** 239f.
  and size of the earth, **VIII** 41
  and speech, **IV** 243f., 277, 287
  structures involved in, **IV** 231

Error
part played by, in scientific advance, **VIII** 201 (fn. 196)
science, a search for, **II** 25 (fn. 29); **IV** 143
Escapism, **III** 239
Eskimo(s), **I** 156ff.; **II** 159ff.; **IV** 129, 253
ability to repair sewing machines, **I** 159
attitude toward nature, **IV** 300
cold weather clothing, **II** 159
diet of, **IV** 256
"fawn" mother, **II** 278
fishing gear of, **II** 161
hunting techniques, **I** 160, 161; **II** 160f.
igloo construction, **I** 157f.; **II** 160
infanticide, **II** 304f.; **III** 138
ingenuity of, **I** 156; **II** 159
meaning of name for *man*, **VII** 201 (fn. 80)
morphological changes with age, **VIII** 244ff.
as paleolithic man, **II** 158ff., 162f.; **IV** 161ff.
snow goggles, **I** 157, 162; **II** 162
"stethoscope," **I** 161
tailored clothing, **I** 158; **II** 159
"telephone," **I** 161; **II** 161
use of block and tackle principle, **I** 160f.
view of White Man, **II** 111
"wolf-killer," **I** 160
ESP. *See under* Extrasensory perception.
Eternal security, **VI** 67
Eternity
experienced in time, **V** 326, 330
vs. time, **VI** 10ff., 38-44
from time into, **VI** 42
timelessness of, **VI** 13
Ether as a cosmic ocean, **VI** 15
Ethics
vs. morality, **I** 29; **III** 66

and warfare, **III** 267; **VIII** 139 (fn. 106)
Ethnology, **I** 51-141
Etruscan
carpenter's tools and lathes, **I** 202
indebtedness of Roman civilization to, **I** 198f.
language affinities, **I** 109f.
origin of, **I** 108ff.
religion, **IV** 124
Eugenics, **III** 12, 121, 162, 273; **IV** 306f.; **VIII** 215
unclear goals of, **VIII** 150 (fn. 100)
Evaporative cooling. *See under* Sweating.
Eve, **II** 254, 276f.
carrier of immortal seed, **V** 139
formation of, out of Adam, **I** 234f.; **V** 87, 146f., 173, 202, 381
immortality of Adam and, **V** 119-140
the mother of all living, **V** 88
naming of, **V** 147; **IX** 186
temptation of, **V** 147
unique body of, **V** 87f.
why not created independently? **V** 203
"Every creature," meaning of the phrase, **IX** 17, 19
Evil(s)
act of God, **VI** 170f.; **IX** 111
foreseen by God in creation, **IX** 111
vs. goodness, **VI** 171f.
human capacity for, **III** 14ff.
law for restraint of, always negative, **III** 35
leavan as a principle of, **V** 109
nature of, **III** 9
not all the consequences of particular sin, **IX** 112
problem of, **VII** 32; **IX** 107-163
problem of, in nature, **III** 64f.

restrained that good may come, **IX** 146
vs. sin, **VI** 166ff.
sin often the cause of, **IX** 163
Evolution, theory of. *See also under* Darwinism.
acceptable only as a working hypothesis, **VIII** 162
applied everywhere, **VIII** 134
bad philosophy, **IV** 170, 179
benefits of, as a challenge, **IV** 112
circular reasoning in, **II** 26, 163, 250 (fn. 2); **IV** 62, 175
compellingness of, **II** 24
consciousness, emergence of and, **III** 257f., 324; **VIII** 85, 136, 142
and convergence, **IV** 140ff.
and crowding of animals, **IV** 186f.
culture and, **II** 65, 68f., 102, 250f.
defined, **I** 347
and definition of *fitness*, **II** 24; **IV** 45
and definition of *higher*, **IV** 45, 46
degeneration admitted, **III** 50, 159
vs. devolution,**II** 45, 70, 106
a divinely guided process? **IV** 13, 73, 86f.
and dogma, **IV** 172, 179
dogmatism of, replaces hard facts, **VIII** 159
effect of, on attitude of naturalists, **III** 56
and embryology, **IV** 82, 147. *See also under* Recapitulation.
evidence is equivocal, **VIII** 49
excessive flexibility of, **II** 24; **IV** 201
as a fact? **IV** 172f.
as a faith, **II** 12-22; 25, 28, **III** 18; **IV** 62, 69, 110f., 142, 173f.; **VIII** 130f.
fatal to Christian theology (Wells), **V** 79

generative power of the word, **VIII** 133
goal of (Huxley), **VIII** 146
heuristic value of, **II** 133
human e., and consequences for man, **VIII** 97
human e., "undoubted," **VIII** 161f.
and involution, **II** 106
an irrational faith, **IV** 172-180
language and, **VI** 188 (and fn. 28)
the "magic" of the word, **VIII** 133, 138
man as a mere by-product of? **VIII** 125, 145, 146
and man: "critical point" concept, **IV** 320
is mechanistic, **VIII** 97
as a mental prison, **IV** 174
miracles required by, **II** 75; **IV** 25; **VIII** 160 (fn. 129)
modern inquisition by, **VIII** 160, 166
moral consequences of, as philosophy, **VIII** 151, 167
as a myth held compulsively, **IV** 173
natural selection and, **IV** 75, 175, 187; **VIII** 133
and nature, false attitude of, **IV** 178f.
opportunism and, **IV** 68f., 144
and origin of language, **II** 250
and origin of man, **II** 12, 145f.; **IV** 305
and origin of plants, a puzzle to, **IV** 55f.
parallelisms between Galileoism and Darwinism, **VIII** 159
as philosophy, **IV** 170
philosophy of, determines lines of research, **VIII** 160
and problems of interdependence, **IV** 71

a "proven" fact, **IV** 172 (Simpson); **VIII** 161 (Beck, Braidwood, Linton), 162 (Pearl), 159 (fn. 127)
of religion, **II** 74; **IV** 114, 126, 132
as a religion, **II** 25; **III** 58, 84; **VIII** 149, 151, 159f.
social effects of, **III** 10, 162, 267; **IV** 170, 178
truth; criterion for, **VIII** 160f.
theistic, **IV** 13, 73, 86f.
theological implications of, **IV** 320ff.; **V** 79, 172
"vital force" and vitalism rejected by, **I** 353f.; **III** 323; **IV** 35, 144, 150; **VIII** 84, 91f., 136, 138
what constitutes proof? **VIII** 161
Evolutionary base line, **IV** 42f., 65
Evolutionary bias, severity of, **II** 67; **IV** 148
Evolutionary credulity, **IV** 69; **VIII** 8
Evolutionary culture sequences, fallacy of, **II** 71-75
Evolutionary faith
an alternative to, **II** 30-39
optimism of, **II** 25, 28; **III** 18; **VIII** 62, 69, 110f., 130f., 142, 173f.
without sufficient reason, **II** 24-29
Evolutionary philosophy
and Big Business, **IV** 86, 178
moral consequences of, **III** 275
Evolutionary process, often inconceivable, **VIII** 25
Evolutionary progress defined, **IV** 45
Evolutionary "Trees," **II** 16, 236, 243f., 246; **IV** 59, 146
Evolutionists
admit the fall of man, **III** 33

definition of sin, **III** 12, 17, 162, 273
Examinations, value of, **IX** 152
Exeter Hall Papers, **II** 63
Existentialism, **III** 271
Exodus, possible date of, **VII** 182, 188
Expanding Universe, **VIII** 18f., 26, 28ff.
bubble concept, **VIII** 31
rubber balloon analogy, **VIII** 30
Explanation
chance as, **III** 62
vs. description, **III** 63, 326
Explosives, **I** 205
Extinction(s)
mass, of animals, **I** 359; **IV** 92ff., 253
of primitive tribes, **II** 114f., 155f.
Extrasensory perception, **III** 264f.
and instinct, **III** 264f.
problem of experimental design for, **VIII** 90 (fn. 74)
unjustified skepticism about, **III** 264f.
Extraterrestrial life, **IV** 31; **VIII** 37
Extrovertism, **III** 30ff., 345
Eye(s)
bifocal in fishes, insects, **IV** 155
vs. the camera, **VII** 85f.
convergence and the, **IV** 155f.
Darwin and the, **IV** 37
development of, **VIII** 75
evolutionary view of development of the, **IV** 155
in octopus and man, **IV** 222
Paul's trouble with his, **III** 228
Sherrington and the, **IV** 37f.
stereovision and culture, **IV** 242
supposed imperfections in, **VIII** 148
widespread occurrence of the lens in different forms, **IV** 155

F

Fables, Aesop's, **I** 199
Fabrics. *See also under* Weaving.
  batik, **I** 181
  brocade, **I** 184
  crocheted, **I** 179
  decorating methods, **I** 180, 181, 184
  dyeing and finishing, **I** 180f.
  dyes, **I** 163, 184
  embroidery, **I** 184
  feather work, **I** 180
  felt, **I** 180
  gauze, **I** 179
  gingham, **I** 184
  gold and silver threaded, **I** 180
  Hamitic inventiveness of, **I** 317
  knitted, **I** 179
  lace, **I** 184
  linen, to be worn by priests, **IX** 213f.
  lists of, **I** 39
  nonwoven, **I** 180, 181
  paper, **I** 180f.
  raw materials used: buckskin, **I** 164
    : cotton (wild), **I** 162, 180
    : flax, hemp, **I** 180
    : pulp, **I** 180, 182
    : wood, **I** 180
  silk, **I** 180, 205, 207f., 209
  tapa cloth, **I** 180
  tapestry, **I** 180
  tie-dying, **I** 181
  voile, **I** 179
  weaving techniques, **I** 179ff., 324
  woven, **II** 94, 97f.
Face
  Hebrew word for, **III** 90; **IX** 214 (fn.)
  masks, Indian, **III** 334

  photography of the, **V** 180
Facial
  characteristics of the Mongoloids, **II** 220
  distance, **IV** 185
  expression: asymmetry in man, **IV** 180
    : in chimpanzees, **IV** 270f.
    : in man vs. animals, **IV** 170, 180, 271 (fn. 147)
    : mobility of, in man, **IV** 170f.
  reconstructions, problems of anthropological, **II** 233f.
Fact
  evolution as a fact? **IV** 172; **VIII** 127, 159 (fn. 126), 161, 162
  vs. hypothesis, **II** 12; **VIII** 154, 155, 162
  vs. truth, **VII** 95
Faculties, human, definition of, **III** 265
Faith
  exercised by anthropologists, **II** 12f.
  the fundamentals of Christian f., **V** 78, 80
  how to defend the, **VIII** 202
  key to new knowledge, **VIII** 199
  and logic, relationship of, **V** 174
  monotheism preceded polytheism, **IV** 110-137
  necessity of some system of, **VIII** 211
  not engendered by proof, **VIII** 208 (fn. 204)
  not the asylum of ignorance, **VIII** 212
  part played by, in discussion of origins, **VIII** 188

place of, in healing processes, **II** 155

and the premises, **VIII** 202f.

proof of, not subject to logic, **VIII** 201

and reason, **I** 246; **V** 78; **VIII** 119, 184f., 191, 194, 201f.

and reason, conflict between, **VIII** 126, 184

in relation to ends, **VIII** 188, 191

saving, a gift of God, **VI** 158

and science, Vol. **VIII**

and science, growing conflict between, **VIII** 122, 152f., 158, 172

and science, intellectual apartheid, **VIII** 172

and science, nature of the conflict, **VIII** 52-64

science as a, **IV** 172f., 199

system of, coherent, **V** 79

and understanding, **V** 175; **VIII** 117, 185

where f. is an improper substitute for reason, **VIII** 191

without reason, **II** 24f.

Fall, the

as "dirt" in mechanism of nature, **VIII** 57

effect on DNA code, **VIII** 50f.

effect on human life span, **VIII** 50

effect on microbiology, **VIII** 50

effect on nature, **VIII** 57ff., 61, 63, 89; **IX** 115

effect on thinking processes, **VIII** 196

effect upon creation, limited, **VIII** 8

made man alien to the natural order, **VIII** 96

miracle necessary because of, **VIII** 89

mutation due to? **VI** 229

physical consequences of; to man, to woman, **IX** 113f., 129

Fall of man, the, **I** 261; **III** 33, 185; **IV** 210f., 321

admitted by evolutionists, **III** 33

aggressiveness and, **III** 27f.

biblical view of, **III** 161

body affected by, **VI** 229f.

consequences of, for animal world, **IV** 248; **VI** 229f.

created a new species, **III** 338; **IV** 210f.

and disease, **IV** 314

effects of, according to Jung, **III** 38

evidence of, **IV** 177

freedoms and, **III** 158

Freud on the nature of, **III** 159

historical reality of, **III** 18, 26, 342

his three-dimensional potential upset by the, **I** 264

and human savagery, **II** 155f.; **IV** 321f.

influence of, on appetite, **IV** 312

loss of "image" in man, as result of, **III** 110f.

nature of, **III** 11ff., 103; **V** 205

results in pseudo-man, **III** 124, 186

suicidal nature resulting from, **III** 163, 296; **IV** 321

summary of consequences of, **III** 45f.

and sweating, **IX** 129

traditions regarding, **V** 94ff.

true manhood lost in, **III** 124, 186, 338; **IV** 236f.

view of T. H. Huxley and G. G. Simpson on, **III** 161

war as evidence of, **IV** 177 what is wrong with man, viewed by eugenicist, evolutionist, educationalist, sociologist, **III** 11, 18ff., 273; **IV** 321; **VII** 24; **VIII** 12

why allowed, **V** 78, 399, 400

and wound healing, **IV** 314

Fallen angels, **VI** 127f.
Falling in love, insane? **II** 299
Falsehoods, essential to abstract thought, **I** 272
Family life
human vs. animal, **IV** 284
monogamy preceded polygamy, **IV** 289, 305
among our primitive contemporaries, **II** 156f.
unique features of, in man, **IV** 288f.
Fans for winnowing, **I** 205
"Far Cathay," **I** 104, 107
Farming and desertification, **IX** 120f.
Father
duties of, **II** 289; **III** 231
honored or dishonored in his son, **I** 26; 145-148; **II** 305f.
vs. husband, **II** 315, 327
as "special friend," **II** 292
as supplying the spirit of the child, **III** 138
"Father Divine," **IX** 242
Fatherhood. *See under* Physical paternity.
Fatherhood of God
in Jewish belief, **VII** 70
not based on fact of creation per se, **III** 100
restricted, **III** 100ff., 125
as a unique relationship, **IX** 265
"Faults" in design, **VIII** 148 (and fn. 94)
"Fawn mother" in Chukchee society, **II** 278
Fear
animal's response to human's f., **IX** 208
"cast out" by perfect love, **IX** 209
and loss of appetite, **III** 65
sweating from, **IX** 197, 208, 209f.
Fear of punishment
as the basis of religion, **IV** 111
necessity of, **IV** 134f.

Feathers
into scales, **VIII** 160 (fn. 129)
origin of, a mystery, **IV** 49, 69
"Federation of the world" (Tennyson), **VIII** 131
Feedback systems, **VIII** 54, 63
Feet, human vs. animal, **IV** 218, 232f., 234f.
Feletabs, **II** 289
Fellowship
and guilt, **III** 279
vs. loneliness, **III** 276
in sharing a meal, **IX** 246
with God, broken by sin, **III** 276, 279
Felt, **I** 180f.
Feral man, **II** 83, 130, 140, 260ff., 270
Caspar Hauser, **III** 212
without language, **II** 252, 261, 270
modified dentition of, **II** 200
Fermentation of wine, **V** 106f.
Fertile Crescent, **II** 91
Fertility in man, cessation of, **IV** 290
Fertilization
manipulation of, **V** 173
as pure "mechanism," **VIII** 71, 80
in vitro, **V** 196; **VIII** 71
Fertilizers developed by American Indians, **I** 168
Fetalization in man, **V** 19, 57
Fetus
development of, **V** 183f.
"memory" of? **V** 198
status of, **V** 263 (fn. 1), 276, 279f.
vegetative nature of, **V** 212f.
Feudal system, causes of breakdown of, **VIII** 120
Fibers, Hamitic invention of, **I** 317. *See also under* Fabrics, Weaving.
"Field" concept in biology, **III** 326
Fig(s)
leaves to cover nakedness, **VI** 73
as a symbol, **VI** 52ff.

and wasps in symbiosis, **IV** 57

Fig tree
omnipotence of God and the, **VI** 132
parable of, **VII** 44, 47
possible identity of, **VI** 73
as a symbol, **VI** 70f.; **VII** 44

Fiji Flood tradition, **IX** 31

"Filling," (as N.T. term)
as content in personality, **V** 207
Jesus Christ as the, **III** 176f.
in the New Testament, **III** 171

Finches, Galapagos, **IV** 83, 264

Fingernails, **IV** 44

Fingerprinting, early Chinese use of, **I** 205, 213, 335

Fins, first appearance of, **IV** 42

Fire
animal use of, **IV** 266; **VIII** 40
art of making, lost, **II** 119f.; **IV** 266
critical size of man and, **VIII** 40
drill, **I** 183
of London, foretold, **VII** 114
use of, by man, **IV** 265

Fireflies used as lamps, **I** 187

Firmament, **VII** 300

First Causes involve purpose, **III** 64

Fish, **III** 96, 263
anticipating earthquakes, **IX** 90
communication among, **IV** 276
death of, natural? **V** 136
do not senesce, **V** 136
in Flood traditions, **IX** 72, 90
life spans of, **V** 133
methods of catching, **I** 168-170
schools of, and group mind, **III** 263f.
size of, factors governing, **V** 132f.
spawning, **V** 136
sudden interment of, **IV** 103
swimming levels of, **VII** 214
symbiosis among, **IV** 196f.
variability in number of vertebrae in a species of, **IV** 159

Fishing
lines with cuttlefish attached, **I** 169
use of birds, **I** 168f.
: of dogs, **I** 168
: of fish, **I** 169
: of kites, **I** 169
: of plant drugs, **I** 169, 170
: of traps, **I** 170

Fitness
and dauermodifications, **VIII** 219-249
of the earth for man, **I** 348ff.; **IV** 27-33; **VIII** 35f., 38
evolutionary definition of, **II** 24; **IV** 45
how acquired, **VIII** 219-225
mechanism guaranteeing, **VIII** 232
in nature, **VIII** 9, 148 (fn. 94), 219ff.
and survival, concept of, **II** 24, 65; **III** 23, 71. See also under Survival of the fittest.
unfitness of man, **IV** 176f.; **VIII** 237

Flame-throwers, **I** 205, 208f.

"Fleece," praying for a, **IX** 277f. See also under Golden Fleece.

Flesh
and blood vs. flesh and bones, **V** 360f.
as a N.T. term, **III** 308

Flies, breeding of, in the dark, **VIII** 222

Flint, **III** 223
effectiveness of, **II** 150
preferred to metal, **II** 151
"rifled" arrow heads, **I** 184 (fn. 62)
sharper than metal, for razors, **II** 150
vs. steel, **II** 150
tools, early perfection of, **II** 90
weapons, Folsom and Yuma, **II** 115. See also under Eoliths.

Flintlock, preferred to cartridges, **II** 69, 150

Flood, the, **IV** 97f; **V** 135; **IX** 13-63
 atmospheric changes at time of, **II** 132; **VII** 239
 biblical account of, unique, **IX** 28, 81
 biblical record of, as a ship's log, **VII** 203; **IX** 25, 79, 82
 birds used in, **IX** 38ff.
 Carbon 14 dating and, **II** 132
 and climatic change, **V** 25
 "coming up" of waters of, **IX** 82
 deposits of, in Mesopotamia? **VII** 202; **IX** 46
 and discontinuity in civilization, **II** 80, 81
 effect of, on life span, **VII** 234ff.
 effect of, on population, **VII** 238; on population growth, **V** 45
 extent of, **II** 30; **IX** 13-63
 four commonly held views regarding, **IX** 14
 global, would require excessive miracle, **IX** 41-43
 inbreeding after, **VII** 234f.
 length of calendric month during, **IX** 22, 25
 local or global? **VII** 202; **IX** 13-63
 locality of, not in Mesopotamia, **VII** 202; **IX** 44-58
 physical causes of, **IX** 44-58
 possible date of, **IX** 44-58
 rate of recession of waters of, **IX** 82
 record of, examined, **IX** 15-27
"Flood deposits" at Ur, **VII** 202; **IX** 46
Flood geology, **IV** 15; **IX** 59f.
Flooding, evidence of recent; in Asia Minor, **IX** 45f.
Flood story
 evidence of biblical priority, **IX** 82

substitution of *land* for *earth* in the, **IX** 16
use of hyperbole in, **IX** 13, 18-21
Flood tradition(s)
 animals used in: birds, **IX** 72, 90, 91
  : dogs, **IX** 90
  : eagle, **IX** 90
  : fish, **IX** 74, 90
  : llama, **IX** 90
  : loon, **IX** 91
  : muskrat, **IX** 32, 91
  : waterfowl, **IX** 91
 biblical record, sobriety of, **IX** 81
 causes of Flood varied, **IX** 31, 69, 71, 77
 common basis in fact, yet independent? **IX** 69f., 83
 common factors in, **IX** 29f., 67, 68, 71-80, 88-93
 cuneiform accounts of, **IX** 76, 78
 depth of water, **IX** 32
 of Egypt, unique, **IX** 30
 evident priority of biblical story, **IX** 82
 few from Africa, **IX** 84
 Higher critical nonsense and, **IX** 81
 lists of: Barton, Frazer, Lenormant, Nelson, Paterson, Rehwinkel, Titcomb, Urquhart, **IX** 94-98
 nature of, **IX** 69-87
 number of survivors, **IX** 31, 32, 70-72, 85f., 88, 92, 106
 overdramatization in extrabiblical, **IX** 29, 76, 79
 punishment a cause of Flood, **IX** 69f.
 relation between Bible and pagan, **IX** 29, 81, 93
 repeopling of the earth afterwards, **I** 119f.; **IX** 73, 89, 90
 true signification of worldwide distribution of, **IX** 33, 80

worldwide distribution of, **VII** 203; **IX** 28

Florisbad Skull, **I** 127

Flowers
created for man, **IV** 66
evolution of? **IV** 57
first appearance of, **IV** 28
symbiosis with insects, **IV** 57, 71

Fo-hi, Chinese "Noah?" **IX** 85f.

Folsom Man, **I** 127

Fontechevade Man, **I** 127; **II** 185, 197f.; **IV** 239; **V** 67

Food(s)
acquisition of, **I** 168f.
alcoholic beverage, **I** 163
baking powder, **I** 162
candy and chewing gum, **I** 162
coffee, **I** 199
condiments, **I** 162, 166
dehydrated potatoes, **I** 326
methods of gathering, list of, **I** 40
miraculous multiplication of, **VI** 33f.
powdered milk, **I** 325
salt, **I** 162, 212

Food gathering techniques. *See under* Fishing, Hunting.

Food preparation and utensils
drinking straws, **I** 202
naphtha gas for cooking, **I** 203, 205
pottery tripod for cooking, **I** 172
rubber flasks, **I** 179
salt, extraction of, **I** 214
tipiti for extracting poison from manioc, **I** 172
watertight woven baskets, **I** 162, 172
whistling "kettles" of earthenware, **I** 181

Foodstuffs, list of, **I** 40

"Foolishness" of preaching, **VII** 18

Foot, human; preadaptation in, **VIII** 145, 245

Footbinding in China, **IV** 85; **VIII** 223

Foramen magnum, position of, **IV** 236f.

Forbidden fruit, **V** 77-114
contained a poison? **I** 234; **III** 289f.; **IV** 321; **V** 86, 93-101
introduced death for man and by man, **V** 83, 110, 142, 148-151, 156f.; 188, 190; **IX** 114
specifications regarding nature of, **V** 100f.
traditions regarding **V** 93-111

Forces of nature, viewed as "wills" by primitive man, **II** 170f.

Forehead, kinds of sweating in, **V** 310; **IX** 200, 214

Foreordination
of good works, **III** 131, 175
of "structure" of personality, **III** 175

Foresight
and the concept of teleology, **IV** 34-38
vs. prophecy, **VII** 115, 142

Forest fires, **III** 69

Forever, meaning of, in Gen. 6:3, **IX** 35

Forgetting, **III** 238ff.
divine vs. human, **III** 277ff.
vs. forgiving, **III** 239
impossibility of, as a disease, **III** 245

Forgiveness, **III** 238-281
vs. cleansing, **III** 298, 305
divine vs. human, **III** 240ff., 277f., 280f.
and forgetting, **III** 239, 277ff.
healing in conjunction with, **VIII** 41
legal problems of, **III** 281
moral implications of, **III** 280, 281
or punishment, **IV** 135
and the subconscious, **III** 238-281
true meaning of, **III** 274, 280

unnecessary if man a machine, **III** 269f.

Forks at first rejected, **II** 177

Form and function, **III** 56; **IV** 145
decline of interest in, **II** 245ff.

Former creation, **VI** 76ff.

Fortune tellers, dangerous, **VII** 116f.

Forty, significance of number, in Scripture, **VII** 60

Fossil(s)
sequences artificially reversed, **II** 241
upside down in rocks, **IX** 60

Fossil fuels, **II** 32; **IV** 85

Fossil Man. *See under specific names:* Abbeville, Australopithecines, Boskop, Canstadt Race, Chou-koutien Man, Cro-Magnon Man, "Dawn Man" (Eoan-thropus), Florisbad, Folsom Man, Fontechevade Man, Galley Hill Man, Gigantopithecus, Grimaldi Man, Heidelberg Man, Hesperopithecus, Homo habilis, Hotu Man, Java Man, Kanjera Man, Kenya finds, Krapina Man, La Chapelle, Logoa Santa, La Quina Woman, Mauer Jaw, Meganthropus, Modjokerto Skull, Monte Cicero, Mount Carmel, Neanderthal Man, Obercassel, Olduvai Skull, Paranthropus, Pekin Man, Piltdown Man, Pithecanthropus, Predmost skull, Sinanthropus, Skuhl Man, Solo Man, Stein-heim Man, Vertesszolles Man, Vestonice finds, Tabun finds, Talgai Skull, Wadjak Skull.

Fossil Man, **I** 129ff.; **II** 12-57
cranial capacities of, **IV** 224f.
criterion for humanness of, **III** 124
and dentition, **II** 21

distribution of, and its significance, **II** 41f.; **IX** 50f.
estimates of age of, **II** 194f.
factors influencing forms of, **II** 49
as "heralds," not ancestors, of man, **IV** 64
in the light of Genesis 10, **I** 54; **IV** 64
longevity of, **III** 49; **V** 56f.
map showing locations of, **I** 127
migrations of Hamites and, **I** 124, 128; **II** 53
modern skulls in ancient strata. *See under* Fontechevade, Galley Hill, Kanam, Kanjera, Stein-heim.
possible links between, **II** 52
and power of speech, **IV** 267f.
pre-Adamic, not human? **VI** 239
skull forms of, **IV** 160ff.
variability of physical type, **VI** 230f.
wide variability, in single loca-tion, **II** 50f.

Foundation, biblical words for, **VI** 117f.

Fowl, ingenious way of capturing, **I** 169

Foxes
diplomacy of, with respect to "neighbors," **IV** 301
hunting habits of, **III** 65f.; **IX** 125
wisdom of, in sickness, **III** 62

Fragmentation
of knowledge: for convenience, **VIII** 124 (fn. 36)
: effect of, on man himself, **VIII** 125
: price paid for, **VIII** 72
of life, due to mobility and rapid communication, **VIII** 177f.
of Medieval Synthesis, **VIII** 120ff.
of thought and life, **VIII** 168-183

Frankincense and myrrh, source of, **I** 20

Freedom
of choice, and responsibility, **III** 268
in confinement, **III** 211, 212
dangers of, **IX** 132
definition of perfect, **III** 35, 89, 92
Dostoyevsky and, **III** 159
of fallen man? **III** 158
limits of human, **VI** 165
penalties of, **III** 87
religious, Jesuit view of, **IV** 118
to sin only, **III** 35
some bondage essential to, **III** 200
of speech in Greco-Roman world, **VII** 28
of thought vs. free-thought, **VIII** 168
true expression of, in man, **III** 37, 92
under strict control, **IX** 152
where observed in nature, **VIII** 60

Free-thought vs. freedom of thought, **VIII** 168

French Revolution, **III** 43

Friendship with God, **III** 93

Friend vs. servant relationship, **III** 93; **VI** 164; **IX** 191

Fruit, forbidden, **III** 289. *See also under* Forbidden fruit.

Fruit(s)
of the Spirit, nature of, **VI** 159f.
vs. works, **III** 131, 192f.; **VI** 163ff.

Frog(s) **VIII** 234f.
decerebrate, experiments with, **V** 213; **VIII** 66
heart preparation of, beating autonomously, **V** 123f.
incipient speciation among, **VIII** 163f.
insensitive to pain? **IX** 127
survival of cripples, **IV** 203

Frontal region of the brain, **IX** 214

Function and form, **IV** 145; **VIII** 148 (fn. 94)

Fundamentals of the faith, **V** 77
logical connections between, **V** 78, 80

"Fullness of time," special significance of, **VII** 18, 20

Furniture, Hamitic inventions of, **I** 41f.

Future life, Hebrew concept of, **V** 280

G

Gadarene swine, **VII** 228

Gainsborough's *Blue Boy,* **II** 202f.; **IV** 162f.

Galapagos finches, **IV** 83

Galatians as Celts and Gauls, **I** 83

Galaxies, number of, **VIII** 32

Galileo
supposed experiments from the Tower of Pisa, **VIII** 157

trial of, **VIII** 152ff.

Galley Hill Man, **I** 127; **II** 195

Games
card, **I** 334
list of early, **I** 42
as public entertainment in Rome, **VII** 29
violence in, **VIII** 177

Ganges River, floodings; and recession rates of, **IX** 24

Gap(s). *See also under* Missing links.
admitted by paleontologists, **IV** 58ff.
between creative acts of God, **IV** 50, 85
called saltations by Goldschmidt, **IV** 49, 61, 175
and circular reasoning, **II** 26 (fn. 32), 250 (fn. 2); **IV** 62, 175
as evidence of divine activity, **IV** 49f.
genealogical, **VII** 221, 222, 260; **IX** 44
in the geological record, **IV** 48-63
in the "Great Chain of Being," **I** 363
various forms of g. or missing links discussed, **IV** 51ff.
: between coldblooded and warmblooded animals, **IV** 58
: between life and no life, **IV** 51
: between nonflowering and flowering plants, **IV** 56
: from scales to feathers, **IV** 69
: between vertebrates and invertebrates, **IV** 55

Gap theory, **IV** 16; **VI** 76ff.
traditions and, **VI** 106-114

Gardens, significance of, **VIII** 62f.

Garment(s). *See under* Clothing, Fabrics.
Universe to be folded up as a, **VIII** 31

Gas. *See also under* Naphtha gas.
ethics of g. warfare, **III** 267
law of diffusion of, **I** 349; **III** 75
used for cooking by early Chinese, **I** 203, 213
for warfare, **I** 209

Gautama (and Buddhism), **VII** 32f.

Gazelle, rescued by lioness, **III** 73

Geese
avoidance of overcrowding among, **IV** 185
unique preparations, for long migrations, **III** 202

Gender vs. sex, **V** 397f.

Gene(s)
mutant, damaging effects of, **VII** 235
nuclear vs. cytoplasmic, **VIII** 222ff.

Genealogy (-ies), **VII** 215-269
of Abraham's family, **VII** 155
alternative interpretations of, **V** 39f.
the "blotting out" of some generations in, **VII** 258
can be fun to study, **VII** 217f.
in the female line only, **VII** 259
found at Elephantine, **VII** 259
gaps in biblical? **V** 35ff.; **VII** 221, 222, 260; **IX** 44
as historiography, **VII** 218, 222
of the Jews, destroyed in 70 A.D., **VII** 259
in Luke vs. Matthew, **VII** 254ff.; 262f., 268
Messiah provided with a continuous inspired g., **VII** 223
of nations in Genesis 10, **VI** 195ff.
in the N.T., **VII** 252-269
in the N.T. to establish unbroken line from First to Last Adam, **VII** 218, 221f., 260, 337
in the O.T., **VII** 220- 246
quartet of fathers begetting sons, **VII** 216
reversed order of names in Matthew and Luke, **VII** 268
rewarding discoveries to be made in, **VII** 220f.
significance of, in four Gospels, **VII** 100, 103, 252f.
significant omissions in, **VII** 223
two lines of descent from Adam in O.T., **VII** 223f.

use of term *son* in Hebrew, **VII** 260f.

Generalization(s)
  vs. concreteness, particulars, **I** 34f., 258, 272, 273 (fn. 65); **VI** 214
  and the construction of a World View, **I** 269f.
  language determines capacity for, **I** 275, 314
  man's propensity for, **IV** 315ff.; **VIII** 113
  the philosopher's aim, **I** 297f.
  vs. practicality, **I** 191, 315
  science based on, **I** 191, 287 (fn. 106), 297f.

Generations, as meaning "histories," **II** 276f.; **VI** 53

Generosity
  without love, **III** 29
  wrongly motivated, **III** 28

Genesis
  chapter 1 analyzed, **VII** 271-316
  chapter 1 not written as poetry, **VIII** 204
  chapter 1:1-2 analyzed, **VI** 77-118
  and geological ages, **VII** 295f.
  meaning of the word *generation*, **II** 276f.; **VI** 53
  multiple authorship of? **I** 75-79
  not allegory, **V** 367
  Table of Nations (chapter 10), **I** 51-141
  traditions regarding chapter 1:1-2, **VI** 106-114

Genetic(s)
  affinity and morphology, **VIII** 214
  coding and the peacock's tail, **VIII** 25
  coding in DNA, **VIII** 49f.
  engineering, **II** 61, 81
  human inbreeding and, **VI** 224ff.
  personality: part played by g. in, **III** 145f.

and "structure" of personality, **III** 171
and theology, **V** 81-92

Geneticist, definition of sin by, **III** 12, 162, 273

Genius
  expressed in simplicity, **II** 252
  hereditary? **III** 145

Gentile(s)
  conversions of, in apostolic times, **VII** 53
  indifference of, to signs and wonders, **VII** 16, 61
  kingdom handed over to, **VII** 50f.
  specific meaning of word? **I** 17
  "times of the Gentiles," **I** 46
  use of the word in O.T., **VII** 165

Geocentric universe
  concept of, **IV** 27
  philosophy of, **VIII** 118, 119, 204

Geographic isolation, effect on species of frogs, etc., **VIII** 163, 234f.

Geological ages
  in Genesis, **VII** 295f.
  later ages may be contemporaneous, **II** 33
  morphology used to determine, **II** 194f.
  possible comfort in contemplation of? **I** 359ff.; **VI** 27ff.

Geological "clocks." validity of, **VI** 27f.

Geology
  circular reasoning in, **II** 26 (fn. 32), 250 (fn. 2); **IV** 62, 175
  datings of, often misconceived, **II** 31ff., 101, 132f.
  of the Flood. *See under* Flood geology.
  fossil arrangements often need reversing, to fit, **II** 241
  and preparation of the earth for man, **I** 345ff.

Geometry
  arose for practical reasons, **I** 191f.
  Sumerian and Egyptian, **I** 189
Germ cell(s). *See also under* seed.
  housing of, **V** 139
  origin of, **V** 112
Germ plasm, **III** 60; **V** 112
  continuity of, **V** 86, 184ff.
  immunity of, to outside influence, **V** 85
Gerontology, **V** 12, 17
Gethsemane, Garden of, **V** 313
"Ghost in the machine" of life, **III** 269; **VIII** 59, 72
Ghosts in fiction, **V** 299, 343
Giants, **VII** 227f.
  modern, **VIII** 240, 241
  origin and significance of, **II** 311
"Giant self," **III** 181ff., 340, 344
Gibbon, **II** 13
Gift(s)
  saving faith as a, **VI** 158
  and talents, **VI** 159
Gigantopithecus, **II** 219
Gihon, spring of, **VII** 130, 132, 135
Gill slits, **IV** 42
Giraffes
  long necks of, **IV** 77; **V** 84
  pygmy, **VIII** 241
Gland(s)
  apocrine, **IX** 201
  adrenal, **II** 219
  endocrine, **II** 185, 220
  pineal and thyroid, **II** 219; **III** 147
Glandular disturbances and morphology, **II** 216ff.; **IV** 168f.
Glass
  malleable? **I** 202
  mirrors, **I** 183, 204; **II** 94
  tools and weapons, **II** 151
  weapons, made by Australian aborigines, **II** 150f.
  windows, **I** 204
  working, by Sumerians, **I** 192

Gliders, early Chinese, **I** 205, 211
Glosso-labial limitations in animals, **II** 257, 262; **IV** 269, 275
Glossolalia. *See under* Tongues.
Gloves
  Chinese sleeves as, **I** 213
  Cretan, **I** 201
  Eskimo design, **II** 159
  paleolithic, **II** 158
Glyptodon clavipes, **IV** 201
Goal in life
  appropriate to the age, **VIII** 14
  essential to meaningful life, **VIII** 150
Goal-seeking, as evidence of life, **VIII** 65f.
Gobi Desert, **IX** 119
God. *See also under* Creator
  activity of, in nature since the Fall, **VIII** 58, 88, 95
  as the Ancient of Days, **VIII** 41
  angels comprehend only His holiness, not His love, **I** 230
  armies of, **III** 218
  attributes of, personified, leads to polytheism, **IV** 117; **V** 250-257
  boundaries of the nations set by, **I** 318; **IX** 154
  character of, **I** 229f.
  common grace of, as restraint of society, **IX** 163
  concept of, unmanageable to science, **IV** 36
  as Designer, and perfection of His works, **VIII** 54f.
  as Designer, wisdom of, **VIII** 35-45
  Economizer of miracle, **IX** 26
  and evil, **VI** 170f.; **IX** 111
  fatherhood of, in Jewish belief, **VII** 40
  fatherhood of, restricted, **III** 100ff., 125

forgetting, divine vs. human, **III** 277ff.

forgiveness of, **III** 277ff.

"of the gaps," **IV** 49; **VIII** 53

governments appointed by, **VI** 139f.; **IX** 151

as the great "Experimenter," **IV** 43

as the great First Planter, **IV** 39

as the great Mathematician, **III** 54, 106

as the great Planner, **VIII** 109

the "ground of all being," **VIII** 53

as a "hilarious giver," **IX** 267

holiness of, **I** 230

how related to every man, **VIII** 199

identity of, in O.T. by use of different type, **V** 240ff.

and idols, **I** 219; **VIII** 109f.; **IX** 110

in the image of man, **III** 110

judgment of, upon Jesus Christ, **V** 328f.

kindness of, **IX** 271

love of, demonstrated by the Cross, **I** 218, 229f.; **V** 400

love of, not self-evident, **I** 231, 234

man made in the image of, **III** 110

multiplication of names of, **IV** 114

name of, meaning of, **VI** 40

names of, and symbols for, corrupted in antiquity, **IV** 117; **V** 250-257

nature as, **II** 272; **IV** 36; **VIII** 93

no man's debtor, **VI** 138

"objectified" by incarnation, **IV** 209, 325

omnipotence of, **I** 233 (fn. 20); **VI** 121-174. *See also under* Omnipotence.

of one substance, **V** 290

permissive will of, **VII** 59

personal intervention to be expected, **VIII** 53

plan of redemption. *See under* Redemption.

plural form of word for, **VII** 281f.

plurality of persons, **V** 221

power of, as Creator, **VIII** 16-27

private vs. public relations, **VII** 13, 14

prophecy as his prerogative, **VII** 120

purpose in creating man, **V** 78; **VIII** 199

relationship to Jesus, **V** 191, 199, 283f., 286f., 359

repentance of, **VI** 157f.

the "rest" of, **VIII** 54, 62f.

revealed in Jesus Christ, **I** 229ff.

saving faith a gift of, **VI** 158

silences of, **VII** 11-63. *See also under* Silences.

sovereignty of, **III** 218f.; **VI** 121ff.; **VIII** 95, 109, 120

universe as His immense handiwork, **VIII** 28-35

unknowable by man's wisdom, **VII** 20, 33

value of man to, **V** 399f.

as the "Watchmaker," **VI** 123; **VIII** 55

"weapons" used by, **IV** 138

will vs. "wish" of, **VI** 173f.

wisdom of, as a designer, **VIII** 35-45

words for, in Hebrew, **VII** 292

God, as a generic term, **V** 227

"God is dead" concept, **I** 231; **III** 275

Gods
  Babylonian, **IV** 114
  Chinese, **IV** 121f.
  Etruscan, **IV** 124
  Greek, **IV** 124
  Indian, **IV** 120

names of, confused with character of, **IV** 116
Persian, **IV** 120
Peruvian, **I** 183
primitive, **IV** 125-130
Roman, **IV** 119, 124
of Shem, Ham and Japheth, distinct, **I** 30, 263 (fn. 47); **IV** 115f.

Goddess of chaos, **VII** 289
Gold, **I** 20; **II** 93
decline in art of, **II** 120
early common use of, **II** 93
Golden age, traditions of, **II** 77f.
Golden Bough, the **II** 77 (fn. 37)
Golden Fleece, **II** 76; **V** 48; **IX** 47
Golden Gate, **VII** 108, 136
Gomer, **V** 82ff.; **VI** 196

Goodness
can be a fault, **IX** 146
vs. evil, **VI** 171ff.
governments, function of in relation to, **IX** 146
human, accidental, **III** 20
human, not inherent, **III** 31

Gorilla, **II** 13, 201, 204, 238-240; **IV** 317
cranial capacity of, **IV** 224
and daisy and man, differentiated, **III** 118; **IV** 320
illustrations of skull of, **II** 205, 209; **IV** 165
skull of, **IV** 162f.

Gospel, the
vs. "religion," **III** 279
resurrection as part of, **V** 345, 347

Gospels
basis of true "harmony" between, **VII** 97-105
compared with one another, **VII** 75, 79, 88, 99ff.
composite portrait of Jesus Christ in, **V** 209, 325; **VII** 96, 103

"contradictions" between, **VII** 67-106
cumulative effects of, **VII** 79ff.
genealogies in, **VII** 100, 103, 252f.
of John, a "fourth dimension," **VII** 88
language of, **VII** 73
necessity for four, **VII** 67-104, 252
reason for four, **VI** 48
reconciliation of contradictions in, **VII** 95f.
synoptic: for Shem, Ham and Japheth, **IV** 116; **VII** 233
synoptic: significance of and order, **I** 16ff.
and verbal inspiration problems, **VII** 78

Government(s)
appointed by God as required, **IX** 151
better than anarchy, **IX** 143f., 146
civil and religious authority, **IX** 148
to choose between evils, **IX** 146
the divine purpose of, **IX** 150
nations have the g. they deserve, **IX** 145
necessity of, **IX** 143f.
when not to be obeyed, and why, **IX** 144, 147

Grammar. *See also under* Hebrew language.
importance in communication, **IV** 274
and logic, **I** 288
nouns vs. verbs, **I** 277f.
pluperfect, expression of in Hebrew, **VI** 87, 90; **VII** 275, 285f.
plural of majesty, **VII** 281f.
superlatives in Hebrew, **I** 26f., 149; **VII** 232f.

vs. vocabulary, as the key to a World View, **I** 274

Grapes, first cultivation of, **I** 25; **V** 102

Grapevine, as the forbidden tree? **V** 96

Gravitation, size of earth and, **IV** 27f.

Gravity
"has no history," **VIII** 61
where law of, is superceded, **I** 349; **III** 75f.

"Great Chain of Being," **IV** 48, 65, 213; **VIII** 84, 134, 136, 141

"Great" man vs. "great" ape, **IV** 298

Great Synagogue, the, **VIII** 195

Great White Throne, the, **III** 246

Greatness
God's view of, **III** 199ff.
and individuation, **IV** 297f.

Greece
Athenian life, effect of war on, **VII** 21f.
early religion of, **IV** 124
Golden Age of, **VII** 18ff.

Greek(s)
astronomy, **I** 191
attitude toward life, **I** 295
attitude toward technology, **I** 299
attitude toward the dead, **V** 349
broad jumping at the Olympics, **III** 201
Flood tradition, **IX** 33, 89
gods of, **IV** 124
humanism, **VII** 22f.
influence on Medieval Synthesis, **III** 81
mathematics, **I** 35, 190f.
nature, their view vs. mystical, **III** 80
nonpractical, **I** 35
philosophy, **I** 31, 35, 257, 278,

280, 295; **VII** 18ff., 26; **VIII** 126, 196
progenitor, **I** 266
sin as defined by the, **III** 12, 29, 162; **VII** 24
skepticism in philosophy, **VII** 25
slaves, **VII** 27
system of values, **I** 162, 295
view of bodily resurrection, **V** 334
view of man, **I** 266f.
view of the soul, **I** 266f.
word for *tower*, **II** 86f.

Greek language
contrasted with Hebrew, **I** 265ff., 289
rapid diffusion of, **VII** 25
as vehicle for logical reasoning, **VII** 23
as vehicle for theology, **I** 265f., 289; **III** 286; **VII** 23
verbs vs. nouns in, **I** 277

Greek thought vs. Hebrew thought, **I** 266, 278

Grenades, **I** 209

Grief, muscles used in expressing, **IV** 245f.

Grimaldi Man, **I** 127, 136

Ground, cursed because of man, **IX** 115

Growth rates of man vs. animals, **IV** 285ff.

Group
behavior, **III** 345
consciousness, **III** 263f., 336
mind, **III** 142, 263f.; **V** 387

Gua, the chimpanzee, **IV** 269f.

Guidance, problems of, **III** 213ff.

Guilt
burden of, but no sense of sin; modern man's dilemma, **III** 273
disrupts fellowship with God, **III** 276, 279

innocence becomes, **III** 290
sense of, **III** 267f., 270, 273; **IV** 135
Guinea pigs, **VIII** 245

Gunpowder, **I** 205, 209f.
effect of invention of, **VIII** 119, 120
Gustatory sweating, **IX** 198

H

Habiru, identity of, **VII** 186, 189
Habitable world, Hebrew word for, **IX** 16
Habits of living, influence of; on skull form, **II** 201f.
Hagar, **I** 15; **II** 318f.; **VII** 98, 171
Hair as a covering, **V** 103
Hairiness, in man and apes, **II** 18, 19
Hairpins, **I** 327
Hall of Man, **II** 229
Hallucinations, criteria for determining, **V** 342
Hallucinogens, **I** 174
Ham
 Al-Hami and alchemy, **VI** 202; **VII** 200
 first to be scattered, **VI** 211ff.
 meaning of name, **I** 72; **VI** 202; **VII** 200
 the sin of, **I** 25ff., 144-150; **II** 313
Hamites
 biblical definition of the term, vs. ethnologists, **I** 11, 13, 14
 Canaanites as H., early high civilization of, **I** 91f.
 civilization created by, **I** 26, 257
 as colored people, **I** 13, 69, 72, 102f.; **VII** 233
 contribution of, to physical life, **I** 26, 247, 251, 257f., 261, 263f.
 current use of the term, **I** 11
 descendants of, **I** 101-112
 domestication of animals by, **I** 304ff.

early scattering of, **I** 122ff.; **II** 35; **VI** 212f.
extended use of the term, **I** 69
fossil man as, **I** 137f.
ingenuity of, **I** 42, 162f., 187 (fn. 77), 204, 285, 298, 300f., 320, 336, 337; **II** 152, 159, 160f.
inventiveness of, **I** 36, 38-43, 154-216, 257, 258 (fn. 42), 273, 300, 304, 317f., 320-338
languages of, and consequences, **I** 272, 274, 288f.
Mongols as, **I** 31, 69
Negroids as, **I** 69
nonphilosophical, **I** 291f., 295, 313f.
nontheological, **I** 285
as pioneers, **I** 27, 48, 120, 122, 140f., 258f., 273f.
practicality of, **I** 34, 275, 290ff., 293f., 295, 316f., 329
religion of, **I** 30, 257, 282, 284, 293
Sumerians as, **I** 36
technology of, **I** 153-216
technology of, vs. science, **I** 11, 37, 252f., 264, 284f., 286, 287
Tower of Babel built by, **VI** 211
wisdom of, vs. philosophy, **I** 31-34, 257, 278f., 279f., 283, 288, 294
World View of, **I** 272, 275, 287

Hamitic languages, **VI** 189
confusion of, at Babel, **VI** 211f.

excessive multiplication of, **I** 273ff.; **VI** 208ff.

grammar stable, vocabulary unstable, **I** 274

reason for diversity of, **VI** 214f.

specificity of, **I** 272; **VI** 215, 218

unique characteristics of, **VI** 218

Hamlet, the ghost in, **V** 299

Hammocks, **I** 186

Hammurabi

as Amraphel? **VII** 166

Code of Laws of, **VII** 171, 264f.

Hamsters, **III** 248

Hand

brain connections with, **IV** 242

evidence of design in, **IV** 37, 73, 241

as an extension of mind, **IV** 231, 241, 277

vs. feet for walking, **IV** 233f.

human, **VIII** 149

human vs. animal, **IV** 218

and mind "in concert," **IV** 242

purposeful design of, **I** 354f.

Handedness, **IV** 227

Hand grenades, **I** 208

Handicap(s), **III** 195- 235

among animals, **IV** 203

and disease, **III** 202f.

effect of, on an author, **III** 202f.

natural endowment and, **III** 199f.

paradises as, **III** 207, 208

of stress and tension, **III** 209

Handwriting, changes in, **III** 167

"Hansard" in Jewish courts, **VII** 39

Happiness, conditions for, **III** 207

Haran, a crossroads city, **VII** 151

Harbors, construction of breakwater design for, **I** 336f.

Hare and rabbits, interspecific sterility of, **III** 346

Harems, marriage and, **II** 283

"Harmonies" of the Gospels, **VII** 69, 79, 83

analogous to fusion of stereoscopic vision, **VII** 91

not altogether desirable, **VII** 77

basis of a true, **VII** 97-105

Harmony

in nature, **III** 66f., 71, 72; **IV** 191f., 194-205, 323; **IX** 127f.

in nature, denied, **VIII** 148 (fn. 94)

vs. unity, **IX** 157

Harness, Chinese produced earliest effective, **I** 205

Harpoons, **I** 161; **II** 158, 161

Harvard College, founding principle of, **VIII** 124 (fn. 37)

Hate, chemical effects of, **III** 309

Hatshepsut, favored foreigners, **VII** 182

Hawaiian

brother-sister marriages among, **VI** 224f.

Flood tradition, **IX** 31

inventiveness and ingenuity of, **I** 258 (fn. 42)

terms of relationship, **VII** 242

Hawthorne experiments, **VIII** 175

Headache remedy, **I** 332

Head shape, study of change of; in immigrants, **VIII** 242f.

Healing(s). *See also under* Miracle.

of cancer by faith? **VIII** 207

comparative absence of miraculous h. today? **VII** 57

in man vs. animals, **IV** 312f.

not always God's will, **III** 229

place of faith in, **II** 155

place of forgiveness in, **VII** 41

Tree of Life, leaves of for healing, **V** 382; **VI** 69, 73; **IX** 113f.

Heart

cells, autonomous reorganization of, *in vitro,* **VIII** 76

cells, maintaining autonomous pulsation, **VIII** 76

excised human, kept alive, **V** 124

rupture of, **V** 296, 302ff., 307ff.

sudden emotion, and rupture of, **V** 307

tissue, pulsating in isolation, **III** 332, 333

Heart, the deceitfulness of the, **III** 36f.

Hearth and home, significance of combination, **VIII** 178

"Heat," time of animal ovulation, **IV** 304

Heat death of the universe, **VIII** 20

Heat regulation in animals, **IV** 152

Heaven
as the animals might see it, a poem, **IX** 241
Hebrew concepts of, **V** 280
language of, **II** 268; **VI** 203ff.
space in? **VIII** 111f.

"Heavenly Father" in India, Greece, and Rome, **VII** 32

Hebrew
concept of future life, **V** 280
conception of man, vs. Greek, **I** 266f.
vs. Greek thought, **I** 266
philosophy of man's place in nature, **III** 85

Hebrew language
as appropriate vehicle for O.T. revelation, **I** 265f., 276f.; **III** 286
conjunction, use of, **VI** 87f.; **VII** 284
construct form, use of, **VI** 80f.
grammar and syntax, **VI** 78ff.
vs. Greek, **I** 265f., 289
of heaven? **VI** 203ff.
ideal vehicle for revelation, **I** 266, 276; **III** 286
in the N.T. (Matthew)? **VII** 74
nonphilosophical, **I** 279
nontheologically oriented, **VII** 23
philosophy of "tense" usage, **VI** 86

poetry, how expressed in, **VII** 276

use of pluperfect (or past perfect) tense, **VI** 87, 90; **VII** 275, 284ff.

as vehicle of religious experience, **III** 286

verbs vs. nouns, **I** 277

verb tenses, philosophy of time, **VI** 23

verb *to be* in, **VI** 89f.; **VII** 273; **IX** 185

word for darkness, **VII** 288

word order in the sentence, **VI** 86f.

Hedgehogs, **IV** 44

Hedges, God's vs. Satan's, **III** 197; **IX** 152

Heidelberg man, **I** 127; **II** 50

Height of man
and erect posture, **VIII** 40
kinetics of, **IV** 241; **VIII** 40f.

Helicopters, **I** 205

Helium and hydrogen, importance of, **VIII** 36

Hell, reality of, **V** 280

Hellas, Elishah of Genesis 10? **VI** 197

Hematidrosis, **V** 311

Hemoglobin vs. chlorophyll, **IV** 154

Hens
in early Egypt, **VII** 158
and foxes, **III** 65

Heraldry, not totemism, **III** 84

Herd leaders
role of, **IV** 298, 301
as "sense-organs," **II** 255; **III** 336

Herds, large size of; in O.T., **VII** 160

Heredity
and criminality, **III** 30f., 145
and intelligence, **III** 146f.
and moral responsibility, **III** 140
and personality, **III** 145f.

Heresy
  defined, **IV** 134
  humanism as, **VIII** 122
  part played by, in progress of
    truth, **IX** 148f.
Hermaphroditism, **V** 180, 397f. *See
  also under* Bisexual.
Hermit crab, **IV** 247
Hesperopithecus, **II** 230; **III** 57; **IV**
  50
Heth, meaning of name, **VII** 229
Hibernation, **III** 121; **IV** 257f.
Higher criticism
  and distortion of truth, **II** 67
  Flood traditions and the non-
    sense of, **IX** 81
  integrity lacking in, **VII** 168
  invalidation of, **VII** 147f., 150,
    153, 158, 180, 188
  mistaken regarding Abraham,
    VII 153f.
  and prophecy, **VII** 141
  Punch's view of, **VI** 52
  and the Spartoli Tablets, **VII** 167
High jump, African style, **III** 201;
  IX 152
High Priest
  duties of, on Day of Atonement,
    V 316
  Jesus as, **V** 359f.
Hindrances, as help in achievement,
  III 199-212
Hindu
  attitude toward Hamitic techni-
    cians, **I** 296
  Flood tradition, **IX** 32, 88
  mathematics, **I** 34f., 281
  philosophy, **I** 34ff., 280, 296, 308
  philosophy and religion, **VII** 32
  religion, **I** 296; **IV** 117f.
  science and philosophy, **I** 308
Hinduism
  emergence of, **I** 281f., 296
  in China, **I** 282f.
Hindustani, as a language of
  philosophy, **I** 280

Hippopotamus, **VIII** 236; **IX** 217
Historiography, genealogies as, **VII**
  218
History
  a biblical view of, Vol. **I**
  climate, its influence on, **IX** 51
  a cyclic view of, **I** 311; **II** 137; **III**
    19; **VI** 55f.; **VIII** 128
  as "drift of culture," **VIII** 118
  ethnocentrism, its effect on the
    writing of h., **I** 154
  generations, word used for h. in
    Genesis, **II** 276; **VI** 53
  "great man" view of, **IV** 298
  imposition of order upon, **VIII**
    128, 129
  omnipotence of God in, **VI** 130ff.
  organic view of, **VI** 55f.
  as philosophy, **I** 279
  is it predictable? **VII** 118f.
  providence of God in, **IX** 144f.
  repeats itself, **VIII** 152-167
  Scripture and, **VI** 194f., 204-206,
    239; **IX** 75, 83
  in three dimensions, Vol. **I**; **VI**
    55-59
History of Israel
  national, **VI** 52f., 60ff.
  religious, **VI** 52f., 70ff.
  spiritual, **VI** 52f., 66ff.
  in three dimensions, **VI** 55-59
  as three trees, **VI** 51-73
Hittite(s)
  domestication of the horse, **I** 327
  invention of spoked wheels, **I** 327
  possible connection with early
    Chinese, **I** 104f., 210
  proliferation of words, **I** 273
"Holidays." a modern concept,
  VIII 175
Holiness
  replaced by truth, **VII** 23
  true and false, **III** 128ff.
Holy of Holies, the earthly and the
  heavenly, **V** 359f.

Holy Spirit
 Juno as? **V** 256
 as Lord, **V** 225
 in the O.T., **V** 237ff.
 as the Voice of the Lord, **V** 237f.
 work of, **III** 129, 177, 190
Homa tree, **V** 100
Home heating, penalties of, **IV** 260
Homeotherm, man the supreme, **III** 120; **IV** 257
Homeothermism, **IV** 68f. *See also under* Thermoregulation.
Homicide, uniquely human, **I** 322
Homo erectus, **II** 15, 28, 29
Homo habilis, **II** 15
Homology(ies). *See also under* Convergence.
 and convergence, **VIII** 78, 235
 as evidence of design, **II** 247; **IV** 222
Homo sapiens
 the body of Adam as, **V** 387
 Neanderthal Man as degenerate, **I** 133
 psychic unity of, **III** 337
 as a single species, **II** 48, 50
 the two species of, **III** 315-350
Honoring parents, **I** 146; **II** 305, 313
"Hopeful monsters," **IV** 61
Hopi
 and abstract thought, **I** 273
 a modern story of, **VIII** 107
 sense of time, **VI** 22
 World View of, **VIII** 107
Hormones
 influence of, on racial morphology, **II** 217f.
 "tyranny" of, **IV** 303f.
Hornet, **III** 215
 Thotmes III as a, **VII** 187
Horns, development of, **IV** 157f.
Horse(s), **III** 120
 breeding of, **IV** 297f.
 can be run down by a man, **IX** 41, 206
 domesticated by Hittites, **I** 327
 evolution of? **IV** 147
 harness for, **I** 205
 prayer for an injured, **IX** 262f.
 prized in early Egypt, **VII** 159
 and tiger story, to illustrate survival of fittest, **IV** 76
 sweating of, **IV** 261; **IX** 197, 201, 202
Hospitals, early Peruvian, **I** 184
Hostages, treatment of; in antiquity, **III** 27
Hottentots
 "joking" relationship among, **II** 303
 meaning of name for "men," **I** 63, **VII** 201 (fn. 80)
Hotu Man, **I** 127
House(s)
 igloos, **I** 157ff.; **II** 160
 of reeds, **I** 177
Household furnishings, **I** 41
 air conditioning, **I** 333
 bamboo piping, **I** 231f.
 "bathrooms," **I** 189, 333
 camp stools, **I** 201
 glass windows, **I** 204
 hammocks, **I** 186
 heating: central, **I** 333
  : coal, **I** 333
  : gas, **I** 205, 213f., 333
 rocking stools, **I** 199
 running water, hot and cold, **I** 189
 wallpapering (with a sponge), **I** 197
 wax candles, **I** 333
Housing for man's soul, very special, **IV** 323ff.
Howling vs. barking, **II** 266
Human
 achievement and handicaps, **III** 195-235
 brain, complexity of, **IV** 221-230
 body, low efficiency of, **IV** 297, 311; **IX** 204

life, future prolongation of, **V** 16

longevity, and achievement, **V** 168

need: punishment as a basic, **IV** 134

race, as an organism, **III** 183; **V** 389

race, of one blood, **IV** 254; **V** 201

sacrifice when founding a city, **VII** 207f.

society, as Leviathan, **V** 388

thermostat, sensitivity of, **IX** 196

Human(ness), **III** 89, 91f., 94; **IV** 281ff.

by acquisition of language, **III** 117

activity as expression of, vs. accomplishment of animals, **IV** 316f.

criteria for, vs. animalness, **IV** 208, 316ff.

criterion for, in fossil man, **III** 124

cultural factors in, **I** 241

definition of true, **III** 186

expression of, in man, **IV** 281ff., 319

is the possession of selfconsciousness, **III** 105

is the power of moral judgment, **III** 107, 268f.

is the power of reason, **III** 106

is the power of reflection, **III** 260

is the power to create, **III** 106f.

language a criterion of, **IV** 266f.

laughter belongs to, **IV** 283

of the Lord Jesus Christ, **V** 153

lost by the Fall, **III** 338

physiological factors in, **IV** 215f.

rationality, a trait of, **III** 106, 117; **IV** 315

recovery of true, **III** 186

is redeemableness, **I** 231; **II** 191, **III** 124, 338; **IV** 20f., 209

speech and, **III** 116, 117; **IV** 216, 266f.

test for, **IV** 265, 266

tool-making as a sign of, **IV** 265

true, exemplified in Jesus Christ, **III** 186

urge to organize, a unique quality of, **IV** 315ff.

worship unique to, **IV** 317

Human behavior

abnormal, nature of, **III** 157ff.

vs. animal, **IV** 281f.

how it is to be corrected, **III** 170ff.

and its essential "fallenness," **III** 14-46

noninstinctive, **IV** 282

tending towards aggressiveness, **III** 17, 23, 114f.

uniquely suicidal, **I** 322; **III** 163; **IV** 321

unpredictability of, **IV** 298

Humanism

among the Greeks, **VII** 22f.

as heresy, **VIII** 122

inadequacy of, **VIII** 211 (fn. 210)

replaces spiritual concern, **VII** 23

Humanist

definition of, **VIII** 91

false optimism of, **II** 66; **VIII** 131f.

Human nature. *See also under* Natural man.

basically evil, **III** 14-46, 159ff.

four reasons why basically evil, **III** 11f., 162

goodness of, accidental, **III** 20, 31

how it must be changed, **III** 170ff.

Humidity, effect of; on morphology, **II** 216

Humility

counterfeit, **III** 37

vs. humiliation, **III** 219

Humming birds and humming moths (Simpson), **IV** 152

Hunger
in man vs. animals, **IV** 295, 312
out of register with need, in man, **IV** 311f.; **IX** 133, 205

Hunting techniques and tools. *See also under* Fishing.
African, **I** 169
of the Ainu, **I** 168
of the Australian aborigine, **I** 170
bolas and boomerangs, **I** 170, 171
for catching wildfowl, **I** 168f.
Eskimo, **I** 160, 161; **II** 160f.
Japanese ingenuity in, **I** 169f.
for killing wolves, **I** 160; **II** 161
in Oceania (Java, etc.), **I** 169
Samoan ingenuity in, **I** 169f.
for seals, **I** 161
Tierra del Fuegan, **I** 170
for walrus, **I** 161

Hunting wasps, study of, **III** 58ff., 65

Husband, as distinct from father, **II** 315, 327

Huxley's falsified diagrams, **II** 233, 240

Hybrids, virility of, **VI** 230

Hydrogen and helium, importance of, **VIII** 36

Hyksos, **VII** 178f.

Hyperbole
examples of, in Scripture, **IX** 18-21
extent of use, in Scripture, **IX** 13

Hypnoanalysis, memory regression in, **V** 198, 276, 278f.

Hypnosis
counting under, **III** 246
regression in time under, **V** 198, 276, 278
and time sense, **VI** 23

Hypothalamus, **IV** 259; **IX** 196

Hypothermia and death, **V** 122

Hypothesis
built on deliberate "lies," **I** 272
vs. fact, **II** 12; **VIII** 154, 155, 162
not used in astronomy by Sumerians, **I** 191

Hysteria
mass, **III** 142
in multiple personality, **III** 167

I

Iapetos, as Japheth, **VI** 195

Ice, protective effect on aquatic life, **III** 75

Ice Age, causes of, **IV** 95, 104f.

Iceland, Vikings discovered, by use of birds, **IX** 40

Ichthyosaurs, **IV** 62

Idea(s)
hard to dislodge, **IX** 296
popularization of, **VII** 11

Idealism
Christian, and class distinctions, **VIII** 116
secular, **III** 41f.

Identical twins
alpha brain waves of, **III** 265
studies of, in psychology, **III** 146

Idleness. See also under *Labor*.
a curse, **IX** 136
far from satisfying, in itself, **VIII** 176

and sin, **III** 132

Idol(s)

absence of, in Chinese religion, **IV** 122

Egyptian worship of, **IV** 117

why not destroyed by God, **I** 219; **VIII** 109f.; **IX** 110f.

worship of, **I** 219; **IV** 326

Idolatry, **III** 110

Igloo, construction of, **I** 157f.; **II** 160

Ignorance

of the Jews regarding Christ's identity, **VII** 37

as sin, **III** 12, 17, 29, 161, 273f.; **VII** 24

sometimes as advantage in research, **VIII** 105 (fn. 2)

Ignoring leads to denying, **VIII** 127, 205, 214

Iguvine Tablets, **IV** 124

Ill health, some, as the secret of long life, **III** 209

Illegitimacy, **II** 278

Illustrations. *See under* Pictures.

Image(s). *See also under* Idols, Imago Dei.

as adornment in churches, **IX** 239

as animals would design them! **IX** 241

dangers inherent in use of, **IX** 239

vs. likeness, **III** 99-133

without likeness, **III** 127

and pictures of Christ, dangerous, **V** 210, 391

possible meaning of, in Genesis, **VII** 312

Imagination

compensates for scarcity of data, **II** 16, 242, 245

dangers of, in anthropology, **II** 69

hindrances to the exercise of, **IX** 244

use of, by anthropologists, **II** 248

use of, justified, **IX** 36

Imago Dei, **III** 102-126

as creativity, **III** 106f.

loss of, **II** 110f., 114f.

in man, **V** 221f., 390; **VIII** 44

as possession of self-consciousness, **III** 105

as the power of making moral judgments, **III** 107f.

as rationality, **III** 106

as relationship, **III** 110

Imbeciles, happy people, **IX** 136

Immanence of God, **III** 334

Immigrants, Franz Boas's study of, **VIII** 242

Immortality, physical, **V** 12

of Adam, **I** 234, 237; **III** 290, 320; **V** 82f., 116ff., 125, 179, 182, 370; **VIII** 50

of Adam and Eve, **V** 141-158

of Adam originally, **I** 235; **V** 87, 89, 139

of asexual cells, **V** 128

of asexual reproduction, **V** 17

Augustine on, **V** 125, 181f.

biological definition of, **V** 117, 124f.

of Cain's descendants, **II** 310ff.

of cancer cells, **V** 133

consequences of, **V** 159-169

of First and Last Adam, **III** 302; **V** 87, 89, 139

immortal children born to Adam unfallen, **V** 180

of Jesus Christ, **I** 236ff.; **V** 191, 235f., 376

Jewish traditions regarding, **V** 179f.

loss of, **III** 290

lost by Adam, when? **V** 150

means of recovering, **III** 289; **V** 151

Nahmanides on, **V** 180

of the ovum, **V** 89, 189f.

of plants, **V** 126

and population growth, **V** 18, 166

possessed by billions of living organisms, **V** 176

possible for man, **V** 119-140

Roman Catholic Church acknowledges, **V** 182

undesirable? **IX** 114f.

of unicellular life, **V** 124f., 145, 276

vicarious sacrifice requires, **V** 164, 191

Immortality (nonphysical), of angels, **V** 117

Impaling, **V** 304

Imperfections labelled as "character," **VIII** 56

"Implacable offensive" of science, **III** 55; **VIII** 52, 65, 135; **IX** 26

Implications

of evolution for theology, **IV** 79, 320ff.; **V** 79, 172

important to attend to, **I** 53f.

Imprinting, **III** 239; **VII** 171

Improvement, not the same as invention, **II** 148

In Memoriam, **II** 65; **III** 14f.; **IV** 126, 181; **VIII** 219

"In the day that," meaning of phrase, **V** 182

Inbreeding, **II** 222; **V** 27; **VI** 223, 226, 229

deaf-mutism and, **II** 263, 300; **IV** 307; **VI** 231; **VII** 235

and decline in intelligence, **VI** 231

and diversification in small populations, **IV** 67

effect of, on animals, **II** 28; **VII** 237

after the Flood, **VII** 234f.

harmful effects of, in man, **III** 121; **VII** 235, 237, 239

harmless among Toda? **VI** 225f.

human, and genetics, **VI** 224ff.

mutations and, **IV** 306f.; **VI** 222ff.; **VII** 235f., 239

Inca

brother-sister marriages, **VI** 222ff.

weaving, **I** 324

Incarnation, the, **III** 144, 292, 323, 327; **V** 162ff., 193-200. *See also under* Birth of Jesus Christ.

and birth of Jesus Christ, **V** 176-200

God objectified by, **IV** 209, 325

key to man's creation, **I** 234; **IV** 328

key to the universe, **I** 218, 233f.; **VIII** 44

man designed for, **IV** 20f., 212, 323ff., 328

moment of, **V** 282ff., 359; **VII** 36

necessary, even if Adam had not fallen? **V** 160

preparation of the human body for, **IV** 323f.

propriety of, **IV** 325f.; **V** 161

and rebirth, **V** 201-214

as revelation, **VIII** 198

timing of, **I** 239; **VII** 20, 34

truths revealed by, **V** 162

universe designed for, **VIII** 44

virgin birth and, **V** 172-214

Incest, **II** 281f., 300, 328; **III** 121; **IV** 307; **VII** 251

among the Alii, Hawaiians, Singhalese, **VI** 224

and brother-sister marriages, **VI** 222-237

Cain's wife and, **VI** 219-240

deaf-mutism and, **II** 300; **IV** 307 (and fn. 222)

endangers intelligence level, **VI** 231

mutations and, **VI** 226f.

as a near "universal," **II** 300

when not damaging, **VII** 329f.

"Incomprehensibility" of reality, **VIII** 24

"Incomprehensibles" and "incredibles," III 325; VIII 21, 23f., 32
Indeterminacy, principle of, VIII 60, 90
India(n)
    caste system, I 296
    Flood tradition (Manu), IX 74
    gods of, IV 120
    medicine in early, I 329
    philosophy, I 280; III 179; VII 19, 30ff.
    religion, IV 119f.; VII 32
    why no industrial revolution in, I 298
Indians of North America. See under North American Indians, American Indians.
Indians of South America, agricultural achievements of, I 166f.
Indians of the Sonoran Desert, resourcefulness of, I 162-164
Indifference of God? VII 13
Individualism, discouraged in primitive society, II 170, 176
Individuation, II 175f.; IV 219
    in man, IV 297f.
    slight, among animals, IV 298f.
Indo-European, II 98. See also under Aryan, Japheth.
    descendants of Japheth, I 11, 80-100; VII 97
    language of, VI 188f.
    philosophical nature of, I 295
    uninventiveness of, I 36, 300, 303, 305, 317, 337
Indulgences, sale of; to build the cathedrals, IX 228, 253
Indus Valley Cultures, I 27, 188; II 38, 78, 95f.; V 61
    beads found at, II 95
    destroyed by Aryans, II 114
    founders of, black skinned? VI 202; VII 200
    Sumerian links with, I 72
Industrialization, cost of, VIII 174

Industrial Revolution, III 14
Indwelling of Christ in the believer, III 168f.; V 206
"Inequality of man," III 147
Infant(s)
    baptism of, III 307; V 279
    death of, III 291; IX 173
Infanticide, II 265, 284, 304f.
    corollary to test-tube babies, VIII 72
    Eskimo, II 304f.; III 138
    reasons for, among natives, IX 172
    of the still unnamed, IX 172
Infection and wound healing in man, IV 312
Infinity, not merely a large number, VI 39
Ingenuity
    affected by the Fall, II 86
    importance attached to, by natives, I 187 (fn. 77)
    of primitive man, I 162f.
    unaccountable, I 204
Inheritance, legal
    rules governing, II 285, 307, 318
    time of receiving, II 239
Inheritance of acquired characters, I 357 (fn. 281). See also Cytoplasmic inheritance.
Ink blot test, III 153
Inquisition, science as the modern, II 75; IV 25; VIII 160, 166
Inscription on the cross, VII 79
Insect(s)
    earlier studies of, III 57
    fixity of species among, IV 188
    flowers in symbiosis with, IV 57, 71
    "inspired activity" of, IV 248
    pain free? IX 126f.
    as plant food, VIII 70
    and size, VIII 40
    societies of, "cultureless," IV 292
    societies of, vs. human, IV 281f.

Insecticides
American Indian's invention of, I 163
loss of potency of, VIII 234
Insemination, V 173
Inspiration
from music, short lived, IX 235
necessity of, for spiritual truth, IV 136
of Scripture, evidence for, III 90; VII 91f.
of Scripture, witnessed by consistent use of symbols throughout, VI 53f.
and revelation, IV 136
of unworthy people, IX 251f.
verbal, problems of, VII 78
"Inspired" art, Christian and non-Christian, IX 252
Instinct(s)
absent in man? III 116, 143; VIII 69
of animals vs. human cultural behavior, IV 263, 282
in bondage to circumstance, III 65
conferred on animals, when sin disrupted nature? IV 248
demand for order by man as an i.? IV 315f.
domestication, effect of on, IV 198f.
and ESP, III 264f.
and expression of emotion, II 257
homing, of pigeons, III 265
and insect behavior, III 58ff.
as "inspired activity," III 97; IV 248; V 168; VIII 96; IX 72
as the law written "within," III 55, 89
as mechanism only, VIII 68
possible decay of, III 265
war as an "aggressive instinct" in man? III 24, 25f.
Instinctive vs. learned behavior, III 60

Institutes of Menu, I 35
Insulin, IV 309
common to unrelated species, IV 153
Integration of knowledge
becoming more difficult, VIII 172
felt need for, VIII 128, 130
the new search for, VIII 124 (fn. 36)
Intellectual
"apartheid," religion vs. science, VIII 122, 172
vs. religious life, I 246
Intelligence
and brain convolutions, IV 226, 228f.
and cranial capacity, II 164, 180, 205; IV 177
decline in, III 49f.; V 169; VI 231
definition of, II 143
of early man, II 144f.; 166
effect of sin upon, III 13, 39, 162, 272, 285, 313; IV 136, 210; VIII 196
endangered by inbreeding, VI 231
exercised in choice of means, not ends, VIII 189, 191
expression of, limited by level of culture, II 166
and heredity, II 146f.
vs. inventiveness, II 147-153
vs. knowledge and wisdom, II 148, 154; III 82f.
as man's chief defense, II 247f.
not related to appearance, II 109, 179, 186, 234ff.
of the "paleolithic" Eskimo, II 159
of primitive vs. civilized man, II 131, 165f.
of primitive vs. modern man, II 108, 154f.
Intelligibility vs. accuracy, III 322
Intention as basis of reward, III 193

Interdependence. *See under* Symbiosis.

International morality, **I** 47; **III** 27, 267; **VIII** 113 (and fn. 18)

Intertestamental period, **VII** 14, 18-35; **VIII** 196

Intertidal communities, **IV** 187ff.

Intertidal crowding, **III** 71

Intra-specific competition, a doubtful concept, **IV** 183f., 186

Introvertism, social advantages of, **III** 30

Intuition, female, **VII** 117

Invention(s)
    classified list of Hamitic, **I** 38-42
    encyclopedias of inventions, early Chinese, **I** 187
    fate of, among primitives, **II** 173f.
    vs. improvement, **I** 170, 181, 207f., 205; **II** 148
    initial hostility to new, **I** 202; **II** 176f.
    necessity the mother of? **I** 48; **II** 149f.
    vs. scientific discovery, **I** 286f.; **VIII** 105 (fn. 2)
    simplicity of, a virtue, **I** 159, 164, 170, 323; **II** 148
    simultaneity of, **VIII** 133
    as a stimulus to exploration, **I** 332
    when not acceptable, **I** 296f.

Inventions, miscellaneous, **I** 38-42. *See also under* Agriculture, Architecture, Food gathering techniques, Hunting, Medicine, Metallurgy, Pharmacology, Pottery, Sanitation, Weaving.
    air conditioning, **I** 333
    aircraft, **I** 205, 211
    asbestos, **I** 322
    ball-and-socket joint, **I** 335
    bellows, **I** 201, 205
    bird-banding, **I** 335
    boatbuilding, **I** 185, 202, 203, 326
    bolas, **I** 170

boomerangs, **I** 171f.

breakwater design for harbors, **I** 336f.

building construction, **I** 159, 185, 193, 194, 202, 323, 324; **II** 160

calendars, **I** 183

camera obscura, **I** 328

camp stools, **I** 201

canals and locks, **I** 326

cartography, **I** 190

children's go-carts, **I** 186

cigar holders, **I** 186

cigarettes, **I** 203

cire perdu casting, **I** 214

clocks, **I** 205, 206, 213, 321

compass, **I** 205, 332

crankshaft, **I** 206

drills, **I** 192, 205, 206, 212f.

enema, **I** 176, 178, 199

fingerprinting, **I** 205, 213, 335

fire drill, **I** 183

fireflies as flashlight," **I** 187

gear trains, **I** 213, 321

glass, **I** 192, 202, 204

gunpowder, **I** 209f., 332

hairpins, **I** 327

hammocks, **I** 186

harness, **I** 205, 326

ink, **I** 212

insecticides, **I** 163

irrigation control systems, **I** 165

kites, **I** 211

looms, **I** 201, 205

malleable glass, **I** 202

mirrors, **I** 183, 204; **II** 94

paint brushes, **I** 209

paper-making, **I** 182f., 205, 209, 212, 332

piping (bamboo and clay), **I** 201, 213f., 333

pottery water vessels to prevent spilling, **I** 181

printing, **I** 209, 212, 325, 332

pumps of all types, **I** 186, 205, 206, 215

rainmaking, **I** 334f.

road-rollers, **I** 182
ropes, **I** 182, 196
rotary fan and winnowing machine, **I** 205
rotary quern, **I** 215
rubber technology, **I** 178f., 214
safety pins, **I** 204 (fn. 137)
"sandpaper," **I** 186
sedan chair, **I** 199, 201
smelting furnace, **I** 201
snow goggles, **I** 157 (fig 5), 162; **II** 162
soap, **I** 163, 201
soldering, **I** 322
spectacles, **I** 204
"stethoscope," **I** 161; **II** 161
stirrups, **I** 215
sunshades, **I** 202
suspension bridges, **I** 211f.
"telephone," **I** 161; **II** 161
thimbles, **I** 158; **II** 159
tipiti, **I** 172
tools, **I** 163, 185, 192, 202, 335
traps, **I** 169, 170, 336; **II** 161
truth serum, **I** 174
tweezers, **I** 178
umbrellas, **I** 201
underwater breathing apparatus, **I** 336
wax candles, **I** 333
weapons, **I** 184, 205, 208, 209f.
wheels, **I** 202, 326, 327
windmill, **I** 206, 214
Inventor(s)
fate of, in primitive society, **II** 173
as heroes, **I** 187
identified with his invention, **II** 174
as "peculiar" people, **II** 149
recognition of, **I** 295
Invisible mending, developed by Aymara, **I** 184
Involution
cultural, **II** 106
vs. evolution, **II** 106

Ion exchange, the sweetening of bitter water and, **VII** 213
Ipswich Skull, **II** 199
I.Q., in search of a paleolithic, **II** 143-192. *See also under* Intelligence.
Iranian Highland Plateau
Cradle of Civilization, **II** 95
Cradle of Man? **IX** 45f.
cultural beginnings in, **V** 65
and distribution of races, **IX** 51
evidence of recent flooding of, **IX** 47f.
Garden of Eden in? **IX** 46, 47
home of domesticated species, **IV** 49f., 52
ideal temperature conditions of, **IX** 51
source of species, **I** 193
starting-point of migrations, **IX** 49
Irish
peasants, displacement of, **II** 183, 221; **IV** 167
wake, purpose of? **V** 122
Iron. *See also under* Cast iron.
smelting of, **I** 305
Sumerian word for, **II** 312f.; **VII** 227
Iroquois Keeper-of-Names, **II** 298; **IX** 179
Irrationality of man, **III** 17
Irrigation works
Nabataean, **I** 165
New World, **II** 117
Irritability of living tissue, **VIII** 85
Iscah as Sarah, **VII** 155
Isolation
absolute i. equals death, **III** 274, 276
consequences of, **II** 139; **III** 210f.
effects of, on culture, **II** 119
geographic, effect on species, **VIII** 163, 234f.
and physical degeneration, **II** 113; **IV** 168

Israel
covenant relationship of, **VII** 16,
35, 36, 38, 41, 46, 47, 50, 60, 63
divine omnipotence in history of,
VI 144-154
history of, in cameo, **VI** 144-154
history of, symbolized in three
trees, **VI** 52-73
natural suicide of, **VII** 44, 45

signs and wonders, purpose of
vis-a-vis Israel, **VII** 51f.
Italics, use of in King James Ver-
sion, **VII** 273ff.; **IX** 185
"I-thou" vs. "me-it" relationship to
nature, **I** 28; **III** 80; **VIII** 106
Ituri Forest Pygmies, **VIII** 241
Ivory from mammoths, **IV** 98f.

J

Jackal, **II** 260
Jackdaw, counting, **IV** 318
Jacob, name found in Egyptian
King List, **VII** 178
Jamdet Nasr, **I** 114; **II** 90; **IV** 114
Janus, two-faced deity, **V** 180
Japheth(ites), **VI** 179, 195f.
ancient form of the name, **VI** 195
blessing of, **I** 27f., 338; **VII** 230
as colonizers, not pioneers, **I** 49,
120, 123, 140f., 259
contribution of, to intellectual
life, **I** 12, 14, 27f., 30f., 47, 247,
251, 256, 259, 261, 263-302
cradle of, **II** 46
culture created by, **I** 27, 259
descendants of, **I** 80-100
displaces Ham, **II** 38
early evidence of, in Iran, **I** 98
as an early linguistic group, **I**
114; **VI** 179
enlargement of, **I** 27f.; **II** 35f.;
VII 230
gods of, **I** 30, 263 (fn. 47); **IV**
115f.
as Indo-Europeans, **I** 11
Luke's Gospel written for, **I** 17;
VII 97, 99, 102f.
nonpractical, **I** 295, 296, 297,
299, 308

philosophy defined, **I** 29, 30, 278,
298
philosophy of, **I** 31, 34ff., 256f.,
265, 280f., 289f., 294, 296
religion of, **I** 30, 281f.
responsibility devinely appointed to, **I** 27f., 43, 251,
255f.
science originated with, **I** 31, 32,
37, 70f., 252, 264, 285, 297,
303-319; **II** 139
spread of, **II** 35
in the tents of Shem, **II** 140
theology originated by, **I** 31, 37,
252, 264f., 285, 296, 303-319;
II 139
uninventiveness of, **I** 35f., 37,
206f., 300f., 303, 305, 313, 317,
337
World View, **I** 272, 275, 290
Jarmo, early settlement of, **II** 86,
100; **V** 66
Jasher, Book of, **VI** 211; **VII** 76
Java Man, **II** 42, 52. *See also under*
Pithecanthropus.
Jaw
diet, influence of, on structure of,
II 213
first appearance of, **IV** 42
language, and form of, **IV** 268f.

mechanism, and skull form, **II** 201f.

mechanism, influence of diet on, **II** 183f.

structural modifications of, **IV** 162ff.

structure, and simian shelf, **IV** 164, 244

structure of, in man vs. apes, **IV** 162f., 243

Jealousy and love
and polygyny, **II** 282
primitive's attitude toward, **II** 299

Jebusites, **VII** 143

Jehovah
Jesus Christ as, in the O.T., **V** 234ff.
name and identity of, **II** 310
pagan parallels of the name? **V** 254, 256

Jellyfish, **III** 263, 336; **IV** 53

Jerboa and the desert rat, **IV** 157

Jericho, **II** 99f.
burning of the city, **VII** 191
date of the fall of the city, **VII** 187f.
excavation of, **VII** 187f.

Jerusalem, **VII** 129-140
as Aelia Capitolina, **VII** 136
destruction of, by Titus, **VII** 135
edict to rebuild, **VII** 36
growth of, in modern times, **VII** 137-140
growth of ancient, **VII** 132-137
meaning of the name, **VII** 164, 169
prophecies concerning its building-up, **VII** 127ff.
rebuilding of, map showing, **VII** 138
successive boundaries predicted, **VII** 132, 133

Jesuit Relations, **II** 79; **V** 48

Jesuits, **IV** 118

attitude of, towards Galileo, **VIII** 154

and Chinese astronomy, **VIII** 154

view of religious freedom, **IV** 118

Jesus Christ. *See also under* Adam, First and Last, Birth of Jesus Christ, Incarnation, Redeemer, Sacrifice, Vicarious sacrifice.
agony of soul, **V** 313f.
as Angel of the Lord, **V** 227, 237f.
appearances of, in the O.T., **V** 228ff., 244f.; bibliography regarding, **V** 248f.
ascension of, **V** 244; **VII** 47
basis of man's condemnation of, **III** 43f.
begotten of the Father, **V** 286f.
birth of, **I** 218, 233; **V** 172-200
blood, presentation of in heaven, **V** 359f.
body, nature of resurrected, **V** 338f.; **VI** 37
body of, **IV** 20f., 326ff.; **V** 381
character of, faultless, **VII** 96
chose to die, **I** 237; **V** 191, 294ff.
"coma theory" of His death, **V** 295f., 337f.
composite portrait of, in the Gospels, **V** 209, 325; **VII** 96, 103
creative acts, a succession of, **I** 367f.
as Creator, **I** 367f., **V** 218. *See also under* Creator.
crucifixion of, **III** 43f.; **V** 294-331
death of, **I** 231; **V** 249ff., 315ff.
death of, active not passive, **V** 325, 330, 379
death of, unique, **V** 376, 315-331
death on the cross, a reality, **V** 337
dismisses His life, **V** 326f.
divine/human nature of, **VII** 104
exemplifies true humanness, **III** 186
fetal life of, **III** 292; **V** 283f.

in the Garden of Eden, **V** 218f.

gender and temperament of, **V** 398

genealogies of, **VII** 100, 221f., 254, 262ff., 268

as God in the N.T., **V** 230

heart rupture, the cause of His death? **V** 302-314

as High Priest, **V** 359f.

His Second Coming, **I** 366f., **VI** 42

how did He die? **V** 293-331

immortality of, **I** 236ff.; **V** 191, 325f., 376

importance of the body of, **V** 161

incarnate anew in the believer, **III** 176; **V** 206f.

incarnate as man, **V** 160

incarnation as an "objectification" of God, **IV** 209, 325

innocence of, **V** 317f.

as Jehovah in the O.T., **V** 234ff.

as the Lamb, **V** 328, 359, 380

as the Last Adam, **V** 368ff.

of the line of David, **VII** 263

lordship of, over nature, **VI** 132

made sinful for us, **V** 329

magnificance of His presence, **VII** 103f.

manhood of, **V** 153f.

moment of incarnation, **V** 282ff., 359

above nationality, **III** 187

necessity of death by crucifixion, **V** 302, 326

not truly dead? **V** 295, 298, 337f.

as perfect Man, **IV** 210, **VII** 104

perfection of His life, **III** 43f.

physical appearance of, as viewed by other cultures, **V** 181; **IX** 239f.

physical immortality of, **V** 191, 325f., 376

pictures of, harmful? **IX** 239, 241, 243

preparation of the world for His coming, **VII** 29

as the Promised Seed, **V** 246f.

relationship to God as Father, **V** 199; **VII** 40

relationship to God as God, **V** 359

relationship to Joseph, **VII** 264f.

as representative Man, **V** 391; **IX** 188f.

resurrection, **V** 297, 299, 300, 334-365. *See also under* Resurrection.

righteousness of, and man's reaction to, **III** 43f.

sacrifice of, **V** 326f., 328, 348, 373. *See also under* Substitutionary death.

as the Second Adam, **V** 368ff.

as Son of Man, **III** 187; **V** 393

sonship: time when it was established, **V** 199, 286f.

sonship relationship to the Father, **V** 191, 283f., 286f., 359

soul of, **V** 282ff.

summation of human potential in, **III** 185ff.; **V** 393

temptation of, from "without," **III** 302

titles of, in the Gospels, **VII** 103, 104

total human potential in, **III** 171f., 187

transfiguration of, **V** 18, 163f., 377f., 399

trial of, **V** 317f.; **VII** 44

true manhood realized in, **V** 153ff.

true nature of man seen in, **IV** 320, 329

as unfallen Man, **V** 159ff.

an uninventable character, **VII** 96

universe designed for His death, **I** 232f.

virgin birth of, **I** 234; **III** 302; **V** 172-212

wisdom of, **III** 281

"within" the believer, **III** 169, 172, 177

witnesses to His faultlessness, **V** 319

as the Word, **V** 219, 246

worship accepted by, **IV** 326

wound received on the cross, **V** 306

Jew(s). *See also under* Israel.

chosen by God for a purpose, **I** 276

committed national suicide, **VII** 44

demanded crucifixion of Jesus, **VII** 38

disbelief of Jesus' identity, genuine, **VII** 37f.

not technically minded, **I** 303, 308, 310

religion of, as experience vs. theology, **I** 257; **III** 286

and science, **I** 303f., 310

Jewish

beliefs regarding certification of death, **V** 123, 349f.

beliefs regarding the Fatherhood of God, **VII** 70

beliefs regarding reincarnation, **III** 139; **IX** 173

concept of future life, **V** 280

covenant relationship with God, **VII** 16, 36, 37, 38, 41, 46, 47, 50, 60, 63

expectations of the Messiah, **VII** 35

genealogies destroyed in 70 A.D., **VII** 259

legal requirements for adoption, **II** 289, 329; **III** 231

methods of reckoning time, **V** 354f.

traditions regarding original immortality, **V** 179f.

traditions regarding the creation of man, **V** 179f.

Job's "hedge," **III** 197; **IX** 152

"Jod" as a wrench, **I** 271

Johannes bread tree, **V** 98

John the Baptist, as Messiah's forerunner, **VII** 36

John the Evangelist, **III** 178

Joking relationship in primitive society, **II** 302f., 327

Joktan, sons of, **I** 117f.

Jordan River held back, **III** 223f.; **VII** 192

Joseph, genealogy of, in Matthew, **VII** 262

Joseph (Jacob's son)

in Egypt, **VII** 177

runner before his chariot, **VII** 180

Josephus

chronology of, **V** 33f.

on Genesis 1:2, **VI** 88

writes in Greek and Aramaic, **VII** 74

Joshua's long day, **VII** 75

Jot (Jod, Yod), **III** 284; **VII** 71

Judeo-Christian value system, **III** 41f.

Judgment, **III** 256

basis of, **III** 91, 175f., 192f., 260, 293

day of, **III** 240, 246, 256, 278

Hebrew words relating to, **VII** 288f.

of Israel, **VII** 47

recall on the Day of, **III** 240

self-judgment, **III** 243, 278

sudden, in O.T., **VII** 49

sudden, of believers, **VI** 67f.; **VII** 49f., 54ff.

time discounted during periods of, **VI** 46

time kaleidoscoped on Day of, **III** 245f.

unfair if delayed, according to primitive people, **VI** 21
when suspended, **VII** 15

Jupiter, **IV** 27; **VII** 199
eclipse of, **VI** 14
Justification, **III** 281; **VI** 168ff.

K

Kaikari, **II** 297
Kalahari Desert, sudden revival of, **IX** 121
Kallikak family, history of, **III** 146
Kalmuks, **II** 297
Kamtchadales, **II** 296
Kanjera Man, **I** 127
Kant, on man as a mathematician, **III** 106
Kantian argument, **VIII** 209
Karaikees, **II** 296
Keel, **II** 184f.; **IV** 163 (fig. 7), 165 (fig. 9), 164. *See also under* Sagittal crest.
Keeper-of-Names among Iroquois, **IX** 179
Kelts. *See under* Celtic.
Kenya finds, **II** 42
Kepler, his method of calculation, **VIII** 201
Kidney
cells, and reorganization, **III** 333; **VIII** 76
stones, treatment of, by native doctors, **I** 329
Kinds of Genesis, **III** 110, 113; **VII** 302f.; **VIII** 225
Kingdom of God, **III** 51-97
in animal life vs. human life, **III** 60
broader definition of, **III** 52ff.
children as part of, **III** 97
encompasses the universe, **III** 54f.
man and, **III** 87-97

nature as part of, **III** 52-72
Kingdom of Satan, **III** 55
King James Version, advantages of, **VII** 273ff.
King lists, **V** 51f.; **VII** 203f.
Kings
chronological contradictions of, in O.T., **VII** 70f., 181
of England, average lengths of reign, **V** 56
the four whom Abraham fought, **VII** 161ff.
Kites, **III** 201
in China, for measuring distances, **I** 211
in China, for military signaling, **I** 211
man-flying, **I** 211
use of, in fishing, **I** 169
Kittens "counted" by mother, **IV** 318
Knossos, tradition regarding, confirmed, **V** 48
Knowing
God, **III** 91; **VIII** 198
God, by non-Christians, **VIII** 198f.
and willing, **VIII** 184
Knowledge. *See also under* Fragmentation, integration.
Christian faith as an integrator of, **VIII** 196
Christian faith as a source of, **VIII** 212

Christian faith as key to new, **VIII** 199

increase of, becoming unmanageable, **VIII** 172

vs. intelligence, vs. wisdom, **II** 148, 154; **III** 82f.

revelation, essential to complete k., **IV** 14, 20, 63, 210

vs. science, **I** 290

scientific k. always fragmentary, **VIII** 172

three avenues of, **VIII** 173

two kinds: reason and experiment or revelation, **VIII** 172

vs. understanding, **III** 62

Koala, **IV** 201

Koreans
builders of first metal-clad battleship, **I** 203

inventors of moveable type, **I** 317, 325

Krapina Man, **I** 127

Krakatoa, blowing up of, **VII** 173

L

Labor. *See also under* Idleness.
absence of, and boredom, **IX** 131

dehumanization of, **VIII** 174

factors which dignify it, **VIII** 173f.

freedom from, not ideal, **IX** 131

spiritual quality of, **VIII** 114

value of, **IX** 116

Laboratory experiments not always valid, **VIII** 244

Labyrinthodonts, **IV** 43

LaChapelle Skull, **I** 127, 136; **II** 53; **III** 48; **V** 24

Logoa Santa, **I** 127

Lamarckianism, **VIII** 220f. *See also under* Acquired characters, Dauermodifications.

Lamb of God, **V** 315ff., 328f., 359, 380; **VII** 37, 44. *See also* Passover Lamb.

Lamb raised in artificial womb, **VIII** 81

"Lamb" vs. "Messiah," **VII** 37

Lamech, vengeance of, **VII** 199

Lamprey, **IV** 42

Land, Hebrew word for, **IX** 14

Landscaping and "back to nature" movement, **IV** 315f.

Lango, **II** 288, 290; **III** 138

Language, **II** 249-271; **IV** 266-277; **VI** 175-218

African, **VI** 185

animal cries and the l. of emotion, **IV** 269, 272

among animals, **II** 252f.; **IV** 269ff., 276

animals have no conversation, **II** 257 (fn. 19)

Aramaic in the Gospels, **VII** 73

Aryan linked to Semitic, **VI** 180f., 186

barrier to race mixture, **I** 274, 317f.

benefits from the confusion of, **VI** 217f.

biological foundation of, **II** 251

Broca center and, **IV** 267

Chinese, **VI** 184

Chinese vs. Indo-European, **I** 288

vs. communication, **II** 253

conceptual, **IV** 278

confusion of, **VI** 175-218
"confusion" caused by technical jargons, **VI** 216f.
and culture, **I** 254, 269f.; **IV** 266
culture, effect of l. on, **II** 137
Dante on, **II** 137, **VI** 216f.
determines "reality," **I** 266f., 270f., 274, 288
determines the ability to classify or specify, **I** 272f., 275; **II** 258
emotional, **II** 257; **IV** 272
erect posture and, **IV** 243f., 277, 287
and ethnic values, **VI** 214
Etruscan, origins of, **I** 109f.
evolution of, from complex to simple, **VI** 188 (and fn. 28)
faculty of, universal, **I** 254
feral children without, **II** 252, 261, 270
in Fossil Man? **IV** 267f.
grammar and logic of, **I** 288
grammar vs. vocabulary, **I** 274; **IV** 274
Greek l. and theology, **I** 265, 289; **III** 286; **VII** 23
of Hamites, highly specific, **I** 272; **II** 259; **VI** 215, 218
Hamitic, proliferation of, **I** 273f.; **IV** 267 (fn. 130); **VI** 208ff.
of heaven, **II** 268; **VI** 203ff.
Hebrew, for revelation, **I** 266, 276; **III** 286
Hindustani, appropriate for philosophy, **I** 280
human association, essential to, **II** 253ff.
Indo-European, **VI** 188f.
influence on thought, **I** 266ff.
Lapp, **VI** 215
and logic, **I** 269f., 288
major families of, relative confusion of, **VI** 188
man the speechmaker, **IV** 266ff.
national and racial character and, **I** 254f., 271f.

none are simple, **VI** 213
no primitives without, **II** 251, 260f., 270
onomatopoeic words and, **VI** 191
original, **VI** 192-207
original unity of, **II** 137; **VI** 178-191
origin of, **II** 75, 129, 249ff.; **III** 116; **VIII** 136
origin of, by mutation? **II** 129 (fn. 171), 253, 268
origin of, by "revelation," **II** 270
pathology of, **II** 257f.
personality development and, **II** 266
predetermines thought, **I** 266ff.
of primitives, complex, **II** 251, 259; **IV** 296; **VI** 213
proliferation of Hamitic, **I** 273f.; **IV** 267 (fn. 130); **VI** 208ff.
propositional, **II** 257
restraints resulting from confusion of, **VII** 196; **IX** 154f.
root vocabulary of all? **VI** 191
scientific concepts determined by, **I** 280f., 286
and self-consciousness, **II** 254
signifies a new "day in creation," **IV** 320
sign language, **II** 253; **IV** 272ff., 274
specificity of, among primitives, **I** 272f., **II** 259f.; **VI** 214ff.
specificity of, for O.T. and N.T., **I** 265f.
and stages of learning in man, **IV** 273f.
Sumerian, nonphilosophical, **I** 290
technical jargon as, **VI** 217
and theology, **III** 286
and thought, **I** 255, 266ff., 270, 288
time as expressed in verb tenses, **VI** 22f.
treasured by society, **VI** 214

and truth, **I** 290

uniquely a human capacity, **II** 261

World View and, **I** 255f., 267f., 288

Language, confusion of, **VI** 175-218

benefits arising from, **VI** 217f.

a safety device used by God, **IX** 154

traditions of, **IX** 29

a universal l., not desirable, **IX** 154, 156f.

Lapps, multiplicity of terms for reindeer, **VI** 215

LaQuina Woman, **I** 136; **II** 52

Last Adam, summation of man in, **III** 185f.; **VII** 316. *See also under* Adam, First and Last.

Last Supper, the; scenes in different cultures, **IX** 240

Lathes, **I** 202, 335

Latitude, influence of; on marine life, **IV** 159

Laughter, **II** 255

muscles involved in, **IV** 245

uniquely human, **IV** 283

vs. weeping, **IV** 245f.

Law

civil, as restraint of evil (i.e., negative), **III** 35

moral, and the problem of forgiveness, **III** 281

natural, and divine intervention, **VIII** 58

natural, three reversals of, fundamental for life, **I** 349; **III** 75f.

reign of, in nature, **III** 54

Lawlessness, **III** 270

Law of prudence, **III** 68

Lazarus

raising of, **IV** 108; **V** 123, 351f.; **VII** 43; **VIII** 87

re-creation of his body, **III** 144 (fn. 12); **VI** 34

Laziness in the scholarly life, **III** 205

Leaders

among men, **IV** 297ff.

among minnows! **IV** 301

herd l. among animals, **III** 336; **IV** 298, 301

League of Nations

failure of, **IX** 145

original ideals of, **III** 41

Learning

animal vs. human, **IV** 263, 283, 284f., 292f.

bacteria capable of? **VIII** 234

without a brain, **III** 257 (fn. 41)

brain size, and ability to l., **IV** 224, 228

culture as learned behavior, **IV** 263, 292

in paramecia, **III** 331

in relation to culture, **IV** 281ff.

transfer of, within the cortex, **III** 252; **IV** 226

Leaven, as a principle of evil, **V** 109

Lebzelter principle, **I** 126, 128; **II** 43, 175, 222; **IV** 67; **VI** 230

Leeward Islands Flood tradition, **IX** 69f.

Legs, first appearance of, **IV** 43

Leisure. *See also under* Holidays, Vacations.

as a "curse," **IX** 136

"l. class," need of a, **II** 152

sometimes a burden, **VIII** 176 (fn. 164)

Lemurs, **IV** 44, 236

Leopards, **II** 260

Leucocytes

consciousness in, **III** 257, 328

movements of, **III** 328

Leviathan

body of Adam as, **III** 184f., 341

human society as, **V** 388

Levirate marriage, **II** 302, 314ff., 325f.; **VIII** 155f., 241, 266

Liberal arts, importance of, **I** 221f.

Liberalism, **III** 9, 36

Libraries, common in Greco-Roman world, **VII** 28

Library at Alexandria, **VII** 28

Lichens, **IV** 40

Life

bacteria essential to, **IX** 161

basic principle of, everywhere the same, **IV** 222; **VIII** 49

and carbon chains, **I** 349; **IV** 28

complexity of elemental forms of, **III** 261 (fn. 50)

conscious, three orders of, **I** 226

creation of, **I** 359, 367. *See also below:* origin of.

death as an advantage to? **V** 17, 128

death not a necessary concomitant of, **V** 141

definition of, **VIII** 64, 139

earth uniquely fitted for, **VIII** 35f.

elsewhere in the universe? **IV** 31f.

"ghost" in the machinery of, **VIII** 59

and global temperatures, **I** 349

goal-seeking of, mechanistic, **VIII** 65

indistinguishable from nonliving? **III** 258, 325; **VIII** 85f., 142

man's early attempts at the creation of, **VIII** 73

may arise automatically? **VIII** 79

mechanical in function, **VIII** 59, 65, 73

more than the sum of its components, **VIII** 83

nature of, **III** 262f.; **VIII** 59, 92

and nonlife, link between? **IV** 51

not an epiphenomenon of cell substance, **VIII** 74

not just chemistry and physics, **III** 262f.; **IV** 35; **VIII** 83, 84

not physcochemically inevitable, **III** 324; **VIII** 91f.

originated only once, **IV** 222

origin of, **III** 324f.; **IV** 30, 34, 51f., 222; **VIII** 73

powers of, defined, **IV** 51

powers of reorganization of, **VIII** 74, 77

preparation of the earth for, **IV** 39; **VIII** 35f., 38

as pure mechanism, **VIII** 59

resistance of, to extreme cold, **VIII** 74

reversal of three natural laws essential to, **III** 75f.

as "the secret of DNA," **VIII** 59

self-regulating organization of, **VIII** 65

successive introduction of higher forms of, **I** 357; **IV** 87ff.

survival power of, extraordinary, **VIII** 74

unpredictability of, **VIII** 139

in utero, vegatative only? **V** 195, 212ff.

viruses, and origin of, **IV** 51

what is alive? **VIII** 59

Life sciences, extreme dogmatism in, **VIII** 166

Life span. *See also under* Aging, Longevity, Old age.

effect of the Fall on, **VIII** 50

factors influencing, **V** 23

of fish, **V** 133

and fossil man, effect on form, **II** 49

and inbreeding, **VI** 233f.; **VII** 235

limitations placed upon, **VII** 238

maximum of 120 years, **V** 29

in modern vs. ancient times, **III** 47

and population growth, **V** 166

post-Flood decline in, **V** 29ff.; **VI** 233f.; **VII** 235

time of maturity and, **V** 34f., 41f.

Life Story of an Irish Saint (Ann Preston), **IX** 261

Lift locks, a Chinese development, **I** 326

Light
basic "substance" of the universe, **VIII** 22
as clothing for the body, **V** 103
contradictory definitions of, **VII** 95
curved path of, **VIII** 32
and darkness alternating, **I** 349; **IV** 28
matter as "bottled l.," **III** 321; **VIII** 22
nature of, **VIII** 31f.
spectrographic analysis of, **VIII** 17
speed of, **VI** 14f.
as "unbottled" waves, **III** 321; **VIII** 22

Light years, distances measured in, **VIII** 18, 32

Likeness, **III** 100-133
as character, **III** 128ff.
vs. image, **III** 100ff.
possible meaning of, in Genesis, **VII** 312

Limb/spinal column proportions, **IV** 217

"Limbo," place of unbaptized children, **V** 279; **IX** 173

Linear progress, concept of, **III** 15f., 36; **VIII** 132

Linen vs. woolen clothing, and sweating, **IX** 213ff.

Links, missing. *See under* Gaps, Missing links.

Lion, **III** 64, 97, 214
area of territory, **IV** 251

Lioness
gentle in captivity, **IX** 123
raising sheep dog, **III** 66
refuses meat diet, **IX** 123
rescues gazelle, **III** 73

Lips, structure of; in man and ape, **IV** 269

Literalism, value and dangers of, **V** 76

Literary arts, loss of, **II** 124

Literature
"Animal Tales," from Africa, **I** 199
cartoons, **I** 201
libraries, **I** 189, 194; **VII** 28
Maya, **I** 183
moving pictures, **I** 201
schools, **I** 189, 194
Sumerian, **I** 194

"Little Tyke," story of a lioness, **IX** 123f.

Liturgy
place of, in worship, **IX** 245
pro and con, **IX** 223

Living vs. nonliving. Distinction between blurred, **V** 123f.

Lobolo, **II** 279, 293; **VII** 245. *See also under* Bride price.

Lobotomy, prefrontal, **III** 165

Logarithms, Sumerian use of, **I** 190, 327

Logic
Chinese vs. Aristotelian, **I** 289
going wrong with confidence, **IV** 203
and grammar, **I** 288
Greek development of use of, **VII** 23
Greek language vehicle for, **VII** 23
and language, **I** 269f., 288f.
limitations of, for understanding, **VIII** 88
powerless to convince, **VIII** 21
relationship of, to Christian faith, **V** 174; **VIII** 201
strict need for, in theology, **VIII** 202

Logical fallacy, how to discover a, **III** 11, 161

Logical implications, as critical test of any system of thought, **V** 78f.

Logos, meaning of the term, **IX** 182

Longaroni Dam (Italy) disaster, **IX** 72

Longevity, **V** 12-74. *See also under* Age, Life span.
and acceleration of cultural growth, **II** 136; **V** 68
in antiquity, **V** 33-60
archaeological evidence of, **V** 61-70
biological view of, **V** 15-32
causes of decline in, **V** 142; **VIII** 235
consequences of, for the future, **V** 69
curve of decline in, **VII** 237f.
decline in, after the Flood, **II** 39; **VI** 234
of early man, **II** 135
effect of, on cranial form, **II** 18, 39
effect of, in pre-Flood times, **IX** 16
examples of, in historical times, **V** 20f.
of fossil man, **III** 48; **V** 56f.
ill-health as the secret to, **III** 209
in Genesis, **II** 18
in modern times, **III** 47f.
and population growth rate, **V** 167
and potential for human development, **V** 168
pre-Flood, **VII** 234f.
a purpose for the record of l. in Genesis, **VII** 237f.
recipe for (Tennyson), **III** 209
suddenness of reduction in, **VII** 234
traditions in antiquity of, **V** 50
of trees, **V** 15, 178

Long jump, Greek method of, **III** 201

Long life. *See under* Longevity.

Long term memory vs. short term, **III** 254

Looms, African, **I** 195

Lord, as a title of the Godhead, **V** 223ff.

LORD God vs. Lord GOD, **V** 240ff.

Lord's Prayer, the, **III** 125, 131

Lot
rescue of, **VII** 162ff.
wife of, turned to salt, **VII** 175

Love. *See also under* Mother love, Romantic love.
apparent and real, **III** 28f.
as chemical neutralizer of hate, **III** 309
effect of perfect, on fear, **IX** 209
of God, abuse of the concept, **IV** 134
of God, demonstrated in the Plan of Redemption, **I** 218, 229f., 230; **V** 400
of God, not self-evident, **I** 231, 234
of God, to be witnessed to all nations, **I** 366
human vs. animal, **IV** 308
Ruskin's definition of, **VIII** 189

Lowell Observatory, **VIII** 18

Luke, Gospel of
Gentile emphasis in, **VII** 102
for whom written, **VII** 97, 99, 102
medical language of, **III** 231

Luke as Paul's personal physician, **III** 225, 228ff.

Luminous organs, convergence and, **IV** 156

Lunacy, demon possession and, **III** 166f.

Lung fishes (Dipnoi), **IV** 42

Luxury, definition of, **II** 149

Lying
essential to abstract thinking, **I** 272f.
unique to man, **IV** 278

M

Macadamized roads, **II** 177

Machine(s)
efficiency of, **IV** 311f.
the "ghost" in the, **III** 269; **VIII** 59, 72
man as a ? **III** 11, 268f.; **IV** 321; **VIII** 82ff., 140, 181
to save labor, a mixed blessing, **IX** 130
universe as only a, **VIII** 205

Madagascar, **IV** 129f.

Magi, **I** 18ff.

Magic, **III** 79ff.
black and white, **II** 172
as a "me-thou" philosophy, **VIII** 106
nature of, **III** 80f.
vs. religion and science, **VIII** 106
vs. science, **III** 80

Magnification, not an "open sesame" to all understanding, **VIII** 169

Magog, **I** 89ff.

Majesty, plural of, **VII** 312

Majority rule, dangers inherent in, **III** 42

Make
distinct in Hebrew from *create*, **VII** 283f., 297, 313
meaning of Hebrew word for, **VI** 115ff.

Making alive vs. resurrection, **III** 304

Making vs. creating, **III** 104f.; **VI** 115f.

Malaria, Paul's thorn? **III** 227

Malchus's ear **IV** 33, 108; **VI** 32

Male
and female, in one person? **V** 393

in procreation, various views of, **II** 281, 290f., 292; **III** 138
raising young, **IV** 290f.
role of, in a family, **IV** 220, 291f.
role of, in animal society, **IV** 290
"socially indigestible," **IV** 291f.

Malthusian doctrine, **III** 58, 71

Mammals, egg-laying, **IV** 44

Mammoths, **IV** 97

Man. *See also under* Human nature, Humanness, Manhood, Natural man.
abolition of (Lewis), **IX** 187f.
an accident? **I** 223, 355; **III** 268
in Adam and in Christ, Vol. **III**
in Adam's image, not God's? **III** 109
age of accountability in, **III** 55, 97, 295, 297f.
aggression of, vs. animal aggression, **I** 243; **II** 155; **III** 14f., 16, 23, 25, 27f., 342; **IV** 322
aging, effect of on appearance of, **II** 18
alien in nature, **III** 14, 17, 55, 84, 103; **IV** 323, 327; **VIII** 95, 96, 144, 181
anatomical uniqueness of, **IV** 215ff., 217
vs. angels and animals, **I** 226ff., 230, 240f., 264; **IV** 212
an animal? **IV** 208-309
an animal plus, **IV** 208; **VIII** 72
vs. animals, **I** 242f.
annihilated as such, **III** 54, 85; **VIII** 179; **IX** 188
an anomaly in nature, **IV** 319
antiquity of, current vs. biblical view of, **IX** 44ff.

as the archdestroyer of nature, **III** 55, 115; **IV** 211

attitude toward nature, **III** 78

basis for his survival, **IV** 249f.

behavior of, its basis, **III** 158f.; **IV** 263, 281f.; **VIII** 68, 137

biblical definition of true, **III** 113

biblical vs. evolutionary view of, **III** 10

biologically considered, **III** 122

body, importance of to, **V** 161. *See also under* Body.

body of fallen m., still not "animal," **IV** 327

body of unfallen m., **V** 162f.

as body/spirit entity, **III** 303; **V** 267; **VIII** 81

body structured to permit worship, **IV** 245f.

brain of, unique, **I** 344; **IV** 221-230

brain size, **IV** 223f.

a by-product of evolution merely? **VIII** 125, 145, 146

capacity for good and evil, **I** 261f.

capacity for moral judgment, **III** 107f., 268f.

as the center of the universe, **IV** 27

chief end of, **VIII** 184-191

chin vs. simian shelf, **II** 207; **IV** 243f.

clothed with light originally? **V** 103

concept of m., Hebrew vs. Greek, **I** 266f.

conceptual thought unique to, **IV** 278; **VIII** 44

constitutionally diseased, **III** 287

constitution of, **VIII** 72, 80f.

convergence and its implications for m., **IV** 166

created for God's pleasure, **VIII** 199

creation of, displays God's love, **V** 78

creative abilities of, **III** 106f.; **VIII** 54f.

culturally considered, **III** 117, 122

culturally unique, **IV** 216

the culture-maker, **IV** 263-280, 283

dauermodifications in, **VIII** 238ff.

death, a process not an event, **V** 381

death as penalty; as blessing, **V** 18; **IX** 113, 114

death entered through m., not woman, **V** 190

death inevitable for? **V** 17, 134, 178. *See also under* Death, physical.

death of, "passive," **V** 315ff., 325, 378f.

defenseless by nature, **IV** 247ff.

definition of, **II** 192

definition of *man*, by primitive people, **I** 63; **VII** 201 (fn. 80)

dehumanization of, **VIII** 94f., 125f.; **IX** 187

dependency of childhood, long, **IV** 288

dependent on others in sickness, **IV** 314

depersonalization of, **III** 84

depravity of, total, **III** 20, 32, 37, 158, 185, 341f.

designed specifically for the Incarnation, **IV** 20f., 212, 323ff., 328

determines the size of the universe, **VIII** 43f.

dichotomy or trichotomy, **III** 303f.; **V** 265ff.; **VIII** 81

diet of, originally herbivorous? **VII** 314; **IX** 124, 206

disease in early, **V** 24

diseases of, **IV** 239f.

divine nature in, **III** 186

earth uniquely fitted for m., **VIII** 35ff.

emotion of, vs. animal e., **II** 255

erectness of, **IV** 231-246. *See also under* Erectness, Posture.

erect posture of, its cost, **IV** 240f.

evolution of, "undoubted," **VIII** 161f.

facial expression of, **IV** 170f., 180, 271 (fn. 147)

as a fallen creature, **I** 244f., 261

fallen m., a different species, **III** 338, 346; **IV** 210f.

fallen m., and his relationship to God, **III** 87-97

fallen nature of, variously diagnosed, **III** 11, 18ff., 162, 273; **IV** 321; **VII** 24

fallenness of, **IV** 177

fallen to sub-animal status, **IV** 327

Fall of, and its consequences, **III** 45f., 124, 186; **IX** 113f., 129. *See also under* Fall of Man.

family life of, unique, **IV** 288f.

fertility in, **IV** 290

fire, use of by, **IV** 265

is foolish, incurably, **III** 19

forgetting, divine vs. human, **III** 277

and forgiveness, **III** 240f., 269f., 277, 280f.

fossil, ancestor or "herald" of, **IV** 64

and genealogical trees, fallacies of, **II** 16, 236, 243f., 246; **IV** 59, 146; **VIII** 49

goodness of, fortuitous, **III** 31

"the great disturber," **IV** 185

growth rates of, vs. animal's, **IV** 285ff.

hair, his original "clothing," **V** 103

hairiness, comparative lack of, **II** 18, 19

hearth and home unique to m., **IV** 284ff.

height of, **IV** 241; **VIII** 40f.

as a "house" for God, **IV** 323ff.

his clothing, unique, **IV** 219, 296

his dominion over the earth, nature of, **VIII** 62f.; **IX** 115

his humanness, expression of, **IV** 181-319

his "inhumanity" to man, **IX** 143

his relation to the animal world, **IV** 213

and immortality, **V** 119-140. *See also under* Immortality.

immortal originally? **I** 234; **V** 116ff., 178; **VIII** 50

and instincts, **III** 116, 143; **VIII** 69. *See also under* Instincts.

irrationality of, **III** 17

key to the universe, **I** 225-239

and language, a unique capacity for, **II** 261

and law "written within," **III** 89

limited variability of, **IV** 253

lives in three dimensions, **I** 44-49, 240-247, 248ff., 264

longevity of, before the Flood, **II** 18; **VIII** 234f. *See also under* Longevity.

as a machine, implications of, **III** 11, 268f.; **IV** 321; **VIII** 82ff., 140f., 181, 207

a "made-over ape"? **IV** 214

maturing processes, advantages of its slowness, **II** 128; **IV** 219, 284f.

meaning in life, a basic need, **I** 228; **VIII** 8f., 97, 98

the "measure of all things"? **I** 221; **VIII** 193

is the measure of animal worth, **I** 221 (fn. 5)

as a mechanism, **III** 11, 268f., 271, 279, 319; **VIII** 82f.

and memory, **III** 259f.

mind of, unique, **IV** 229f.

mind of, vs. animal's, **IV** 229f., 271, 273, 275

moral accountability of, **I** 227; **III** 268

moral responsibility, **IV** 276, 288; **IX** 16

more than an animal (Dobzhansky), **IV** 208f.; **VIII** 72

mortality, an acquired inherited character, **III** 289f.; **IV** 327; **V** 87, 151f., 189

nature, and destiny of, **VII** 24

nature of his "superiority," **II** 128

neck, vs. animal's, **IV** 219, 236, 287

needles, use of by m. vs. animals, **IV** 314

needs of, are basically three, **I** 44-49, 240-247

neoteny in, **II** 18, 19

the "new man," how initiated, **V** 206

a new species of, sinned into being, **III** 338, 346; **IV** 210f.

noetic effects of sin, **III** 13, 39, 162, 272, 285, 313; **IV** 210; **VIII** 196

omnivorous, **IV** 256f.

one species, **IV** 254; **V** 201

the organizer of time, space, things, **IV** 315f.; **VIII** 113

origin and destiny related, **IV** 211, 329; **VIII** 14f., 81, 188f.

origin of, **I** 133f.; **II** 12, 64; **IV** 140-170

origin of, some acute observations regarding, **IV** 320ff.

overcomplex for survival, **IV** 176

paedomorphism in, **II** 18, 19; **IV** 287

and pain, **III** 67; **IX** 111f., 128f., 138, 210

perfectability of? **III** 16

perfectability of, assured! **IV** 178

a philosophy of life, necessary, **I** 228, 248f.

phylogenetic trees, inadequacies of, **II** 242

phylogeny of, based on morphology, **II** 16, 236, 243f., 246; **IV** 59, 149; **VIII** 49

physiologically unique, **III** 119f.

place in nature, Babylonian view, **III** 79; Greek view, **III** 80; Hebrew view, **III** 85; Medieval view, **III** 81f.; the modern view, **III** 82f.

a poor animal, **II** 126f., 177; **III** 116

poorly equipped by nature, **III** 88

potential of, fragmented, **I** 44-49, 242-262; 264

psychologically considered, **III** 123

purpose of his creation, **III** 274; **IV** 20, 322ff.

qualitatively or quantitatively unique? **IV** 208ff., 221

a rational animal, **IV** 211f., 322, 327

rationality of, **III** 106, 117; **IV** 315

recollection and reflection, implications of, **III** 260

redeemableness of, **I** 231; **II** 191; **III** 124, 338; **IV** 20f., 209

relation to nature, **I** 28; **III** 78-86

resemblances vs. relationships, **II** 12ff.

reproduction of, vs. animal, **IV** 303ff.

and self-consciousness, **III** 260; **VIII** 42, 87

sex life of, **IV** 303ff., 308

his significance within the universe, **VIII** 33f.

sinfulness of his will, **III** 34, 36f., 270

size of, **IV** 241; **VIII** 39ff. *See also under* Size.

skin and its significance, **I** 342; **III** 120; **IV** 312ff.; **VIII** 148 (fn. 94)

social life of. *See under* Social life.

a solecism in nature, **II** 131

the speechmaker, **IV** 266ff.

speech of, related to posture, **IV** 243f., 277, 287. *See also under* Speech.

spirit, when given, **V** 194, 277

spirit of m., what is revealed regarding, **III** 303; **V** 266

"spirit" of m. vs. "spirit" of animals, **VIII** 80f.

spiritual, intellectual and physical life of, **I** 44ff., 240f., 246, 248ff.

suffering, benefit of, **IX** 111f.

suicidal nature of, **III** 163, 196; **IV** 321

supreme as a homeotherm, **III** 120; **IV** 257

temperature regulation in, **I** 342; **III** 119f.; **IV** 257f.; **VIII** 40, 238ff.; **IX** 197f.

temptation of, **III** 301f., 308

and time sense. *See under* Time.

the toolmaker, **IV** 263f.

trilogy of capacities in, **I** 248f.; **II** 138f.

true nature of, seen in Jesus Christ, **IV** 320-329

two distinct species of, **III** 315-350 (esp. 343f.) **IV** 210f.

ubiquity of, **I** 341f.; **III** 120; **IV** 219, 247-262

unfallen, and his relationship to nature in a perfect world, **VIII** 62

unfallen, how maturity to be achieved in, **V** 165

unfallen, in Jesus Christ, **V** 159ff.

unfit to survive, **IV** 176f.; **VIII** 237

unique, in relation to God, **III** 123f.

uniqueness of, **I** 340f.; **IV** 213-220

universe designed for m.? **VIII** 11-45

value of, to God (Mascall), **V** 399f.

"wasp waist" of, **IV** 219

what is he for? **IV** 322f.

what is wrong with m., **III** 14-29

why the last to be created? **IV** 65

will of, how free? **III** 34, 36f., 37, 92

world created for m., **I** 343f.; **IV** 23f.; **V** 127f., 162; **VIII** 35ff.

Man distinct from animals by,

absence of instincts, **III** 116

possession of language, **III** 116

possession of rationality, **III** 117

power of reflection, **III** 117

skin structure, **III** 120

social behavior inimical to his welfare, **III** 117f.

thermoregulation, **I** 342; **III** 119f.; **IV** 259, 260; **IX** 196f., 201

unlikelihood of improvement by breeding, **III** 121

Mandu, identity of, **VII** 165 (fn. 28), 167

Manhattan Island, **VII** 132

Manhood. *See also under* Humanness.

biblical definition of true, **III** 89, 113, 114; **IV** 209ff.; **V** 154, 369, 383, 390

concept of, among primitives, **I** 63; **VII** 201 (fn. 80)

realized in Jesus Christ, **V** 153ff.

recovery of true, **III** 344; **V** 390

lost in the Fall, **III** 124, 186, 338; **IV** 236f.

true nature of, **IV** 320-329

"Manifesto" of Helmholtz et al., **I** 353 (fn. 273); **III** 272

Manioc, extraction of poison from, **I** 172

Mankind
as "Adam," **III** 341; **V** 387
as the "Body of Sin," **V** 389
of one blood, **IV** 254; **V** 201
as a single organism, **III** 183; **V** 389

Maori chief's genealogy, **VII** 219

Marah, bitter waters of; made sweet, **VII** 213

Marduk, **IV** 116

Marginal zones, concept of, **II** 46

Margin of survival, **I** 329
effect of a small m., **II** 167f.
effect on attitude toward nature, **II** 168f.

Marmosets, **II** 182

Marriage
basis of, **II** 304
brother-sister, **VI** 222-237; **VII** 239f.
in Cana, **VII** 38f.
and child legitimacy, **II** 278
of close blood relatives, **VI** 222f., 231f.
complex laws of, among aborigines, **III** 118
as a contract, **II** 283, 302, 318ff.
as a contract for the bearing of children, **II** 283, 304
of cousins, **II** 301; **VII** 155, 241
customs, early, **VII** 154ff.
and domicile, of husband or wife? **II** 277f., 287f.
economic basis of, **II** 280
ideal partner relationships in, **II** 281, 301
levirate and, **II** 302, 314ff.
not for provision of sex, **II** 290
in other cultures, **IV** 305
and polygyny, **II** 279, 282f., 303, and provision of substitute wife, **II** 295, 318ff.
purposes of, **II** 280

relationships within a family (brother-sister), **II** 281, 292f.
romantic love as basis of, **II** 280, 299
status as a "man," achieved by m., **II** 280
strict requirements for, among primitives, **II** 294ff.

Marsupials, **II** 213; **IV** 44, 79, 156

Martyrdom vs. death from disease, **III** 230

Marxism, **III** 9

Mary
genealogy of, in Luke, **VII** 262, 265
tradition regarding her parents, **VII** 262

Masochism, **III** 239

Mass production, penalty of, **VIII** 174

Materialism
its effect upon personal worth, **VIII** 33
tendency towards, in Chinese religion, **IV** 121
and time sense, **VI** 26

Materialists, prejudices of, **IV** 38f.

Materials, structural; and others, list of, **I** 38f.

Maternal
instinct, not universal, **II** 305; **III** 148, 157; **IV** 294; **IX** 172
instinct, unusual expressions of, **III** 66
"m. uncle," role of, **II** 279, 281, 292; **VII** 245f.

Mathematical ability, earliest known evidence of, **II** 251

Mathematician, God as the Great, **III** 54, 106

Mathematics, **I** 41, 327
abacus, **I** 204
algebra, **I** 189f., 191, 327
of American Indians, **I** 183
of Arabs, **I** 307
and art, **III** 54

Babylonian, **I** 291; **V** 55
Chinese, **I** 327, 328
and communication, **IV** 316
concept of zero, **I** 328
and deaf-mutes, **II** 266
earliest known evidence of, **II** 251
Egyptian, **I** 189, 293
feats of mental calculation, **III** 246
geometry, **I** 189f., 191
Greek, **I** 35, 190f.
Hindu, **I** 34
Kepler's errors in, **VIII** 201 (fn. 196)
logarithms, early, **I** 190, 327
and music, **III** 54
place system, used by Central Americans, **I** 183, 327f.; used by Chinese, **I** 327, 238
as a pure, pure mental activity, **I** 297
as pure philosophy, **I** 34f., 297
Sumerian, **I** 189f., 308, 327
and time divisions, **I** 190
value of pi, **I** 189
zero, invention of, **I** 183, 328
Mating, barriers to
in animals and in man, **IV** 302
psychological, **IV** 253
Matrilinear descent, **II** 281, 327
significance of, for incest, **II** 300f.
Matrilocal residence
psychology of, **II** 288
reference to, in Genesis, **II** 276
significance of, **II** 277, 287, 308
Matronymy, **II** 297, 311ff.
Matter
annihilation of, **VI** 35
as "bottled" light, **III** 321; **VIII** 22
as "congealed" consciousness, **III** 317
as congealed energy, **VIII** 22, 53
has consciousness? **III** 258, 324
creation of (Eddington, Gamow), **VIII** 20f.

eternal? **VIII** 135
as mindedness, objectified, **III** 325
mind independent of, **III** 262, 264
and mind interaction, **III** 259, 261f., 318, 325
original form of, **VIII** 20
the origin of, **VIII** 135
in relation to spirit, **III** 256
spiritual nature of, **III** 261, 322f.; **VIII** 23
Matthew and his Gospel
in Aramaic or Greek? **VII** 74f., 100
authorship of, **VII** 99f.
circumstances preceding his call, **VII** 102 (fn. 20)
emphasizes fulfilled prophecy, **VII** 101
financial matters and, **VII** 101f.
for whom written, **VII** 75, 82, 97
Maturing rate, in animals and in man, **IV** 219, 284ff.
Mauer Jaw **I** 127, 137
Maypures, **II** 157
Meaning
vs. actual words used, **VII** 76f., 78, 83
a basic human need, **VIII** 8f., 97, 98
defined in terms of size and duration, **I** 220
of life, discovered in concentration camp, **III** 210ff.
loss of, **I** 219; **III** 271
vs. mere description, **VIII** 64
Nietzsche on the importance of, **VIII** 180
related to man's origin and destiny, **VIII** 14
search for, **III** 210f.; **VII** 18; **VIII** 14, 107f., 198
Meaninglessness, specialization results in, **VIII** 190f.

Means. *See also under* Ends.
  in adult education, **VIII** 190
  and the chief end of man, **VIII** 184-191
  and ends, **VIII** 94
  intelligence to be used in choice of, **VIII** 188, 191
  replacing ends, **VIII** 183, 184ff., 187, 190
Meat eating, **V** 24
Mechanical efficiency of machines, **IV** 311f.
Mechanical principles and engineering developed by Hamites, **I** 38
  ball-and-socket joint, **I** 335
  bellows, piston and others, **I** 201, 205
  bilge pump, **I** 186
  block and tackle, **I** 161
  breakwater designs for harbors, **I** 336f.
  building construction: vaulting, suspension, truss, etc., **I** 159, 185, 193, 194, 202, 323, 324; **II** 160
  canals and locks, **I** 326
  chain pumps, **I** 186
  cire perdu casting, **I** 214
  clockwork escapement, **I** 205, 213, 321 (fn. 196)
  crankshaft, **I** 206
  drilling rigs, **I** 212. *See also* Drilling.
  electricity, **I** 216
  explosives, **I** 205, 208, 209
  force pump, **I** 206
  gear trains, **I** 213, 321
  gimbal suspension, **I** 205
  harness, **I** 205
  looms, **I** 201, 205
  piping systems (bamboo and clay), **I** 201, 213, 333
  pot chain pump, **I** 206, 215, 305
  printing, **I** 209, 212, 325, 332
  repeating crossbow, **I** 205
  rotary fan and winnow, **I** 205
  rubber technology, **I** 178f., 214
  smelting furnaces, **I** 201
  suspension bridges, **I** 211
  traps of various kinds, **I** 169, 170, 336; **II** 161
  umbrellas (folding), **I** 201
  wheeled vehicles, **I** 205
Mechanics, temperament of, **III** 154f.
Mechanism(s). *See also under* Feedback systems, Servo-mechanisms.
  biology as, **VIII** 92
  brain as, **III** 24f.
  conception (fusion of sperm and ovum) as pure m., **VIII** 71, 80
  concept of, essential to scientific progress, **VIII** 72, 92
  vs. conscious activity, **VIII** 68
  determinism, an incomplete view of reality, **VIII** 214f.
  guaranteeing fitness, **VIII** 232
  God's use of, in creation, **I** 361
  life as, **VIII** 59, 65, 73
  man as, **III** 11, 268f., 271, 279, 319; **VIII** 82f.
  manufacture of protein as a, **VIII** 70
  meaning of, in nature, **VIII** 64
  and miracle, **VIII** 53, 79
  as natural law, **VIII** 58
  in nature "dirtied" by the Fall, **VIII** 57,60
  in nature, perfect apart from the Fall, **VIII** 48ff.
  in nature, widespread evidence of, **VIII** 47ff., 65-81
  in plant life, **VIII** 59, 69
  and purpose, opposed, **III** 271
  when perfect, needs no superintendent, **VIII** 55, 58
Medes, **I** 91
Medical language of Luke, **IX** 216

Medical treatments, **I** 41. *See also under* Drugs, Pharmacology, Surgery.
anemia, **I** 329
anxiety, **I** 174
boils, **I** 163
burns, **I** 163
catheterization, **I** 329
constipation, **I** 163
coughs, **I** 163
diagnostic techniques for hernia and intestinal T. B., **I** 329
diarrhea, **I** 329
enemas, **I** 176 (fig 9), 178, 199, 329
fevers, **I** 163
gangrene, **I** 331
headaches, **I** 163
internal bleeding, **I** 331
migraine, **I** 332
procedures used, **I** 163, 176, 178, 184, 199, 202, 204, 329
pulse reading, **I** 330
respiratory diseases, **I** 163
scurvy, **I** 331
snake bite, **I** 330
sore eyes, **I** 163
spectacles, **I** 204
stomach aches, **I** 163
toothaches, **I** 163
vaccines, **I** 202, 329f.
venereal disease, **I** 331
Medici Chapel, **VII** 95
Medici family, inbreeding within, **VI** 223
Medicine. *See also under* Surgery.
as a choice of evils, **IX** 146
developed by American Indians, **I** 166ff.
diseases diagnosed and treated, **I** 163, 174, 186, 329, 332
foundations of Indo-European, **I** 328
preventive, **I** 202, 329f.
primitive practitioners as M.D.s, **I** 173f.; **II** 154

psychosomatic, **I** 175; **II** 154
use of psychology, **I** 173f.
Medieval Synthesis, **VIII** 104-117
and modern fragmentation of thought, **VIII** 99-216
a reason why it failed, **VIII** 204
Medieval world
beauty of portraiture in, **VIII** 114f.
criteria for truth, **VIII** 112f.
drama of life in, **VIII** 146
educational objectives of, **VIII** 109
goal of life in, **VIII** 189f.
seamy side of life in, **VIII** 114
war in, vs. modern world, **VIII** 182
wealth linked to responsibility, **VIII** 115
Medieval World View, **III** 78ff.; **VIII** 109ff. *See also under* World View.
basic objective of, **VIII** 112
causes of the collapse of, **VIII** 118ff.
contrasted with modern World View, **VIII** 101f., 144, 146, 147, 152ff., 166f., 180, 181, 189f.
fatal weaknesses of, **VIII** 117
final fragmentation of, **VIII** 117
labor given a spiritual coloring, **VIII** 114
life seen as a pilgrimage, **VIII** 147
miracle accomodated easily, **VIII** 111
monumental unity of, **VIII** 113
nothing surprised anyone, **VIII** 173
philosophy of, **III** 81f.; **VIII** 110, 115f.
provided a "map" for "everyman," **VIII** 116
"purpose" seen everywhere, **VIII** 115

Saw things as a *Uni*verse, **VIII** 110

Megalithic structures, **I** 185; **II** 121

Meganthropus, **II** 20, 219

"Me-it" vs. "I-Thou" relationship to nature, **I** 28; **III** 80; **VIII** 106

Melanism in moths, **IV** 75

Memorization, native feats of, **V** 47; **VII** 258

Memory, **III** 238ff.
  animal experiments and, **III** 248f., 256
  of animals, contingent, **III** 259; **IV** 317
  "blotting out" by God, **III** 240f.
  blotting out of name (*Damnatio Memoriae*), **VII** 257
  without a brain, **III** 257 (and fn. 41)
  and brain surgery, **III** 244, 252, 256
  brain unnecessary for, **III** 250
  electro-chemical cost of, **III** 253
  erasure of, **III** 248-255
  faculty of, in man and animals, **III** 259f.
  fetal memories? **V** 198
  as a filing cabinet, **III** 242f., 277, 278
  and forgetting, **III** 238ff.
  indestructibility of, **III** 248, 253, 278
  "inheritance" of m., by cannibal paramecia and planaria, **III** 250f., 331
  long term and short term, **III** 254
  as mechanism, **III** 249
  permanence of, **III** 240f.
  persistence of, despite brain tissue removal, **III** 248
  persists through death, **III** 254
  power of, among primitives, **VII** 258
  "progression" and, **V** 198, 278
  "regression" and, **V** 198, 276, 278

resident in the brain? **III** 249
  and RNA, **III** 251
  the seat of, **III** 256f., 278
  surgical erasure of, **III** 248f.
  time required to fix, **III** 253
  too much memory, a pathological condition, **III** 245
  wanted and unwanted, **III** 278

Memra, meaning of the word, **V** 219; **IX** 182

Mental
  deterioration, **III** 47-50
  feats of m. calculation, **III** 246
  illness, and art therapy, **IX** 167
  illness, cause of, **VIII** 125 (fn. 38)
  mathematics as a pure, pure, m. activity, **I** 297
  vs. spiritual life, **I** 246
  sweating, **IX** 197
  sweating, loss of during unconsciousness, **IX** 200
  sweating, sites of, **IX** 198

Menu, Institutes of, **I** 35

Merchant princes, ancient and modern, **VII** 160f.

Mercury, **IV** 27

Merodach as Nimrod? **VII** 197

Messiah
  the "Coming Prince" of Daniel, **VII** 36
  the inspired provision of a continuous genealogy, **VII** 223
  Jewish expectations of, **VII** 35
  vs. Lamb of God, **VII** 37
  miracles as credentials of, **VII** 38f., 40f.
  widespread hope for, in Roman world, **VII** 30

Metabolic cost of thinking processes, **VIII** 143

Metabolism
  as the burning of food, **VIII** 73
  effect of erectness upon m. of the brain, **IV** 245
  and energy available to primitives, **II** 126f.

Metal(s)
  development of steel, **I** 214, 321
  vs. flint, for razors, **II** 150
  loss of use of **II** 37
  precious, **II** 98f.
  at Sialk, an early settlement, **I** 193
  working of, in antiquity, **II** 99
Metallurgy, **VII** 197, 226
  alloys, **I** 189
  early appearance of, **I** 193, 197
  beading, **I** 196
  Bessemer process, **I** 214
  bronze, **I** 189, 214, 322
  case-hardening technique, **I** 214
  cast iron, **I** 205, 210, 214
  chain making, **I** 186, 211
  copper beads, **II** 92
  copper smithing, **II** 98f.
  electroplating, **I** 196
  flint vs. steel, **II** 150
  filigree, **I** 196
  gilding, **I** 196
  gold smithing, **II** 93
  hammered metal, **I** 201
  hollow casting, **I** 196
  inlaying, **I** 196
  intaglio, **I** 196
  iron and steel, **I** 214, 321f.
  repoussé, **I** 196
  sheeting, **I** 196
  smelting furnaces, **I** 201
  soldering, **I** 322
  welding, **I** 196
Metaphysical reality, **III** 53
Miao (China) Flood tradition, **IX** 106
Mice, **II** 216; **III** 66
  experiments with (Sumner), **VII** 226; (Weismann), **VII** 222
Michelson-Morley experiment, **VI** 16f.
Middle Ages, spirit of, **III** 82. *See also under* Medieval.
Middle Class, rise of, **VIII** 121

Middle East, Cradle of Civilization, **II** 95, 102; **V** 61
Midrash, **VI** 107
Migraine therapy in Sumeria, **I** 332
Migration(s)
  alternative to ark building, **IX** 26f., 33ff.
  of animals, factors governing, **IV** 189
  barriers to animal m., **IX** 40-43
  culture, effects of m. on, **I** 122, 221f.; **II** 36ff., 69, 112
  date of early, **I** 131
  forced, effects of, **II** 123, 125, 221f.; **IV** 167
  of geese, **III** 202
  Hamites were first waves of m., **I** 258; **II** 35f.
  of man, starting-point of, **IX** 49f., 53
  physical degeneration and, **II** 113, 221f.
  routes of early man, **I** 73, 119-141; **II** 40f.
  technological cost of, **II** 70, 119
  time taken for, **I** 141(fn.); **II** 56, 101, 115f., 122, 188; **IX** 55ff.
  under excessive pressure, **IX** 57
Milk
  inducing flow of, **I** 325
  powdered m., early use of, **I** 325
Millenium, **I** 49, 260, 262
Mind. *See also under* Brain.
  of animals vs. man, **IV** 229f., 271, 273f., 275, 317f.
  vs. brain, **I** 289; **III** 239f., 256ff., 320; **IV** 229f., 277f.; **VIII** 87
  without brain, **III** 251, 257, 328
  "change of," as repentance, **III** 39
  Christian life and the importance of the, **I** 253; **VIII** 197f.
  in decerebrates, **V** 213
  dimensionless quality of, **III** 261
  energy cost of, **VIII** 87, 143
  group, **III** 142, 263f.; **V** 387

hand as extension of, **IV** 231, 241, 277

and hand "in concert," **IV** 242

independent of matter, **III** 262, 264

as a machine, **III** 269

of man, ably supported by his body, **IV** 250

and matter: "interaction," **III** 259, 261f., 318, 325

mindless behavior, **VIII** 66

necessity of, to harmonize visual input, **VII** 91

in need of redemption, **III** 313

noetic effects of sin on, **III** 13, 39, 162, 272, 285, 313; **IV** 136, 210; **VIII** 197

not to be identified with brain, **III** 256ff., 263

in organisms without a brain, **III** 251, 257, 328

and origin of consciousness, **III** 257ff.

persists through death, **III** 254, 256f.

physiological basis of? **III** 320

reduced to electrochemistry? **III** 123, 251, 269ff.

renewing of the, **III** 39; **VIII** 196f.

resident in every cell, **III** 251f.

"size" of, **III** 261, 328, 331

when does mind emerge, **III** 257, 321

Mindedness

in all living substance? **VIII** 141

in amoeba? **III** 257

in atoms? **III** 321

and brainless animals, **III** 256ff., 328

vs. consciousness, **III** 321, 330

defined, **III** 321f.

of leucocytes? **III** 328

objectified in matter? **III** 325

progressive manifestations of, **III** 326

ubiquity of, **III** 328-339

of unicellular life, **VIII** 65, 75, 80, 86

Mind-less but alive and responsive, **V** 212f.; **VIII** 66f., 70

Minnows, leaders among! **IV** 301

Minoa(n)

bibliography, **I** 197 (fn. 102)

chronology, **II** 32

civilization, **II** 120

Palace of Minos, **I** 196f.

piping systems and sewage disposal, **I** 195 (fig. 11), 196

Miracle(s). *See also under* Divine intervention.

Augustine's definition of, **IV** 19

blind man healed going in and out of Jericho, **VII** 73

cessation of, as Paul ministered, **VII** 53, 56

vs. chance, **VIII** 37

and conversion, **VII** 53

as credentials of the Messiah, **VII** 38f., 40f.

in the crossing of Jordan, **III** 223f.; **VII** 192

in daily life, on aspect of, **VII** 192

of deliverance from prison, **VII** 51

and evolution of the eye! **IV** 155

of the gift of tongues, **VII** 53

a global flood requires excessive use of, **IX** 41-43

God's economy of, **IV** 19; **V** 196f.; **IX** 26

healing of bedevilled daughter: contradiction in the record of, **VII** 79f.

healing of maniac of Gadara: contradiction in the record of, **VII** 81f.

at marriage in Cana, **VII** 38

vs. mechanism, **VIII** 48ff., 53

Medieval world easily accommodated m., **VIII** 111

in the midst of mechanism, **VIII** 79

natural explanations of, **VII** 212, 213

and natural law, **VIII** 58, 87

nature of, **VIII** 207ff.

necessary because of the Fall, **VIII** 89

performed by Paul, **VII** 53

performed by Peter, **VII** 48

vs. providence, **VIII** 87

in the provision of food, **VI** 33f.

raising of the dead, **III** 144 (fn. 12); **IV** 108; **V** 123, 351f; **VI** 34; **VII** 42f; **VIII** 87

redemptive nature of, **VIII** 58, 88

requirement of, by the theory of evolution, **II** 75; **IV** 25; **VIII** 160 (fn. 129)

revival of, in end times, **VII** 62

vs. science, **II** 66

timing of, **III** 223; **IV** 19; **VII** 191, 192, 213; **VIII** 87

of the ten lepers, and the "feet of God," **VII** 82

and theistic evolution, **I** 358

unaccompanied by saving faith, **VII** 62

and unbelief, **VII** 61

where appropriate, **I** 29

where explaining is explaining away, **IX** 26

Mirrors, **I** 183, 204; **II** 94

Miscarriage, ancient law regarding, **V** 263

Missing links. *See also under* Anthropology, Gaps, Fossil Man.

categories of links still missing, **VIII** 135, 141

frequent claims of discovery of, **VIII** 134f.

improbability of, **II** 128f.

locations of so-called, **I** 132

"popularity" of, **II** 26, 27

variant forms mistaken as, **II** 20, 27

Mithraism, **IV** 120; **VI** 112

Missionaries

and anthropology, **II** 63

influence of, on spread of civilization, **II** 140

and spread of culture, **II** 140

to Tierra del Fuego, **II** 191

Mnemonist, professional, **III** 245

Moabite Stone, **VII** 282

Mobility; present excessive m. dangerous, **VIII** 177f.

Modal personality, **I** 45, 251; **III** 142f.

and national character, **IX** 155f.

Modern Synthesis. The, **VIII** 118-151

Modjokerto Skull, **II** 218

Mohenjo Daru, **I** 197; **II** 95, 96

Moles, marsupial and placental, **IV** 157

Mollusc shells, **IV** 159

Monastic life, "penalties" of, **III** 205

Money, paper; in early China, **I** 205f.

Mongoloid(s)

facial characteristics of, **II** 220

migratory routes of, **I** 138f.

Mongoloid races as Hamitic, **I** 69

Monism, **I** 267; **III** 319

Monkeys, *See also under* Cebus monkeys.

as experimental animals, **III** 119

fighting among, **IV** 190

intelligence of, vs. cranial capacity, **II** 181, 182; **IV** 228f.

painting done by, **IV** 317

sharing of food among, **IV** 194

territories of, **IV** 251, 299

Monk's Mound, **II** 116

Monogamy, precedes polygamy, **IV** 289f., 305

Monophyletic origin of man, **I** 133ff.; **II** 64; **V** 201

Monotheism, **IV** 110-138

in early China, **IV** 121f.

among the Midianites, **VII** 183
preceding polytheism, **II** 74; **IV** 110ff.
primitive, **II** 74; **IV** 110-137
uniquely Semitic, **I** 278
Monte Cicero finds, **II** 232
Moon, importance of, to the earth, **I** 352; **IV** 30f.
Moral(s). *See also under* Accountability.
 accountability of man, angels, animals, **I** 226f.; **VI** 229 (and fn. 12)
 consequences of evolutionary philosophy, **III** 275; **IV** 86, 178; **VIII** 151, 167
 of the gods, **VII** 29f. *See also under* Flood traditions.
 judgment, capacity for, a criterion of humanness, **III** 107, 268f.
 vs. mores, **III** 267
 none, in a mere machine, **III** 268
 private vs. public, **VII** 22
 responsibility: of animals? **IX** 16
  :capacity for, in man, **IV** 276, 288
  :extent of man's, **IX** 16
  :and heredity, **III** 140
 sense is universal, **III** 107f.
 and social implications of science, **VIII** 187 (fn. 185)
 standards, cost of present decay in, **VIII** 113f.
Morality
 and air warfare, as viewed in sixteenth century, **VIII** 139 (fn. 76)
 vs. ethics, **I** 29; **III** 66
 international, **I** 47; **III** 27, 267; **VIII** 113 (and fn. 18)
 of primitives, **II** 156
 and psychologists, **III** 270
Mores vs. morals, **III** 267; **VIII** 97
Morgan's three stages of culture, **II** 71f.

Moriah, Mount, **VII** 130, 132, 134
Morphology
 and degeneration of type, **II** 45
 diagnostically inconclusive, **II** 19f.
 effect of age on, **IV** 167; **VIII** 244f.
 effect of climate on, **IV** 159; **VIII** 234
 effect of disease on, **II** 216; **IV** 168
 effect of displacement on, **IV** 167f.
 effect of foods and soils on, **IV** 157, 159; **VIII** 234
 effect of humidity on, **II** 216f.
 effect of population size on, **II** 222
 effect of temperature on, **II** 215, 220
 glandular disturbances of, **II** 216ff.; **IV** 168f.
 and phyletic relationship, **IV** 140f., 147
 vs. relationship, **II** 12f.
 similarity no proof of relationship, **II** 12f., 19f., 198
 vs. stratigraphy, **II** 194; **IV** 149f.
 and tooth size, **II** 27f.
 used as base to determine geological age, **II** 194f.
 and wide variation within a species, **II** 20
Mortality, physical. *See also under* Death.
 an acquired character in man, **I** 234; **IV** 327; **V** 87, 152, 189
 acquisition of, in man, **III** 289f.
 of Adam, acquired, **I** 234; **IV** 327; **V** 87, 152, 189
 of body cells, **V** 140
 of man, and his DNA, **VIII** 50
 a tragedy for man, **I** 235
 and virgin conception, **V** 153
"Mortification" of the flesh, process, **III** 129f., 190

Morula stage of embryonic development, **V** 183
Moscow, **I** 96f.
Moses
divine education of, **III** 220f.
Egyptian education of, **VII** 184
marries a Nubian princess, **VII** 185
rod of, **IV** 33
role as Egyptian general? **VII** 184
Moslem uninventiveness, **I** 36f., 306
Mosquitos, **I** 350
Mother
to any child in a primitive community, **II** 279
brother of, important, **II** 279, 281, 292
and child relationships, **VII** 171
"fawn" m., among Eskimos, **II** 278
love, absence of, **II** 305; **III** 148, 157; **IV** 294; **IX** 172
Moths, melanism in, **IV** 75
Motives vs. actions, **VI** 149ff., 166f., 201f., 247ff.
Mound Builders, **II** 116
Mount Carmel finds, **I** 129; **II** 50, 221, 223
Mount Moriah, **VII** 130, 132, 134
Mount Ophel, **VII** 130, 134, 135
Mount of Transfiguration, **III** 215f.; **V** 18, 163, 377f., 399; **VIII** 97; **IX** 116
Mount Palomar Observatory, **VIII** 18
Mount Wilson Observatory, **VIII** 18
Mouse. *See under* Mice.
Movies, violent emotional shifts in; and effect on children, **VIII** 177
"Moving pictures," early Egyptian, **I** 201
Multi-culture, by American Indian farmers, **I** 168
Multiple births, **II** 284

Multiple conception, **IX** 137
Multiple personality, **III** 167; **IX** 187
Multi-verse vs. *Uni*-verse, **III** 53f.
Multi-versities, **VIII** 123 (fn. 35)
Mundugumor, absence of feminine temperament among, **III** 148; **IV** 294
Murder, uniquely human, **III** 322
Muscles
in the lips of man and apes, **IV** 270f.
involved in emotion, **IV** 245f.
involved in human erectness, **IV** 233
involved in speech, **II** 257, 262; **IV** 268f., 275
tension of m., for thermoregulation, **IV** 258
Muscular strength, blood supply and, **IX** 206
Music
among animals, **IV** 316f.
effect of, on pulse, respiration, etc., **IX** 235
and growth of crops, **III** 334
inspiration from, short-lived, **IX** 235
and mathematics, **III** 54
for meditation, **IX** 233
and science, **III** 54 (fn. 4)
and worship, **IX** 234
Musical instruments
list of early inventions of, **I** 42
pipe organ, **I** 202
Muskrats, **IX** 32, 91
Mutation(s), **IV** 49, 61, 81
agents causing, **V** 131
and aging, **V** 131f.
conditions of lethality, **V** 28; **VI** 228f.
damaging effects of, **VI** 228; **VII** 235; **VIII** 223
of disease germs, **IX** 159f.
divinely guided, **I** 362; **IV** 74
due to the Fall? **VI** 229

inbreeding and, **IV** 306f.; **VI**
222ff.; **VIII** 235f., 239
and incest, **VI** 226f.
increasing number of, throughout history, **VI** 232f.
language arose by m.? **II** 129 (fn.
171), 253, 268
not entirely random, **VIII** 90
reversibility of, **IV** 72; **VIII** 60,
90
self-correcting mechanism, **VIII**
60 (fn. 12)
"sudden" nature of, **VIII** 233
usually harmful, **IV** 76
Muti Ali (Arabia), **II** 290, 301; **VII**
156 (fn. 9)

Mutiny on the Bounty, The **II** 123
Mutual aid in nature, **III** 23, 24; **IV**
195f.
Myrrh and frankincense, source of,
I 20
"Mystery of iniquity," **III** 341
Myth(s)
Adapa, **V** 96
African, on death, **V** 94
Babylonian and Assyrian, re-
garding creation, **VI** 113
in the Bible? **VII** 195, 204, 205
Greek, regarding their own
genealogy, **I** 59f.
Mythology, the underlying source of
all pagan, **VI** 114

N

Nabataeans
capital city, Petra, **I** 165
irrigation works of, **I** 165
Nabonidus, prayer of, **VII** 152
Nain, widow of, **V** 350f.
Nakedness
consequences of, in Eden, **I** 144;
V 102f., 150
fig leaves to cover, **VI** 73
rights to uncover n., in primitive
societies, **II** 302, 327
Namelessness, psychological significance of, **IX** 167
Name(s), **IX** 165-192
attributes of deity as names of,
IV 116f., 120; **V** 250-257
"blotted out" *(Damnatio Memoriae)*, **VII** 257f.
change of: equals personality
change, **IX** 167f., 176f., 190f.
: meaning and reason for, **IX**
170, 177, 186

: in Scripture, **VI** 205f.; **VII**
242; **IX** 190f.
: in sickness, **II** 265, 298; **III**
139f., 164
: as therapy, **IX** 176
of deities, confused with characters of, **IV** 116
determines nature (the "Wrench"
experiment), **I** 271
equals the thing named, **IX** 181,
186
in Genesis 10, meanings of, **VI**
193
of God, meaning of, **VI** 40
of God, pagan, **V** 254f.
identified with the person, **II** 265;
III 139
identified with the soul, **II** 265;
III 137; **IX** 169, 171
importance of, **II** 265ff., 298, 299
Iroquois Keeper-of-N., **II** 298;
IX 179

knowledge of, gives power over the person, **IX** 174, 177f.

learning of, a function of child development, **II** 267; **IX** 175

mention of a person's n., tabu, **II** 298; **IX** 179

misuse of a, an instance of, **IX** 179

new, at spiritual rebirth, **IX** 188

new, for Christian in heaven, **IX** 188

as opposed to *title*, **V** 224

of person, secret, **III** 139; **IX** 170

of the redeemed, known unto God, **IX** 189

as a reflection of character, **II** 298; **IX** 186

rites of giving, **III** 137; **IX** 171

significance of, **VII** 229: **IX** 167ff.

in the Table of Nations, **I** 80-118

three kinds of, **II** 297f.

used by child for its own mother, in a polygynous family, **II** 280f.

as viewed by different societies, **IX** 169-180

as viewed by Scripture, **IX** 181-192

who may use a given n., **II** 297f.

"written in the dust," **IX** 189

Naming

of the animals by Adam, **II** 269; **V** 147, 270; **IX** 183

ceremony, **III** 137; **IX** 171

and ensoulment, **II** 265

to establish sonship, **II** 329

of Eve, **V** 147; **IX** 186

by father in adoption, **VII** 264

after the mother, **II** 297, 311f.

of sickness, first step towards control, **IX** 175

things, child's interest in, **IX** 175

things, gives reality to them, **VI** 204; **IX** 169, 174

wrongly is cause of sickness, **IX** 170

Naphtha gas, **I** 203, 333

Napoleon

attitude towards the Bible, **III** 33, 160

evasion of conscription under, **V** 373

Narcotics, **I** 174

Naros, **V** 55

Naskapi Indians

and family life, **II** 300

meaning of word for *men*, **VII** 201 (fn. 80)

National character, **I** 45, 68, 251, 253; **III** 143; **IX** 155

Nations. *See also under* Races.

boundaries of, set by God, **I** 318; **IX** 154

have the government they deserve, **IX** 145

language as a natural hedge between n., **I** 254, 274, 317f.

life of, in three dimensions, **I** 45, 251

as "personalities," **I** 45, 251, 252

as wild beasts, **III** 342

Native view of "White Man," **II** 110ff.

Nativity scenes in different countries, **IX** 240

"Natural communities," **III** 73; **IV** 194ff.

Natural death. *See also under* Death.

a legal fiction, **V** 17

not inherent in life, **V** 125

rarity of, **V** 177

Natural disasters in relation to the Fall, **IX** 140

Natural gas, used in early China, **I** 213

Naturalism, an incomplete view, **IV** 37

Naturalists

pre-Darwinian, main interest of, **III** 56; **IV** 38; **VIII** 148 (fn. 94)

World View of the, and of the Christian, **IV** 23-33

Natural law (or order)
control of, vs. understanding of, **VIII** 169
and divine intervention, **VIII** 58, 87
in embryological development, **V** 196, 198
evidential value of, **VIII** 58
mechanism as, **VIII** 58
and predictability, **VIII** 61, 139
and procreation, **V** 196; **VIII** 72, 79f.
rule of, in the universe, **VIII** 41
vs. supernatural, **II** 170; **IV** 70; **VIII** 91, 208 (fn. 204)
where superceded, **I** 349; **III** 74ff.

Natural man
abnormal behavior and, **III** 22
barbarism and, **III** 22
bias toward unrighteousness, **III** 38
culture as restraint of conduct of, **III** 18, 42, 45, 158
God's standard of righteousness not acceptable to, **III** 38
goodness of, **I** 261; **III** 18, 27, 31, 33, 39f., 45
and his "inhumanity to man," **IX** 143
optimism of, **II** 66; **III** 14, 29, 39, 40f.; **VIII** 120, 131f.
sinfulness of, **III** 35, 158
suicidal nature of, **III** 163, 296; **IV** 321

Natural Selection, **IV** 21, 64f., 81f., 147f., 181f.; **VIII** 236
to account for complex organs? **IV** 150
and animal behavior, **III** 25
cultural evolution and, **II** 108
Darwin and, **VIII** 220, 221
a dogma, **IV** 80, 179
eleminates the extremes, **IV** 187

evolution not advanced by, **IV** 187
fact or fancy? **IV** 181-193
and the formation of eyes, **IV** 155f.
importance of, as a concept, **VIII** 133
ineffectiveness of, **III** 115
not applicable to man, **II** 108f.
overcrowding and, **III** 71
and Supernatural Selection, **I** 346f.; **IV** 64-80; **V** 127
and the survival of the unfit, **IV** 172ff.
an unproven hypothesis, **IV** 75, 175f.
validity of, doubtful, **IV** 79f., 175

Natural vs. supernatural, **II** 170; **VIII** 91

Nature
"abhors a vacuum," **IV** 143
as animate, **II** 168f.; **III** 79, 85; **VI** 132
as a balanced economy, **III** 71f.; **IV** 191f.
beauty of, when ordered, **VIII** 61
convergence, pervasive in, **IV** 140f., 149f., 152f.
cooperation in, **IV** 179, 181ff., 194
as a cooperative "society," **III** 55, 69f.
cruelty in? **III** 64, 66f.; **IV** 197f.
degrees of freedom within, **VIII** 60f., 89, 90
deified, **III** 272; **IV** 36; **VIII** 93
design in, evidence and economy of, **III** 56; **IV** 84f.; **VIII** 49f., 147f.
divine intervention within, **IV** 19f.; **VIII** 48-98
economy of **III** 54, 74
under Edenic conditions, **VIII** 89, 96, 249
effect of the Fall upon, **VIII** 57ff., 61, 63, 89; **IX** 115

efficiency in, **VIII** 70
Egyptian philosophy of, **II** 172
essential orderliness of, **VIII** 51
every element contributes in, **IX** 142f.
failure of, **IV** 77
fallacy of evolutionary view of, **IV** 178
forces of, as "wills," **II** 170f.; **III** 79
as God's "ceased from" work, **VIII** 62, 95
God within, **III** 52-77
harmony in, denied, **VIII** 148 (fn. 94)
harmony within, **III** 66f., 71, 72; **IV** 191f., 194-205, 323; **IX** 127f. *See also under* Symbiosis.
Hebrew view of n., reverential, **II** 171

machinery of, perfected, **VIII** 54
man alien to, **II** 131; **III** 14, 17, 55, 84, 103; **IV** 323, 327; **VIII** 95, 96, 144, 181
man as a "critical point" in, **IV** 320
man as the keeper of, **IV** 323; **VIII** 62f.; **IX** 115
man the archdestroyer of, **III** 55, 115; **IV** 211
man's relationship to, various views, **III** 78-86
man the key to, **IV** 218
man relatively powerless in the face of, **II** 177; **IV** 300; **VIII** 106
mechanism in, "dirtied" by the Fall, **VIII** 57, 60
mechanism perfect in, apart from the Fall, **VIII** 48ff.
not a battleground, **III** 23; **IV** 189
omnipotence of God in, **VI** 132
"personalized," **III** 334; **IV** 81f.; **VIII** 180f.

primitive view of, **II** 169; **III** 85; **IV** 299ff.
primitive view of, vs. that of White Man, **I** 28; **III** 80, 85; **VIII** 106
problem of evil in, **III** 64f.; **IX** 109-163
profligacy of, **VI** 28f.
purpose and plan in, **I** 354 (fn. 275), 355; **III** 56f.; **IV** 37; **VIII** 65f., 91f.
reasons for studying, **VIII** 42f.
redemptive activity of God in, **VIII** 58, 88, 95
"red in tooth and claw"? **III** 23, 25, 64, 72; **IV** 181, 192, 197, 198; **VIII** 219, 244; **IX** 127
remarkable peacefulness of, **III** 68
scientific attitude toward, **VIII** 140
sensitive to imbalance, **III** 61f.
state of beautiful balance in, **IX** 128
and supernature, not separate, **VIII** 173
the unfit cared for in, **IV** 194ff.
the urge to return to, **III** 21
web of life in, **IV** 301
Western bifurcation of n., **III** 85, 334
Nature of man. *See under* Fall of man, Man, Natural man.
Nature–nurture relationship in personality formation, **III** 141, 145ff.
Navel, Adam's, **VI** 33
Navigation, role of birds in, **IX** 39f.
Nazarite vow. *See* Nazirite vow.
Nazirite vow, **V** 103f.
Neanderthal Man, **III** 49; **IV** 166, 225, 238f.; **V** 58
alternative reconstructions of, **II** 233; **IV** 168, 169
average age at death, **V** 58f.

as cave-man prototype, **II** 195f., 230

cranial capacity of, **II** 181; **IV** 225

as degenerate *Homo sapiens*, **I** 133

disappearance of, **II** 114

and disease, **IV** 168, 239

erectness of, **I** 134; **IV** 168 (fn. 70), 238f.

fate of, **I** 131; **II** 47f., 114

I.Q. of, **II** 166

and language, **IV** 267f.

Maurice Tillet as a, **II** 219

original finding of, **II** 230

position within the family of man, **II** 45ff.

preceded by modern man, **IV** 239

and speech, **IV** 267f.

Nebulae, distances from the earth of, **VIII** 18

Necessity, the mother of invention, **II** 149

Neck

human vs. animal, **IV** 219, 236, 287

in relation to erect posture and speech, **IV** 243f., 277, 287

Needles, **II** 94, 159; **IV** 243

use of, by man vs. animals, **IV** 314

Negrito Pygmies, **I** 130f.; **III** 27

Negro. *See under* Black races.

Negro-African languages, **VI** 185

Negroid(s)

in early Indus Valley culture, **VI** 202; **VII** 200

Hamites as, **I** 69

origins of, **II** 46f.

in prehistoric America, **I** 107; **II** 52

Sumerians as? **I** 151f.

types, early, **I** 130f., 136f.

"Neolithic" Revelation (Childe), **II** 82

Neoteny, **II** 18f.

Nephesh (soul), **V** 270, 281; **VII** 307

Nettles, as part of the curse, **IX** 121

New birth. *See also under* Conversion, Rebirth.

consequences of, **III** 95f., 111f., 154, 317f., 346

nature of change in, **III** 154ff.

test of reality of, **III** 348

what is not *new* in, **III** 168

New Covenant (testament), **III** 95

designed for the forgetting of sins, **III** 239

nature of, **III** 239

Newspapers in Greco-Roman world, **VII** 27

New Testament, ethos of, **VIII** 108

New World, effects of discovery of, **VIII** 120

Niagara River escarpment chronology, **II** 32, 132f.

Nicene Creed, **V** 290

Nigeria(n)

metallurgy, **VII** 197, 226f.

possible origin of the name, **VI** 200f.; **VII** 198

Nigger, origin of the word? **VI** 201

Nihilism, **VII** 19

Nile River turned into "blood," **VII** 212f.

Nilotic Negroes, **II** 216; **VIII** 240

Nimrod, **VI** 200; **VII** 200f.

as Merodach? **VI** 200 (fn. 48); **VII** 197

Nineveh, sparing of, **III** 111, 125; **VI** 229 (fn. 12)

Nin-gir-shu, significance of name, **VI** 200; **VII** 197

Nipples, cause of supernumerary, **IV** 168

Nirvana, **VII** 19, 32, 33

Noah

building the ark, **IX** 35

and his curse upon Canaan, **I** 25ff., 144-150

his ship's log, **IX** 25

planting a vine, **V** 99

precise instructions regarding entering and leaving the ark, **IX** 58 (fn 32)

revelation not claimed regarding extent of Flood, **IX** 13, 14, 26

synoptic Gospels written for the three sons of, **I** 16ff.; **VII** 97, 99

three sons of. *See under* Shem, Ham, Japeth.

why he could not simply have migrated, **VII** 33f.

"Noble savage" concept, **III** 21, 28, 36

Noblesse oblige, **VIII** 115

Noetic effects of sin, **III** 13, 39, 162, 272, 285, 313; **IV** 136, 210; **VIII** 196

Noise
as an assist to concentration, **III** 205; **IX** 232
as an assist to worship, **IX** 232

Non-nuclear genes,**VII** 224. *See also under* Genes, Plasmagenes, Nuclear genes.

"Normal" personality, **III** 157ff.

North American Indians. *See under tribal names:* Algonkins, Bella Coola, California, Cree, Crow, Hopi, Iroquois, Naskapi, Pawnee, Pima, Shosone. *See also list,* **IX** 94, 95.

Nostrils, positioning of, **II** 216; **VIII** 236

Notochord, **IV** 42

Noun vs. verbs, **I** 278

Novelty, made a virtue, **II** 149, 174; **III** 36

Nuclear genes, **VIII** 224
resistant to environmental influence, **VIII** 231
species preserved by, **VIII** 224

Numbers (in Scripture)
problem of very large, **VII** 71
with reference to animals, **VII** 160
reporting of, **VII** 71f.
significance of the number forty, **VII** 60

Nunivak Eskimo, **II** 302

Nursing. *See also under* Breast feeding, Suckling.
effect of alcohol upon, **V** 105f.
extended period of, among Eskimo, **II** 305
of infants by father, **V** 155; **VII** 172

O

Obercassel finds, **I** 127, 135; **II** 51, 223

"Objectification" of God in Jesus Christ, **IV** 209, 325

Objectivity in science, **IV** 24, 38, 143f., 205; **VIII** 95

Occasionalism, **III** 318f.

Ochre, red, use of, **I** 137; **II** 53f.

Octopus, eye of, **IV** 222

Odor
of body, and its significance, **II** 285, 306, 330
expressed mathematically as wave length, **III** 54

Oil
in the Jordan Valley? **VII** 174
rapid formation of, **II** 32

Ointment vases, **II** 94

'Olam, meaning of, in Hebrew, **VI** 102; **VII** 295

Old age,
    not the cause of death? **V** 177
    pathology of, **V** 22

Old Covenant ordinances, object of, **III** 239f.

Old nature vs. new nature in man, **III** 127f., 178

Old red sandstone, Hugh Miller on, **VI** 29

Old Testament
    passing of, **VII** 61
    "philosophy" of, **VIII** 108
    the Trinity in the, **V** 215-257

Olduvai (Oldoway) Skull, **I** 136; **II** 20, 52; **V** 127

Olfactory sense in dogs, **VIII** 68

Olive tree
    symbolic meaning of, **VI** 52f.
    symbol of Israel's spiritual history, **VI** 66ff.

Olympic games, **III** 201

Omnicompetence of scientists, **IV** 144; **VIII** 127f., 165

Omnipotence of God, **I** 233; **III** 91; **VI** 121-174
    in history, **VI** 130ff.
    and human responsibility, **III** 192f.; **VI** 163-173
    in Israel's history, **VI** 144-154
    in nature, **VI** 132
    in personal history, **VI** 155-162
    in the universe, **VI** 122-129
    in our world, **VI** 130-143

Onas, extinction of the, **II** 115

Onkelos, Targum of, **VI** 108

Oocyte production, **V** 139

Open fire as focal center of home, **VIII** 178

Ophel, Mount, **VII** 130, 134

Ophthalmia, **III** 228

Opossum, **IV** 201

Opportunism in evolution, **IV** 68, 144

Opportunity, and the expression of sin, **III** 31f., 185, 343; **V** 389

Opposable thumbs, **IV** 44, 233, 235, 242

Opposition, not without value, **IX** 149

Optimism
    of evolutionary faith, **II** 25, 28; **III** 18; **VIII** 62, 69, 110f., 130ff., 142, 173f.
    following the Renaissance, **VIII** 130
    of humanists, **II** 66; **VIII** 131f.
    of the late nineteenth century, **II** 66; **III** 14
    of natural man, **III** 39f.
    unjustified, **III** 29, 40, 41

Oracle Bones of China, **IV** 120ff.

Oracles, always female? **VIII** 116f.

Orangutan, **II** 13
    infant and adult skulls of, **II** 218, 224

Order
    demanded by the mind, **IV** 315; **VIII** 113
    in nature, as orginally created vs. present, **VIII** 62f., 89, 96, 249
    of words in Hebrew grammar, **VI** 86ff.

Organism(s)
    "mind" in o. without brain? **III** 251, 257, 328
    society as an, **III** 340

Organization, man's insistence upon, **IV** 315f.

Organogenesis
    mechanisms in, **VIII** 65, 75, 79
    in response to need, **IV** 150f.

Origin(s). *See also under* Life, origin of.
    of consciousness and self-consciousness, **III** 259f., 262f., 324f., 335; **VIII** 86, 136f., 142
    and destiny related, **IV** 211, 329; **VIII** 14f., 81, 188f.
    the dilemma of, **VIII** 24

of feathers, a mystery, **IV** 49, 69; **VIII** 160 (fn. 129)

of germ cells, **V** 112f.

of language, **II** 75, 129 (and fn. 171), 249ff., 253, 268; **III** 116; **VIII** 136

of life, **III** 324f.; **IV** 30, 34, 51f., 222; **VIII** 73

of man, Christian vs. evolutionary, **I** 133f.; **II** 12, 63ff.

of man, monophyletic, **I** 133f.; **V** 201

of matter, inconceivable, **IV** 19, 135; **VIII** 24

of mind, **III** 257f.

of nations, traditions regarding, **IX** 73, 90

part played by faith in discussion of, **VIII** 188

of religion, **IV** 110f.

science cannot deal with, **VIII** 24f.

of speech, **II** 250; **III** 117

Original sin, **III** 290f., 316

  as an acquired character, **III** 289f.; **IV** 210f.; **V** 188

  as defect in central nervous system, **III** 296

  defined by Calvin, **III** 291

  introduced at conception, **III** 292

  physical basis of, **III** 290; **V** 189f.

T. H. Huxley on, **III** 295

virgin birth escapes original sin, **III** 302

Origin of Religion, The (Zwemer), **IX** 264

Origin of Species, The (Darwin); reception accorded to, **VIII** 133

Orogeny, **IV** 93

Orphic Hymns, **V** 256

Osteoarthritis, **II** 230; **IV** 239f.

Ostrichs

  acquired callosities of, **VIII** 246

  domestication of, **I** 304

Ovaries, complement of seed complete at birth in, **V** 139

Ovid, account of the destruction of Sodom? **VII** 176

Ovulation **IV** 304

Ovum

  immorality of, **V** 85, 89, 189f.

  as a unicellular form of life, **V** 139

  untouched by the poison, **V** 156, 190

Ox(en)

  accountable? **VI** 229 (fn. 12)

  and ass, ploughing together, **III** 347

  stoning of, **IX** 17

Oxygen, early life and, **I** 349; **IV** 40ff.

Ozone, **IV** 41

P

Pacific Ocean, **VII** 302

Pack leaders, **IV** 299

Paedomorphism in man, **II** 18, 19; **IV** 287

Pagan deities, as attributes of God deified, **IV** 115, 120, 124

Pain

  absence of, dangerous, **IX** 128f.

in the animal world, more apparent than real, **III** 67; **IV** 197f.; **IX** 126f.

apparent sense of, in animals, reason for, **IX** 128

in childbirth, **IX** 138, 210

as experienced by animals compared with humans, **IX** 210f.

experienced by brain preparations? **VIII** 77

may bring exhilaration, **IX** 210

necessity of, **IX** 111f.

not inflicted by predators, **IX** 126

not suffered by plants, **VIII** 85

purpose of, **III** 67

sense of, absent in some individuals, **IX** 128, 129

sweating caused by fear and, **IX** 209f.

time sense upset by, **V** 314; **VI** 21, 25f.

Paint brushes, **I** 209

Painting(s)

by animals, **IV** 317

of Christ, culturally oriented, **IX** 241, 243

Paleolithic Man, **II** 143-192

not basically different from us in intelligence, **II** 166ff.

Eskimos as, **II** 158, 159, 162; **IV** 161

intelligence of, **II** 144-192

modern parallels with, **II** 158f.

modern primitive man represents, **II** 107, 158

portraits of, **II** 233 (fig. 14), 234f.

as waifs and strays of early migrations? **IV** 188

Paleolithic-Mesolithic-Neolithic sequences

ages often contemporaneous, **II** 33

concept of, **II** 72

Paleopathology, **V** 24

Palestine, Hebrew invasion of, **VII** 188f.

Palmar and plantar sweating, purpose of, **IX** 199

Palmar bleeding (stigmata), **V** 311

Panpsychism, **III** 323, 326; **VIII** 141

Panther chased by deer, **III** 65

Paper

clothing made from, **I** 332f.

coated stock, rag, fiber, etc., **I** 212

from early China, **I** 205, 212

invention of, **I** 317, 332

Maya and Aztec, **I** 182f.

p. money, **I** 205f., 334

toilet p., **I** 333

Paqadh, dual meaning of Hebrew word, **VI** 138

Parachutes, **I** 205, 211

"Paradises," earthly; not always happy, **III** 207, 208; **IX** 131

Parallel cousins, **II** 282, 301, 316f., 320; **VII** 156

Parallelisms, **IV** 153. *See also under* Convergence.

Paralytic, healing of, **VII** 39

Paramecium(a), **IV** 42

behavior of, **III** 257

immortality of, **V** 145

learning in, **III** 331

Paranthropus, **II** 17

Parasympathetic nervous system, **IX** 199

Parent(s)

credited or blamed, **I** 146; **II** 305, 313

limited of responsibility of, **VI** 169f.

"Parliament of man" (Tennyson), **VIII** 131

Parrot(s)

capacity for speech but not language, **II** 252

sole survivor of an extinct tribe (Maypures), **II** 157

Parthenogenesis, **V** 89, 91, 174, 189

Part used for the whole, **VI** 47

Parzillu, cuneiform word for *iron,* **II** 312; **VI** 202; **VII** 199, 205, 209, 227

Passover(s)

attended by Jesus, **VII** 44

meaning of the ritual, **V** 316f., 359f.

Passover Lamb

"age of accountability" of, **IX** 17

to be of the first year, **VI** 229 (fn. 12)

Past perfect in Hebrew grammar, **VI** 87ff.; **VII** 275, 285f.

Paternal sperm, **III** 290. *(See also* **V** 189f.)

Paternity. *See under* Physical paternity.

Patriarch
archaeological confirmations of the times of the, **VII** 194-209
decline in longevity after the flood, **VII** 237
numbering ten, **V** 51

Paul
appearance of, **III** 227
education of, **VIII** 194f.
his hope of reward, **III** 132
his "thorn," **III** 225ff.
miracles performed by, **VII** 53
validation of his ministry, **VII** 53
wife of? **III** 227

Pawnee, **III** 118

Peace and prosperity as a handicap, **III** 204f.

Peace of God, **III** 280

Peacock's tail, genetic coding and the, **VIII** 25

Peat, rapid formation of, **II** 32

"Pecking order" among scientists, **VIII** 104 (fn. 1)

Peking Man, **I** 127; **II** 51; **IV** 166, 268

Pelasgians, **I** 109, 116

Peloponnesian War, **VII** 21

Penalty of SIN, **III** 310, 311
assumed by God, **III** 304
death a merciful, **IX** 113
physical death as, **III** 287f., 289; **V** 18

People, use of the word by primitives, **VII** 201 (fn. 80)

Pepsin, in plants and animals, **IV** 155; **VIII** 70

Perfectibility of man, **III** 39

Perfection, meaning of the word in Greek, **IX** 116

Perfection of design. *See also under* Design.
eliminates a "Superintendent," **VIII** 54, 57
how far possible for God, **VIII** 54ff.
how far possible for man, **VIII** 54ff.

Peripheral vasodilatation, **IX** 201

Permissive will of God, **VII** 59

Persecution, value of, **IX** 149

Persia(ns)
deities, origin of, **IV** 120
influence of, on Islamic culture, **I** 309
invention of the windmill? **I** 36, 305
uninventiveness of, **I** 305

Persian Gulf, silting up of, **II** 93

Person
composed of spirit and body, **V** 193ff.
each has three kinds of names in primitive society, **II** 297f.
fetus as a? **V** 263 (fn. 1)
name identified with, **II** 265, 298; **III** 139; **IX** 170, 174, 177, 179
vs. personality, **V** 198, 288, 290
worth of, in materialistic society, **VIII** 33

Personality
"blank sheet of paper" concept of (tabula rasa), **III** 141
change, with name change, **IX** 167f., 176f., 190f.
changes in, by artificial and natural means, **III** 164ff.
chemical factors influencing, **III** 147
the Christian content or "filling" of, **III** 176f.
components of, **III** 145-150
and conversion, **III** 150, 164, 170ff.

cultural factors in, **III** 145, 147f.
definition of (Kroeber), **III** 150, 157-163
destruction of, **VIII** 179
development of, **III** 135-193; **IV** 288f.
emergence of, **III** 137-144
formation of the new, in Christ, **V** 206f.
hereditary factors in, **III** 145
human vs. animal, **IV** 317
imprisonment, its effect on, **III** 211
influence of diet on, **III** 165
influence of high altitude on, **III** 146
influence of language on, **II** 266f.
Jung's "X" factor and, **III** 141f.
matching of name with, **IX** 169
modal, **I** 45, 251; **III** 142f.; **IX** 155f.
multiple, **III** 167; **IX** 186f.
national character and, **I** 45, 68, 253; **III** 143
nature-nurture interactions, **III** 141, 145ff.
the new p., and our part in, **III** 189f.
"normal," **III** 157-163
origin of, **III** 137ff.
the physical basis of, **III** 140
and physique and temperament, **III** 145, 149
and projection techniques, **III** 151ff.
sibling age difference and, **IV** 288f.
and soul, **V** 288
split p., **IX** 187
stereotypes of, **I** 143
structure and content of, **III** 154ff., 170-180
structure of, foreordained, **III** 175
"suit of clothes" concept of, **III** 140f.

tension, place of in p. development, **III** 209f., 216
three dimensions in, **I** 249
types of, **I** 249f.; **III** 151-156
"Personhood," time of achievement of, **V** 260
Peruvian(s), weaving, **I** 324f. See also under Aymara.
Pessimism, **I** 223f.; **III** 16, 196; **VI** 19, 29; **VII** 19, 29, 33
of the evolutionary view (Monod), **VIII** 97
Peter
  first sermon, **VII** 45
  miracles performed by, **VII** 48
  personality type, **III** 179
Pharaoh
  of the Exodus, **VI** 134f., 149
  of the Oppression, **VII** 185
"Pharaoh's daughter," identity of? **VI** 182
Pharmacology
  anaesthetics, **I** 176, 184
  antibacterial and antifungal salves, **I** 329
  antiseptics, **I** 184, 329
  astringents, **I** 331
  cascara, **I** 166
  cocaine, **I** 166, 176
  contraceptives, **I** 329 (fn. 221)
  diuretics, **I** 331
  emetics, **I** 163
  ephedrine, **I** 212
  ergotamine, **I** 332
  euphorics, **I** 174
  excitants, **I** 174
  expectorants, **I** 331
  hallucinogens, **I** 184
  hypnotics, **I** 184
  kidney-stone dissolvants, **I** 329
  laxatives, **I** 163
  mercury (ulcers), **I** 329
  narcotics, **I** 174
  plant sources for drugs, **I** 163
  purgatives, **I** 331
  sedatives, **I** 174

suppositories, **I** 329
tonics, **I** 163
Pharos lighthouse, **II** 148
Philosopher(s)
  primitive man as, **I** 314
  temperament of, **III** 154
Philosophy
  absence of in China, **I** 33, 282; in
    Egypt, **I** 33f., 291, 294; **II** 172;
    in Sumeria, **I** 290, 314f.
  of agriculture among primitive
    people, **I** 168f.
  aim of, to make generalizations, **I**
    297f.
  the Arabs and, **I** 307
  Aristotelian, **VIII** 119
  Aryan, **I** 296
  "chance" in Greek p., **VIII** 26
  "chance" in modern p., **I** 233;
    VIII 106
  Christian p., hope and purpose
    in, **I** 223f.
  contribution of p. to man's wel-
    fare, **I** 252
  definition of, **I** 30, 279
  doubt encouraged by, **VII** 24
  early Indian, **I** 280; **III** 179; **VII**
    19, 30ff.
  evolutionary p. determines lines
    of research, **VIII** 160
  evolutionary theory as, **IV** 170
  Golden Age of Greek p., **VII** 18ff.
  Greek p., **I** 263f.
  Greek p., limitations of, **VIII** 196
  Greek vs. Indian p., **VII** 32
  Hindu, **I** 34, 296, 308; **VII** 32
  Indo-European (Japhetic) p., **I**
    31, 295
  irrelevance of "doctorates" in,
    VIII 213
  of life, necessary, **I** 228
  limitations of, **VII** 18, 19, 20
  materialistic p. of science, **I** 220f.
  mathematics as pure, **I** 34f., 297
  of Medieval World View, **III**
    81f.; **VIII** 110, 115f.

  moral consequences of evolu-
    tionary p., **III** 275; **IV** 86, 178;
    VIII 151, 167
  necessary for man's intellectual
    life, **I** 248f.
  non-existent among Hamites? **I**
    313f.
  pessimism of modern p., **I** 223f.;
    III 196; **VIII** 126
  vs. practical wisdom, **I** 31ff., 257,
    278, 283, 288, 294
  preeminently Japhetic, **I** 31, 70,
    297ff.
  primitives non-p., **I** 314ff.
  vs. religion, **I** 29, 246, 276; **III** 23,
    29
  vs. religion vs. technology, **I**
    263-302
  and technology, **I** 264f., 295f.
Phoenicians, **I** 94
Phosphorescence in nature, **IV** 56
Photographic memory, **III** 246f.
Photography
  giving a false picture of nature,
    IV 184
  of the human face, **V** 180
  phase p., of plants, **VIII** 69
  in three dimensions, **VII** 90
  and "truth," **VII** 85ff.
Photosynthesis, **IV** 28, 40, 41
Phrygian Flood traditions, **IX** 33
Phylogenetic trees, **II** 16, 236, 243f.,
  246; **IV** 59, 146, **VIII** 49
Physical paternity, **II** 280f., 285,
  290; **III** 138; **IV** 292
  father provides spirit only, **II** 285
  ignorance of, in modern times! **II**
    292
Physical world
  essential to God's plan of re-
    demption, **I** 232f.
  spiritual nature of, **III** 318
Physiology
  of man, created specifically with
    redemption in mind, **I** 233
  of man, unique, **III** 119f.

psychology reduced to, **III** 123; **VIII** 94, 209
of redemption, **V** 152f.
Physique
  degeneration of, **II** 45ff., 113, 221f.; **III** 45
  effect of environment on, **II** 189
  effect of migration on, **II** 113, 221f.
  and personality relationships, **III** 140
  Sheldon and, **III** 149
  and temperament, **III** 145, 149; **VIII** 81
  uniformity of culture with diversity of, **I** 126, 128; **II** 43f., 175, 222; **IV** 67; **VI** 230
Pi, value of, **I** 189
Pickaxe sinks 20 feet in hard ground in 60 years, **II** 34
Pictures. *See also under* Portraits.
  of Christ, **V** 209, 325, 391f.; **VII** 103; **IX** 239f., 241, 243
  three-dimensional vs. two-dimensional, **VII** 88f.
Pig(s), **II** 260
  Gadarene, **VII** 228
  of giant size, **V** 132
Pigeon(s)
  counting abilities of, **IV** 317f.
  homing instincts of, **III** 265
Piltdown Man, **II** 195; **IV** 148; **V** 58
  significance of forgery, **VIII** 135, 161
Pima Indians, Flood tradition of, **IX** 33, 72
Pineapples, development of, **I** 167f.
Pine trees in France, **IV** 40
Pipe organ, **I** 202
Piping systems in Crete, **I** 193 (fig. 11)
Piracy, disturbing effects of, **II** 124
Pisa, Tower of; and Galileo's experiment, **VIII** 157
Pithecanthropus erectus, **I** 127, 136; **II** 27, 48, 50, 204, 205 (ill.), 209

(ill.), 221, 218 (ill.), 235; **IV** 45, 162f., 165, 225; **V** 58
  cranial capacity of, **IV** 223
Pithom, **VII** 210
Pituitary gland
  effect of, on morphology, **II** 217f., 219; **IV** 168f.
  effect of, on temperament, **III** 147
Placenta, **V** 277
Placentals, **IV** 44, 154
Plan. *See under* Purpose.
Planarium flatworm(s), **III** 250, 329f.
  "emotional" states of, **III** 251
  experimental mutilation of, **III** 250, 256f.
  experiments involving "cannibal" p., **III** 251
  memory in, **III** 250f., 256f.
  "psyche" of, **III** 330
Plankton, behavior of, **III** 74
Planner, God as the Great, **VIII** 109
Plan of Redemption. *See under* Redemption.
Plants
  carnivorous, **VIII** 70
  creation of p. important to man, **IV** 65ff.
  dauermodifications in, **VIII** 233
  death of, not natural, **V** 15
  domestication of, **I** 166f.; **II** 86, 88; **IX** 49f.
  earliest, **IV** 39f.
  emotional responses in? **III** 334f.
  evolution of, a puzzle, **IV** 55f.
  growth of, and music, **III** 334
  home of domesticated p., **II** 55
  immortality of, **V** 126
  mechanisms, **VIII** 59, 69
  missing links between nonflowering and flowering, **IV** 56
  pain unknown to, **VIII** 85
  pepsin and, **IV** 155; **VIII** 70
  perpetuation of, variety of methods, **IV** 78f.

phase photography of, **VIII** 69
purpose of earliest, **IV** 40
"soul life" of, **III** 69, 335
tropism **III** 322; **V** 395; **VIII** 69, 85
Plasmagenes
  autonomy of, **VIII** 229
  in cytoplasm, **VIII** 224
  responsive to environmental influence, **II** 211; **VIII** 231
Plasmodium of slime mold, **VIII** 74
Plasmotype, definition of, **VIII** 230
Plastic surgery, **I** 329, 330f.
Platypus, Duckbilled, **IV** 44
Plumbing in Palace of Minos, **I** 195, 196
Pluperfect in Hebrew grammar, **VI** 87, 90; **VII** 275, 285f.
Plural of majesty, **VII** 281f.
Plywood, early Sumerian development, **I** 202, 326
Poetry
  method of indicating in Hebrew, **VII** 276
  in O.T., **VII** 276; **VIII** 204
Poison(s)
  alcohol as a protoplasmic, **V** 183
  causing mortality, **V** 189. *See also under* Mortality.
  extraction of cyanide, **I** 173
  of the forbidden fruit, **I** 234; **III** 289, 290; **IV** 321; **V** 86
  of the forbidden fruit, its effect on body and on spirit, **III** 293
  ovum (woman's seed) untouched by, **V** 156, 190
  used in fishing and hunting, **I** 169, 170
Polar bears, **IV** 264
Polyandry, **VI** 225f.
Polydemonism, **IV** 115, 127
Polygamy, a later development, **IV** 289, 305
Polygyny, **II** 279, 282f., 296, 303ff., 311ff., 319
  vs. the harem, **II** 283

Polynesian(s)
  art of pottery lost, **II** 118
  canoe construction, **I** 157, 164
  use of birds in navigation, **IX** 40
Polyp Hydra, as a "missing link," **IV** 48; **VIII** 134
Polytheism, **II** 74
  origin of, **IV** 110-137
  the Trinity not, **V** 251ff.
Ponchos, **I** 179
Pope
  Pius XII, demands proof of evolution, **VIII** 162
  Pope Urban VIII, Galileo and, **VIII** 156
Population(s)
  and birth rate in animals, **IV** 192, 201, 255f.
  controlled naturally in nature, **IV** 182, 185ff., 191, 255f.
  and numbers of animals in a given species, **IV** 182, 192, 225
  variability of type in small p., **I** 126, 128; **II** 43, 175, 222; **IV** 67; **VI** 230f.
Population density and size, **IV** 184ff.
  effect of, upon animals, **III** 63
  effect of, upon culture, **II** 137
  influence of, on morphology, **II** 222
  numbers of animals in a given area, **III** 71
  stability of size of, among animals, **IV** 255f.
Population growth
  birth of twins and, **IX** 137, 138
  and immortality, **V** 18, 166
  and life span, **V** 166
  rate of doubling of, **V** 44
  since the Flood, **V** 45; **IX** 53ff.
Porcupine, **IV** 156
Portrait(s)
  of paleolithic man, **II** 179, 233 (fig. 14), 234f.
  sanctity of a, **IX** 178

Portraiture
  appearance vs. reality in, **VII** 92
  artistic penetration by, **VII** 92
  beauty of, in Medieval times, **VIII** 114f.
  vs. character, **VII** 92
  of Christ. *See under* Pictures.
  multifaceted nature of, **VII** 77f., 85ff., 87f., 94
  truth in, **VII** 84-96
Portugese man-of-war, **III** 263, 336
Post-mortems formerly more frequent, **V** 306f.
Post system, ancient, **I** 182, 189
Posture. *See also under* Erectness.
  cost of erect p. to man, **IV** 240f.
  and disease, **IV** 239f.
  effect of, on civilization, **VIII** 41
  effect of, on culture, **IV** 243f.
  of man vs. animals, **II** 232, 233; **IV** 217f., 232, 243, 277
  and soul, **IV** 245f.
  and speech, **IV** 243f., 277, 287
Potatoes, dehydrated, **I** 326
Potiphar, the "Egyptian," **VII** 179
Pottery, **I** 181
  art of making p. lost, **II** 118f.
  Central and South American, **I** 181
  decay of art of, **II** 118f.
  design and decoration of, **I** 194, 196
  early, **II** 91, 94, 95, 99, 116
  fine, **I** 197
  fired, **I** 189
  metal prototypes, **I** 121, 182, 197; **II** 37, 99f.
  Middle East and Minoan, **I** 182
  modern Zuni, **II** 151
  perfection of early p., **I** 181, 194f.; **II** 89ff.
  porcelain, **I** 205
  pots with two spouts, **I** 181
  p. wheel, **II** 99
  of Tell Halaf, **IV** 64; **V** 64
  Sumerian, **I** 189

whistling kettles, **I** 181
Poverty, not always detrimental, **III** 208; **IX** 132, 135
Powdered milk, **I** 325
Prayer, the Lord's; the only requested instruction in N.T., **IX** 260
Prayer(s) and praying, **IX** 255-286
  as an alternative to action, **IX** 277
  of Ann Preston, **IX** 261
  answered unpredictably, **VIII** 88
  answers to, **IX** 257ff.
  appropriate places for, **IX** 276f.
  asking for signs, **IX** 277f.
  dangers and advantages of written, **IX** 247ff., 285
  Elijah's, regarding rain, **IX** 20, 21
  for guidance, **IX** 279f.
  hindered for undiscoverable reasons, **III** 198
  for an injured horse, **IX** 262f.
  on keeping records of, **IX** 275
  liturgical, advantages and disadvantages of, **IX** 245ff.
  about lost articles, **IX** 269f.
  of a Medieval architect, **IX** 228
  of Nabonidus, **VII** 152
  of Naskapi Indians, **II** 169
  the necessity and propriety of, **IX** 260
  of non-Christians, **IX** 261
  in the O.T. "for the Lord's sake," **IX** 265
  one man's answers to, **IX** 255-286
  pagan, **IX** 264f.
  public, **IX** 284ff.
  of saved vs. unsaved, **III** 125f.
  specificity of, less as one matures, **IX** 267
  as simple communion, **IX** 257
  and thankfulness, **IX** 275, 285
  unanswered, **VII** 13; **IX** 281f.
  unnecessary? **VI** 41

for "unnecessary" things, **IX** 271f.

what to pray about, **IX** 266-275

when inappropriate, **III** 235

when in need of books! **IX** 273f.

when in need of money, **IX** 268f.

when to, **IX** 283f.

where to, **IX** 284

whose p. are answered? **IX** 260-265

written vs. extempore, **IX** 285

Preaching, "Foolishness" of, **VII** 18

Pre-Adamic man? **VI** 234, 238f.; **VIII** 80, 246ff.

Preadaptation(s), **I** 356 (and fn. 279), 363; **IV** 68, 70

as evidence of purpose, **I** 356; **VIII** 144, 145

example of, in man, **VIII** 145

Pre-Cambrian, sterility of? **IV** 52

Pre-Columbian New World cultures, **II** 116f.

Predation, **III** 64f.; **IV** 322

little evidence of, in the Darwinian sense, **IV** 189f., 197

Predestination, biochemical, **IV** 31; **VIII** 82f.

Predictability, natural law and, **VIII** 61, 139

Prediction(s)

in history, inaccurate, **VII** 118f.

inherent difficulties of making, **VII** 118f.

in science, **VII** 118; **VIII** 139

Predmost Skull, **I** 136

Prefrontal lobotomy, **III** 165

Prehistoric animals, absence of beauty in, **VI** 28f.

Prejudice

vs. objectivity, **IV** 38

power of, **II** 60

Prelogical thought, **I** 287 (fn. 106), 313f.

Premise(s)

base for logical extension, **VIII** 200, 201

held as an act of faith, **VIII** 200

importance of, in Christian faith, **VIII** 202

of science vs. Christian faith, **VIII** 200

Premonitions

feminine, **VII** 116

as a form of prophetic insight? **VII** 115f.

Present Day Tracts, **II** 64

Prestige, how achieved in different societies, **III** 28

Presuppositions, importance of; in research, **III** 39

Pride, **III** 13

of grace, **III** 216

in the scientific community, **I** 302

spiritual p. in giving one's testimony, **IX** 275, 286

of spiritual success, **III** 197, 219, 222

Primate(s)

"anticipators," not "ancestors," **I** 54; **IV** 64

brain of, **VIII** 44

proliferation of, prior to man, **VIII** 248

Primitive culture(s), **II** 60-141

abnormal individuals in, **I** 314

abstract thought absent in, **I** 272f.; **II** 258

and attitude toward nature, **II** 169

breakdown of, **III** 28

conservatism of, **II** 105, 126, 150, 178

and divorce, grounds for, **II** 294

educational practices in, **II** 169

do not elevate themselves, **II** 73, 107

and the joking relationship, **II** 302f., 327

and magic, **VIII** 106

and marriage customs, **II** 277ff., 287f.

and marriage tabus, **VI** 224f.

meaning of their word for *men*, **I**
63; **VII** 201 (fn. 80)
monotheism found in early, **II**
74; **IV** 125ff.
names, their importance, **IX**
169-180
peripheral nature of, **II** 105f., 117
polygyny in, **II** 279, 282f., 296,
303ff., 311ff., 319
and reincarnation, **III** 137f.; **IX**
171, 174 (fn. 5)
and sense of sin, **III** 274f.
and sex, place of, **II** 280, 283
social behavior of, and the Bible,
II 273-331
sociology of, **I** 173f., 175; **II** 287
status, how achieved in, **II** 280
studies of, early anthropological,
II 66f.
their historical origins, **II** 60-141
Primitive man('s). *See also under*
Hamites.
attitude toward nature, **II** 168ff.;
III 85; **IV** 299f.
attitude toward the aged, **II** 112,
154, 170, 173
building techniques of, **I** 159,
177, 322ff.; **II** 160
conservatism of, **I** 300; **II** 126,
150f.
cradle of, **II** 40f.
educability of, **II** 108, 164f.
effects of small margin of survival
on, **I** 329; **IV** 300
exhibited by P. T. Barnum, **II**
229
extinctions of, **II** 114, 115, 155ff.
family life among, **II** 156f.
geographical distribution, reason
for, **II** 105
gods of, **IV** 125-130
high civilizations and their effect
on, **II** 140
high intelligence of, not inferior
to modern man, **II** 108, 131,
154f., 165f.

honesty characteristic of, **I** 272
individualism less pronounced,
II 170, 176
ingenuity of, **I** 162, 187 (fn. 77).
See also under Ingenuity.
inventiveness of, **I** 154ff., 162. *See
also under* Inventions.
languages of, not simple, **II** 251,
259; **IV** 296; **VI** 213
marriage and romantic love,
jealousy, **II** 282, 299
medical practices of, **I** 162f., 173;
II 155. *See also under* Medicine,
Pharmacology, Surgery.
memorization, feats of, **V** 47f.;
VII 258
morality of, **II** 156
more "noble" than we are? **III** 28
and names. *See under* Names.
no p.m. without language, **II**
251, 260f., 270
not different from civilized man,
II 131, 165f.
not philosophically inclined, **I**
314ff.
our "contemporary ancestors,"
II 73
pain, comparative insusceptibil-
ity to, **IX** 126
as "paleolithic man," **II** 107, 158
as philosopher, **I** 314
physical appearance of, related
to style of living, **II** 183, 221;
IV 167
and physical paternity, **II** 280f.,
285, 290; **III** 138; **IV** 292
practical nature of, **I** 313
proverbs, **IV** 130
psychology of, **I** 173; **II** 288
religion of, **II** 122; **IV** 113f.,
125ff., 133
religious beliefs not system-
atized, **I** 293
specificity of vocabulary, **I** 272f.;
II 251, 258ff.; **VI** 214ff.
suicide, attitude toward, **IV** 296

time as viewed by, **I** 273; **VI** 22f.

tools of, **II** 165

true man, words for, **I** 63; **VII** 201 (fn. 80)

truth, attitude toward, **I** 272f.

twins, attitude toward, **VII** 228

"unexpected" humaness of, **II** 155; **III** 19

view of "delayed judgment," **VI** 21

view of White Man, **II** 110ff.

vocabularies, extensive, **I** 272f.; **II** 251, 258ff.; **VI** 213ff.

vocabulary vs. grammar, **I** 274; **IV** 274

wisdom of, **II** 110ff.

World View in personal terms, **I** 28; **II** 171; **III** 80, 85; **VIII** 106

Primitive society

fate of an inventor in, **II** 173

neither more nor less wicked than civilized s., **III** 27f.

philosophy of agriculture and food gathering, **I** 168f.; **II** 169

Primitive tribes. *See under the following names:* Ainu, Aleuts, Alii, Alorese, Ancasmarca Indians (Peru), Andaman Islanders, Araphesh, Arunta, Australian aborigines, Aymara, Aztecs, Bakairi, Banyoro, Basques, Bedouin, Bushmen, Carib (Orinoco), Dobuans, Fiji, Hottentots, Incas, Ituri Forest pygmies, Kaikari, Kalmuks, Kamtchadales, Karaikees, Lango, Lapps, Leeward Islanders, Maori, Maypures (extinct), Miao (China), Mundugumor, Muti Ali, Negrito Pygmies, Nilotic Negros, Nunivak Eskimo, Onas, Polynesians, Pygmies of Central Africa, Reddi (Bison Hills), Samoans, Semang (Malay), Singhalese, Singphos, Sumatra, Swiss Lake Dwellers, Tchambuli, T'honga, Tierra del Fuegians, Tlingit, Toda, Toltec, Trobrinanders, Twsana, Wabemba, Yoruba. *See also list,* **IX** 94, 95.

Primitive World View, **III** 85, 334

asks "how," not "why," **III** 64

asks "who did it?," not "what happened?" **II** 170f.

is personal, **I** 28; **II** 171; **III** 80, 85; **VIII** 106

"Princess" as a term of endearment, **VII** 156, 242

Principle of Constancy (Einstein), **VI** 18

Principle of Indeterminacy (Heisenberg), **VIII** 60

Printing

in early China, **I** 212

effect of invention of, **VIII** 119, 120

materials relating to, list of, **I** 39f.

with moveable type, **I** 205, 325

technology for, Hamitic in origin, **I** 317

Prism of Sennacherib, **VII** 282

Prisoners, treatment of; in ancient and modern war, **III** 27

Prison experiences, **VII** 51

Private armies, **VII** 160, 162

Privilege, linked to responsibility, **VIII** 115

Procreation, and natural law, **V** 196; **VII** 72, 79f.

Productivity, and day of week, **IX** 134

Progeria, **V** 22

Progress, concept of

automatic linear p., **III** 15f., 36; **VIII** 132

makes novelty a virtue, **III** 36

not automatic, **II** 107; **III** 17

real evidence of, **II** 82

Progression. *See under* Regression.

Projection techniques, **III** 157ff.

Promised Seed, **II** 309f.; **V** 246f.
  Abel as, **VII** 227
  line of the, **VII** 237
Promotion, as from the Lord, **III** 219
Proof
  does not engender or strengthen "faith," **VIII** 208 (fn. 204)
  nature of, **V** 79; **VIII** 162
Prophecy
  criteria of "fulfillment" of, **VII** 109f.
  divine purpose of, **VII** 120
  dual fulfillment of, **VII** 142
  as God's perogative, **VII** 120
  and Higher Criticism, **VII** 141
  vs. human foresight, **VII** 115, 142
  human vs. divine, **VII** 112ff.
  regarding Jerusalem and its rebuilding, **VII** 127-140
  Matthew's Gospel emphasizes fulfillment of, **VII** 101
  and the ministry of condemnation, **VII** 120
  pagan p. not too successful, **VII** 107
  practical value of, today, **VII** 143
  prophetic poems (Mother Shipton, etc.), **VII** 112
  purpose of, **VII** 119f.
  retrospective value of, **VII** 140
  some modern "howlers," **VII** 117f.
  striking fullfillments of, **VII** 107-143
  to "tell the time," **VII** 120
  of Tyre's destruction, **VII** 121-127
Prophetic utterance, the last in O.T., **VII** 46
Prophets
  false, in Roman times, **VII** 108
  replaced by scholars, **VII** 29
  who are p.? **VII** 112-120
  woman as, **VII** 116

Prostitution, enforced, **II** 297
Protein(s), speed of manufacture of, **VIII** 70
Protestantism, the rise of the middle class and, **VIII** 121
Protoplasm, functioning, death not inherent in, **V** 15f., 126, 130, 176
Protoplasmic consciousness, **III** 329
Protoplasmic poison, alcohol as, **V** 183
Protozoa(n), **III** 72
  possessing a will? **III** 261
  sensations experienced by, **III** 324
Proverbs, primitive, **IV** 130
Pseudo-man, definition of, **III** 124
Psychedelic drugs, **I** 174
Psychiatry
  art and, **III** 164; **IX** 167
  and guilt, **III** 273f.
  and moral standards, **III** 270
  and music, **IX** 235
  and the problem of life's meaninglessness, **III** 210ff.
  punishment, a basic human need according to p., **IV** 134
  religion and, **III** 270
  and "repressions," **III** 35
Psychic sweating, **IX** 211f. *See also under* Emotional sweating.
Psychic unity
  of any "species," **III** 317
  of man, **III** 337
Psychokinetics, example of, **III** 318
Psychologists and morality, **III** 270
Psychology
  animal p., no substitute for human p., **III** 122
  case of split personality, **III** 167; **IX** 187
  crowd, **V** 387
  historical development of, in a nutshell, **VII** 179
  native use of, **I** 173
  of primitives, **II** 288

projection techniques and, **III** 151f.

reduced to physiology, **III** 123; **VIII** 94, 209

shifts in interests and emphasis of, **III** 269f.

and simple forms of life, **III** 251

Thomistic, **V** 288

and worship, and the Trinity, **V** 249f.

Psychosomatic medicine, **I** 173, 175; **IX** 181

Psychosurgery, **III** 165f.

Pteridophyta, **IV** 59

Ptolemies

astronomical tables of, **VIII** 158 (fn. 125)

inbreeding in the family of, **VI** 224

Publishers, Christian; responsibility of, to authors, **IX** 305

Publishing

ease of, in N. T. times, **VIII** 28

mode of, in classical times, **VII** 27

Pulsation, of heart cells autonomous, **VIII** 76

Pumps

bellows, chain, and piston type, **I** 205, 305

self-acting bilge, p., **I** 186

Punch, on Higher Criticism, **VI** 52

Punishment. *See also under* Chastisement.

a basic human need, **IV** 134f.

basis of, **III** 91f.

the Flood, traditionally seen as a, **IX** 69ff.

lack of, among some primitives, **III** 300

need for fear of, **IV** 135

as a public manifestation of God's concern, **VII** 15

reward and, **III** 92, 131f., 192f.; **VI** 165ff.

Roman forms of capital p., **V** 379f.

"sudden p." in the early Church, **VII** 49ff.

in Tlingit society, **V** 373f.

Puranas, **VII** 33

Purgos, meaning "tower" and "town," **VI** 199f.

Puritan influence on science, **I** 301

Purpose. *See also under* Teleology.

as admitted evidence of God, **VIII** 145 (fn. 90)

argument for, inconceivable to scientists, **I** 362

concept of, foreign to philosophy of science, **I** 220

concept of, rejected by science, **I** 353ff., 362; **IV** 73f., 151f.; **VIII** 125ff.

denied by science, **IV** 23, 34; **VIII** 127

equated with vitalism, and "forbidden," **IV** 35, 144f., 150

evidence of, almost compelling, **VIII** 93

evidence of, in nature, **I** 354 (fn. 275), 355; **III** 56f.; **IV** 37; **VIII** 65f., 91f.

exists chiefly in relation to man, **VIII** 144

idea of, diametrically opposes mechanistic view, **III** 271

lack of, paralyzing society, **VIII** 149

loss of, and sickness, **VIII** 125 (fn. 38)

in Medieval world, **VIII** 115

mutations as evidence of p., **I** 362

necessity of, in life, **I** 220, 222f., 228; **VIII** 188

preadaptation as evidence of, **I** 356; **VIII** 144, 145

the search for, **VIII** 108, 116

the ultimate p., found in God, **I** 225

ultimately relates to human destiny, **I** 225f.
in the universe as a whole, **I** 352f.; **III** 272; **VIII** 105, 144
why rejected by science, **VIII** 127
"Purposeful" activity
without mind, **VIII** 66f., 70
and plant tropisms, **VIII** 69

Pygmies of Central Africa, **IV** 126, 129, 253, 266; **VIII** 240
reason for morphology, **II** 216
in "refuge" areas, **I** 130

Pyramids of Egypt, **I** 194f.; **II** 89
accuracy of construction, **V** 63
early stonework of, **I** 194f., 324
in the New World, **II** 116

Q

Quadrumana vs. quadruped, **IV** 218
Quails in the wilderness, **VII** 194, 213
Quakers, **IX** 234
Queen Mary, the, **IX** 37
Queen of Sheba, **I** 20f.

Questions
of primitive man vs. Western man, **II** 170f.
which kind most important, **III** 118; **VIII** 94, 139 (fn. 76)
"why" vs. "how," **I** 49, 294; **III** 63f.
Quietness and worship, **IX** 232f.
Quills, as a defence, **IV** 156

R

Rabbinical literature, **IV** 107f.
and wisdom regarding worship of idols, **I** 219; **VIII** 109f.; **IX** 110f.
Rabbits, **III** 346
development of decapitated, **V** 213; **VIII** 67
and foxes, **IV** 301
neutral effects of crowding on, **IV** 187
rapid maturing of, **V** 166

surviving though badly injured, **IV** 203
and wound healing, **IV** 313
Race(s)
colored, **I** 12f., 53, 72, 101
differences between, **I** 50
gods of the three branches of, **IV** 115f.
as listed in Genesis 10, **I** 71ff., 80-118, 155
routes of migration of the white r., **II** 46

three main branches of, **I** 155, 251ff.; **VII** 97f., 229f.
unity of, **I** 133
Racial
causes of r. differentiation, **I** 126f.
character, **III** 129, 254
differences, **I** 50
divisions of man, **I** 12
influence of hormones on r. types, **II** 217
language as a barrier to r. mixture, **I** 274, 317f.
mixture, advantages of, **I** 137f., 311ff.; **II** 138
mixture, as a policy, **VII** 26
mixture, in China, **I** 312
purity, penalties of, **I** 311f.; **II** 137f.; **III** 121
stocks, biblical view, **I** 13f.
stocks and skin color, **I** 72
Radiation
cosmic, **IV** 233f.; **V** 25
effect of, on life span, **V** 131
Radio, foretold by Mother Shipton? **VII** 112
Rain, "Bloody," **VII** 212
Rainbow, as a sign, **V** 25
Raincoats (American Indian), **I** 179
Rain dance, Hopi, **I** 334; **II** 172; **III** 334
Rainmaking, **I** 334f.
Raising of the dead, after three days, **V** 348; **VII** 42f. *See also under* Dead, raising of.
Ramses, **VII** 210
Randomness, difficulty of designing for, **VIII** 90
Ras Shamra, **II** 91
Rat(s)
ability to recognize signs, **IV** 318
"camp followers" of man, **IV** 185
canny wisdom of, **IV** 293f.
desert, and jerboa, **IV** 157f.
dietary wisdom of, **III** 62f.; **IV** 309

experiments with (Washburn), **II** 224; **III** 248
"learned" behavior of, not inherited, **IV** 293
mutual aid among, **IV** 195
skull form modified, **II** 224
Weismann's experiments with, **V** 85f., 189
Rate of living, **V** 23, 27
Rate of maturing, **V** 27
in man vs. animals, **IV** 284-290
Rate of revolution of the earth, **I** 349; **IV** 28f.; **VIII** 39
Rationalism, inadequacy of, as a creed, **VIII** 211 (fn. 210)
Rationality
a human trait, **III** 106, 117; **IV** 315f.
man is, **IV** 315
Rationalization of miracles, dangers of, **IX** 26
"Rato-morphic" view of man, **III** 254
Raven, **III** 96, 223; **VI** 132; **IX** 39
Reality
determined by language, **I** 266ff., 270, 274, 288
"incomprehensibility" of, **VIII** 24
mechanistic determinism, an incomplete view of, **VIII** 214f.
spiritual nature of, **III** 261f., 326f., 333; **VIII** 22f.
vs. truth, **VII** 94f.
two aspects of, **VIII** 205
Reason
affected by sin, **III** 13, 39, 274; **VIII** 95, 196
distrust of, **VIII** 121
and faith, **I** 246; **V** 78; **VIII** 119, 184f., 191, 194, 201
and faith, conflict between, **VIII** 126, 184
and false premises, **VIII** 118f.
and revelation, **VII** 29, 34; **VIII** 189

theology as a system of, **V** 77f., 152f.

Reasonableness of the created universe, **VIII** 34

Reasoning capacity of man, **III** 106, 117; **IV** 315

Reasoning, circular; in evolution **II** 26, 163, 250; **IV** 175; **IX** 81f. *See also under* Circular reasoning.

Reassembly of cells teased apart, **III** 332; **VIII** 74, 76, 80

Rebirth. *See also under* Conversion, New birth.
  and incarnation anew, **V** 201-214
  new name as a new personality, **IX** 188
  real, not merely symbolic, **III** 343f.

"Rebirth" of mentally ill child, **IX** 167

Recall
  under electrode stimulation of cortex, **III** 242ff.
  under hypnosis, **III** 245f.
  in the Judgment, **III** 240
  recognition vs. reminiscence, **III** 259
  short term (STM) and long term (LTM), **III** 254
  time factor in, **III** 245

Recapitulation, theory of, **II** 241
  disregards functional morphology, **IV** 147

Recession of flood waters
  rate of, **IX** 22f., 25
  of Tigris and Ganges rivers, **IX** 24

Recognition vs. cognition **III** 259f.

Reconstitution theory, **IV** 92ff.

Reconstruction(s), **IV** 145
  fallacy of anthropological, **II** 162, 226-248
  falsified, **IV** 231f.
  from a single bone, **II** 247; **III** 57; **IV** 145

Reddi of the Bison Hills, **II** 299

Redeemableness of man, a criterion of humanness, **I** 231; **II** 191; **III** 124, 338; **IV** 20f., 209

Redeemer
  qualifications for, **V** 117f., 192, 202f.
  truly represents man and woman, **V** 201ff.

Redemption
  of angels and animals? **I** 226, 231; **IV** 212
  applies specifically to the body, **V** 205, 274
  impossible any other way, **I** 232
  key to creation, **IV** 21
  man created for, **IV** 21, 325
  manner of, and application of, regarding man's body and spirit, **V** 161
  of the mind, **III** 313
  of the natural order, **VIII** 58, 88, 95
  the parameters of God's plan of, **V** 191f.
  physical world essential to plan of, **I** 232f.
  physiology of, **V** 152
  and the problem of the concept of pre-Adamites, **VI** 234, 238f.
  as the purpose of the universe, **I** 218
  requirements of the plan of, **V** 117, 157f.
  scope of plan for, **V** 210
  time factor in, **VI** 45-49
  wholeness of, **III** 46

Redemptive activity, God's work since the Fall, **VIII** 58, 88, 95

Red ochre, widespread prehistoric use of, **II** 53f.

Red shift, **VIII** 18ff., 26

Reductionism, **III** 261f., 266, 268f., 272, 279, 319; **IV** 87, 214; **VIII** 48ff., 52, 72, 86, 93, 138

applied to the phenomenon of
life, **III** 262f.; **IV** 35; **VIII** 83,
84
and behavior, **III** 255
doubts regarding, **VIII** 79
and personality, **III** 40
understanding by, **VIII** 132
Reed houses, **I** 177
Reflection
mental, not found in animals? **IV**
274
uniquely human? **III** 260
Reformation, science scorned by
the, **VIII** 122
Reformation of the self, **III** 159, 163,
170
Reformed theology, the result of
controversy, **IX** 150
Regeneration. *See also under* Conversion, New Birth.
and the renewing of the mind, **III**
39; **VIII** 196f.
the nature of, **III** 170ff.
Regression, **V** 278
Reign of law, **III** 54
Reincarnation, **IX** 169, 171
of Christ in the believer, **III** 169,
172, 177; **V** 155f., 206f., 363ff.;
IX 188
and ensoulment, **IX** 171
Jewish belief in, **III** 139, **IX** 173f.
among primitive people, **III**
137ff.; **IX** 171, 174 (fn. 5).
Rejuvenation in old age, **V** 141
Relationship(s)
based on homology, **II** 12ff., 247
similar morphology not a proof
of, **II** 12f., 19f., 198
Relativism, cultural, **III** 108
Relativity
creation and the Theory of, **VI**
27-37
historical background of, **VI**
14-19
and size, **VI** 25
special theory of, **VI** 11ff., 17f.

of time in experience, **VI** 20-26
Religion(s)
ancestor worship, **IV** 123f., 126,
131
animism, **II** 170f.; **III** 79f. 334;
IV 110, 127
based on fear? **IV** 111
broadmindedness in, **IV** 118
Buddhism reaches China, **I**
282ff.
Chinese, **I** 284; **IV** 120ff.
contribution of Shem to, **I** 251,
257; **VII** 99
corruption of, in civilized vs.
primitive society, **IV** 125
vs. culture, **IV** 133
and culture not parallel, **II** 109
decline in primitive, **II** 122
development of, contrary to
evolutionary theory, **IV** 126,
132
difference between Semitic and
native (primitive), **I** 257
effects of civilization on, **IV** 133
Egyptian, **IV** 116
an essential part of human activity, **VIII** 150 (fn. 99)
Etruscan, **IV** 124
evidence of monotheism in the
ancient world, **IV** 113ff.
evolution as a r., **II** 25; **III** 58, 84;
VIII 149, 151, 159f.
evolution of? **II** 74; **IV** 114, 126
vs. the Gospel, **III** 279
Greek, early, **IV** 124
Hindu, **IV** 117f.
of India, **IV** 119f.; **VII** 32
Israel as a unique vehicle for, **I**
276
an "I-Thou" philosophy, **III** 80;
VIII 106
vs. magic vs. science, **VIII** 106
possible origins of, **IV** 110f.
vs. philosophy, **I** 29
in primitive societies, **I** 293; **IV**
126f.

of primitives once a purer faith, **IV** 133

sacrifice common to all, **V** 334

science as a, **VIII** 145 (and fn. 90)

in sophisticated societies, **IV** 113f.

Sumerian, **IV** 113f.

vs. technology vs. philosophy, **I** 263-302

Religious

art, **IX** 223ff.

vs. civil authority, **IX** 147, 148

vs. Christian faith, **VI** 56

faith, degeneration of, **IV** 110f.

freedom, as defined by Jesuits, **IV** 118

vs. intellectual life, **I** 246

vs. philosophical thought, **I** 246, 276; **III** 23, 29

vs. psychological view of sin, **III** 270

r. history of Israel symbolized by fig tree, **VI** 70-72

vs. spiritual life, **I** 246 (fn. 30) thought, evolutionary development of? **IV** 74

Reliving the past, **III** 240f., 243ff.

Reminiscence, a faculty of man, **III** 259f.

Renaissance, **VIII** 117

gains and losses, **VIII** 114

optimism engendered by, **VIII** 130

Renewing of the mind, **III** 39; **VIII** 196f.

Repentance, **III** 39

of David vs. Ahab, **III** 31f.

a gift of God, **VI** 156, 157

Replenish, Hebrew word for, **VII** 314

Reproduction

asexual, in plants and animals, **V** 17

cessation of, in humans, **IV** 290

and death, **V** 136, 137

history of the sperm and ovum after fusion, **V** 183f., 196

in man vs. animals, **IV** 303ff.

Reptiles

vs. amphibians, **IV** 70

mass extinction of, **IV** 93f.

profound changes in form of, with time, **IV** 188

Research

definition of, **II** 25

idea of mechanism essential to, **VIII** 72

ignorance sometimes an advantage in, **VIII** 105 (fn. 2)

lines of, determined by evolutionary philosophy, **VIII** 160

must exclude God, **VIII** 92

the nature of the "tools" determines the findings, **VIII** 55

popular misconception of, **I** 104f.

presuppositions important in, **III** 39

scientific r. cannot introduce the supernatural, **I** 355

where errors cancel each other out, **VIII** 201 (fn. 196)

Resen, city of, **I** 108

Respiration, artificial, **III** 90, 144

Responsibility

and age of accountability, how early? **III** 55, 97, 295, 297, 298

and freedom of choice, **III** 268

for growth in Christian life, **III** 189

human, and omnipotence of God, **III** 192f.; **VI** 163-173

in man vs. animals, **IV** 288; **IX** 16

and omnipotence of God, **VI** 163ff.

parental, limits of, **I** 146; **II** 305, 313; **VI** 169

personal r. absent in modern warfare, **III** 27

privilege linked with, **VIII** 115

social and moral r. of scientists, **VIII** 139 (fn. 76), 140; **IX** 291f.

for what? SIN or SINS, or both? **III** 293, 304

Restitution theory. *See* Gap theory.

Restraint(s)

civilization as a, **III** 19

necessary for progress, examples of, **IX** 153

necessary to curb wickedness, **III** 19f., 34

rejection of older forms of r. by evolutionists, **III** 36

sin caused by? **III** 35

thrown to the winds in modern war, **III** 26

Resurrection, **V** 334-365. *See also under* Dead, raising of.

appearances of the Lord, **V** 165, 338, 357ff.

bodily, necessary for consciousness, **III** 249, 254

bodily, of Jesus Christ, **V** 297ff., 338; **IX** 297f.

of the body, nature of, **V** 297; **VI** 35f.

of the dead, **IV** 108; **V** 123, 351f.; **VII** 43; **VIII** 87

the drama of, in the Gospels, **V** 340

early emphasis of, in preaching, **V** 335

effect of Jesus' r. upon the disciples, **V** 339ff.

events following the, **V** 165f.; **VII** 47ff.

experiential aspect of the, **V** 363-365

Greek view of bodily r., **V** 334

historical aspect of Jesus' r., **V** 337-346

importance of the, in the founding of the Church, **V** 335, 339

of Jesus, a hallucination? **V** 342

of Jesus, "explanations" of, **V** 295, 298, 337f.

of Lazarus, special significance of, **V** 123

less believable even than the sacrifice itself? **V** 334

messianic, importance of, **VII** 37

vs. making alive, **III** 304

as part of the Gospel, **V** 345, 347

the passage from time into eternity, **VI** 42

for the presentation of the blood of the Lamb, **V** 358ff.

sets consciousness free of present limitations, **III** 326

theological importance of the, **V** 347-362

to be universally applied to all men, **III** 306

validation of the, as a fact, **V** 344ff.

Resuscitation of the apparently dead, **V** 119f.

Retreats, dangers of, **III** 133, 215

Retrotensive concept, **VIII** 142

Return of Christ, alternative views regarding purpose of, **III** 14

"Return to nature," **III** 21, 36, 97

Revelation

contradiction essential to, **VII** 67-104; **IX** 78

the corruption of an original r., in traditions, **V** 250ff.

effect of its absence or denial, **VII** 33

essential to complete knowledge, **IV** 14, 20, 63, 210

essential to complete the scientific World View, **I** 348

Hebrew language for, **I** 266, 276; **III** 286

the incarnation as, **VIII** 198

and inspiration, **IV** 136

must come afresh to each generation, **IV** 135f.

need of, and place of, **IV** 209;
VIII 63, 196f.
to Noah, regarding depth of
Flood waters, **IX** 22
to Noah, regarding extent of the
Flood, **IX** 13, 14, 26, 80
and origin of language, **II** 270
place of, in understanding, **III**
272
and reason, **VII** 29, 34; **VIII** 189
reason for absence of, **VII** 14f.
replaced by reason, **VII** 29
of spiritual truth given to man at
the beginning, **IV** 133
and when effective, **IV** 135
Revival, may be intellectual as well
as spiritual, **I** 252
Revolution of the earth, rate of, **I**
349; **IV** 28; **VIII** 39
Reward(s)
basis of, **VI** 165ff.
intention as basis of, **III** 193
vs. punishment, **III** 131f.
and punishment, basis for, **III**
92, 192f.; **VI** 165ff.
Rhesus monkeys
brain preparation of, reveals con-
tinued EEG tracing, **VIII** 76
territories of, **IV** 299
Rhind Papyrus, **I** 34, 293
Rhodesian Man, **I** 127, 136; **II** 42,
52, 197, 205 (fig. 6); **IV** 165; **V** 24
absence of dental caries in? **III** 48
Ribonucleic acid (RNA)
learning and, **III** 251
memory stored in? **III** 251
Righteousness
God's standard of, not acceptable to natural man, **III** 38
man's reaction to the r. of Jesus,
III 43f.
true vs. false, **III** 130
vindicated in the Lord by his ac-
cusers, **V** 159f.
Rig Veda, **I** 152; **II** 78; **IV** 120; **V** 48

Ritual
conservatism of, **II** 176
Peruvian r. for making fire, **I** 183
place of, in worship, **IX** 245
of sharing a meal, **IX** 246
Road building in Central America, **I**
182
Road rollers, **I** 182
Rockets and rocket arrows, **I** 195,
210
Rocking chairs, **I** 199
Rodents, thermoregulation in, **IX**
203
"Rod of Christ." Welsh word for,
III 226
Rod of God, **III** 213ff., 217
Role of the male
among animals, **IV** 290ff.
vs. female, **IV** 294
in human society, **IV** 291f.
in primitive society, **II** 281
reversal of, **IV** 294
Roman(s)
adoption laws, **II** 289
assessment of Britons as slaves!
II 111
attitude towards cast iron, **I** 214
capital punishment, forms of, **V**
379f.
citizenship, **III** 41
civilization on Etruscan base, **I**
198f., 309
deep sense of sin, even among
pagans, **III** 274
education, **VII** 27
entertainment, **VIII** 176f.
"games," in relation to religious
festivals, **VII** 29
gods, less moral than the wor-
shippers, **VII** 29
gods of early R., **IV** 119, 124
origin of the name of their capital
city, **I** 199
rule favored early spread of the
gospel, **I** 239
slaves, numbers of, **VII** 27, 41

suicide rate, **VII** 19, 29
uninventiveness of, **I** 36, 305, 309
world, ideal setting for the N.T.,
 I 239
Roman Daily News, **VII** 27
Roman Catholic Church
 immortality acknowledged by, **V**
 182
 their view of the soul, **V** 288ff.
Romance in marriage, **II** 280, 282
Romantic love, **II** 280, 299
 not the basis of marriage, **II** 282,
 289
Rome, sack of, **VIII** 109
Romulus and Remus, **VII** 207
Rope(s)
 Egyptian, **I** 196
 very large size of native Ameri-
 can r., **I** 182
 piece of charred r., found in
 Jericho, **VII** 191
Rorschach tests, **III** 152
 John, Peter, Thomas and, **III**
 178

Rotary querns, **I** 215, 305
Rotifers, behavior of, **III** 330f.
Round worms, survive deep freezing, **VIII** 74
Royal Society, founding members
 of, **VIII** 122f.
Royalty and the acceptibility of incest, **VI** 224
Rubber
 development of, by American
 Indians, **I** 166
 products, made by American Indians, **I** 178f.
 solid and hollow r. balls, **I** 178
Rudder, stern-post, **I** 203
"Rule of law." evidence of; in the
 universe, **VIII** 41f.
Rupture of the heart, **V** 296, 302ff.,
 307ff.
 sudden emotion and, **V** 307
Russia(n)
 national character, **III** 239
 origin of name? **I** 90
 railway ticket, **V** 356

S

Sabbath day, healings performed
 on, **VIII** 88
Saber-toothed tiger **II** 213, 214 (ill.)
Sacrifice(s). *See also under* Substitutionary death, Substitutionary sacrifice.
 common to all religions, **V** 334
 common to human idealism, **V**
 334f.
 death of Jesus Christ as a vicarious, **V** 326f.
 essential for the expression of
 God's love, **I** 230
 kinds of, that man can make, **V**
 372ff.

the Lord's, and presentation of
 His blood, **V** 357ff.
the Lord's, differs from all others,
 V 328f., 373
substitutionary nature of, proven
 by the resurrection, **V** 348
why made to demons, **IV** 135
Safety pins, invention of, **I** 204
Sagittal crest, **II** 201, 204
Sahara desert, caused by man? **IX**
 117f.
Saint(s), the making of, **III** 196ff.,
 215
 place of bodily affliction in, **III**
 233

self-imposed sanctions are necessary for, **III** 205
St. Bernard and Chihuahua cross, **IV** 253
Salamanders, **VIII** 234
Salisbury Cathedral, endangered by vibration, **VII** 190
Salmon, death of, **V** 136f.
Salt
　accumulations of, in the Dead Sea, **VII** 175
　Christians as, **II** 141; **III** 184
　s. water as a barrier to the spread of animals, **IX** 41
Saltations, **IV** 49, 61, 175
Salutations, forms of, **II** 307
Salvation
　gift of God, **VI** 158
　logic of, **III** 284-313
　plan of, simply stated, **III** 307, 310, 311
　steps in, **VI** 156
　of the whole man (body and spirit), **III** 303-309
Samaritan Pentateuch, Chronology of; in Genesis, **V** 33
Samoa(ns), **II** 299, 306
　Utopia, **VIII** 176
　live in chronic state of war, **III** 207; **IX** 132
　tradition of creation, **V** 97
Samson and the Nazirite vow, **V** 104ff.
Sandpaper, invention of, **I** 186
Sanitation
　ancient, **II** 95f.
　sewage disposal systems, **I** 189, 326, 333; **II** 95
　soap, **I** 201
　street drains, **I** 197 (fig. 11)
　tiled baths, **I** 189
　toilet paper, **I** 333
　toilet seats, **I** 333
Sanskrit, **VI** 181
Santal tradition of creation and the Fall, **V** 94

Sarah
　as Abraham's "princess," **VII** 150ff.
　as Abraham's "sister," **VII** 154f.
　change of name, **VII** 156, 242
　consequences of her barrenness, **VII** 171ff.
　hazards to, in Egypt, **VII** 157
　as Iscah, **VII** 155, 241
　as one of Abraham's three wives, **I** 15; **VII** 98, 233
Sarah, the chimpanzee, **IV** 274f.
Sarai as a title, **II** 317
Sargon, Annals of, **I** 20
Saros, values of the, **V** 51ff., 71; **VII** 204
Satan, **VI** 128; **VII** 300
　area of operation, **VIII** 89
　and the destruction of the body, **VII** 56
　as the dragon of paganism, **VI** 113
　in Eden, **V** 147f.
　kingdom of, **III** 55
　limitations of his control over animals, **III** 96, 111
Satisfaction, conditions required for, **III** 207
Saturnalia, **I** 111
Saul, the king and the apostle compared, **III** 199
"Savage of Aveyron," **II** 261
Savagery
　among animals, **IV** 197f.
　in our culture, **II** 109
　of the White Man, **II** 155f.
"Savagery-barbarism-civilization," concept of, **II** 71f.
Saxons, **I** 85-88
　use of red ochre, **II** 54
Saws with glass-cutting edges, **I** 185
Scales into feathers? **IV** 49, 69; **VIII** 160 (fn. 129)
Scarabs, a means of dating, **VII** 189
Schizophrenia, **II** 265; **III** 164
　increasing incidence of, **VIII** 179

Scholarship. *See also under* Christian scholarship.
  Christian s. defined, **IX** 292
  general rules regarding, **IX** 289, 291
  social and moral responsibility of, **IX** 290
  specifically Christian, **IX** 289ff.
Scholars replace prophets, **VII** 29
Science
  absence of, in China, **I** 286; in Egypt, **I** 315; in Sumeria, **I** 315
  aim of, to reduce man to pure mechanism, **III** 255
  the "as-if-ness" of its explanations, **VIII** 170
  atheism demanded by? **VIII** 93
  automatically eliminates evidence of the Creator, **VIII** 55f.
  basic credo of, **III** 13; **VIII** 63
  basic premises of, held by faith, **VIII** 200f.
  benefits of, in doubt, **VIII** 171
  bias necessary in, **IV** 143
  vs. common sense, **VIII** 158
  a comparative latecomer, **I** 315ff.
  concept of God unmanageable in, **IV** 36
  as a contribution of Japheth and Ham together, **I** 315ff., 328
  creation concept rejected by, **IV** 35f.
  and the detection of divine intervention, **VIII** 62ff.
  determinism essential to philosophy of, **VIII** 86f., 91f., 206f.
  detrimental effects of bias upon, **II** 67
  not directed to practical ends, **I** 297
  a disadvantage to society? **VIII** 140
  disregard leads to denial, **VIII** 127, 205, 214

  dogma in modern, **II** 75; **IV** 25, 170, 179
  doubt essential to, **VII** 24
  early confidence regarding fruits of, **VIII** 130
  emergence of, causes of, **I** 297f.
  emergence of, time of, **I** 264, 296, 315
  error, part played by, in the advance of, **VIII** 201 (fn. 196)
  and ESP, **III** 264
  and Faith, Vol. **VIII**
  as a faith, **IV** 172f., 199
  and the Faith: bifurcation between, **VIII** 172
    : growing conflict between, **VIII** 122, 152f., 158, 172
    : nature of the conflict, **VIII** 52-64
  as a form of religion, **VIII** 145 (and fn. 90)
  goal of, is to predict, **VIII** 118, 139
  as "the good life," **VIII** 171, 187 (fn. 185), 209
  harbinger of the millenium, **VIII** 132
  Hindu s., **I** 308
  and human conduct, **VIII** 140, 151
  "implacable offensive" of, **III** 55; **VIII** 52, 65, 135; **IX** 26
  an incomplete World View, **VIII** 91, 214
  and the Jewish community, **I** 303f., 308, 310
  vs. knowledge, **I** 290
  language influences concepts of, **I** 280f., 286
  limitations of, **VIII** 91, 95, 102, 151, 210f.
  vs. magic and religion, **III** 80; **VIII** 106
  as a "me-it" philosophy, **III** 80; **VIII** 106

mechanism, an essential concept in progress of s., **VIII** 63f., 72, 92

mechanism of s., and divine intervention, **VIII** 47-98

and miracle, **II** 66

miracles unnecessary to (Shapley), **VIII** 79

as a modern "inquisition," **II** 75; **IV** 25; **VIII** 160, 166

moral implications of, **VIII** 187 (fn. 185)

and music, **III** 54

nonutilitarian, **I** 297

objectivity vs. prejudice in, **IV** 38

omnicompetence of, **IV** 144; **VIII** 127f.

origins of, **VII** 31

partial view of reality, **VIII** 94, 127, 128

philosophy and technology combined produce s., **I** 32, 37, 48, 70f., 252, 263f., 287 (fn. 106), 303-319; **II** 139; **VII** 31

philosophy of, materialistic, **I** 220f.

predictive value of, **VII** 118; **VIII** 139

without presuppositions? **VIII** 210

pretended infallibility of, **VIII** 128

Puritan influence on, **I** 301f.

purpose excluded from, **I** 353ff.; **IV** 23, 34, 73, 151f.; **VIII** 125f., 127

by rejecting revelation, s. gives a limited view of earth's history, **I** 348

a search for error, **II** 25; **IV** 143

the search for purposes discouraged by, **VIII** 52, 65, 135

specialization in s. results in meaninglessness, **VIII** 190f.

study of, in relation to the search for meaning, **I** 121f.

"stultifies life" (Marx), **VIII** 171

and the supernatural, **VIII** 91, 208 (fn. 204)

vs. technology, **I** 11f., 32, 286f., 298f., 302, 318

teleology rejected by, **IV** 23; **VIII** 222

and theology, **I** 297, 303-319

and "truth," s. the only avenue to? **VIII** 164

and values, **VIII** 210, 211

Scientific

bias, and its baneful effects on publishing, **III** 264

determinism and divine intervention, **VIII** 47-98

discovery, nature of, **VIII** 105 (fn. 2)

discovery, vs. invention, **I** 286f.

hypotheses depend on "telling lies," **I** 272

instruments, limitations of, **VIII** 56, 63

instruments, self-validating by design, **VIII** 56, 63, 205, 206

knowledge, always fragmentary, **VIII** 172

knowledge, incomplete apart from revelation, **IV** 14, 20, 63, 210

materialism, **IV** 24

objectivity not as rigid as claimed, **IV** 24, 38, 143f., 205; **VIII** 95

prediction, **VII** 118; **VIII** 139

questions not the most important ones, **VIII** 40

theory only overthrown by a better theory, **VIII** 167

"understanding" in terms of as-if-ism, **VIII** 72, 170

World View, incompletness of, **VIII** 209

Scientific method

"convictions" frowned upon, **VIII** 213, 214

designated limitations of, **VIII** 94, 95, 98, 206, 207, 209

emergence of, **I** 37, 315

failure of, in social sciences, **III** 10; **VIII** 95, 139 (fn. 76), 211

the "implacable offensive" of, **III** 55; **VIII** 52, 65, 135; **IX** 26

limitations of, **III** 262

objectivity limits its range, **VIII** 95

as a prejudiced filter, **IV** 143

provides only deterministic answers, **VIII** 205, 206

a search for error, **II** 25 (fn. 29); **IV** 143

successful in dealing with nature but not with man, **III** 10

Scientist(s)

bigotry and conceit among, **VIII** 104f. (fn. 1)

credulity of, **VIII** 80

moral responsibility of, **IX** 291f.

pecking order among, **VIII** 104 (fn. 1)

and pride, **I** 302

resistant to innovation, **VIII** 157

social responsibility of, **VIII** 139 (fn. 76), 140; **IX** 291f.

undue conservatism of, **VIII** 157

Screw principle, invention of, **I** 206

Scripture(s). *See also under* Bible.

animation in the Psalms, **II** 171 **III** 85

anticipates scientific findings, **VIII** 31

care taken by the scribes, **III** 284

chronology of. *See under* Chronology.

confirmed by archaeology, **VII** 145-214

contradictions, four types of, **VII** 68

contradictions, true method of resolving, **VII** 97f.

contradictions in, apparent only, **V** 224, 228f.; **VII** 67-106

contradictory genealogies in, **VII** 254

cultural behavior illuminating incidents in s., **II** 274-331

drama in, **V** 146-151; 340

Genesis as the original account of the Flood, **IX** 83

Genesis not allegory, **V** 367

grounds for confidence in, **VI** 220f.

historicity of, **VI** 194f., 204-206, 239

historicity of the Flood account in, **IX** 75

inspiration of, evidence for, **III** 90

inspiration of, nature of, **VII** 91f.

and its implications, **I** 53f.

its inner consistency, **III** 132

language of the Gospels, **VII** 73f.

language specific for O.T. and N.T., **I** 265

literal interpretation of, **VI** 219, 221

memorization of, its value, **IV** 136

methods of interpretation of, **III** 95

multiple authorship of? **VI** 52f.

names, meaning and importance of, **IX** 181-192

N.T. elucidates the O.T., **V** 224

numbers. *See under* Numbers.

poetry in, **VII** 276; **VIII** 204

its precision in its use of terms, **III** 285

recognition in S. of man's three-dimensional needs, **I** 15ff., 253, 260f.

relation of Flood story to pagan traditions, **IX** 29, 73, 81, 82, 89, 90

significance of the number 40 in, **VII** 60

supernatural power of, to convince its critics, **V** 297

symbols used consistently throughout, **VI** 53f.

to be taken seriously, **I** 239; **V** 151, 297, 361; **VII** 220, 234, 268

as the touchstone of truth, **II** 61

translation, problems of, **VII** 73f., 76

trilogies in, **I** 15-24, 260; **VII** 98f.

universality of appeal to all ages, **VII** 7

verbal inspiration of, **VII** 78

Sculpture, **I** 196

Scurvy, **I** 331

Scythians, **VII** 167

Seal cylinders of the Tree of Life, **V** 97

Sea otter, **IV** 264

Season(s)

as a check on disease, **I** 350; **VIII** 39; **IX** 142

significance of, **IV** 28f.; **IX** 141

variation of, beneficial to health, **I** 350; **IX** 142

Second Adam, the summation of man in, **III** 185ff. *See also under* Adam, First and Last.

Second Coming of Christ, **I** 366. *See also under* Return of Christ.

imminence of? **VII** 63

in relation to time, **VI** 42

Secular. *See under* Civil authority.

Sedan chair, **I** 201

Seed, **V** 352

immortality of woman's s., **V** 89, 139, 190

Jesus Christ as the, **III** 168ff., 172ff.

Luther on the male seed and original sin, **III** 290

of the man, **V** 87, 156f., 188f. *See also under* Sperm.

the Promised S., **II** 309f.; **V** 157, 246f.; **VII** 227f., 237f.

separation of the two s. (male and

female), **I** 235; **V** 89, 113, 139, 192

which is Christ introduced into the new man, **III** 168f.; **V** 208, 363ff.

of the woman, **I** 234; **V** 86, 91f., 154ff., 188f., 190; **VII** 268. *See also* Ovum.

of the woman and Satan, **II** 309ff.; **III** 287

of the woman and the man, **III** 287; **V** 86f., 156

Sefer Hazzohar, **VI** 107

Seismology, use of animals for prediction, **IX** 90

Selection, **I** 346f.; **IV** 64ff.; **V** 127. *See also under* Artificial Selection, Natural Selection, Supernatural Selection.

Selective breeding, limits of, **I** 346 (fn. 262)

Self, a community of selves, **V** 386

Self-awareness

emergence of, in man, **III** 106, 259; **IV** 276

of a species, **V** 387

Self-confidence vs. self-reliance, **III** 220

Self-consciousness, **I** 241, 243; **III** 326f.

of cell-life? **III** 181; **V** 385

vs. consciousness, **III** 105f., 182f., 259; **VIII** 42, 92

as a criterion of humanness, **III** 105

the evolution of? **III** 259, 324; **VIII** 85, 136, 142

and language, **II** 254; **IV** 276

in man, **II** 255; **III** 105, 260; **VIII** 42, 87

mystery of, **V** 386

nature of, **III** 182, 260

origin of, **III** 259, 260, 262f., 325, 335; **VIII** 136f., 141

problems regarding, **V** 385

uniquely human, **III** 105

Self-discipline and scholarship, **III** 205

Selfishness
civilization breeds "enlightened" s., **III** 19
parades as generosity, **III** 28f.

Self-reformation, futility of, **III** 159, 163, 170

Self-reliance, when appropriate for a Christian, **III** 219ff.

Semang (Malay), **IX** 133

Semites (Semitic), Vol. **I**; **VI** 179
blessing of, **I** 27f., 338
as carriers, not inventors, **I** 36f., 303, 306f.
contribution of, defined, **I** 29f., 263-302
contribution of, to spiritual life, **I** 14, 27, 29f., 41, 47, 49, 247, 251, 257, 259, 261, 263f., 275; **II** 139
descendants of, **I** 113-118
languages, **VI** 189f.
language suited for religious expression, **I** 266f., 276f.
links with Aryan language, **VI** 180, 186
not philosophical, **I** 33, 266, 279, 281, 307
not theological, **I** 37, 252
as the original language, **VI** 192ff., 194, 203ff.
religion defined, **I** 29, 251, 257, 276, 278; **VII** 99
uninventive, **I** 36, 305ff., 308, 313, 316f.
World View, **I** 272, 275

Senescence
and death not necessarily related, **V** 140f., 177
need never have occurred, **V** 168
not observed in fish, **V** 136
probably begins at birth, **V** 133

Senile decay, elimination of, **V** 16

Senility, **V** 22

Sennacherib, translation of the name from cuneiform, **VI** 105

Septuagint, **V** 320, 324; **VII** 30
chronology of, **V** 33f.
rendering of Genesis 1:2, **VI** 88
word *foundation* in, **VI** 117f.

Serabit Temple, **VII** 183

Serengeti National Park, **III** 73

Serpent in Eden, **V** 147f.

Servant(s)
all men as s. of God, **IX** 191
emphasized in Mark's Gospel, **VII** 100f.
vs. friend relationship, **III** 93; **VI** 164; **IX** 191
unbelievers as s. of God, **VI** 135-140

"Servant of servants," meaning of the phrase, **I** 16f., 26f., 149, 156; **VII** 232f.

Servo-mechanisms, **VIII** 54, 63

Sewers, early, **I** 195 (fig. 11), 196; **II** 95

Sewing machines, **I** 156

Sex
vs. gender, **V** 397
hormonal control of, **IV** 304ff.
life of men vs. animals, **IV** 303ff.
perverted only in man, **IV** 308
in primitive cultures, **II** 280
roles of primitive society, **IV** 294
and social organization, in man and animals, **IV** 302f.
and temperament, **III** 148; **IV** 294; **V** 155

Sex cells
immortality of, **V** 89
origin of, **V** 89

Sex chromosomes, **V** 91

Sexual activity in man vs. animals, **IV** 303f.

Sexual reproduction and death, **V** 128

Sexual sweating, **IX** 198

Seymouria, **IV** 43

Shaman, sweating of blood by, **V** 311; **IX** 217
Shambles, the, **VII** 55
Shangri-la, not always a happy place, **III** 207, 208; **VIII** 176; **IX** 131f.
Sheep
in early Egypt, **VII** 158
and wolves, **III** 66
Shekinah, the Lord as the, **V** 246
Shem, Descendants of, **I** 113-118. *See also under* Semites.
Shem, Ham and Japeth. *See under* Three sons of Noah, and each name.
She'ol, **V** 280
Shepherd Kings, **I** 104; **VII** 159, 178
Ships. *See also under* Boats.
compartmentalized, **I** 326
iron clads (early), **I** 203
Ship's log kept by Noah, **IX** 26, 79, 82
Shipton's prophetic poem, **VII** 112
Shivering, **IV** 258f.
Short term memory (STM), **III** 254
Shrew
ground and tree, **IV** 44
significance of size of, **IV** 77, 200
Shrimp, **IV** 196
Shroud, history of the, **V** 337 (and fn. 2)
Sialk
early settlement of, **II** 96; **V** 65
use of metals at, **I** 193
Siberia
animal cemeteries in, **IV** 97f.
early high civilization in, **II** 116 (fn. 123)
Sibling relationships, personality development and, **IV** 288f.
Sibylline Books, **VII** 30
Sickness
caused by a wrong name, **II** 265, 298; **III** 139f., 164; **IX** 170
naming of, first step in its control, **IX** 175

Sidon, meaning of the name, **VII** 229
Sign(s)
s. language, use of, **II** 253
s. language, use of with animals, **IV** 269, 272, 275, 318
vs. symbols, **II** 254ff.
Signs, seeking of; in a prayer, **IX** 277
Signs and wonders
in the apostolic age, **VII** 48, 49
and covenant relationship with Israel, **VII** 16, 35f., 38, 41, 46f., 50, 60, 63
as credentials of divine commission, **VII** 39
Gentile indifference to, **VII** 16, 61
have ceased? **VII** 51, 61f.
in Paul's ministry, **VII** 52, 56f.
purposes of, strictly vis-a-vis Israel, **VII** 51ff.
reappearance of, in modern times, **VII** 62, 63
significance of, **VII** 14f., 38f., 52, 57
significance of, in early Gentile conversions, **VII** 53
temporary cessation of, reasons for, **VII** 35, 51ff.
Silence(s) of God, **VII** 11-63
by absence of miracle, judgment, and revelation, **VII** 14
broken, by the Incarnation, **VII** 36ff.
in the intertestamental period, **I** 265; **VII** 18-35; **VIII** 196
methods of rationalizing, **VII** 57f.
since apostolic times, **VII** 47-63
types of divine s., **VII** 7, 13, 14, 15f.
Silk, **I** 180f., 207f.
Silk screen, **I** 181
Silver, **II** 93
Simian shelf, **II** 207f.; **IV** 164, 244
Similarity vs. relationship, **II** 12, 19f.; **IV** 140-170

Simon of Cyrene, **I** 23
Simplicity
  of design, not due to lack of in-
    telligence, **II** 110
  virtue of, in technology, **II** 152
Sin, brother of Heth, **I** 105
Sin, moon-god
  prayer of Nabonidus to, **VII** 152
  temple of, **VII** 151f.
SIN. *See also under* Original sin.
  as an acquired character in-
    herited, **III** 289f., 292f., 295,
    302; **IV** 210f.; **V** 188
  awareness of, in earlier genera-
    tions, **V** 96
  Barth on, **III** 34, 112, 158
  biasing effect of, **III** 40
  cleansing of, what it does not
    mean, **III** 306f.
  consequences of ignoring fact of,
    III 162
  covered, not forgiven, **III** 163
  definitions of, **III** 12, 161f., 273f.
  as "dirt" in the mechanism of na-
    ture, **VIII** 57, 60, 63
  as a disease, **III** 287, 289, 296,
    305
  Dostoyevsky on, **III** 35f., 158
  education, its lack as cause of, **III**
    12, 161f., 273f.
  effects of, on the natural order,
    VIII 58, 88, 95; **IX** 115
  eugenicists' view of, **III** 12, 161f.,
    273f.
  vs. evil, **VI** 166f.
  evolutionary definition of, **III** 12,
    161f., 273f.
  and the existence of war, **III** 159
  as a form of "sabotage," **VIII** 60
  Freud's view of, **III** 159
  as ignorance, **III** 12, 17, 29, 161,
    274; **VII** 23, 24
  inherent in man, **III** 131
  as a "lack," **III** 11f., 161f., 273f.
  as malfunction or sickness, **III**
    268

  as "mechanical" failure, **III** 11,
    268f.; **IV** 321
  modern views of, **III** 267
  noetic effects of, **III** 13, 39, 162,
    274; **VIII** 63, 95, 196
  as "normal" human behavior,
    III 158f.
  as original sin, **III** 290
  penalty of, physical death, **III**
    287f., 289; **IX** 113
  positive nature of, **III** 10ff., 29,
    162, 273f.
  as the root of many evils, but not
    all, **IX** 163
  as the root of sins, **III** 285
  sense of, real among primitives
    and pagans, **III** 274f.
  sense of guilt vs. sense of sin, **III**
    267ff., 273; **IV** 135
  suicidal nature of, **III** 163, 296;
    IV 321
  uniquely human, **V** 368
  war the ultimate expression of,
    III 24, 159
  where to be observed in nature,
    VIII 58, 88, 95
  will affected by, **III** 30-44, 92,
    270
SIN and SINS, **III** 284-313, esp.
  312, 313
Sinanthropus, **I** 127; **II** 27, 204, 205
  (fig. 6), 221; **IV** 45, 162f., 225; **V**
  58
  age at death, **V** 59
  cranial capacity of, **IV** 225
  flint weapons of, **II** 113
Singhalese, Brother-sister marriages among, **VI** 224
Singphos of Burma, Flood tradition
  of, **IX** 73
Sin(s). *See also under* SIN.
  Barth on, **III** 34, 112, 158
  blotting out of, **III** 240, 277, 279,
    280
  break fellowship with God, **III**
    276, 279

caused by restraints? **III** 35
of David and of Ahab, **III** 31f.,
  184, 185; **V** 388, 389
definitions of, **III** 12, 161f., 273f.
Dostoyevsky on, **III** 35, 36, 158
of Eve vs. Adam, **V** 147f.
as an expression of man's freedom, **III** 35
forgiven and forgotten, **III** 239f.,
  277, 281
forgiveness, **III** 238ff., 304f.
forgiveness of our hidden s., **III**
  279
Greek definition of, **III** 12, 29,
  162; **VII** 24
and idleness, **III** 132
of ignorance, **III** 17, 29
Lamont's definition of, **III** 18
Liberal definition of, **III** 18
New Testament designed for the
  "forgetting of" sins, **III** 239
not forgiven under Old Covenant, **III** 239
opportunity and, **III** 31f., 185,
  343; **V** 389
penalty of, applied over several
  generations, **I** 145
symptoms vs. disease, **III** 129
victory over? **III** 37
Sinlessness
  of the believer? **III** 177f., 189f.; **V**
    365
  vs. innocence, **V** 159
Sister-brother relationship, special
  nature of, **VII** 157
Sister-brother marriages, **VI** 222-
  237
Sisters, marriage of; to one man, **II**
  283, 293, 325
Size
  of animals: factors governing, **IV**
    241; **V** 132
    :food intake in relation to, **IV**
      200f.;
    :and temperature mainte-
      nance, **IV** 200f.

civilization and the effect of
  man's s. upon, **VIII** 41
of the earth, in relation to the
  universe, **VIII** 39
of the earth, its importance, **I**
  348; **VIII** 38f.
importance of s., **IV** 241; **V** 132
of man, **IV** 241f.; **VIII** 39f.
mind, without "size," **III** 261,
  328, 331
in relation to time, **IV** 32; **VI** 25,
  32
relativity of, **VI** 25
of the shrew, **IV** 77, 200
of the universe, and man's in-
  significance, **I** 219
Skepticism
  answered by logic, ineffective,
    VII 67
  as faulty vision, **VII** 95
  in Greek philosophy, **VII** 25
Skin
  color, **I** 148, 151f.
  color and beauty, **IX** 239, 242
  grafts in man vs. animals, **IV** 302
  human, fitness of, **VIII** 148 (fn.
    94)
  human vs. animal, **III** 120; **IV**
    313
  insulating value of, **IV** 258
  need for suturing s., in man vs.
    animals, **I** 342; **IV** 312f.
  and wounds, healing of in ani-
    mals, **IV** 313
Skuhl Man, **II** 50, 223; **IV** 289
Skull(s). *See also under* Cranium.
  ancient moderns, discovery of, **II**
    194ff.
  ballooning of, **II** 206, 224
  chronological sequences of, and
    morphology, **II** 194
  facial reconstructions on, of
    doubtful value, **II** 162, 234ff.
  influence of food and environ-
    ment on, **II** 200f.

influence of migration on, **II** 210f.

influence of soil on, **II** 202

jaw mechanism of, **II** 201

modern types found early, **II** 195, 199, 228

modifications of, **IV** 160ff.

morphology of, influenced by diet, **II** 200ff.

plasticity of, **II** 212

supposed evolution of the human s., **II** 194-224

sutures obliterated by age? **II** 39; **V** 57

thickening of cranial vault, **II** 27, 206f.

Skull form(s)

and disease, **II** 185

modified by old age, **II** 39

various factors modifying, **II** 17f., 183f.; **IV** 160f., 168

Skunks, **III** 66

Slave(s)

adoption of, **II** 289

as educators in Greco-Roman world, **VII** 27

enormous numbers of, in Greco-Roman world, **VII** 27

labor of, prevents industrial development, **I** 298f.

position of, in Rome, **III** 41

Slavery

important to the spread of culture, **VII** 27

to obtain a wife, **II** 296

Sleep, palmar sweating declines during, **IX** 200

Sleeves, Chinese design of; for cold weather, **I** 213

Slime-molds, **VIII** 74

Smell. *See also under* Odor, Olfactory sense.

expressed in terms of wave length, **III** 54

recall of, under ferradic stimulation, **III** 244

Smith, meaning of the word, **II** **VII** 198

Snake bite, protection against; African natives, **I** 330

Snow goggles, Eskimo, **I** 157, 162; **1** 162

Soap

invention of, **I** 201

s. substitute, from Yucca tree, **I** 163

Social

behavior, endangering survival, **III** 117; **IV** 295f.

environment and crime, **III** 31f.

order, contributes to spiritual well-being, **IX** 143

organization, its determinants in man vs. animals, **IV** 281, 305f.

organization often complex among primitives, **I** 175; **II** 287

restraint, value of in Christian life, **III** 215

security, good or evil, **IX** 131

status: achieved by marriage, **II** 283

: of slave educators, in classical world, **VII** 27

Social life

of animals, **III** 23, 88

of animals vs. culture of man, **IV** 292

of man: causes of the modern fragmentation of the, **VIII** 177f.

: and how recognition achieved among primitives, **III** 28

: in three dimensions, **I** 248ff.

Social sciences, scientific method not suited to, **III** 10; **VIII** 95, 139 (fn. 76), 211. *See also under* Sociology.

Society

ant vs. human, **III** 60, 118; **IV** 249, 263, 292

ner-sister marriages, why orbidden by, **VI** 224
ring for the widow in primitive s., **II** 283, 302
vs. culture, **IV** 292
enlightened selfishness encouraged by modern s., **III** 18
evolutionary influence on Western s., **III** 275; **IV** 178
human s. as Leviathan, **V** 388
human vs. animal, **IV** 220, 281f.
lack of purpose, paralyzing modern s., **VIII** 149
modern s., atheistic? **III** 274ff.
omnipotence of God in, **VI** 130-143
as an organism, **III** 340
practical atheism in Western s., **III** 275
role of male in, **IV** 291
science, a disadvantage to s.? **IV** 86; **VIII** 140
sex behavior in human vs. animal s., **IV** 305
sociological vs. biological, **IV** 281
three-dimensional nature of, **I** 250, 252f.
violence in, **III** 267
Sociology
definition of sin by, **III** 12, 162, 274
developed by Australian aborigines, **I** 175
faulty premises of, **III** 10f., 162
and native concepts, **I** 173f., 175; **II** 287
survival concept and, **IV** 178
unrealism of, **III** 281
Socratic method, **VII** 22
Sodom and Gomorrah
archaeological expeditions, **VII** 174f.
changed ecology of the area, **VII** 173
destruction of, **VII** 173, 174
similar event in Phrygia, **VII** 176

in the Table of Nations (Gen. 10), **I** 77f.
Soil
erosion, **IX** 117
first appearance of, **I** 357
generation of, **IV** 39
influence of, on morphology, **IV** 159
Solar radiation, **IV** 41
Soldering, **I** 322
Solitary confinement, effects of, **III** 211
Solitude, **III** 211
Solo Man, **I** 127; **II** 52; **IV** 225
Somatic cells
mortality of, **V** 140
origin of, **V** 184
Soma tree, **V** 100
Son
cognate words for, in antiquity, **VII** 208f.
rules governing legal status of a, **VII** 263
use of term, in Hebrew genealogies, **I** 67f.; **VII** 260f.
Sonia Shankman Orthogenic School, **IX** 167
Son of man, a title of Jesus Christ, **V** 393; **VII** 39, 252
"Son of man" in the Book of Enoch, **V** 98
Sonship
by adoption, **II** 278, 289f., 318, 331
claimed by the Lord to the Father in very personal terms, **VII** 40
of the Lord, when was this initiated? **V** 199f., 286f.
spiritually created, **III** 102f.
two conditions for legal status of adoptees, **II** 329
Sophistication, detrimental to spiritual perceptions, **IV** 133
Sophistry, **VII** 22
Sossos, **V** 55

Soul, the, **V** 259-291
  of Adam, **III** 144; **V** 194
  of animals, **V** 262, 270; **VII** 307
  and the blood, **V** 273
  as body-spirit interaction, **III**
    303; **V** 265, 268f.; **VIII** 81
  and the central nervous system,
    V 271f.
  definition of, **V** 261ff., 280f.
  as electro-chemical action sim-
    ply, **VIII** 68
  emergence of, **V** 268-274
  fate of, in death, **V** 275
  Greek and Hebrew view of, con-
    trasted, **I** 266f.
  identified with the name, **II** 265;
    III 137, 139; **IX** 169, 171
  "informs" the body, **V** 290
  of Jesus Christ, **V** 282-285
  nature of, **III** 138f.; **V** 261ff.
  in the newborn, **V** 279
  origin of, primitive view, **III**
    138f.
  vs. personality, **V** 288
  posture and the, **IV** 245f.
  and reductionism, **III** 140
  relation of, to spirit, **V** 194f.
  as a "resultant," **V** 268f.
  Roman Catholic view of, **V** 288-
    291
  and the senses, **V** 271
  suffering as "education" of, **IX**
    111f.
  time of admission of, **III** 140,
    144; **V** 173, 193ff., 196, 198
Soul life
  of cells, **III** 324
  of plants, **III** 69, 335
Sovereignty of God, **III** 218f.; **VI**
  119-174
  challenged by the Black Plague,
    VIII 120
  on history, **VIII** 109
Space
  curvature of, **VIII** 30f.
  nature of, considered, **VIII** 30f.

problems of, in heaven, **VIII**
  111f.
  and time, **VI** 11ff., 19, 32f.
Space-time relationships. *See under*
  Relativity.
Sparta, **VII** 21
Spartoli Tablets, **VII** 167, 168
Speaking in tongues, **VII** 52, 62f.
Spearheads made from glass, **II**
  150f.
Spearman Rank Order Formula, **V**
  42
Specialization
  beginning of, **VIII** 121
  effect of, **VIII** 181
  price of, **VIII** 168f., 172, 185, 190
  as a step toward meaningless-
    ness, **VIII** 191
  technical importance of, **II** 152
Speciation, **VI** 81f.
  competition not a contributing
    factor, **IV** 187ff.
  by geographic isolation, **IV** 61;
    VIII 163, 234, 235
  intra-specific competition? **IV**
    183ff., 186
  new environments and, **IV** 66f.
  relation of DNA to, **VIII** 50
  supposed example of, **VIII** 162f.
Species
  appear in orderly succession in
    creation, **I** 357
  as a "body," **III** 317
  concept of, applied to the Body of
    Adam and of Christ, **V** 394
  consciousness of, in Adam and in
    Christ, **III** 181ff.
  cradle of, in Asia Minor? **II** 41,
    55f.
  creation of, **IV** 13
  death allows expression of varia-
    bility in a, **V** 128
  diversification of, in a new envi-
    ronment, **II** 43
  of *Homo sapiens*, two, **III** 316-350,
    esp. 340ff.; **IV** 210

as an interbreeding community, **V** 394

a new "definition" of, **III** 316

a new s. of *Homo sapiens* formed by the Fall (Lewis), **III** 338; **IV** 210

number of, in an animal community, **IV** 255

preserved by nuclear genes, **VIII** 224

as a psychic entity, **III** 142, 263, 316f., 337, 345

requirements for the survival of a, **III** 347f.

self-awareness of, **III** 387

single mindedness of, **III** 337

struggle between vs. within species, **IV** 183, 322

variability, limits within a, **I** 346 (fn. 1)

vs. variety, **IV** 77

viability of, basic requirements for, **III** 347f.

wide variability within a, **III** 20ff., 27

Species-specific psyche, **III** 142, 263, 316f., 337, 345

Spectacles, invention of, **I** 204

Speech, **II** 249-271; **IV** 266ff. *See also under* Language.

acquisition of, **II** 250

birds and, **II** 263; **IV** 277

the brain and, **IV** 262f.

of chimpanzees, **IV** 269ff.

diversification of s., advantageous, **I** 255

and emotional cries, **IV** 272

and erect posture, **IV** 243, 277, 287

and humanness, **IV** 216

importance of, to man, **II** 249ff.

jaw and, **IV** 268f.

of man vs. animal, **II** 255 (fn. 16), 257f., 262

muscles involved in, **II** 257, 262; **IV** 268f., 275

organs of, **IV** 268f., 275

origin of, **II** 250; **III** 117

power of, in fossil man? **IV** 267

sign language and, **IV** 269ff.

slowing of, at high altitudes, **VI** 23

taught to blind deaf-mutes, **II** 263

uniquely human, **III** 116, 117; **IV** 266f.

vs. vocalization, **II** 263; **IV** 244f.

who taught Adam? **II** 249-271

Speed of light, **VI** 14f.

Sperm

cytoplasm of, **V** 189f.; **VIII** 229

not immortal, **V** 189

original sin conveyed by, **III** 290 (Luther); **V** 156, 189f.

primitive view of its significance, **II** 290f.

Spermatogenesis, **V** 189

Sphinx, inscription found on, **VII** 186

Spinal column, human vs. animal, **IV** 218, 231, 236, 238 (ill.), 287

Spinal consciousness, **III** 329

Spiny Anteater, **IV** 44

Spirit. *See also under* Soul.

in animals, **V** 197f., 266, 272

and body interactionism, **III** 303; **V** 161, 261-267; **VIII** 81

body without s., a corpse, **V** 273

and breath, **V** 198, 262

departure of, in death, **V** 264f.

and dichotomy of man, **VIII** 80f. *See also under* Dichotomy.

dulled by the civilizing process, **IX** 133

and the emotions, **V** 271

the father as originator of (primitive view), **II** 291

given at the drawing of the first breath, **V** 194, 263, 276, 277

in man, list of verses regarding, **III** 303; **V** 266

of man vs. animal, **VIII** 80f.

relation of, to the soul, **V** 194f., 268ff.

vs. the soul, **V** 271f.

Spirit, as ultimate reality, **III** 261, 326f., 333; **VIII** 22f.

Spiritual

death vs. physical death, **IV** 321

history of Israel symbolized by olive tree, **VI** 66-69

vs. intellectual life, **I** 246

vs. mental life, **I** 246 (fn. 30)

nature of matter, **III** 256, 261, 322f.; **VIII** 23

nature of the physical world, **III** 318

pride, **III** 197, 216, 219, 222; **IX** 275, 286

vs. religious life, **I** 246 (fn. 30)

truth, culture hostile to, **IV** 133

understanding, new birth necessary to, **III** 55

Split-personality, a case of, **III** 167; **IX** 187

"Sponges" used by chimpanzees, **IV** 264

Sports, violence in, **VIII** 176f.

Spray painting by primitives, **I** 203

Squirrels, **III** 52

Staff and rod of God, **III** 217

Stalagmites, rapid growth of, **II** 34

"Standing" vs. "state," **III** 133

Star(s)

and the concept of an expanding universe, **VIII** 18f.

numbers of, **VIII** 32f.

sun as an "insignificant" s., **VIII** 33

Starvation, effect of, on animal form (aphids), **III** 63

Statuary in churches, **IX** 239

Stature. *See also under* Giants, Pygmies, Environment, Size.

influence of temperature on, **VIII** 245

polar bears, limb proportions of, **VIII** 245

pumas, limb proportions of, **VIII** 245

Status, achievement of, in primitive society, **II** 280; **III** 28

Steady State theory (Hoyle), **VIII** 25f., 135

Steam engines, efficiency of, **II** 148; **IX** 204

Steel, development of, **I** 214, 321

Steinheim Man, **II** 195

Stereoscopic vision, **VII** 90

in dogs, **VII** 91

vs. monoscopic, **VII** 88ff.

and opposable thumbs, important to culture, **I** 242; **IV** 242f.

and the three Gospels, **VII** 88

Stereotype personality, **III** 143

Stethoscope, Eskimo invention, **I** 161; **II** 161

Stigmata, **IX** 217

Stirrups, **I** 205

Stoat, extent of "territory," **IV** 251

Stoicism, **VII** 19

Stone Age(s). *See also under* Paleolithic.

every baby a Stone Age baby, **II** 109, 166; **III** 31; **VIII** 131 (fn. 54)

conservatism of Stone Age cultures, **II** 102

contemporaneity of, **II** 33, 72, 114

recency of, **II** 72

Stone masonry, early perfection of, **II** 89

Stones of a temple, Christians as, **III** 176

Store cities, building of, **VII** 210

Storms, beneficial, **IX** 141

Stoves, Chinese cast iron, **I** 200

Stratigraphy vs. morphology, **II** 194

Straw, as a binder in bricks, **VII** 211f.

Strength, muscular; of man is small, **IV** 247

Strength in weakness, **III** 219f.

Stress
  and the aging process, **V** 131
  and heart rupture, **V** 309
  value of, in character develop-
    ment, **III** 209f., 216
Structure(s)
  developed in response to need,
    IV 150, 157
  and function, **IV** 145; **VIII** 148
    (fn. 94)
  and survival, **IV** 204f.
  for temporary use in an or-
    ganism, **IV** 79
"Structure" of personality, **III**
  152f., 170f.
  genetically determined, **III** 171
  as "vessel" in N.T., **III** 171
Struggle to survive, **II** 65; **III** 23, 71
  concept encourages violence as a
    philosophy of life, **IV** 170
  fallacy of, **II** 24; **IV** 23, 148f.,
    181ff., 189f., 199
  sociological concept of, **IV** 178
Subconscious, **III** 238-281. *See also
  under* Unconscious.
  offensive content of, cleansed, **III**
    280
"Substance" of the soul in Roman
  Catholic theology, **V** 290
Substitutionary death, **I** 237; **V**
  164f., 191, 294-331, esp. 315ff.,
  348
  examples of human, **V** 372ff.
Substitutionary sacrifice, requirements governing, **V** 191f.
Suckling of infants
  by barren women, **VII** 172
  by males, **V** 155; **VII** 172
Suddenness of God's judgments, **VI**
  67f.; **VII** 49ff., 54ff.
Suffering
  effect of, **III** 203, 211
  of the godly, problem of, **VII** 59
  is it all due to sin? **IX** 111f.
  modes of escape from, **VII** 32f.

in nature, apparent only, **III** 64,
  66f.; **IV** 197f.; **IX** 125ff.
necessary for the education of the
  soul, **IX** 112
for the perfecting of the saints, **IX**
  111
to preserve sympathy, **IX** 112f.
to preserve the world from total
  corruption, **IX** 111
problem of, and God's silence,
  VII 60
problem of undeserved s., and
  Indian philosophy, **VII** 32
Suffering Servant, **VII** 37
Suicidal nature of human behavior,
  III 163, 296; **IV** 321
Suicide, **IV** 296; **VII** 19, 29; **IX** 135
  when Israel committed national
    s., **VII** 44
Suidas, on the saros, **V** 55, 72
Sumatra Flood tradition, **IX** 33
Sumeria(ns), **I** 112
  absence of true science among,
    I 315f.
  accounting practices, **I** 308
  algebra, **I** 187, 327
  astronomy, **I** 191
  banking houses, **I** 192
  as black-headed people, **I** 72,
    151f.; **VI** 202; **VII** 200
  bronze, **I** 188
  and Chinese languages links? **I**
    106; **VI** 186, 210
  drinking straws used by, **I** 200,
    202
  early high civilization of, **II** 92;
    V 64f.
  geometry, **I** 189
  glassworking, **I** 192
  Hamitic, **I** 36
  inventiveness of, **I** 36, 202
  lack of interest in generaliza-
    tions, **I** 290f.
  language links with other na-
    tions, **VI** 186

language of, nonphilosophical, **I** 290f., 314

literature, **I** 193f.

logarithms, **I** 189f., 327

mathematics, **I** 188f., 308, 327

medical practices of, **I** 192f., 331f.

metallurgy, **I** 188

migraine therapy, **I** 332

nonphilosophical, **I** 290, 314f.

nontheological, **I** 291

pottery, **I** 189

relationship to Indus Valley culture, **I** 72

religion of, **IV** 113f.

vocabulary with its proliferation of words, **I** 273

wheels of plywood, **I** 202, 326

word for iron, **II** 312f.; **VII** 227

Summa Theologica, **III** 84

Sun

distance of, from the earth, **VIII** 38

as an "insignificant" star, **VIII** 33

Sunshades, **I** 202

Supercentenarians, **V** 20f.

Supercultural, concept of, **III** 158

Superdense state, theory, **VIII** 20

Superlative, expression of; in Hebrew, **I** 26f., 149; **VII** 232f.

Superman

goal of eugenics, **VIII** 150 (fn. 100)

goal of evolution (Huxley), **VIII** 146

Supernatural and natural, not distinguished by primitives, **II** 170

Supernatural Selection, **I** 346f.; **IV** 18-22, 64-80, 86ff.; **V** 127

Supernatural vs. natural order, science and, **IV** 70; **VIII** 91, 208 (fn. 204)

Supernatural vs. unnatural, **VIII** 88

"Superorganic," concept of (Kroeber), **II** 83 (fn. 47)

Supraorbital ridges, **II** 209

Supreme Being, early belief in, **IV** 113

Surgery, **I** 41, 176f.; 329ff.

of American Indians, **I** 176

amputations, **I** 184

anaesthetics, **I** 176, 184

bladder-stone removal, **I** 329

bone setting, **I** 192

bone transplants, **I** 184

Caesarian, **I** 199, 330

cauterizing, **I** 184

excision, **I** 184

eye operations, **I** 192

operating rooms, preparation of, **I** 184

Peruvian, **I** 183f.

plastic surgery, of the face and artificial noses, **I** 329, 331

primitive, Ackerknecht's bibliography on, **I** 178 (fn. 48)

Sumerian and Babylonian, **I** 192f., 332

suturing method, **I** 178

trephination, **I** 176, 184, 330

tweezers, **I** 178

Survival. *See also under* Margin of survival.

of animals, not dependent on beauty, **IV** 205

conservatism necessary for, among primitives, **II** 169f., 178; **IV** 300; **VI** 230

man unfit for, **IV** 176f.

and structure, **IV** 204f.

Survival of the fittest, **II** 24, 65; **III** 23, 71

tautology of, **IV** 202

Survival of the unfit, **IV** 172-205

Susa

early civilization of, **V** 65

early pottery of, **I** 197

Suspension bridges, early, **I** 211

Sutures (of the skull)
  obliteration of, in fossil man, **V** 59
  rate of closing of, with age, **III** 39, 48; **V** 57
Suturing
  use of ants for, **I** 178
  of wounds, not needed in wild animals, **IV** 312f.
Swanscombe Man, **I** 127; **II** 185, 195; **V** 67
Sweat, **IX** 193-218
  bloody s., **V** 310ff.; **IX** 216ff.
  glands, **IV** 259f., 313f.; **V** 310f.
  high water loss via, **IX** 197
  as part of the curse, **IX** 193- 218
  purest of body fluids, **IX** 197, 211
  and Roman baking! **IX** 135
  themoregulatory, **IX** 129f. *See also under* Thermoregulation.
Sweating, **I** 341; **VIII** 239f.; **IX** 193-218. *See also under* Thermoregulation.
  animal vs. human, **IX** 196-203
  bibliography on, **IX** 218f.
  caused by fabrics, **IX** 213
  cold s., sites of, **IX** 198
  diet and, **IX** 206
  emotional or psychic s., **IX** 197, 207ff.; sites of, **IX** 198
  the Fall and human s., **IX** 129, 204-213
  by the First and the Last Adam, **IX** 216, 217
  on the forehead, **V** 310f.; **IX** 200, 213-217
  gustatory, sites of, **IX** 198
  in man, unfallen? **IX** 211
  in man vs. animals, **I** 342; **III** 120; **IV** 259, 260; **IX** 196f., 201
  mechanism of, **IV** 259f.
  mental and emotional, distinguishable, **IX** 200
  mental s., **IX** 197, 200; sites of, **IX** 198

  odorless character of thermogenic, **IX** 211
  palmar vs. plantar, **IX** 199
  references to, in Scripture, **IX** 213ff.
  in relation to body efficiency, **IV** 311
  sexual, **IX** 198; sites of, **IX** 198
  sympathetic nervous system, **IX** 198f.
  thermal, **IV** 260f., 313f.; **IX** 129f., 197, 200; sites of, **IX** 198
Sweden, high crime rate in, **IX** 131
Swine, **III** 96
Swiss Lake Dwellers, **II** 121
Symbiosis, **III** 70, 73; **IV** 57, 71, 196f.
Symbol(s)
  in animal language, **IV** 272, 275
  of deity, Babylonian, **V** 252f.
  fig tree as s. of Israel's religious history, **VI** 70ff.
  Israel's history portrayed by s., **VI** 52-73
  olive tree as s. of Israel's spiritual history, **VI** 66ff.
  in Scripture used with remarkable consistency, **VI** 53f.
  vs. signs, **II** 254ff.
  used for Christ, **VII** 103; **IX** 243f.
  vine as a s. of Israel's national history, **VI** 60ff.
Sympathy, the need of, **IX** 112f., 158
Synoptic Gospels
  composite account of the Lord's words, **VII** 79f.
  composite portrait of Christ in, **VII** 103f.
  composite record of the inscription on the cross, **VII** 79
  and the Lord's genealogies, **VII** 268f.
  significance of the order of, **I** 16ff.

a three-dimensional picture of Christ, **VII** 88
for whom each was designed, **I** 16ff.; **VII** 97ff., 233f.

Synthesis of thought, Medieval vs. modern, **VIII** 99-216
Syphilis, **I** 331 (fn. 227)
Syria (Tell Halaf), **V** 64

T

Table of Nations, **I** 12ff., 43, 52-141; **VII** 201, 224, 229f.
  assessment of its value, **I** 57ff.
  date of, **I** 75-79
  significance of the meaning of the names in the, **VI** 193f.
Tabun finds, **II** 50, 223
Tale of Two Cities, A, **VII** 121ff.
Talgai Skull, **I** 127
Tallness, kinetics of, **VIII** 40f.
Talmud
  on leaven, **V** 108f.
  tradition regarding the dead, **V** 349
Taoism, **I** 287
Tapa cloth, **I** 180, 181
Ta panta, as meaning the universe, **VII** 24f.
Targom, House of, **I** 89
Targum(s), **VI** 108f.
  of Onkelos, **V** 71, 219; **VI** 82, 88, 106
  of Pseudo-Jonathan, **V** 219
Tarshish, **I** 93f.
Tarsioids, **IV** 45
Tartars, **II** 297
Tartessos, **I** 94
Tasmania(ns), **II** 119
  attitude toward the dead, **V** 349
  extinction of, **II** 155f.
Tasmanian wolf, **IV** 157, 158 (fig. 5)
Tautophone Test, **III** 152f.
Taxonomy, abortive use of, **II** 22
Tchambuli, reversal of sex and temperament, **III** 148; **IV** 294

Technical contribution of Ham, **I** 153-216, 257ff., 320-338. *See also under* Ham.
Technology
  in China, **I** 205-214, 321f., 325f.
  converted into science, **I** 252, 264, 296
  effects of migration on, **II** 70
  of the Eskimo, **I** 158ff.; **II** 159ff.
  of the Hamitic peoples, **I** 38-42, 153-216, 320-338
  of non-Indo-Europeans, a characteristic simplicity, **I** 323
  vs. philosophy vs. religion, **I** 263-302
  vs. science, **I** 11f., 286, 287f., 297, 298f., 302, 315, 318
  where found, **VII** 30f.
Teeth
  absence of decay of, in early man, **V** 24
  canine t., developed in feral children, **II** 200
  fillings for (pre-Inca Indians), **I** 186
  gold capping of, in early China, **I** 334
  worn down to the gums, **II** 202; **V** 23, 24, 59
Tehom, meaning of word, **VII** 288f.
Teleology, **I** 222f.; **III** 56f., 271; **IV** 23f.; **VIII** 66. *See also under* Purpose.
  anathema to scientists, **I** 353
  concept of, **IV** 34-38

Teleonomy, **VIII** 65

Telepathy, **III** 263f., 265, 336

Telephone
Eskimo "invention," **I** 161; **II** 161
influence of, on modern life, **VIII** 177

Television, violence on, **VIII** 177

Tell Asmar, **IV** 115

Tell el Amarna Tablets, **VI** 61; **VII** 169, 186

Tell Halaf
pottery of, **I** 182, 197; **II** 91; **V** 64
settlement of, **V** 67

Temperament
of the artist, **III** 154f.
and body chemistry, **III** 147, 166
and environmental factors, **III** 147
genetic basis of, **III** 145f.
and physique, **III** 145, 149; **VIII** 81
and sex, **III** 148; **IV** 294; **V** 155

Temperature. *See also under* Thermoregulation.
effect of, on breeding cycle, **VIII** 235
effect of, on organisms, **VIII** 227
effect of, on time sense, **VI** 24
effect of high environmental t., **IX** 196
influence of, on morphology, **II** 215f., 220
levels of, endurable by man, **IX** 196
range for carbon chain viability, and for life, **I** 349f.; **IV** 28; **VIII** 38
ranges of, on the earth, **I** 349f.; **IV** 28f.; **VIII** 38
and rate of chemical reactions, **III** 76
regulation of, in animals, **I** 342f.; **III** 120; **IV** 152, 260; **IX** 197, 201
regulation of, in the human body, **I** 342; **III** 119f.; **IV** 257f.; **VIII** 238; **IX** 196f.
and seasonal variations and disease, **I** 350; **IV** 29; **VIII** 39; **IX** 142

Temple
Body of Christ as a, **VII** 191
Christians as stones of a, **III** 176
destruction of, foretold, **VII** 110, 135
destruction of the, **VII** 47, 61, 135
and the Passover ceremony, **V** 316, 359f.
visited three times by Jesus Christ, **VII** 44

Temptation
of Adam and Eve, **III** 308; **V** 147, 381f.
of anthropologists! **II** 20
of Christ, **III** 301f.
from within and from without, **III** 301f., 308

Ten
generations, significance of in inbreeding, **V** 28; **VI** 29, 234; **VII** 237, 239
"magic" value of, in antiquity, **V** 51

Tenses in Hebrew grammar, philosophy of time and, **VI** 23

Tension, value of; in development of personality, **III** 309f., 316

Tepexpan Man, **II** 232

Terah, **VII** 154ff.

Termite societies, **IV** 291

Territorial confidence of animals, **IV** 191

"Territorial imperative," **IV** 189

Territorial rights and free passage, **VII** 170

Territory(ies)
  of animals: comparatively small
    size of, **I** 341; **IV** 251f.
    : extent of, **I** 341; **IV** 251ff.
    : and mode of recognition, **III**
      250
    : not overcrowded, **III** 71f.; **IV**
      182, 186, 190
  defense of, by animals, **IV** 190ff.
  of primates, suprisingly small, **I**
    341 (and fn. 258)
"Test-tube" babies, **V** 173; **VIII** 61,
  71, 80
Teutonic uninventiveness, **I** 36
Textiles. *See also under* Fabrics,
  Weaving.
  Aymara (invisible mending), **I**
    184
  Chinese, **I** 180f.
  Egyptian, **I** 181
  Hamitic inventions of, **I** 317
  Inca broadloom, **I** 324
  Peruvian, **I** 179f., 184
  Polynesian (tapa cloth), **I** 180f.
Thankfulness, an essential part of
  prayer life, **IX** 275, 285
Theistic evolution, **IV** 13, 73, 86f.
Thematic Apperception Test, **III**
  152f.
Theological colleges
  and problems of recognition and
    accreditation, **VIII** 125
  and the sciences, **VIII** 124 (fn.
    37)
Theology. *See also under* Christian
  faith, Christian theology
  absence of in China, **I** 285; in
    Egypt, **I** 292; Eskimo, **I** 293;
    primitives generally, **I** 293; in
    Sumeria, **I** 291
  advantages of bias in, **VIII** 124
    (fn. 37)
  anathema to the scientists, **IV** 36
  "apartheid" between science
    and, **VIII** 122, 172

  emergence of, **I** 14, 264f.
  function of, replaced by science,
    VIII 128
  and genetics, **V** 81-92
  Greek language as vehicle for, **I**
    265f., 289; **III** 286; **VII** 23
  Hebrew language not appropri-
    ate to, **III** 286
  implications of evolution for, **IV**
    320ff.; **V** 79, 172
  language and modes of thought
    for, **I** 266f., 276ff.
  necessary to account for man, **III**
    271f.
  need of strict logic in, **VIII** 202
  as philosophy applied to religious
    insight, **I** 14, 37, 48, 252, 263f.,
    303-319; **II** 138
  as the queen of sciences, **III** 81;
    VIII 112, 120f.
  of redemption, its importance, **V**
    347ff.
  of redemption, rooted in physiol-
    ogy, **V** 152f.
  relationship to science, **I** 297,
    303-319
  of the resurrection, **V** 347-362
  as a system of reasoning, **V** 77f.,
    152f.

Theophanies, **V** 228-231, 244f.
Theory
  abstraction vs. the concrete, and
    language used, **I** 191, 272,
    275; **VI** 214
  dangers of emotional attachment
    to a particular t., **VIII** 98
  dangers of well-established t., **V**
    79f.
  vs. fact, **VIII** 154, 155
  factors governing general ac-
    ceptance of a, **VIII** 233f.
  false t. valuable: false observa-
    tions damaging, **II** 75
  to be useful, must be challenge-
    able, **II** 25

useful t. only overthrown by a better t., **VIII** 167
value of false t., **I** 10f.
Therapsids, **IV** 44
Thermal sweating, **IX** 197, 199
Thermoregulation. *See also under* Heat regulation, Sweat, Sweating.
  in animals and in man, **I** 342; **III** 119f.; **IV** 219f., 257; **VIII** 40, 238ff.; **IX** 196ff.
  innervation connected with, **IX** 198, 201
  loss of, in Eden, **V** 150
  and sweating, **IX** 196
Thiamine, **IV** 309
Thimbles, **I** 158; **II** 159
"Thing"
  vs. "act" orientation, **I** 289
  vs. person, **VIII** 94
  and relationship to its name, **II** 265, 266f.; **IX** 181
Thinking, Human vs. animals, **IV** 271, 273f., 275, 317
Thirst
  in man and animals, **IV** 312
  and need, out of register in man, **IX** 205
Thirty-nine Articles, **III** 291; **V** 215
Thomas (Didymus), personality of, **III** 179
Thomistic psychology, **V** 288
T'honga, **II** 295
"Thorn," Paul's, **III** 225-234
Thorns
  crown of, **V** 293,
  and thistles as part of the curse, **IX** 120, 121
Thought. *See also under* Conceptual thought, Freedom of thought, Telepathy.
  abstract t. applied to technology equals science, **I** 315
  abstract t. requires falsehood, **I** 272f.
  of animals, contingent, **IV** 271, 273f., 275, 317
  conceptual character of human t., **IV** 216, 278
  energy cost of, **VIII** 87, 143
  fragmentation of, **VIII** 168-183
  modern fragmentation of, vs. Medieval Synthesis, **VIII** 99-216
  Modern Synthesis of, **VIII** 118-151
  molded by language **I** 266, 270, 288
  necessity of language for, **I** 255
  "prelogical" t. of primitives, **I** 313f.
  relation between words and t., **I** 268ff.; **II** 261
  as silent language, **I** 270
  t. transferance in birds, **III** 336
  wordless t.? **I** 255, 270f., 275
Thracians, **I** 97
Three. *See also under* Trilogies.
  branches of the human race, **I** 9-50, 80-118
  hours of darkness on the cross, **V** 314; **VI** 26
  vs. two-dimensional pictures, **VII** 88ff.
Three days
  for certification of death, **V** 123; **VII** 43
  dead, significance of, **V** 123 (fn. 5), 124, 348, 350; **VII** 42
  diagram of the, regarding the Lord's entombment, **V** 356 (fig. 13)
  reckoning of, and the use of a whole or parts, **V** 353ff.
Three sons of Noah. *See also under* Hamites, Japhethites, Semites.
  contribution and responsibilities of each, **I** 12, 14, 29-43, 44ff., 69ff., 140, 247, 251f., 256ff., 260f., 263, 275, 317ff.; **II** 138
  the gods of each branch, **I** 30

and languages of each, **I** 254ff., 272, 274, 287, 290

order of contribution, **I** 47, 256

Scripture's recognition of the threefold division of man, **I** 15ff., 24, 260f.

as three branches of the human race, **I** 13f., 43, 68ff., 72ff., 120, 139, 256; **II** 134, 138; **VII** 229

and the three dimensions of life, **I** 44-49, 246f., 248ff., 337

World View of each, **I** 275

Threefold needs of man, **I** 12, 44-49, 240ff., 244f.

Threshing-floor, David's purchase of, **VII** 71

Thumbs, opposable; significance of, **I** 242; **IV** 44, 233, 235, 242

Thymus gland, growth and, **II** 220

Thyroid, **II** 219, 220f.; **III** 147

Tiamat, **VI** 93; **VII** 289f.

Tibareni, origin of, **I** 96f.; **II** 312

Tiber, the god of the, **VII** 198

Tiber River, **I** 97

Tierra del Fuegians, **IV** 129

fate of, **II** 114

ingenuity in trapping, **I** 170

mission to, and Darwin, **II** 140, 190

their surprise at Darwin's skin color, **I** 148

Tidal (King), possible identity of, **VII** 165

Tides and the moon, **I** 352

Tie-dyeing, **I** 181

Tiger

and the horse story, **IV** 76

saber-toothed, **II** 214

Tiglath Pileser, **I** 20

Tigris River, recent flooding and recession rate of, **IX** 24

Tilt of the earth's axis, **IV** 105; **VIII** 39

Time. *See also under* Chronology, Dating.

alcohol and its effect on t. sense, **VI** 21

animal's sense of, **VI** 24

carbon dioxide and its effect upon t. sense, **VI** 23

and creation, simultaneous, **VI** 19; **VIII** 111

during the crucifixion, **V** 313f.

during torture, **V** 314, 326, 330; **VI** 25f.

eclipsed in death, **VI** 42

vs. eternity, **VI** 10-49; esp. 38-44

as experienced, **III** 246; **VI** 20f., 38

as a factor in creation, **VI** 10, 19, 25, 27f.; **VIII** 247

as a fourth dimension, **VI** 12f., 18f.

as the forth dimension in John's Gospel, **VII** 88

as the great "creator," **VIII** 136

Hopi sense of, **VI** 22

inversion of, **VI** 41

Jewish method of reckoning, **V** 354f.

kaleidescoped in the Day of Judgment, **III** 245f.

materialism, and the value of t., **VI** 26

native attitude toward, **VI** 21f.

as past, present, and future combined, **VI** 39f.

in redemption, **VI** 45-49

reductions in the dating of prehistoric t., **II** 31f., 101, 133

and the Resurrection, **VI** 42

and the Second Advent, **VI** 42f.

sense, in men, women, and children, **VI** 24f.

sense and temperature, **VI** 24

sense of, and drug disorientation, **VI** 21

sense of, and Hebrew verb system, **VI** 23

sense of, in darkness, **VI** 24
sense of, in dreams, **VI** 21, 24
sense of, in pain, **VI** 21, 25f.
sense of, under hypnosis, **VI** 23f.
as sequence, **VI** 36
size and, **IV** 32; **VI** 25, 32
and space, **VI** 11ff., 19, 32f.
when not counted by God, **VI** 45ff.
Time factor in migration, **I** 141 (fn.); **II** 56, 101, 115f., 122, 188; **IX** 55f.
Timing
as an element in miracle, **III** 223; **IV** 19; **VII** 191, 192, 213; **VIII** 87
of the Incarnation, **VII** 20, 34
Timelessness
of eternity, **VI** 13
in relation to spiritual life, **VI** 26
Tissue organization, self-regulation of, **VIII** 80. *See also under* Bone, Brain, Heart, Kidney, Organogenesis.
Titles, as opposed to names, **V** 224
Tittle, jot and, **III** 284
Tlingit society, **V** 373f.
Tobacco
cigar holders (American Indian invention), **I** 186
cultivation and use of, **I** 203
Tobolsk, **I** 97
Toda, effects of inbreeding among, **VI** 225, 226
Togarmah, **I** 88f.
Tohu, **VII** 298
Tohu wa-bohu, **VI** 92ff.; **VII** 287
Toilet(s). *See also under* Sewage systems.
facilities, **II** 95
paper and seats, **I** 333
Toledoth of Genesis. *See under* Generations.
Tolerance, Jesuit view of religious freedom, **IV** 118
Toltec Flood tradition, **IX** 31

Tongue
not essential to speech, **IV** 268
use of, in man and apes, **II** 207
Tongues. *See under* Language.
Tongues, speaking in,
in the N.T., significance of, **VII** 52
in the O.T., **VII** 48 (fn. 31)
the phenomenon of, **VII** 62
as a sign, **VII** 52f.
Tool(s)
animals using, **II** 14; **III** 107; **IV** 263ff.
Australopithecines and, **II** 13f.; **IV** 264f.
effectiveness of flint for, **II** 150
making of, and culture, **II** 14
making of, vs. using of, **II** 14 (fn. 4); **III** 106f.; **IV** 263ff.
perfection of early t., **II** 90, 115
of primitive man, **II** 165
unnecessary care taken in manufacture of, **IV** 295
Toolmaker, man the, **IV** 263ff.
Tooth. *See also under* Dentition, Teeth.
convergence of form of, **II** 213f.
morphology and size of, **II** 27f.
Toothbrush, early Chinese, **I** 177 (fig. 8), 334
Toothpaste, early American, **I** 186 (fn. 67)
Torture, time sense in, **V** 314
Total depravity of man, **III** 20, 32, 158, 185, 341f.
definition of, **III** 37
Totemism, **II** 170, 291; **IV** 114
vs. heraldry, **III** 84
not Indo-European, **III** 84
Tower
Greek word for, **II** 86f.
origin of the word, **VII** 207
Tower of Babel, **VII** 196. *See also under* Babel.

Town
    ancient word for, **I** 108; **VII** 207
    origin and meaning of the word,
        VII 225
Toy(s)
    dolls, made from rubber, **I** 179
    helicopter, **I** 205
    rubber balls, **I** 179
    with wheels in Central America,
        I 182
Trachoma, **III** 228
Trade and commerce, **I** 41
    banking houses, **I** 189, 192
    economy controlled by liquidat-
        ing competition, **I** 202
    industrial automation (Sume-
        rian), **I** 189
    inspection for quality control, **I**
        189
    interest rates, **I** 189
    medical fees controlled legally,
        with penalties, **I** 192f.
    mortgage firms, **I** 192
    overseas trade and commerce
        (Minoan), **I** 197
    paper currency, **I** 205ff., 334
    price and wage control, **I** 189
Tradition(s)
    Arabian, regarding a former
        creation, **VI** 112
    of Babel, **IX** 29
    Babylonian, regarding a former
        creation, **VI** 113f.
    Chinese, regarding a former
        creation, **VI** 112
    confirmation of, **V** 13
    continuity of, **VI** 106ff.
    of creation and deluge, **V** 97
    of creation and the fall of man, **V**
        94ff., 97
    of creation prior to Adam, **VI** 112
    of the dispersion of man, **IX** 29
    of Eden, **V** 93ff.
    of the Flood, **IX** 28ff., 67-106. See
        also under tribal names.
    of the Flood, as the worldwide
        shared t., **IX** 28, 29, 33, 78, 80;
        VII 203
    of a former creation, **VI** 112,
        113f.
    of the founding of the first city,
        VII 207
    and the Gap theory, **VI** 106-114
    increasing respect for t., **V** 12
    Jewish, regarding man's crea-
        tion, **V** 179
    of longevity in ancient times, **V**
        50; **VII** 203
    oral, perfectly preserved, **II** 77
    of original immortality of man ,**V**
        179f.
    of an original revelation, **V** 250ff.
    pagan, **V** 47ff.
    persistence and stability of, **II** 79
    preservation of, **V** 47f.
    regarding Vulcan, **VII** 199, 226f.
    remarkable stability of, among
        N. Am. Indians, **V** 48
    value of, **II** 76f.; **V** 93
Traditions of the Flood
    comment on significance of, **VII**
        203
    extended collection of, **IX** 65-106
Tranquilizers, **III** 147, 165, 174
Transfiguration, **V** 377f.
    instead of dying, **V** 18f., 398f.
    significance of, **V** 163f.
Transfiguration, Mount of, **III**
    215f.; **V** 18, 163f., 377f., 399;
    VIII 97; **IX** 116
    as a place of retreat, **III** 215f.
Transformation to replace death, **V**
    18f., 151, 163f., 399; **IX** 116
Translateableness of the Bible, **IX**
    243
Translation
    problems in, **VII** 76
    are versions inspired? **VII** 73f.
Translation into heaven. *See under*
    Transformation.
Transvestites, **V** 181

Traps
for catching a wolf, **I** 160f.; **II** 161
for catching mice and rats, **I** 336
for catching wild fowl, **I** 169
for fishing, **I** 170
Travel
by air: balloons, **I** 205, 211
: dirigibles, **I** 211
: gliders, **I** 205
: jet-propelled rockets, **I** 210
: kites, **I** 205, 211
: parachutes, **I** 205
: rockets, **I** 205
compass, **I** 205
ease of, in Greco-Roman world,
VII 28, 34
by land: bridges, stone, **II** 121
: chariot wheels of plywood, **I**
202, 326, 327
: graticules on maps, **I** 206
: harness for horses, **I** 205, 326
: roads, cement and surfaced,
I 182; graded, **II** 121
: road-rollers, **I** 182
: sedan chairs, **I** 199, 201
: suspension bridges of rope,
I 182; of chains, **I** 211f.
: wheels, spoked, **I** 327
means of conveyance, list, **I** 40
by water. *See also under* Boats.
: breakwaters for harbors, **I**
336f.
: canal and locks, **I** 203, 326
: canoe (Polynesian), **I** 157
(fig. 6), 164
: cantilever principle, **I** 202
: compass, magnetic, **I** 332
: ironclad battleships, **I** 203
: sailing boats, **I** 185
: ship's propeller, **I** 172
: stern-post rudder, **I** 203
: underwater repair work, **I**
336
: use of birds in navigation, **IX**
39f., 71, 74f.
Traveling vs. arriving, **VIII** 14, 187

Tree(s)
evolutionary, as "bundles of
twigs," **IV** 146
evolutionary, how they are con-
structed, **IV** 140f.
fallacy of genealogical t. of man,
II 16. *See also under* Phylogenetic trees.
fig, as symbol of Israel's religious
history, **VI** 70-72
great age achieved by, **V** 15, 178
olive, as symbol of Israel's spiritual history, **VI** 66-69
parable of fig, that was left one
more year, **V** 44f.
ring dating, **II** 132
symbolic of Israel's history, **VI**
52-73
Tree of Knowledge, **III** 289; **V** 93f.,
381f.; **VI** 73
confused with Tree of Life, **V**
99f., 148
as the Homa or Soma tree in
India, **V** 100
Tree of Life, **III** 289; **V** 178
dangers arising from, **V** 83f.
forbidden to fallen Adam, **V** 151,
179
leaves of, for healing, **V** 382; **VI**
69, 73; **IX** 113f.
Trent, Council of, **VIII** 121
Trepanation. *See under* Trephination.
Trephination, **I** 176, 330
Trial
of Jesus Christ, **V** 317f.; **VII** 44
by ordeal, principle of, **II** 172
Trichotomy of man. *See under*
Dichotomy of man.
Trilogies in Scripture, **I** 15-24; **VII**
98f.
Trinil Ape-man. *See under* Pithecanthropus.
Trinity, **VII** 312
Babylonian and Egyptian
trinities, **V** 252f.

Chinese and Indian trinities, **V** 254

Greek and Roman trinities, **V** 253f.

Lord, a term of the, **V** 223-227

not to be equated with polytheism, **V** 251ff.

in the Old Testament, **V** 216-257

pagan recollections of the, **V** 250f.

psychological factors in the, **V** 249f.

Tripoli, **IX** 120

Trobrianders, **II** 290, 291, 293; **IV** 292

views of, regarding physical paternity, **III** 138

Tropisms (plant), **III** 322; **V** 395; **VIII** 69, 85

Troy, excavation of, **II** 76, 120; **V** 48

Truth(s)

arrived at by deception? **VIII** 168f.

in art, contradictory? **VII** 85ff.

attitude of primitives toward, **I** 272f.

clarified by heresy, **IX** 148f.

communicated by contradiction, **VII** 77f.

discovered by magnification, **VIII** 169

doubt, essential to discovery of truth, according to Greeks, **VIII** 24

evolutionary criterion of, **VIII** 160f.

vs. fact, **VII** 95

faith not a necessary part of, according to Greeks, **VII** 24

Greek skepticism, **VII** 25

heresy as part of the t. taken for the whole, **IV** 134

Higher Critics and, **II** 67

vs. holiness, which has priority? **VII** 23

and language, **I** 290

Medieval method of assessing what is t., **VIII** 112f.

Medieval vs. modern criteria for, **II** 75; **IV** 173f.; **VIII** 119

more than one kind of? **VIII** 53

as perception, vs. reality, **VII** 84f., 94f.

photography and, **VII** 85ff.

Plato's method of judging what is t., **VIII** 160f.

in portraiture, **VII** 87

vs. reality itself, **VII** 84, 94f.

revealed in the Incarnation, **V** 162

revealed t., powerless unless freshly revealed, **IV** 135f.

science, the only avenue to? **VIII** 164

Scriptures as the touchstone of, **II** 61

search for, in the intertestamental period, **I** 18

search for, vs. search for holiness, **VII** 23

spiritual, acquired only by inspiration, **IV** 136

spiritual, not perceived by logical argument, **VII** 67f.

the test of, **V** 173

words vs. meanings in conversation, **VII** 78

Truthfulness of native people, **I** 272

Truth serums (native), **I** 175

Tswana, **II** 296

Tubal, Tubil, **VI** 201

Tubal-Cain, **VI** 201

as Bar-Zillah, **VII** 199

as founder of brass metallurgy, **VII** 198, 226

possible equation with Vulcan, **VII** 198

Tubilustrum, **VI** 201; **VII** 199

Turin shroud. *See under* Shroud.

Tweezers, **I** 178

Twin(s), **II** 284f., 304, 309, 311; **III** 146f.

brain waves of, identical, **III** 265
and personality formation, **III** 145f.
and population growth, **IX** 137, 138
sentiments regarding, **VII** 228; **IX** 173

Type, moveable; for printing, **I** 183

Typographical errors in the Bible, **VII** 71

Tyre, **I** 77; **VII** 121-127
beseiged by Nebuchadnezzar, **VII** 124
biblical prophecies regarding, **VII** 122f.
captured by Alexander the Great, **VII** 125f.
coast city abandoned, **VII** 125
its columns laid in the sea, **VII** 128
commercial enterprise of, **VII** 123
destruction of, **VII** 121ff.
maps of the island and site, **VII** 122, 127
population moved from shore to island, **VII** 124

U

Ubiquity of man, **I** 341f.; **III** 120; **IV** 219, 247ff., 262

Ugarit tablets, **I** 93

Umbrellas, **I** 202

Unbaptized infants, in limbo, **IX** 173

Unbelief, effect of miracle upon, **VII** 61

Uncle, **II** 279, 281, 292, 317; **VII** 245f.

Unconscious, the, **III** 32, 38, 160, 163, 242f., 279. *See also under* Subconscious.
the collective, **III** 142
Freud's view of, **III** 158ff.
shared, at the species level, **III** 263

Unconsciousness, loss of mental sweating in, **IX** 200

Understanding
"as-if-ism" in scientific u., **VIII** 72, 170
biblical meaning of the word, **III** 90ff., 111
faith as a means to, **V** 175; **VIII** 117, 185
vs. knowledge, **III** 62
limitations of logic for, **VIII** 88
never complete, **VIII** 170
new birth essential to spiritual, **III** 55
not essential to control, **VIII** 169
place of revelation in, **III** 272
by "reduction," **VIII** 132

Underwater breathing apparatus, invention of, **I** 336

Unfallen man
and achievement of maturity, **V** 165
portrait of, in Jesus Christ, **IV** 210; **V** 159ff.
relationship to nature in a perfect world, **VIII** 62
value of, to God, **V** 399f.

Unfit
care of the, in nature, **IV** 195f., 204

man supremely unfit to survive! **IV** 176f.

survival of the, **IV** 172-205

Unicellular animals, consciousness in, **III** 257. *See also under* Amoeba, Paramecia.

Unicellular life, **V** 145

characteristics of, **V** 385

immortality of, **V** 124f., 145, 176

mindedness of, **III** 251f., 257, 261 (fn. 50); **VIII** 65, 75, 80, 86

Unified consciousness of cell aggregates, **III** 182f., 260, 263, 335

Uniformitarianism, **II** 61; **IV** 15

Uniformity of human physique, **IV** 253

Uninventiveness

Indo-Europeans are, **I** 37, 207, 301

most people are, **I** 36, 37, 305f., 309; **II** 147f.

of Semites, **I** 36, 305ff., 308

Unions, purpose served by, **II** 175

United Nations, ideals of, **III** 89

Unity

vs. harmony, **IX** 157

vs. trinity, psychological significance of, **V** 149f.

Universality of Christ's personality, **III** 187; **V** 393

Universals, cultural, **III** 21, 157

incest as a, **II** 300

moral sense a, **III** 107f.

mother-love not a, **II** 305; **III** 148, 157; **IV** 294; **IX** 172

the search for, in psychology, **III** 157f.

Universe

and Big Bang theory, **VIII** 19f., 28f.

circumference of, **VIII** 32

concept of geocentric, **IV** 27; **VIII** 118, 119, 204

created on man's account, **VIII** 7

and Cyclic theory, **VIII** 27

denial of purpose in, **VIII** 66

designed for the crucifixion, **I** 218, 231ff.

designed for the Incarnation, **I** 218, 233f.; **VIII** 44

designed for the introduction of life, **VIII** 73

designed for man? **VIII** 11-45

elements and their relative proportion in the, **VIII** 36

evidence of design in, **VIII** 38

expanding, **VIII** 18ff., 26, 28ff.

as God's great thought (Jeans), **III** 321; **VIII** 42

great age of, **VI** 27f.

Greek term for, **V** 231

heat death of, **III** 196; **VIII** 20

immensity of, **VIII** 28-34

key to, **I** 218, 225-239

kingdom of God encompasses the u., **III** 54f.

life elsewhere in? **IV** 31; **VIII** 37

light as basic "substance" of, **VIII** 22

as a machine only, **VIII** 205

man as key to the understanding of the, **I** 225-239, 339, 345f.

man determines the size of, **VIII** 43f.

man the center of? **IV** 27

meaning of, **I** 218, 219, 225-239; **VIII** 14, 44

vs. multi-verse, **III** 53f., 74

nature vs. purpose of, **VII** 24

omnipotence of God in, **VI** 122-129

as a perfect clockwork, **VIII** 54

plan or accident? **VI** 122f.

purpose in the universe as a whole, **I** 352ff.; **III** 272; **VIII** 105, 144

rationality of, **VIII** 34

reality of, nonmaterial, **III** 53

redemption was the purpose of the u., **I** 218

red shift and, **VIII** 17ff.

as a setting for the world, **I** 345-365

significance of its size, **IV** 32; **VI** 32

significance of man within, **VIII** 33f.

size of, relative to man, **I** 219f., 339f.; **VIII** 41

as the skin of a balloon, **VIII** 28f.

spiritual nature of, **VIII** 22f.

Steady State concept of (Hoyle), **VIII** 25f.

as a suitable habitat for man, **VIII** 35f.

superdense state of, **VIII** 20

and super-physical agency, **VIII** 22f.

ta panta, as the u., **VI** 124f.

to be folded up as a garment, **VIII** 31

as a true *uni*-verse, **I** 238; **VIII** 37

two models of, **VIII** 16, 28ff.

ultimate collapse of, **VIII** 31

ultimate fate of, **VIII** 33

viewed as a political arena, **II** 172

wisdom of God revealed in design of the, **VIII** 35-45

youthfulness of, **IV** 18f.

Uni-verse, evidence of its oneness, **I** 238; **III** 45

Universities,
abrogate interest in ends, **VIII** 213

founded by theologians, **VIII** 124 (fn. 37)

original concept of, **VIII** 123, 124 (fn. 37)

Uratom, **VIII** 28f.

Urea, synthesis of, **VIII** 73, 135

Ur of the Chaldees, **VII** 151
flood deposits found at, **VII** 202

Uruk, **VII** 207
excavation of, **IV** 114

history of the name of, **I** 108; **VI** 198

named after Enoch, **VII** 205f., 224f.

Uru-Salem, meaning of the word, **VII** 164

Us, use of the pronoun in the O.T., **V** 221f.

Utnapishtim, as biblical Noah, **V** 54

Utopia(s)
chronic warfare in, **VIII** 176 (fn. 165)

not always a happy place, **III** 207, 208; **VIII** 176; **IX** 130f.

philosophy of, **VII** 24

V

Vacations, concept of; is modern, **VIII** 175

Vaccines, **I** 202, 329

Vale of Siddim, **VII** 175

Value(s)
of anything, ultimately means v. to man, **I** 339

judgments, and science, **VIII** 210, 211

of man as created but unfallen, **V** 399f.

of man to God, to society, **I** 64

qualitative vs. quantitative, **VIII** 33

system, Judeo-Christian, **III** 41f.

Variability
allowed for in the DNA mechanism, **VIII** 50
of culture, **I** 126, 128; **II** 43, 175, 222; **IV** 67; **VI** 230
"explosive" diversification, **IV** 67
expression of, requires death, **V** 128
limitations of, **IV** 78, 187
limited in man, **IV** 253f.
limits of, within a species, **I** 346 (fn. 262)f.
not random, **IV** 72f.
of physical type, **I** 126, 128; **II** 43, 175, 222; **IV** 67; **VI** 230
in small populations, **I** 126, 128; **II** 43, 44, 175, 222; **IV** 67; **VI** 230
within a species, underestimated, **II** 20ff., 27
of a species in a new environment, **I** 128ff.; **II** 44; **IV** 67, 84
Variance
of form often misconstrued, **II** 27f.
of inbred forms (Lebzelter), **VI** 230
Variation, biological,
allowance for, within limits, **IV** 187; **VIII** 60f., 90f.
via non-nuclear genes, **VIII** 224f.
Varieties vs. species, **IV** 77
Varve counting, **II** 132
Vasoconstriction, **IV** 258
Vasodilatation, causes and effects of, **IV** 259; **V** 102
Vatican Septuagint, chronology of, **V** 33f.
Vedas, **IV** 120; **VII** 33
Vegetables, developed by American Indians, **I** 40, 166f.
Vegetarianism, **V** 24; **IX** 124, 206
"Vegetative" animal life, **V** 212f.
Vehicles of transport, list of, **I** 40f.
Veils, wearing of, **VII** 153

Venereal disease, **I** 331 (fn. 227)
Venus flytrap, **VIII** 70, 85
Verb(s)
Hebrew tense peculiarities in the, **VI** 86
vs. nouns, **I** 277
to be in Hebrew, **VII** 273; **IX** 185
Verbal inspiration
contradictions and, **VII** 78
the jot and the tittle, **III** 284
Vertebrae, variability in numbers of; in a species of fish, **IV** 159
Vertebrates and invertebrates, missing link? **IV** 55
Vertesszolles Man, **II** 50
Vessel
the individual as a, **V** 208
as used in the N.T., **III** 171f., 174f.; **V** 292
Vestal virgins at Roman games, **VII** 29
Vestonice finds, **II** 234f.
Viability
reduced by inbreeding, **VII** 235
of a species, basic requirements for the, **III** 347ff.
Vibration, effects of, on walls and structures, **VII** 190, 191
Vicarious sacrifice, **V** 376ff.
defined, **V** 380
of Jesus Christ, **V** 164
and the human body, **IV** 326
light shed on, by nature of Adam, **I** 237f.; **V** 371
nature of, **V** 371
requires immortality, **V** 164, 191
Vicki the chimpanzee, **IV** 270
Victoria Institute, Transactions of, **II** 63f.
Victory
incomplete, benefits of, **III** 213f., 216
with small "weapons," **III** 224 ·
when only partial, reasons for, **III** 213f.

Vikings, use of birds in navigation, **IX** 40

Vine
grape, the forbidden fruit? **V** 96f.
of Noah, **V** 99
as a symbol, **VI** 52ff.
symbol of Israel's national history, **VI** 60-65

Violence
encouraged by evolutionary theory, **IV** 170
in games, **VIII** 177
in society, **III** 267

Virgin birth, **V** 176-192
of Jesus Christ, **I** 234; **III** 302
and the Incarnation, **V** 171-214
the Lord's freedom from original sin by the, **III** 302
in Matthew's and Luke's Gospels, **VII** 102
necessity of, **I** 234f; **III** 302; **V** 152f., 156f., 377
in prophecy, **VI** 142f.
relation of, to the death of Jesus Christ, **V** 326

Virgin conception, **V** 153

Virtue
can be dangerous, **I** 47
innocency turned into, **V** 18f., 163, 399; **VIII** 96f.
novelty made a, **II** 149, 174; **III** 36

Virus, **IV** 51

Vision. *See also under* Eyes, Stereoscopic vision.
binocular, fusion of in the mind, **VII** 91
four-dimensional, in birds, **VII** 90
vs. photography, **VII** 85f.
stereoscopic, **IV** 44f., 242f.

Vision, spiritual; and stereoscopic, **VII** 91

Vision and hallucination regarding the resurrection, **V** 342

"Vital force"
concept of, not rejected by all investigators, **IV** 150
concept of, not welcome in biology, **IV** 144; **VIII** 91f.

Vitalism, **I** 353f.; **III** 323; **IV** 35, 144, 150; **VIII** 84, 92, 136, 138

Vitamins
A and B deficiency, effects of, **II** 221
animals and diet deficient in, **III** 62f.

Vocabulary
vs. grammar, **I** 274; **IV** 274
of primitives extensive, **I** 272f.; **II** 251, 258ff.; **VI** 213ff.

Vocalization
of animals, restricted by jaw structure, **IV** 244
vs. speech, **II** 263; **IV** 244f.

Vocal organs
and erect posture, **IV** 243f.
in man, special nature of, **IV** 279

Vocal tract, structure of; and language, **IV** 231, 275f.

"Voice of the Lord," **V** 227, 237ff.

Volcanoes, benefits of, **IX** 140f.

Voles, **IV** 202

Vulcan
identity of, **II** 312f.
origin of the name? **VI** 201
traditions regarding, **VII** 199, 226f.

Vulgate, Genesis 1:2 according to the, **VI** 88

Vultures, use of stones as tools, **IV** 264

W

Wabema, **II** 297

Wadjak Skull, **III** 49; **IV** 225; **V** 58

Wake, purpose of Irish? **V** 122f.

War
  absence of personal relations in modern war, **VIII** 181f.
  casualties, numbers of in ancient, **VII** 160
  civilian involvement in, **VIII** 181, 182
  civilians, treatment of in ancient vs. modern, **III** 26
  conduct of modern, **III** 267
  effect of, on Greek civilization, **III** 21f.
  effect of long range weapons on the soldier, **III** 27
  as evidence of an "aggressive" instinct in man? **III** 24, 25f.
  as evidence of the Fall, **IV** 177
  high culture favoring, **III** 19
  honor absent in modern w.? **III** 27, 267; **VIII** 182
  increasing barbarity of, **III** 26
  military vs. civilian casualties, **VIII** 182
  modern civilization almost makes necessary, **IX** 153f.
  natural to man, **III** 19
  prisoners, numbers taken in ancient w., **VII** 160
  within a species, unique to man, **IV** 322
  spirit of Medieval vs. modern, **VIII** 182
  and the struggle to survive in nature is mild, **IV** 181ff.
  the ultimate expression of sin, **III** 24, 159
  unknown in some lower cultures, **IX** 133
  when a lesser evil, **IX** 153f.

Warfare
  from the air, immorality of, **VIII** 139 (fn. 76)f.
  ethics of gas, **III** 267
  internecine w. found where least expected, **III** 207
  invention of weapons of, **I** 42
  numbers of troops dead, prisoners, etc., in ancient w., **VII** 160
  private armies, size of, **VII** 160
  psychological use of noisemakers, **I** 209
  sulphur-naphtha compounds, **I** 208
  techniques, etc., **I** 42, 184, 208, 209

Warka, **VI** 199; **VII** 207, 225

Warmbloodedness, **III** 120f.; **IV** 43, 69, 93
  "evolved" independently twice! **IV** 155

Wart hog, **VIII** 246

Washoe, the chimpanzee, **IV** 272ff.

Wasp(s)
  burrowing, and their use of a tool, **IV** 264
  and figs, **IV** 57
  flight ceiling of, **VII** 214
  hunting w. studied by Fabre, **III** 58f.
  as illustration of "mechanism" in nature, **VIII** 66
  stingers as malfunctioning ovipositors, **IX** 161

"Wasp waist" in man, **IV** 219

Water
bitter, made sweet, **VII** 213
exceptional behavior of, **III** 75
freezing of, **III** 75; **IV** 30; **IX** 142
large bodies of, barrier to land
birds, **IX** 41
salt w. a barrier to animal migration, **IX** 42
symbolic washing with, **III** 307
turned into "blood," **VII** 212
unique properties of, **I** 351f.; **IV**
29f.
Waterbuck, territorial extent of, **IV**
251
Wave theory of light, **VIII** 31f.
Ways vs. acts or works of God, **VI**
165; **IX** 258
Weaknesses as strengths, **III** 221f.
Wealth
amassing of, in Greco-Roman
world, **VII** 28
linked to responsibility in
Medieval world, **VIII** 115
maldistribution of, **IX** 136f.
Weapons
arrowheads, **I** 162; **II** 99f.
axes, stone, **II** 121
bolas, **I** 170f.
boomerangs ("guided missile"),
I 171f.
cannon, **I** 208, 210
crossbow, repeating, **I** 205
decline in quality of, **II** 121
of defense among animals, **IV**
156f.
explosives, **I** 205
flame w., **I** 205, 208, 209
of flint, **IV** 265
flint-lock rifles, **II** 150
of glass made by Australian
aborigines, **II** 150
gunpowder, **I** 209, 332
hand grenade, **I** 209
harpoon, **I** 161
incendiaries, **I** 209
"irritating" gases, **I** 209

jewelled w., **I** 196
kites for military observation, **I**
211
psychological, to stampede
horses, **I** 209
repeating "magazine" crossbow, **I** 208
rifled arrowheads, **I** 184f.
rocket arrows, **I** 209
screaming arrowheads, **I** 209
smoke bombs, **I** 208
spearheads, stone and glass, **II**
151
"Wear and tear" theory of aging, **V**
131
Weasel, territory, extent of, **IV** 251
Weather forecasting, **I** 205, 211
Weaving, **I** 179ff., 184; **II** 97. *See also*
under Fabrics.
broadloom in ancient Peru, **I** 324
decline in art of, **II** 120
fibers for, **I** 162, 180, 205, 207f.,
209
list of Hamitic achievements in, **I**
39
Peruvian achievements, **I** 180,
181, 324
types of cloth, **I** 179, 180, 184
Web of nature, **III** 61
"Weeds" in spiritual life, **III** 129f.,
173
Weeping vs. laughter, **IV** 245f.
Weismann
his concept of the continuity of
germ plasm, **V** 86
his experiments with rats and
mice, **V** 85f., 189; **VIII** 222
Weld Dynastic Prism, **V** 52
Wellcome-Marston Expedition,
VII 188
Westminster Confession, **VIII** 185
Whale(s), **II** 182; **III** 96
brain weight relative to body
weight, **IV** 228
life span of, **V** 132f.
swallowing Jonah, **VII** 193

Wheel(s)
  plywood, **I** 202, 326, 327
  spoked, **I** 327
  for toys, used by Central and South American Indians, **I** 182
Wheelbarrows, **I** 205
Whistling kettles, **I** 181
White Man, the,
  as judged by primitives, **II** 110f.
  unforgiveable savagery of, **II** 109, 155f.
  uninventiveness of, **I** 35f., 37, 206f., 300f., 303, 305, 313, 317, 337
Whole, part used for the, **V** 355; **VI** 47
"Whole creation," meaning of the phrase, **IX** 17
"Whole response," **III** 151f.
"Whole world," use of the phrase, **IX** 20
Wickedness
  is it greater in modern man? **III** 13
  more destructive in modern civilization, **IV** 170
  is in the motive, not the act, **III** 34
  unpunished, **VII** 15
Widows, care of, in primitive society, **II** 283, 302
Wife, in primitive cultures, **II** 295, 302, 303, 318ff. *See also under* Polygamy.
Wildebeest, extent of its territory, **IV** 252
Wildfowl, device for catching, **I** 169
Will, the,
  evidence of, in simple organisms, **III** 261 (and fn. 50)
  freedom of, only to sin, **III** 34, 36f.
  to life, in nature, **IV** 51, 110
  and problem of sin, **III** 30-44, 92, 270

power of, over the body, **IX** 182
Willing vs. knowing, **VIII** 184f.
Will of God
  and omnipotence, **I** 233 (fn. 20), **VI** 121-174; **VII** 120
  performance of, **III** 92
  permissive, **VII** 59
  summary observations of, **VI** 173f.
  vs. the "wish" of God, **VI** 173f.
Wills, the making of, in primitive society, **II** 285, 307, 330
Windmills, Persian invention of, **I** 36, 206, 215, 305
Windows, **I** 159, 204
Wine
  in the Communion Service, **IX** 226
  fermentation of, **V** 106f.
  as a symbol of blood, **V** 108
Wings
  angels have w.? **VI** 31
  of bats vs. the fly, **IV** 157
  development of, by aphids when crowded, **III** 63
Wisdom
  of animals, unlike human rationality, **IV** 319
  belongs to the elders in primitive society, **II** 169f.
  fear an essential part of, **IV** 134
  vs. intelligence and knowledge, **II** 148, 154; **III** 182f.
  vs. knowledge, **III** 83
  limitations of human, **VII** 18f., 20
  of primitives, **II** 110f., 154
  vs. rationality, **IV** 319
"Wisdom" literature
  of the Chinese, **I** 283f.
  of Hamites, entirely practical, **I** 294f.
  of the Hebrew people, **I** 278
Witch-doctor(s)
  as men with medical expertise, **I** 154f., 173

true function of, **VII** 116
Witches, male or female? **VII** 116
Witnesses
two or more required, **VII** 40
value of contradictory, **IX** 32
Wives of Abraham, **I** 15; **VII** 98
Wolf
Eskimo method of killing, **I** 160f.;
II 161
European, **IV** 157, 158
North American, **IV** 157, 158
pack leaders, **IV** 298f.
Tasmanian, **II** 213; **IV** 157, 158
Wolsey, death foretold, **VII** 114
Wolves
hunting habits of, **II** 260
savagery of, a misunderstanding,
IX 125
and sheep, **III** 65
Woman
origin of the word, **VI** 204f.
taken in adultery, story of, **III**
281; **IX** 189
Women
as prophets, **VII** 116
rights of, as a wife, **II** 302, 303
Wonders. *See under* Signs and wonders.
Woolen vs. linen clothing, **IX** 213ff.
Word(s)
intimate relation between, **I**
268ff.
liberating power of a w. or term,
VIII 133
vs. meaning, **VII** 76f., 78, 83
numbers of, in primitive speech,
I 272f.; **II** 251 (fn. 3), 258ff.;
IV 267 (fn. 136); **VI** 214ff.
significance of order of, in Hebrew grammar, **VI** 86f.
and thing, **II** 265, 266f.; **IX** 181
vs. thought, **I** 268ff.; **II** 261
and thought, relation between, **I**
255, 268, 275
"Word," the; Jesus as, **V** 219, 246;
IX 182

Wordless thought, **I** 255, 270f., 275
Word of God, precision in, **III** 101.
See also under Bible, Scriptures.
Work. *See also under* Labor.
dehumanizing effect of piece
work, **VIII** 174f.
ethic, **I** 301
of God, not yet "ceased from,"
VIII 54, 58, 89
Works
vs. fruit, **III** 131, 192f.; **VI** 159f.,
163f.
good, foreordained, **III** 131
vs. ways of God, **VI** 165; **IX** 258
World, the
becoming a single society, and
the consequences, **IX** 153f.
end of, predicted, **VII** 119
Hebrew word for, as distinct
from *ground* and *earth*, **IX** 15f.
made for man, **I** 343f., 348ff.; **IV**
23f.; **V** 127f., 162; **VIII** 35ff.,
86
as mechanism or organism, **III**
53
omnipotence of God in, **VI** 130-
143
as the "rod of God," **III** 217
settlement of, **I** 119-141
spiritual nature of, **III** 261, 318-
327, 333; **VIII** 23f.
as a stage, **I** 339-344
suffering preserves w. from total
corruption, **IX** 111
viewed by primitives in personal
terms, **I** 28; **III** 80, 85; **VIII**
106
World View(s), **I** 228f. *See also under*
Medieval Synthesis.
advantages of having a, **VIII** 116
ancient, **III** 78ff.
Babylonian, **III** 78ff.
changing, **III** 53
Christian, as a "map," **III** 82
Christian, for today, **VIII** 192-
216

of the Christian and of the naturalist, **IV** 23-33
Christian vs. scientific, **VIII** 200
Christian vs. secular, **IV** 23f.
a coherent World View shattered by catastrophe, **VIII** 13
difficulty of achieving a modern, **VIII** 165
of early and primitive man, **III** 64, 85, 334; **VIII** 106
four basic, **III** 78ff.
grammar vs. vocabulary, as the key to a, **I** 274
Hopi, **VIII** 107
and language, **I** 255f., 267f., 270, 288
man's need for a, **VIII** 8f.
as a "map," **VIII** 107, 116, 149f.
Medieval, **III** 81; **V** 162; **VIII** 104-216
Medieval vs. modern, **III** 81-85; **VIII** 101f., 144, 146, 147, 152ff., 166ff., 180, 181, 189f.
necessity of some form of a, **I** 229; **III** 83; **VIII** 211
a "needed map" (Huxley), **VIII** 150
non-Western, **III** 78ff., 84
of primitive man, **I** 28; **III** 54, 79, 85, 334; **VIII** 106
of primitive man, did not separate nature from supernature, **II** 170f.
scientific, incompleteness of, **VIII** 209
three kinds of, **I** 275
World War II, **VIII** 13f.

Worldliness, not to be equated with culture, **I** 245

Worms, survive extreme low temperature, **VIII** 74

Worship, **IX** 223ff.
of ancestors, **IV** 123, 126, 131
buildings appropriate to, **IX** 226-237

and familiar surroundings, **IX** 236
of God, by angels, **I** 230 (fn. 15)
of gods in the guise of animals, **IV** 117
and liturgy, **IX** 245-250
man's body structured to permit w., **IV** 245f.
music as an assist to, **IX** 232f.
and physical comfort, **IX** 230
place of art in, **IX** 221-253
purest conception of God in the most primitive societies, **IV** 126
specifically human, **IV** 317
statuary and, **IX** 238-244
structured or unstructured, **IX** 224, 245
washing of feet, ritual of, **IX** 245
Worth of the person. *See also under* Value.
in materialism, **VIII** 33
in quantitative terms,, **I** 220
in terms of function, **I** 64

Wound(s)
healing and infection, **IV** 312
healing of, **I** 342
in man vs. animals, **IV** 312f.

Wrench as a "jod," **I** 271

Writing
the art of, and associated technologies listed, **I** 39, 316f.
advantages of, vs. ideograms, **I** 286
disapproved by Greeks, **II** 79
displaces older people as source of knowledge, **II** 169f.
early development of, in Egypt, **V** 63
early records in, **I** 193
early use of alphabet, **I** 305, 316; **VII** 184
envelopes, **I** 189
great increase of, resulting from Alexander's conquest, **VII** 28

as hindrance to memorization, **II** 79

and invention of paper, **I** 182, 183, 209, 212, 332

and invention of printing, **I** 39f., 183, 205, 209, 325

the Lord writing on the ground, **IX** 189

originating with art? **II** 128

postal systems, **I** 182, 189

success in w., enhanced by handicaps? **III** 202ff.

XYZ

X and Y chromosomes, **V** 91

"X" factor in personality, **III** 141ff.

Xisouthros, the Greek "Noah," **V** 54

Yaghan(s)
  complexity of language of, **VI** 214f.
  meaning of word for *man*, **VII** 201 (fn. 80)
  reason for their degeneration, **II** 117f.

Yankee, uninventive? **I** 301

Years, counted as months in Genesis? **V** 41

Yellow Emperor, medical texts of, **I** 294

Ylem, primordial matter, **VIII** 21f.

YMCA, early history of, **II** 64

Yoruba, **I** 103; **VI** 200f.
  bronze metallurgy of, **VII** 197f.
  of the tribe of Nimrod, **VII** 198

Yucca moth and plant, **III** 70; **IV** 57

Yucca tree, Indians make soap substitute from, **I** 163

Yuma points, perfection of, **II** 115

Zebra, **IV** 184

Zeitgeist
  as a cultural compulsive, **VIII** 160 (fn. 130)
  in Darwin's day, **II** 66; **III** 15; **IV** 148, 181
  influence of, on acceptance of change, **II** 149

Zero, early concept of, **I** 183, 328

Zic-zac, **III** 70

Zillah, **VI** 202; **VII** 199

Zimbabwe, ruins of, **II** 114

Zinjanthropus, **II** 20ff.
  human or not? **III** 124
  reconstructions of, **II** 23 (ill.), 238

Zion
  ancient topography of, **VII** 130, 131, 133, 134
  to be ploughed as a field, **VII** 129, 135

Zohar, **VI** 107

Zondi Test, **III** 152f.

Zoroastrianism, **I** 282; **VII** 32

Zulu, **IV** 130

Zuni pottery, **II** 151

Zygotes, human, **V** 196f.

Index of Names

A

Aaron, **V** 37, 228; **VII** 185, 238, 297
Abel, **II** 309, 311; **V** 38, 83, 247; **VII** 207, 208, 209, 227
Abelard, **VIII** 117, 119
Abelson, P. H., **VIII** 73
Abimelech, **II** 315
Abner, **I** 147; **II** 313, 314; **VII** 232
Abraham, **I** 15, 16, 78; **II** 91, 310, 314–320, 322, 331; **III** 93; **IV** 135; **V** 32, 35, 41, 248, 265; **VI** 39, 40, 43, 164, 193, 194; **VII** 72, 98, 100, 121, 147–159, 168–174, 177, 183, 194, 195, 233, 234, 239–243, 252, 258, 265, 268, 269; **IX** 297, 298
Abrahamson, Hans, **V** 94
Absolom, **II** 328; **VI** 137
Absolon, Karl, **II** 179, 234, 235
Acheson, Edward G., **VII** 211, 212
Ackerknecht, Erwin H., **I** 158, 159, 178, 199; **II** 115, 159, 184, 202; **IV** 161
Acsadi, Gy, **IX** 113
Acton, Lord John, **V** 319
Adah, **II** 311
Adam, **I** 17, 58, 61, 119, 233–235; **II** 30, 35, 64, 80–82, 133, 136, 138, 139, 187, 228, 254, 267–269, 271, 276, 277, 308, 309, 311; **III** 50, 88, 89, 94, 109, 110, 128, 144,
171, 172, 283, 289, 290, 291, 293, 295, 308, 317, 344, 345; **V** 18, 22, 25, 27, 29, 30, 33, 35, 37–41, 50, 82, 83, 86–88, 91, 92, 95, 97, 102-
-104, 106, 109, 110, 116–118, 125, 129, 139, 142, 145–159, 162, 172, 174, 179, 181, 190, 201–203, 228, 244, 368, 370; **VI** 33, 70, 73, 110, 176, 178, 193, 195, 198, 204, 205, 232, 233, 235, 238; **VII** 100, 147–150, 195, 200, 204, 209, 220, 222, 223, 225, 227, 235, 239, 252, 262, 268, 269, 274, 296, 308; **VIII** 89, 96, 248, 249; **IX** 38, 44, 113, 115, 116, 123, 133, 139, 140, 183-
-186, 211, 294, 297, 298
Adam, Leonard, **I** 186
Adrian, Lord, **III** 255, 319; **VIII** 68
Aeschylus, **V** 323, 324; **VII** 23
Aesop, **I** 199
Agassiz, Louis, **I** 359, 360; **IV** 90, 92
Agrippa, **VII** 29
Ahab, King, **III** 31, 184, 185; **V** 388, 389; **VII** 255–257; **IX** 18
Ahitophel, **VI** 137
Ainu, **I** 99, 130, 135, 168; **II** 46, 51, 114, 291, 298; **III** 138
Akhnaton, **VII** 186, 189
Alacalufes, **II** 114
Alaric, **VIII** 109, 120

185

Albrecht, William, **III** 63; **IV** 309, 310

Albrecht–Carrie, Rene, **I** 37, 306

Albright, W. F., **I** 21; **VII** 161

Alcuin, **I** 116

Aldis, A. S., **I** 222

Alexander the Great, **I** 77, 95, 97, 308; **V** 100; **VII** 25–28, 34, 125, 126

Alexander, William, **V** 299, 343

Alhazen, **I** 328

Allee, W. C., **III** 23, 61, 70; **IV** 184, 196, 197

Allen, Frank A., **I** 350–352; **II** 114, 116, 124

Allfrey, V. G., **VIII** 70

Alpenfels, Ethel, **I** 204

Altamira Caves, **II** 164

Altner, Helmut, **IV** 277

Al Ubeid, **I** 114; **II** 86, 90, 92, 94, 98, 101; **V** 64, 65, 67

Amala (feral child), **II** 260, 261, 267

Ambrose, **VIII** 173

Amenhotep II, **VII** 185, 186

Amenhotep III, **VII** 187, 189

Amenhotep IV, **VII** 257

Ammon, **I** 105

Amnon, **II** 328, 329

Amos, C. W. H., **II** 191

Amraphel, **VII** 161, 165, 166

Ananias, **VII** 15, 49

Anaxagoras of Clazomenae, **VIII** 126

Andamanese, **I** 63; **II** 259; **IV** 129

Andersen, F. I., **VIII** 171

Anderson, Sir Robert, **V** 297, 300, 339

Andree, Richard, **IX** 95, 96

Andrew, **I** 18; **V** 303

Andrew, R. J., **IV** 271

Andrews, Alfred C., **III** 84

Angus, S., **VII** 26–29

Anselm, **I** 232; **VIII** 117, 119

Anstey, Martin, **V** 44, 45; **VI** 46, 91, 238; **VII** 222; **IX** 55

Antevs, Ernst, **II** 32

Antiochus II, **V** 51

Apel, Willi, **I** 202

Apollodorus, **V** 51; **IX** 95

Appleton, Sir Edward, **VIII** 105

Aquinas, Thomas, **I** 296; **III** 81, 84, 226; **V** 168, 288; **VIII** 109, 117

Ararat, **I** 85; **II** 95

Arber, Agnes, **IV** 56

Arbib, Michael A., **VIII** 135

Archimedes, **I** 299

Ardrey, Robert, **III** 250, 265; **IV** 191, 199, 255, 299; **VIII** 25

Arensberg, C. M., **I** 254; **III** 28

Aristophanes, **I** 35, 81; **V** 55

Aristotle, **I** 262, 289; **III** 50, 202, 259; **V** 312; **VII** 18, 23–26; **VIII** 111; **IX** 216

Armenia, **I** 83, 86, 87, 89, 96

Arrian, **I** 107, 117

Arundell of Wardour, Lord Henry, **II** 77, 78; **VI** 9, 112, 195; **IX** 74, 75, 89, 91

Aryans, **I** 81, 91, 188, 312; **II** 114

Ashby, Sir Eric, **VIII** 14, 190

Ashkenaz, **I** 85–88

Ashurbanipal, **VII** 124, 163

Ashurnasipal, **VII** 123

Athanasius, **I** 218

Athens, **VII** 14, 21, 27

Atlas, **I** 81

Auerbach, C., **V** 202

Augustine, **I** 94, 223; **III** 34, 81, 84, 88, 158, 171, 226, 292, 302; **IV** 19; **V** 83, 125, 179, 181, 383; **VI** 10, 19, 38, 40, 43, 109, 174, 192; **VII** 87; **VIII** 109, 111; **IX** 42, 149

Augustus, Caesar **VII** 27–29

Austin, C. R., **IX** 138

Austin, John, **IV** 298

Australian Aborigines, **I** 171, 175; **II** 33, 46, 52, 54, 72, 74, 119, 123, 150, 154–156, 165, 170, 208, 220, 222, 258, 259, 287, 290, 291, 305; **III** 208

Australopithecines, **II** 13–15, 17, 20, 21, 28, 198, 201, 212, 213

Ávebury, Lord John, **IV** 133
Avery, J., **IV** 138
Axelrod, Daniel I, **IV** 53, 54
Ayala, Felip Huaman Poma de, **VI** 222

Ayer, A. J., **III** 270
Aymara, **I** 158, 184, 185, 326; **II** 259, 260, 306; **III** 147, 149
Ayres, Eugene, **VIII** 171

B

Bacon, Francis, **II** 66
Bacon, J. S. D., **IX** 160
Bacon, Roger, **II** 66
Baikie, James, **I** 294; **VII** 178, 182, 186
Bailey, Lloyd R., **IX** 63
Baker, E. Á., **III** 184
Baker, Howard B., **IV** 105
Balaam, **III** 96; **V** 148; **VI** 132, 164
Baldwin, James, **V** 210; **IX** 239
Baldwin, James L., **IV** 77, 200, 201
Bales, J. D., **IV** 90; **VIII** 24
Balfour, Arthur, **VIII** 126
Balfour, J. H., **IX** 120, 121
Ballinger, W. L., **IV** 307; **VI** 231; **VII** 235
Balsiger, David, **IX** 103
Bankoff, George, **VIII** 170
Banyoro, **II** 289
Barber, Bernard, **VIII** 157
Barclay, Vera, **V** 337
Barnett, Lincoln, **II** 114, 115, 140; **IV** 197
Barnett, S. A., **III** 25, 56; **IV** 149; **V** 186; **VIII** 163
Barnhouse, Donald G., **I** 185
Barnum, P. T., **II** 228, 229, 242; **IV** 48
Baronides, Samuel H., **III** 253
Barr, James, **I** 266, 267, 277, 278; **III** 286; **V** 194; **VII** 23
Barry, David G., **I** 301
Barth, Karl, **III** 34, 112, 158; **V** 78
Bartolome, Fray, **I** 331

Barton, George, **I** 80, 104; **II** 275, 299; **V** 52, 96; **VI** 186, 204; **VII** 147, 171, 186; **IX** 29, 76, 98
Basil, **V** 55
Bates, Daisy, **IV** 294
Bates, J. A. B., **IV** 227
Bates, M., **II** 76
Bateson, William, **IV** 74; **VIII** 90
Batterson, Hon. J. G., **I** 324
Bavister, B. D., **V** 196; **VIII** 72
Baynes, H. G., **III** 142
Bazett, H. C., **V** 213; **VIII** 67, 137
Beale, G. H., **V** 202
Beals, Ralph L., **VI** 187
Beasley, Walter J., **III** 73; **IV** 57
Beck, Stanley D., **VIII** 161, 162
Becker, Carl, **VIII** 147
Becker, Howard, **VIII** 63, 127
Bede, Adam, **III** 226
Bedford, D. E., **I** 294
Bedouin, **I** 158
Beethoven, Ludwig van, **II** 152
Behrendt, Thomas, **III** 265
Bell, Alexander Graham, **III** 206
Bell, Sir Charles, **IV** 37, 38, 73, 241; **VIII** 149
Bell, Clive, **I** 295; **II** 148, 175
Bell, G. H., **V** 212; **VIII** 67
Bella Coola, **II** 298
Bellarime, Robert, **III** 226
Belsen, **I** 231, 262; **III** 16
Belshazzar, **II** 277; **VI** 136, 203; **VII** 152
Benda, Julien, **VIII** 115, 181–183

Bender, George A., **I** 212
Benedict, Ruth, **I** 68, 334; **II** 73, 130; **III** 60, 118; **IV** 263, 292
Benjamin, A. Cornelius, **VIII** 129, 130, 197
Bennett, H. H., **IX** 118
Bentham, Jeremy, **IX** 146
Benzinger, T. H., **IV** 259; **IX** 196
Berdyaev, Nicholas, **VIII** 168; **IX** 154
Beresford, John, **V** 132
Berg, Leo S., **II** 18, 184, 215; **III** 261; **IV** 35, 81, 145, 148, 150–152, 154–157, 187
Bergson, Henri, **II** 262; **III** 242; **IV** 278
Bergstrom, Sten R., **III** 257, 331
Berl, Ernst, **II** 32
Berna, Kurt, **V** 337
Bernal, J. D., **IV** 34, 222; **VIII** 49
Bernard, Claude, **III** 320; **IV** 36; **VIII** 86, 91, 143
Bernard, Jessie, **I** 33, 37, 303, 304, 310
Bernard (of Clairvaux), Saint, **III** 226
Berossus, **V** 51, 52
Berrigan, Daniel, **V** 335
Bertalanffy, Ludwig von, **IV** 192, 282, 287
Bessemer, Sir Henry, **I** 322
Best, C.H., **IV** 314
Best, Jay, B., **III** 250, 251, 330
Bethuel, **II** 320–323; **VII** 243–246
Bettelheim, Bruno, **II** 265; **III** 164; **VI** 205; **IX** 167
Bevan, Edwin, **VIII** 198
Beveridge, W. I. B., **VIII** 105
Bewberry, R. E., **II** 90; **V** 63
Bhartri-hari, **VII** 33
Bidder, G. P., **V** 136
Bierce, Ambrose, **VI** 25
Bingham, Les, **II** 156
Birch, L. C., **III** 323
Birnbaum, Jesse, **V** 335

Bishop, Carl Whiting, **II** 104
Bishop, Eric F., **I** 19, 20
Bishops, Isabella L., **I** 203
Bismarck, Prince Otto von, **IV** 225
Bissell, Claude, **VIII** 123
Bithynia, **I** 86, 87, 97
Blackett, P. M. S., **I** 318
Blackler, A., **V** 196
Black Sea, **I** 82, 88, 89, 97
Blackwood, Beatrice, **II** 183
Blair, Harold, **II** 165
Blanc, Alberto Carlo, **II** 232; **IV** 168
Blegen, Carl W., **I** 197; **II** 77
Bleibtrue, Herman K., **IV** 208
Bligh, Captain, **II** 123
Blitzer, Charles, **VI** 222, 223
Bliven, Bruce, **V** 105
Bloch, Raymond, **I** 109
Blum, Harold, **I** 351; **III** 76; **IV** 29, 30; **V** 26; **VIII** 35
Blunt, J. J., **I** 53; **VII** 234, 243
Boas, Franz, **II** 79, 108, 109, 180, 211, 212, 236; **IV** 166; **VIII** 242, 243
Bochart, **I** 90, 94–96
Bogoras, W., **II** 294, 296; **V** 311; **VII** 201; **IX** 171
Bohlen, Peter von, **VII** 158
Boigne, Comtesse de, **VII** 115
Boman, Thorlief, **I** 266, 277, 278; **III** 286
Bondi, H., **IV** 88
Boone, Daniel, **II** 187
Boring, E. J., **III** 238
Born, Max, **VIII** 182
Bosanquet, R. C., **I** 197
Boscawen, St. Chad, **I** 36, 192, 308; **V** 95; **VI** 199; **VII** 151, 152, 163, 164, 206, 225; **IX** 45
Bose, Sir Jagdis Chunder, **III** 69, 335
Bosius, Jacobus, **V** 303
Boulding, Kenneth, **VIII** 123
Boule, Marcellin, **II** 67, 113, 181; **III** 48; **IV** 152, 235, 265
Bovill, E. W., **IX** 117

Bowman, Isaiah, **VIII** 140
Boyd, Bill, **III** 69
Boyd, J. D., **V** 112
Brace, C. L., **IV** 214
Brachet, J., **V** 185
Brahe, Tycho, **I** 191
Braidwood, Robert J., **I** 138, 171; **II** 100, 165, 195; **V** 61; **VIII** 161
Branch, D. P., **I** 322, 323
Braque, Georges, **VII** 87, 88
Breasted, James, **I** 194, 308; **II** 89; **V** 63
Bridgeman, Laura, **II** 263, 265, 266; **IX** 112
Bridges, Thomas, **II** 122, 189; **IV** 296; **VI** 215
Bridgman, P. W., **VIII** 144
Briffault, Robert, **II** 131, 166, 262, 290, 296; **IV** 278, 285, 286, 294; **VIII** 131
Briggs, Robert, **V** 185; **VII** 296
Britton, S. W., **IV** 245
Broca, Pierre Paul, **IV** 267
Brody, Samuel, **II** 185, 220, 221; **III** 62, 63; **IV** 285, 286, 289, 303; **IX** 134
Bronowski, J., **VIII** 135
Brooke, Rupert, **IX** 241
Broom, Robert, **II** 28, 198, 199, 212; **IV** 73; **VIII** 145
Brown, A. R., **III** 139, 167
Brown, Gordon, **II** 301; **VI** 224
Brown, R., **I** 110; **IV** 138
Brown, Radcliffe, **IV** 266
Brown, Roger, **II** 270

Browne, E. Harold, **III** 292; **V** 182, 249
Browne, Lewis, **IV** 111
Bruce, F. F., **I** 23
Brues, Charles, **I** 128; **II** 222; **IV** 67, 188
Bruman, Henry J., **I** 167
Bruno, Giordano, **II** 66
Bryan, Ingram, **II** 105
Bryant, J., **IX** 85
Buckland, William, **II** 53; **VI** 107
Buddha, **I** 282; **V** 395; **VII** 32
Budge, E. A. Wallis, **V** 254; **VI** 93; **VII** 289
Buffon, Comte, **II** 250; **IV** 84, 87, 88
Bulfinch, T., **VI** 201; **VII** 199
Bullen, R. A., **IV** 265
Bullinger, E. W., **I** 80; **V** 354
Bunyan, John, **I** 223
Burkhardt, Dietrich, **IV** 277
Burns, Allen, **V** 308
Burrill, Augustine, **III** 209
Burstall, Aubrey, F., **I** 321
Burtt, E. A., **VIII** 158
Buschbaum, Ralph, **III** 331; **IV** 52, 53
Bush, Vannevar, **I** 300, 301; **III** 15
Bushmen of Kalahari Desert, **I** 139; **II** 56, 105, 118, 119, 122, 220
Butler, Alban, **V** 303
Butterfield, Herbert, **I** 316; **III** 20, 22, 26, 39; **IX** 241
Button, Jeremy, **II** 140
Buyssens, Paul, **I** 136; **II** 52
Byron, Lord George, **II** 181

C

Cabell, J. B., **IX** 109, 163
Caesar. *See* Augustus *and* Julius.
Caiaphas, **VI** 164; **IX** 148, 151
Caiger, S. L., **II** 104; **V** 94; **VI** 186; **VII** 186

Cain, **I** 108; **II** 87, 139, 309–311; **IV** 307; **V** 37, 38, 83, 157, 247; **VI** 198, 219ff.; **VII** 149, 198, 205, 207–209, 223–225, 227, 228; **IX** 47

Cain, A. J., **IV** 72

Cairns, Huntington, **II** 295

Cairns, Rev. Principal, **VII** 91, 92

Calder, Nigel, **III** 254

Calder, Ritchie, **VIII** 105

Caldin, E. F., **VIII** 210

Caleb, **V** 280

Calverton, V. F., **II** 33, 66, 119, 131, 166, 183; **III** 15; **IV** 148, 178; **VIII** 131, 133, 160

Calvin, John, **III** 37, 291; **VIII** 122; **IX** 149

Cambyses, **I** 103

Cameron, D. Ewen, **VIII** 169, 209

Campbell, John, **VI** 186

Camps, F., **V** 121

Canaan, **I** 25, 63, 67, 72, 101, 102, 108, 145, 148, 150, 151; **II** 313; **VII** 231, 232

Canaanites, **I** 72f.; **II** 302

Candole, A. de, **III** 145

Cannon, Walter B., **V** 212, 313; **VIII** 67

Canstadt Race, **I** 136; **II** 52

Caransius, Count of the Saxon Shore, **I** 87, 88

Carlson, A. J., **I** 134; **III** 13; **V** 212; **VIII** 67

Carmel, Mount, **I** 129, 131, 134; **II** 44, 48, 50, 221, 223

Carmichael, Leonard, **III** 205; **IX** 151

Carnegie, Andrew, **IV** 178

Carpenter, C. R., **IV** 290, 299

Carrel, Alexis, **V** 124, 178

Carr-Saunders, A.M., **III** 146

Carter, George, **IV** 75; **V** 57

Carthage, **I** 94; **VII** 123

Carthy, J. D., **III** 23, 24, 114

Cartier, Jacques, **I** 331

Casarett, George W., **V** 130

Caspari, E., **VIII** 230

Cassirer, Ernst, **I** 268, 271, 274; **II** 86, 129, 253, 256–258, 265, 267, 299; **III** 105; **VI** 216; **VII** 85, 87; **VIII** 113; **IX** 175

Cassius, **III** 149

Casson, S., **II** 121

Castleley, J. V. Langmead, **VIII** 176

Catchpole, H. R., **V** 213

Cathay, **I** 104, 210

Catlin, **I** 78

Caucasus, **I** 90, 96

Cave, A. J. E., **IV** 168

Celts, **I** 84, 91

Chalk, L., **IV** 55

Chalmers, Thomas, **VI** 106, 107, 109, 111

Chamberlain, A. F., **I** 89; **VI** 183

Chambers, Oswald, **III** 127

Chambers, Robert, **II** 183, 221f.; **IV** 167

Champlain, **III** 203

Chandler, Tertius, **I** 328

Changu Daru, **I** 197; **II** 95, 96; **V** 65

Chapell, F. L., **VI** 173

Chapin, Miriam, **I** 280; **VI** 210

Chardin. *See* Teilhard de Chardin.

C'harma, **I** 35, 81

Charles II of Spain, **VI** 223

Chaucer, Geoffrey, **VI** 53

Chedd, Graham, **III** 331f.; **IV** 198

Chedorlaomer (king of Elam), **VII** 161–165, 167, 173

Cheesman, Evelyn, **IX** 179

Cherokee, **I** 78

Chesterton, G. K., **IV** 298

Chetwood, Thomas B., **V** 182

Cheyenne, **I** 273

Chiang, Mickey, **II** 14

Childe, Vere Gordon, **I** 36, 72, 114, 121, 125, 171, 188, 193, 194, 305, 306; **II** 35, 37, 42, 44, 54, 82, 89, 90, 92, 93, 96–98, 114, 134, 177; **IV** 248, 249; **V** 63–66; **VI** 179, 186; **IX** 48

Choukoutien, **I** 107, 126, 129, 134; **II** 27, 42, 44, 51, 56, 115, 180, 223; **VI** 230

Chukchee, **I** 63; **II** 260, 265, 278, 294, 296, 298, 302, 305, 306; **III** 137–139

Churchill, Winston, **III** 187; **V** 393

Cicero, **II** 111; **VII** 27, 30, 107

Cihak, R., **II** 14

Clapp, Frederick G., **VII** 175

Clapperton, Captain Hugh, **V** 304

Clapperton, R. H., **I** 212

Clark, Gordon H., **III** 15; **VIII** 131

Clark, Harold W., **II** 33; **IX** 62

Clark, J. Grahame D., **I** 36, 166, 305; **II** 101, 126, 168

Clark, Sir Kenneth, **V** 347; **VIII** 114, 115; **IX** 229

Clark, R. E. D., **I** 354, 363; **IV** 199, 226; **V** 16, 133; **VIII** 208; **IX** 136, 159

Clark, Robert A., **I** 297

Clark, R. T., **IV** 90; **VIII** 24

Clark, Wilfred LeGros, **II** 13, 21, 22, 43–45, 51, 214, 236; **III** 58; **IV** 149, 151, 166, 224, 235, 236; **V** 61

Claudius, **VII** 29

Clausen, Jens, **IV** 84

Cleanthes, **VII** 19

Cleckley, Hervey, **IX** 187

Clement, **I** 20; **VI** 89

Clement of Overdyke, **II** 200

Cleopatra, **I** 209; **II** 301; **III** 121; **IV** 282; **VI** 224

Cloudsley-Thompson, J. L., **III** 25

Clymene, **I** 81

Cnossus. *See* Knossos.

Cobb, Stanley, **III** 69, 321, 335; **IV** 225

Cogan, Dr. Thomas, **V** 307

Coggins, Jack, **I** 210

Coghill, George E., **VIII** 211

Cohen, A., **V** 397

Cohen, I. Bernard, **VIII** 153

Cohen, Robert S., **I** 285

Cohn, S. H. and S. M., **VIII** 128

Cole, Mabel and Fay-Cooper, **II** 230

Cole, M. C., **I** 134, 138, 180

Collett, Sidney, **IX** 80

Collingwood, R. G., **II** 83; **VIII** 129

Collins, J. L., **I** 167

Collins, Roy, **IV** 138

Columbus, **VIII** 158

Comfort, Alex, **V** 132, 136, 166

Commodus, **VII** 257

Commoner, Barry, **VIII** 59

Companella, Tomasso, **II** 66

Comte, Auguste, **II** 74

Conant, James B., **I** 11, 286, 297, 315; **VIII** 140, 167

Conder, C. R., **I** 88, 90, 104, 107, 210; **VI** 188–191

Confucius, **I** 30–32, 211, 278, 279, 283, 294; **III** 187; **V** 393

Constable, **IX** 271, 272

Constantine, **V** 55

Cook, Captain James, **II** 190, 191

Cook, F. C., **I** 80, 94; **IX** 74, 80, 92

Cooke, W., **II** 123

Coon, Carleton S., **I** 36, 52, 74, 138, 170, 199, 305, 322, 326, 328, 333; **II** 54, 122, 184, 189, 190, 200, 202, 210, 211, 230, 297, 299, 302, 305, 306; **III** 62, 139; **IV** 168, 239, 265, 266; **VI** 188, 213; **VII** 201; **IX** 75, 92, 126

Coonen, L. P., **IX** 158

Cooper, L. F., **III** 246; **VI** 24

Copernicus, **VIII** 119, 154

Cornelius, **I** 22; **III** 125; **VII** 52, 99

Corner, George W., **IV** 304; **V** 189; **VIII** 92

Cotlow, Lewis, **I** 178

Cotton, Clare M., **I** 169

Coulson, C. A., **VIII** 19, 122, 123

Cousins, Frank W., **II** 236, 243

Cowley, Malcolm, **III** 204

Cowper, William, **IV** 12

Coxinga, **II** 124

Crassus, **VII** 107

Crawford, Dan, **III** 171; **V** 208, 392

Crawford, M. D. C., **I** 167, 180, 317; **II** 88

Crawford, P. J., **III** 123

Creasy, Edward S., **I** 308; **VII** 25
Cree, **I** 78
Creed, J. Mildred, **II** 110, 165
Crew, H., **VIII** 156
Crewdson, G., **VII** 253
Crick, Francis, **III** 258
Crimea, **I** 82
Cro-Magnon, **I** 134; **II** 50, 102, 196; **V** 58, 67
Cronos, **I** 82
Crowe, Leslie K., **IV** 72; **VIII** 60
Crowell, C., **V** 309
Crow Indians, **II** 54, 302, 303
Crowson, R. A., **III** 56

Cuenot, Lucien, **VIII** 234
Cumont, Franz, **VI** 112
Cunningham, William, **IX** 149
Curry, John C., **I** 312, 313; **II** 34, 137; **IX** 48
Curtis, Howard J., **V** 131
Cush, **I** 102, 118; **VI** 200; **VII** 197, 206
Custance, Arthur C., **I** 10, 70; **IV** 259, 260; **IX** 130
Custance, John, **VIII** 126; **IX** 111
Cuvier, Georges, **II** 247, 248; **III** 57
Cymri, **I** 84, 85, 87
Cyrus (the Great) **IV** 118; **VI** 131, 135; **VII** 167; **IX** 19, 20

D

Dachau, **I** 231, 262; **III** 18
Dale, Andrew M., **I** 199
Daltry, Joseph F., **IX** 234
Danby, P. M., **II** 183
Daniel, **III** 96, 222; **VII** 35, 39, 110, 141, 152
Danielli, J. F., **VIII** 75
Daniels, Roy, **VIII** 123
Dante, **I** 223; **II** 137; **VI** 216; **VIII** 117
Darius, **I** 97; **IX** 20
Dart, Raymond, **II** 28, 198
Darwin, Charles, **I** 148, 170; **II** 65, 66, 69, 75, 108, 115, 140, 157, 189, 190, 191, 219, 223, 228, 234, 245, 247, 250, 255, 256; **III** 15, 23, 69, 335; **IV** 16, 47, 56, 58, 71, 73, 86, 88, 90, 91, 96, 110, 125, 145, 146, 172, 177, 178, 181ff., 187, 189, 192, 195–197, 199, 214, 233, 254; **V** 84, 127, 184, 187; **VI** 109, 228; **VII** 201; **VIII** 24, 78, 131, 133, 151, 219, 220, 221
Darwin, Sir Francis, **II** 140; **IV** 86, 88; **VIII** 220, 221

Dathe, Johann August, **IV** 107; **VI** 110
David, **I** 16, 26, 147, 267; **II** 281, 313, 314, 328, 329; **III** 31, 94, 184, 185, 193, 224, 342; **IV** 46; **V** 28, 191, 244, 388, 389; **VI** 43, 44, 47, 138, 164, 172; **VII** 70, 71, 100, 123, 132, 134, 231, 232, 237, 258--260, 262, 263, 265, 268; **IX** 19, 20, 232, 235
Davidheiser, Bolton, **IV** 178
Davidson, A. B., **VI** 86, 87
Davidson, Basil, **II** 152
Davidson, J. N., **V** 212; **VIII** 67
Davies, Benjamin, **VI** 117, 186, 187
Davies, D. R., **III** 24, 26, 27, 35, 88, 159; **VIII** 140, 182
Davies, H. M., **I** 160
Davies, Merson, **IV** 53, 54; **VIII** 208
Davis, George T.V., **VII** 137, 139, 140
Davis, G. H., **I** 202
Davis, J. D., **I** 80
Davy, Sir Humphry, **I** 361; **IV** 87

Dawkins, Boyd, **II** 158

Dawson, Sir J. William, **I** 122, 128, 133, 137, 184, 192; **II** 19, 38, 39, 49, 53, 54, 70–72, 114, 120, 222, 288; **III** 48; **IV** 67, 148, 247, 249, 268; **V** 59, 254; **VI** 112, 183, 184; **IX** 62, 79

Dawson, W. Bell, **IV** 40

Deacon, G. E. R., **I** 336, 337

Deacon, W. A., **I** 173

DeBeer, Sir Gavin, **I** 198, 309; **II** 18, 236, 241, 243; **III** 146, 292; **IV** 72, 147, 187, 255, 287; **V** 19, 57, 59, 188; **VIII** 60

Deevey, Edward, **V** 16, 17, 135, 178

de Haas, Frank S., **II** 120

De Laguna, Frederica, **II** 158

De Laguna, Grace, **III** 117; **IV** 315

de la Loubere, S., **I** 211

de Lana, Francesco, **VIII** 140

Delitzsch, Franz, **VI** 193, 194; **IX** 24

Delitzsch, Friedrich, **IV** 116

Democritus of Abdera, **VIII** 126

de Mortillet, Gabriel, **I** 125; **II** 42

Dench, E. B., **IV** 307; **VI** 231; **VII** 235

Denholme-Young, H. M., **IX** 139

Denmark, **I** 87

Dennett, R. E., **VI** 201; **VII** 198

Dennis, Alfred Pearce, **IX** 130

de Plauzoles, Sicard, **V** 104

de Quatrefages, A., **II** 56; **IX** 57

de Santillana, G., **VIII** 156, 204

Descartes, Rene, **III** 318, 319; **V** 290; **VIII** 179

Deukalion, **I** 81; **IX** 89

Devlin, Lord, **III** 267, 270

Devoe, Alan, **III** 67

DeVries, John, **II** 32

Dewar, Douglas, **IV** 52

Dewey, Thomas E., **VII** 117, 118

de Wit, J. J. D., **IV** 83

Diamond, A. S., **II** 295

Dice, Lee R., **III** 23, 72, 73; **IV** 191, 192, 323

Dickens, Charles, **V** 372

Digger Indians, **II** 122

Dill, D. B., **VIII** 73

Dillmann, A., **I** 62, 67, 72, 80, 106

Dinsmoor, W. B., **I** 197

Disney, Walt, **I** 201; **III** 64

Disraeli, Benjamin, **VII** 114

Dixon, Roland, **II** 78, 117, 118; **III** 208; **VII** 156; **IX** 132

Djapatischta, **I** 82; **VI** 195

Dobell, P., **II** 296

Dobuans, **I** 169; **II** 284

Dobzhansky, Theodosius, **I** 134; **II** 50, 76, 164, 195; **III** 17, 292, 323; **IV** 49, 61, 72, 81, 208, 209; **V** 188; **VIII** 65, 66, 84, 97, 162, 163, 180

Dods, Marcus, **I** 66, 80, 82; **II** 312; **VI** 195, 201; **VII** 198, 226

Dodson, E. O., **IV** 76; **VIII** 234, 235; **IX** 41, 42

Donne, John, **III** 135

Dorozynski, Alexander, **V** 120

Dorsey, George, **II** 185, 220; **III** 49, 121, 181; **IV** 224, 306; **V** 385; **IX** 137, 159, 206

Dostoyevsky, F. M., **III** 35, 36, 88, 159, 187, 239; **V** 393

Drake, Stillman, **VIII** 153

Driberg, J. H., **II** 288, 290

Driver, S. R., **I** 58–60, 65, 80, 93, 113; **V** 53; **VI** 178, 179; **VII** 167, 296

Dryden, Hugh, **I** 44, 70, 221, 248, 339; **VIII** 140

Duane, D. T., **III** 265

Dubberstein, Waldo H., **I** 192

DuBois, Cora, **III** 145, 147, 148, 157; **IV** 294

DuBois, E. F., **IV** 258

duBois-Reymond, Emile, **I** 353; **III** 272; **VIII** 73, 138

Dubos, Rene, **III** 209; **VIII** 181, 206, 207

Dufour, Léon, **III** 58

Dunbar, Carl O., **IV** 239

Duncan, Mrs. George J. C., **VI** 238

Duncan, J. Garrow, **VII** 165, 194, 210

DuNouy, Pierre Lecomte, **I** 204, 340, 354–356; **IV** 33, 57, 68, 70; **V** 17, 128; **VI** 24; **VIII** 169; **IX** 243

Durant, Will, **III** 18; **VII** 21, 23, 24, 26, 28, 33; **VIII** 151, 188

Durkheim, Emile, **II** 67; **IX** 135

DuToit, A. L., **I** 116

E

Easter Islanders, **II** 157

Eber, **I** 62, 115

Eckhardt, Robert, **II** 201

Eddington, Sir Arthur, **VI** 11; **VII** 85; **VIII** 20, 21, 30, 32, 60, 170

Edersheim, Alfred, **V** 99, 123, 249, 349; **VI** 111; **IX** 62

Edholm, O.G., **III** 120; **IV** 261

Edison, Thomas, **I** 262

Edwards, Jonathan, **III** 146; **IV** 135

Edwards, R. G., **V** 139, 196; **VIII** 72

Eells, M., **IX** 92

Egypt, **I** 102; **III** 79, 220, 221

Einstein, Albert, **I** 304, 310; **II** 152; **III** 53, 54; **VI** 12, 13, 17–19, 25; **VIII** 170

Eiseler, R., **VII** 225

Eiseley, Loren, **I** 356; **II** 108, 196; **IV** 70, 256

Eisenberg, Leon, **III** 19, 25, 138

Eisler, Robert, **I** 27, 193; **II** 86

Elam, **I** 113, 118; **IX** 45

Elbing, F. B., **III** 23, 24, 114

el Damieh, **VII** 191, 192

Elijah, **III** 96, 139, 215, 223; **V** 154, 178; **VI** 59, 132; **VII** 255–257; **IX** 18, 20, 231

Elishah, **I** 92, 93; **VI** 197

Elizabeth, **III** 144

Elkin, A. P., **I** 173, 174; **II** 154, 155

Elsasser, Walter, **V** 47

Elton, Charles, **III** 71; **IV** 187, 189, 255

Embery, Winnifred, **III** 167

Emery, Walter B., **II** 89

Emmerson, A. E., **V** 136

Engberg, Martin, **I** 33, 138, 291, 292

Enoch, **I** 108; **II** 87, 187; **V** 37; **VI** 198, 199; **VII** 149, 205, 206, 223-
-225

Enoch (7th from Adam), **II** 133, 134; **V** 18, 34, 40–42, 154, 178; **VI** 43; **VII** 237

Ephrussi, Boris, **I** 357; **V** 113; **VIII** 227, 228

Er, **II** 325–327

Eridu, **II** 93, 94

Esarhaddon, **I** 82, 87; **VII** 124

Esau, **II** 330; **V** 279; **VI** 144, 145, 157; **VII** 224, 246

Eskimo, **I** 135, 158–162, 165, 168, 293, 323, 341; **II** 51, 105, 115, 121, 158–162, 170, 184, 187, 200, 202–204, 260, 265, 289, 304–306; **VII** 201

Ethiopia, **I** 102, 103, 118

Ethiopian (eunuch), **I** 15, 22, 24, 261

Etruscans, **I** 107–111, 116, 198, 202, 204, 308, 309, 335

Euripides, **V** 323

Europe, **I** 83, 85, 88, 96, 99

Eusebius, **I** 83; **V** 51; **VII** 74, 259

Eustathius, **V** 55

Evans, Sir Arthur, **I** 196, 197; **V** 13, 48

Evans, F. Gaynor, **II** 48

Evans, Sir James Lovett, **IV** 261

Evans, W. D., **V** 121

Evans-Pritchard, E. E., **II** 73, 121; **IV** 143

Eve, **I** 234, 235; **II** 228, 254, 267–269, 308–311; **III** 88, 289, 308, 344; **V** 18, 30, 38, 82, 83, 86–88, 91, 92, 97, 103, 104, 106, 109, 110, 118, 125, 139, 147–158, 172, 174, 179, 181, 190, 201–205, 244, 247, 248, 370, 381, 382, 391, 398, 399; **VI** 70, 73, 178, 205, 232, 235, 237; **VII** 147, 148, 195, 209, 227, 235, 239, 274; **IX** 113, 115, 116, 139, 140, 298

Evenari, Michael, **I** 165

Ewing, Sir Alfred, **VIII** 170

Exell, Joseph S., **VI** 207

Eysenck, H. J., **III** 30, 166, 345; **IV** 25; **V** 202; **VIII** 166

Ezra, **II** 79; **VIII** 195, 196

F

Fabre, J. Henri, **III** 57–60, 62, 65, 97, 159; **IV** 248; **V** 168; **VIII** 96; **IX** 72

Fairbairn, P., **I** 80

Fairholme, George, **IV** 96

Farber, Eduard, **I** 213

Farmer, F. T., **I** 348; **IV** 27

Farrand, William R., **IV** 97

Farrar, F. W., **I** 84; **III** 226, 232; **VII** 19

Farrington, Benjamin, **I** 291, 299, 315

Farwell, George, **I** 171, 172

Fayrer, Sir Joseph, **III** 67

Fechner, G. T., **III** 69, 335

Feletabs, **II** 289

Felkin, Robert, **I** 330

Fentriss, J. C., **IV** 202

Ferguson, Elizabeth A., **I** 330

Ferguson, Wallace K., **VIII** 119

Fernel, Jean Francois, **VIII** 84

Fessard, A. E., **VIII** 143

Feuner, Phyllis R., **I** 204

Field, Henry, **I** 19, 125, 138; **II** 42, 55, 217; **IX** 51

Fiesel, Eva, **I** 110

Finch, R. M., **IV** 270

Finkelstein, J. J., **I** 291

Fischberg, M., **V** 196

Fischer, Daniel, **V** 308

Fisher, J., **III** 320

Fisher, James, **III** 66, 114

Fisk, Eugene Lyman, **V** 107

Fitch, J. M., **I** 322, 323

Flanigan, Francis, **III** 167

Fleming, Sir Ambrose, **III** 75

Flesch, Rudolf, **II** 25; **IV** 143

Fleure, H. J., **I** 124, 139; **II** 40, 56, 86; **IX** 50

Fontechevade, **II** 135, 185, 196; **V** 67

Forbes, R. J., **I** 93, 97, 201, 203, 210, 211, 214; **II** 311, 312; **VI** 201; **VII** 198, 199, 226

Forbes, S. A., **III** 61

Foreman, G., **II** 157

Forman, L. L., **VI** 100

Forsdyke, E. J., **II** 99

Forster, E. M., **VIII** 52

Forsyth, P. T., **IX** 244

Fortune, Reo, **V** 349

Fothergill, P. G., **I** 362; **II** 75; **III** 118; **IV** 74, 320; **IX** 160

Fox, George, **III** 341

Fox, Munro, **II** 252, 257; **IV** 317; **IX** 127

Fox, R. H., **IV** 261

Fox, Sidney, **IV** 34, 222; **VIII** 36, 49

Fox, Theodore, **VIII** 24

France, **I** 83, 85

France, Anatole, **II** 181, 236; **IV** 225
France, R. H., **III** 69, 335
Francis of Assisi, Saint, **III** 82, 112, 226; **VIII** 111, 173
Frank, Philipp, **I** 298; **VI** 12, 19
Frankel, H. M., **IV** 260
Frankfort, H. and H. A., **I** 34, 314; **II** 94, 101, 172; **III** 79, 80; **IV** 115, 138; **VIII** 106, 181
Frankl, Viktor E., **I** 44, 70, 249; **III** 210, 249, 271; **IV** 214; **VIII** 13, 14, 164, 165
Franseen, E. B., **IV** 239–241
Frazer, Sir James, **II** 67, 74, 77, 259, 301; **IX** 70, 73, 75, 77, 81, 82, 85, 86, 90, 93, 96, 176

Free, Joseph P., **I** 80; **VII** 147, 153, 158, 194
Fremantle, Anne, **VIII** 114; **IX** 229
French, J. D., **V** 213; **VIII** 68
Freud, Sigmund, **I** 304; **III** 33, 141, 142, 158, 159, 161, 209, 240
Fried, C., **III** 251
Friedman, Herbert, **IV** 153
Frisch, Carl von, **IV** 276
Frisch, O. R., **VIII** 134
Fromm, Erich, **III** 32, 87, 89, 159, 201; **VIII** 129, 172; **IX** 152
Fuller, Thomas, **VII** 216
Furer-Haimendorf, Christoph von, **II** 288, 289
Furness, W. H., **IV** 269, 270
Fyfe, Hamilton, **I** 68

G

Gadd, C. J., **I** 152; **II** 92; **V** 64
Gaffron, Hans, **VIII** 74, 83
Gainsborough, Thomas, **II** 202, 203; **IV** 162, 163
Galef, Bennett, **IV** 309
Galen, **IX** 216
Galileo, **I** 315; **IV** 25; **VIII** 119, 152–159, 162, 165, 173
Gall, Franz Joseph, **II** 181
Gall, James, **III** 296; **IV** 321; **VI** 239
Galley Hill finds, **II** 195
Galpin, F. W., **II** 104
Galsworthy, John, **III** 16, 204
Galton, Sir Francis, **I** 67; **II** 127; **III** 145, 146
Gama, Vasco da, **VIII** 158
Gamaliel, **VII** 38
Gambetta, Leon, **II** 181, 236; **IV** 224
Gamow, George, **I** 352; **IV** 93; **VIII** 21, 26
Gandhi, **III** 187; **V** 393; **VII** 33

Garbar, Clark M., **II** 304; **III** 138; **IX** 172
Garcia, John, **IV** 294, 309
Gardiner, Sir Alan, **I** 33, 292
Gardner, Martin, **IX** 60
Gardner, R. A. and B. T., **II** 262; **IV** 247, 269, 271–274, 276
Garn, Stanley M., **II** 27
Garrod, Dorothy, **I** 125; **II** 42
Garstang, **VII** 189, 191
Gates, Ruggles, **IV** 153
Gayton, A. H., **I** 325
Geertz, Clifford, **III** 17, 18; **IV** 283, 284, 320
Geikie, Cunningham, **II** 117; **VI** 208, 209
Gellius, Alus, **V** 207
Genghis Khan, **I** 209, 322, 325; **III** 187; **V** 393
Geoffroy, Etienne, **III** 57
George VI, **VI** 151

Gerard, Ralph, **III** 246, 248, 253, 254, 256, 329; **IV** 142, 226; **VIII** 99, 139, 169

Gerleman, G., **I** 277

Germany, **I** 85–89

Gesenius, H. F. W., **I** 118; **VI** 92, 93, 117, 186; **VII** 287

Ghirshman, R., **II** 96–98

Gibbon, Edward, **VI** 57

Gibson, R. E., **IV** 25; **VIII** 157, 165, 166

Gideon, **III** 222; **IX** 279

Gillispie, Charles C., **I** 360; **IV** 87; **IX** 62

Ginsberg, Louis, **V** 179, 180

Gissing, George, **VIII** 171

Gladwin, Thomas, **II** 184, 216; **VIII** 241

Glanville, S. R. K., **I** 202

Glass, Bentley, **IV** 307; **VI** 228

Glicksberg, C. I., **VIII** 147

Gliedman, Lester H., **VI** 21

Glucksberg, Samuel, **I** 271

Glueck, Nelson, **I** 165; **V** 99; **VII** 145

Gode, Alexander, **II** 137; **VI** 216; **IX** 156

Goerg, Edouard, **VII** 87, 88

Gog, **I** 89, 90

Goldenweiser, Alexander, **I** 138, 161, 182; **II** 74, 75, 106, 131, 151, 161, 167, 176, 250, 291, 298, 305; **III** 138; **IV** 288, 290; **V** 311; **VIII** 208; **IX** 92, 179, 217

Golding, W. J., **III** 343

Goldschmidt, R., **VIII** 60

Goldschmidt, Ralph B., **II** 44; **IV** 49, 61, 67

Goliath, **I** 26, 147; **II** 311, 313; **III** 234; **VII** 228, 232

Gomer, **I** 82–85, 89; **VI** 196

Gomorrah, **I** 76–78; **III** 178; **V** 232; **VII** 162, 170, 173–175

Good, Ronald, **III** 23, 72; **IV** 56, 191, 192; **IX** 127

Goodall, Jane and Hugo van Lamick, **IV** 264

Goodhart, C. B., **VI** 24

Goodyear, Charles, **I** 179

Gordon, C. A., **I** 350; **II** 297; **IV** 29; **IX** 142

Gordon, Ernest, **II** 274; **V** 104

Gordon, S. D., **IX** 276

Gorer, Jeoffrey, **VIII** 177

Goshen, C. E., **VIII** 163

Goths, **I** 87, 99

Gould, Sir Alfred, **V** 107

Graham, C., **II** 122

Grant, Asahel, **VII** 74

Grant, Verne, **VIII** 229

Grau, R. F., **I** 37, 68, 309

Gray, George W., **VIII** 18

Gray, Sir James, **IV** 147, 175, 176; **VIII** 159

Gray, Thomas, **VII** 114

Gray, Willard F. M., **I** 196

Green, Michael, **III** 177

Greenberg, J. H., **VI** 187

Greene, John C., **II** 250; **IV** 84, 87, 177

Gregory the Great, **III** 82, 226

Gregory of Nyssa, **I** 361; **IV** 65; **VI** 192

Greulach, Victor A., **V** 395; **VIII** 70

Grey, Anthony, **III** 211

Grey, Zane, **VII** 160

Grimaldi Man, **I** 136; **II** 52

Grollenberg, L. H., **VII** 139

Gudger, E. W., **I** 169

Gunstrip, H. J. S., **VIII** 69

Gunter, Gordon, **VII** 212

Gurdon, John, **V** 184

Gurney, O. G., **I** 104

Gyges, **I** 83, 90

H

Hadamard, Jacques, **III** 246

Haddon, A. C., **I** 213; **II** 185, 208, 217; **IX** 57

Hadrian, **VII** 135, 136

Haeckel, Ernst, **II** 241; **IV** 147; **VIII** 79

Hafstead, L. R., **I** 286

Hagar, **I** 15, 16; **II** 318, 319; **VII** 98, 171, 172

Hagemann, R., **VIII** 230

Hagen, Victor W. von, **I** 182, **VI** 222

Haimendorf. *See* Furer-Haimendorf.

Haldane, J. B. S., **III** 147, 325, 340; **V** 70, 132, 135, 136; **VI** 187; **VIII** 139

Hale, John R., **VI** 223; **VIII** 114

Hall, K. R. L., **II** 14; **IV** 264

Hallebrandt, F. A., **IV** 239–241

Hallesby, O., **III** 186, 344; **V** 390

Hallman, H. E., **III** 54

Hallowell, A. Irving, **IV** 227

Hallowell, John H., **III** 9, 11, 117, 162; **IV** 295, 308; **VIII** 124

Ham, **I** 12, 14, 15, 16, 18, 21–23, 25–27, 30, 31, 35–38, 43, 45–49, 69, 71, 72, 74, 81, 101–103, 105, 107, 120, 140, 141, 144, 145, 148--150, 152, 155, 156, 215, 216, 247, 248, 251, 252, 255, 257, 258, 260, 261, 263, 264, 272, 275, 295, 304, 310, 313, 317, 320, 337, 338; **II** 35, 52, 53, 56, 98, 134, 138, 139, 313; **IV** 115; **VI** 197, 200, 202; **VII** 97, 198, 200, 230-234

Hambly, Wilfrid, D., **I** 201; **II** 121

Hamilton, W. J., **V** 112

Hamilton, William, **I** 297

Hamlet, **III** 239; **V** 299

Hammerton, Sir John, **I** 182, 197

Hammer-Purgstall, **II** 258

Hammond, John, **I** 326

Hammurabi, **I** 72, 151; **VII** 164, 166

Hampden-Turner, Charles, **III** 210

Handel, George F., **I** 262; **IX** 252

Handrich, T. L., **V** 136, 137

Hanfmann, George M.A., **I** 202

Hannibal, **III** 187; **V** 393

Hanson, Hazel D., **II** 120

Hanson, N. S., **VIII** 156

Haram al-Raschid, **I** 208

Haran, **II** 314–317

Harappa, **II** 95, 96; **V** 65

Harary, Isaac, **III** 332; **VIII** 76

Hardy, Sir Alister, **I** 346, 357; **II** 18; **III** 263, 336, 337; **IV** 35, 150, 157; **V** 187; **VIII** 234

Hardy, J. D., **III** 119; **IV** 261; **IX** 202

Hare, R., **IX** 113

Harlan, J. R., **I** 137; **II** 55

Harrington, Alan, **V** 138

Harris, Rendel, **I** 201

Harris, Zellig S., **I** 93

Harrison, E. F., **VII** 71

Hart, C. W. M., **VIII** 129, 175

Hartshorn, C., **III** 323

Harvey, William, **I** 294

Harwood, Thomas, **VI** 214

Hatfield, H. Stafford, **I** 179

Hatshepsut, **VII** 182–185, 257; **VIII** 194

Haupt, Paul, **VI** 79

Hauret, Charles, **I** 361; **IV** 65

Hauser, Kaspar, **II** 200; **III** 212

Havermeyer, Loomis, **VI** 208, **VII** 228

Hawke, E. L., **VI** 25

Hayes, K. J. and C., **II** 262; **IV** 269--272, 276

Hayes, William, **I** 33, 292

Heberer, G., **II** 197

Hedin, Sven, **I** 212

Heermance, E. L., **II** 165

Hegel, G. W. F., **I** 281, 295, 296

Heidelberg Man, **I** 125; **II** 42, 44, 50

Heim, Karl, **VIII** 209

Heisenberg, Werner, **IV** 88; **VIII** 53

Heizer, Robert F., **I** 170, 176

Hellas, **I** 81, 93; **VI** 197

Helmholtz, Hermann von, **I** 353; **III** 272; **VIII** 73, 138

Henderson, Lawrence, **I** 349; **IV** 28; **VIII** 35; **IX** 142

Henderson, William, **I** 212

Henri-Martin, Mlle. Germaine, **II** 196

Henry II of France, **VI** 223

Henry, Carl F. H. **VII** 71

Heraclitus, **III** 11, 161

Hero of Alexandria, **II** 148

Herod, **VII** 36, 49, 259; **IX** 174

Herodotus, **I** 21, 82, 86, 89, 95, 96, 99, 109; **II** 76, 123; **V** 48, 49, 349; **VII** 23, 121

Herrick, C. Judson, **VIII** 211

Herrman, Paul, **I** 215; **II** 174

Hershon, Paul Isaac, **I** 145; **V** 99; **VI** 47, 96, 194

Herskovits, Melville, **I** 133, 168, 202; **II** 16, 65, 71, 73, 290, 292; **III** 142; **IV** 266; **VIII** 175, 243; **IX** 178

Hertz, J. A., **VI** 212

Hertz, J. H., **I** 86

Hervas, Lorenzo, **VI** 185

Hesiod, **IX** 96

Hesperopithecus, **II** 226, 229, 230; **III** 57

Heth, **I** 101, 103; **VI** 197; **VII** 229

Heurtley, W. A., **I** 197

Hieronymus, **IX** 30

Hiesey, W. M., **IV** 84

Hilgard, Ernest, **IV** 282

Hill, A. V., **IV** 37; **VIII** 112

Hill, Leonard, **IV** 233

Hillaby, John, **II** 155

Hinde, R. A., **VII** 171

Hindley, Charles, **VII** 114

Hindry, L. Fitz-James, **III** 167

Hinkle, Beatrice, **III** 142; **V** 387

Hinshelwood, C. N., **I** 238; **III** 74; **VIII** 38, 234; **IX** 142

Hippocrates, **IX** 216

Hiram (king of Tyre), **I** 77; **VII** 123

Hirst, J. Cowther, **III** 66, 67; **IV** 197, 198; **IX** 126

His, Wilhelm, **IV** 147, 148

Hislop, Alexander, **I** 30, 257, 263; **II** 77; **IV** 124; **V** 249, 254; **VI** 201; **VII** 198

Hitler, **I** 64; **III** 84, 184, 340; **IV** 306, **VI** 137; **VIII** 151

Hittites, **I** 103, 104, 107, 193, 210, 273, 305, 306, 327; **VI** 197

Hoare, William H., **I** 360; **IV** 89

Hobart, W. K., **III** 231; **IX** 216

Hobbes, Thomas, **III** 184, 185, 341; **V** 388, 389

Hodge, Charles, **IV** 325

Hoijer, Harry, **I** 288; **VI** 22, 187

Hollander, Willard, **IV** 307; **V** 28; **VI** 228, 229, 234; **VII** 235

Holliday, Leslie, **I** 299

Holloway, R. L., **IV** 264

Holmberg, Erik J., **I** 197

Holmyard, E. J., **II** 109; **IV** 177, 211

Holst, Erick von, **IV** 301

Homburger, L., **VI** 185

Homer, **I** 76, 81, 82, 86, 307; **V** 13, 48, 55; **VII** 212

Hommel, Fritz, **V** 53; **VII** 165, 166

Hooke, Robert, **VIII** 157

Hooker, Joseph D., **VIII** 220

Hooten, A. E., **I** 130; **II** 46, 184, 202, 229; **III** 30; **IX** 51

Hope, James, **V** 308

Hopi, **I** 174, 273, 334; **II** 171, 172, 288, 302

Hopkins, Evan, **IV** 102

Horace, **VII** 27

Hornell, James, **I** 203; **IX** 40

Horowitz, S., **III** 251

Horsley, Sir Victor, **V** 105–107

Hottentots, **I** 63; **II** 220, 303

Howard, John Eliot, **I** 196; **III** 69, 335; **V** 254

Howell, F. Clark, **II** 12, 26, 102; **VIII** 246

Howells, William, **I** 130, 138; **II** 35, 46, 50, 166, 184, 204, 206, 221, 236; **III** 48; **IV** 76, 162, 225, 244, 271; **V** 58

Howitt, John R., **IV** 246; **VI** 115

Howorth, Sir Henry, **IV** 97, 98, 101–103

Hoyle, Fred, **IV** 32; **VIII** 25, 26, 35–37, 135

Hrdlicka, Ales, **I** 136; **II** 52, 53, 121, 184, 204; **III** 48; **IV** 162, 164, 215; **V** 24, 58; **IX** 159

Hubble, Edwin P., **VIII** 18, 19

Hudgings, William, **VI** 18

Hudson, W. H., **I** 304; **IV** 186; **IX** 145

Huettner, A. F., **V** 190

Hughes, Philip E., **V** 160

Hugo of St. Victor, **I** 217, 224; **V** 162; **VIII** 110, 193

Humason, Milton L., **VIII** 18

Humboldt, W. von, **I** 268, 271; **II** 157, 250; **IV** 98, 99, 266, 305; **VI** 186

Huntingford, G. W. B., **II** 122

Huntington, Ellsworth, **I** 138; **II** 55, 83; **VIII** 129; **IX** 51, 141, 142

Huntsman, Benjamin, **I** 322

Hurley, H. J., **V** 310

Hustad, Donald P., **IX** 228

Hutton, E. H., **I** 321

Huxley, Aldous, **I** 174; **VII** 115; **VIII** 14, 93, 94, 127, 190

Huxley, H. E., **II** 150

Huxley, Julian, **I** 222, 223, 228, 340, 341, 343, 344, 353; **II** 25; **III** 10, 17, 25, 66, 83; **IV** 24, 45, 81, 83, 175, 214, 216, 217, 219, 225, 226, 255, 318, 323; **V** 15, 18, 80, 90, 126, 130, 178; **VI** 124; **VIII** 42, 44, 83, 95, 106, 137, 141, 146, 149, 150, 159, 211, 215, 222, 233

Huxley, Thomas H., **I** 136; **II** 52, 219, 240, 241; **III** 33, 161, 295; **IV** 88, 231; **VIII** 24, 25

I

Ibn-Sina (Avicenna), **I** 310

Ihde, Aaron J., **VIII** 133

Imbrie, John, **IV** 59

Inca, **I** 173, 182; **II** 116, 301

Indus Valley, **I** 99, 120, 152, 188, 197, 296, 298, 312, 326, 328, 336; **II** 36, 38, 39, 78, 81, 86, 95, 101, 102, 104, 114

Ingersoll, Robert, **III** 168

Inglis, J., **I** 106

Ionians, **I** 81, 91–93, 116; **III** 80

Irenaeus, **VII** 74, 185

Iroquois, **I** 184; **II** 78, 118, 287, 290

Irwin, C. H., **VII** 160

Irwin, L. N., **III** 251

Isaac, **II** 310, 319–323; **V** 30, 248, 265; **VII** 173, 177, 243

Iscah, **II** 314, 316, 317

Ishmael, **II** 319; **V** 30, 265; **VII** 172

Ivan the Terrible, **I** 91

Ivy, Andrew, **VIII** 150; **IX** 116

J

Jaarsma, Cornelius, **VIII** 212

Jackson, Dugauld C., **II** 292

Jackson, J. H., **II** 257

Jacob, **II** 288, 296, 310, 319, 321, 323, 324, 325, 330; **V** 29, 30, 45, 244, 248, 265, 279; **VI** 144, 145, 193, 205; **VII** 177, 180, 237, 239, 244, 246; **IX** 190, 191, 236

Jacob, H. E., **IX** 135

Jacobs, Melville, **II** 166; **IV** 289

Jacobson, Allan L., **III** 251

Jaki, Stanley L., **III** 53; **IV** 174; **VIII** 26, 79

Jamdet Nasr, **I** 114; **II** 90; **V** 62

James, E. O., **II** 74; **IV** 131; **IX** 115

James, William, **III** 167, 168; **VIII** 104

Jamieson, R., **I** 80, 116; **VI** 111

Japetos, **I** 35, 81, 266

Japheth, **I** 12, 14, 16–18, 21–23, 25–28, 30, 31 35–38, 43, 45–49, 53, 58, 69, 71, 72, 74–76, 80–82, 88, 94, 95, 99, 101, 102, 120, 139--141, 145, 150, 152, 155, 215, 216, 247, 248, 251–253, 255, 256, 259--261, 263–266, 275, 279, 295, 304, 310, 313, 317, 337, 338, 366; **II** 35, 56, 98, 134, 138, 139; **IV** 115; **VI** 195–197; **VII** 97, 230, 231, 233, 234

Jarmo, **I** 188; **II** 34, 86, 88, 99, 100; **V** 61, 66

Jarvis, C. S., **VII** 213

Java Man, **I** 125, 132, 136; **II** 20, 27, 42, 48, 50, 52, 208, 218, 236

Javan, **I** 91–94; **VII** 195

Jeans, Sir James, **III** 54, 106, 320, 321; **VI** 11; **VIII** 22, 31, 37, 38, 41, 53

Jeffreys, C. W., **I** 158; **II** 159

Jeffreys, M. D. C., **III** 23

Jennings, H. S., **III** 261, 328; **VIII** 86, 140

Jeon, K. W., **VIII** 75

Jeremiah, **I** 145, 146; **III** 223; **VII** 60

Jericho, **II** 86, 88, 99, 100; **VII** 147, 187, 188, 190, 191, 194

Jerome, **I** 94; **III** 226; **V** 182, 327; **VI** 88, 192; **VII** 74, 125, 284, 294

Jerusalem, **I** 19, 23, 76, 79, 102; **VII** 127ff., 164, 169, 225

Jervis, J. J-W., **I** 103

Jesperson, Otto, **I** 272, 288; **II** 251; **IV** 267

Jesse, the Bethlehemite, **I** 147; **II** 314; **VII** 232

Jesus Christ, **I** 229–239, 367, 368; **II** 192, 329; **III** 43, 94, 125f., 127, 130, 131, 168–170, 172, 173, 175--177, 186–188, 192, 275, 277, 279, 281, 298, 299, 301, 302, 304, 305, 310, 311, 313, 327, 346, 348, 349; **IV** 21, 108, 209, 210, 212, 320ff., 325–328; **V** 117, 118, 123, 152–154, 159–162, 164, 194, 210, 211, 216, 225, 232, 234, 244, 368; **VI** 35, 36, 39, 41, 48, 49, 70, 71, 114, 124, 125, 132, 137, 153, 166; **VII** 14, 18, 20, 34, 37, 39–48, 52, 73, 80–82, 96, 100–104, 110, 140, 142, 232, 252, 262, 264, 268, 269, 316; **VIII** 53, 199

Jevons, F. B., **IV** 138

Joad, C. E. M., **II** 128; **IV** 249; **VIII** 174

Job, **III** 197; **V** 32, 190, 265; **VII** 239; **VIII** 108; **IX** 152

Johannesson, A., **VI** 187

John, **I** 16; **III** 179; **V** 209, 218, 246, 325, 338, 358; **VI** 43; **VII** 79, 97, 104, 252, 268

John, E. Roy, **III** 249, 251

Johnson, Humphrey T., **II** 118, 184, 208; **III** 118; **IV** 166, 320; **V** 59

Johnson, Iris, **VI** 214

Johnson, N. Victor, **V** 212; **VIII** 67

John the Baptist, **III** 130, 139; **V** 235, 236, 316; **VII** 36f., 38, 40, 44, 63, 82, 102; **IX** 174

Joktan, **I** 117, 118

Jollos, V., **VIII** 226

Jonah, **III** 96, 111, 131, 192; **V** 357; **VI** 132, 164; **VII** 60, 193; **VIII** 87; **IX** 17

Jones, F. A., **V** 55; **VI** 238; **VII** 204

Jones, F. Wood, **I** 354; **II** 184, 211, 213, 235, 245, 247, 248; **III** 29, 57, 115, 159; **IV** 38, 55, 68, 77, 79, 145, 150, 156, 157, 167, 176, 203, 211; **V** 397; **VIII** 127, 139, 148, 223, 234, 236, 247, 248

Jones, J. C., **III** 295, 316; **VI** 203

Joseph (son of Jacob), **III** 222; **V** 41; **VI** 145, 148, 168; **VII** 148, 177–181, 187, 194, 282

Joseph (of Nazareth, **II** 327, 329; **VII** 100, 102, 262–264

Josephus, **I** 80, 83, 86–89, 93, 95–97; **II** 76, 316; **III** 220; **V** 33, 34, 51; **VI** 88; **VII** 74, 132, 135, 155, 173, 185, 204, 241, 258; **VIII** 195; **IX** 30, 105

Joshua, **V** 29, 37, 235, 244; **VII** 188, 190, 191, 238

Josiah, **VI** 136; **IX** 148

Jost, A., **V** 213; **VIII** 67

Jourdain, Philip E. B., **I** 192

Joyce, T. Athol, **I** 181

Judas, **III** 96, 111; **V** 347; **VI** 157; **VII** 102

Julien, Stanislas, **I** 210

Julius Caesar, **I** 209; **III** 108, 149, 226; **VII** 27, 28, 107

Jung, Carl G., **III** 37, 141–143, 160, 183, 240, 263; **V** 155, 387, 392, 393

Junod, H. A., **II** 295

Justice, J. N., **II** 121

Justin Martyr, **I** 20; **V** 357

Jyapeti (Japetos) **I** 35, 81, 266

K

Kafka, John S., **VI** 24

Kagemni, **I** 294

Kahan, B. D., **IV** 302

Kahn, Fritz, **I** 335; **IV** 243; **V** 180; **VIII** 68

Kaikari, **II** 297

Kalisch, M. M., **I** 57, 63, 80, 84, 94; **VI** 197; **VII** 218; **IX** 83, 86, 88, 99

Kamala, **II** 260, 261, 267

Kamtchadales, **II** 296

Kant, Immanuel, **III** 106; **IV** 34; **VII** 87

Karaikees, **II** 296

Kardiner, Abram, **II** 67; **III** 142

Karpechenko, G. D., **I** 339; **VIII** 163

Karsner, T., **V** 309

Kass, Leon, **VIII** 81, 94

Katz, Sidney, **III** 167

Kautzsch, E., **I** 58

Keane, A. H., **VI** 215

Keary, Charles F., **II** 77; **IV** 138; **V** 254

Keith, Sir Arthur, **II** 94, 185, 217, 219, 220; **IV** 168, 169

Keller, Helen, **II** 255, 263–265; **III** 206; **IX** 112

Kellog, S. H., **IV** 138; **V** 94

Kellogg, W. N. and L. A., **II** 262; **IV** 269–271, 274, 276, 284, 286

Kelly, William, **I** 214, 322

Kelvin, Lord, **VI** 17

Kent, Kate Peck, **I** 325

Kennedy. *See* Studdart-Kennedy.

Kenyon, Dean H., **IV** 31; **VIII** 82

Kenyon, Sir Frederic G. **VII** 193

Kenyon, Kathleen M., **II** 100

Kepler, Johannes, **I** 191; **VI** 28; **VIII** 153, 201

Kerkut, G. A., **IV** 85; **VIII** 160

Kermack, K. A., **II** 243

Kettering, Charles, **IV** 203

Keturah, **I** 15; **VII** 98

Kety, Seymour, **III** 320; **VIII** 86, 87, 142, 143

Kidd, Charles V., **I** 300

Kidd, Walter, **IV** 71; **VIII** 208

Kidder, Alfred, **I** 141; **II** 55; **IX** 57

King, F. H., **I** 168

King, L. W., **II** 93

King, Thomas, **V** 185

Kipling, Rudyard, **II** 126; **IV** 249; **V** 84

Kirk, Dudley, **V** 45; **IX** 55

Kitto, John, **I** 80; **VI** 211

Kjelgaard, Jim, **III** 62

Klaatsch, Hermann, **II** 248

Klatt, D. H., **IV** 275

Kleiber, Max, **III** 271, 272; **IV** 36, 37

Kline, Morris, **I** 294

Klopsteg, Paul E., **I** 209

Klotz, John, **II** 32, 216; **III** 70; **IV** 56, 57, 72, 75

Kluckhohn, Clyde, **II** 252; **III** 21, 22, 146, 150, 158, 209; **IV** 267; **VI** 188, 213

Knight, G. A. F., **I** 276

Knight, James, **III** 167

Knoblock, Irving W., **II** 16; **IV** 55, 59, 146

Knossos, **I** 333; **II** 32; **V** 13, 48

Knox, W. L., **III** 292

Koehler, Otto, **IV** 318

Koehler, Wolfgang, **II** 256, 257

Koenigswald, G. H. R. von, **III** 20

Koestler, Aurthur, **I** 307, 364; **III** 20, 211, 250, 254, 261, 263, 269, 296, 319; **IV** 168, 179, 214, 216, 274, 296, 297, 321, 322; **V** 213; **VIII** 14, 23, 56, 66, 75, 119, 152--156, 158, 164, 166, 210; **IX** 241

Kohts, N., **IV** 270

Koller, Dov, **I** 165

Koppers, Wilhelm, **I** 124, 126, 133; **II** 41, 43, 49, 175, 199; **IV** 67, 138

Korenchevsky, V., **V** 16, 133–135

Korn, N., **I** 221, 341; **II** 12, 50; **IV** 62, 175, 223

Kortlandt, Adriaan, **III** 118

Kramer, Samuel, **I** 72, 151, 191, 193, 290, 316, 332; **VI** 202; **VII** 200

Kranzberg, Melvin, **I** 302

Krebs, H., **IV** 36, 37

Kreighbaum, Hillier, **IV** 143

Kretschmer, Ernst, **I** 311, 312; **II** 137; **III** 121; **IX** 233

Krieger, A. D., **II** 158

Kroeber, A. L., **I** 32, 34, 35, 254, 274, 279, 280, 287, 288; **II** 17, 31, 75, 83, 101, 129, 133, 197, 198, 251, 252; **III** 21, 150, 158, 207; **IV** 55, 144, 148, 217, 266, 267, 292, 317, 320; **VI** 22, 185, 187, 191, 213; **VIII** 105, 129, 133; **IX** 131

Kroeber, Theodora, **II** 111; **VI** 209

Krogman, W. M., **I** 133; **IX** 141

Kroner, W., **V** 311

Kropotkin, Prince Petr, **III** 23; **IV** 145, 148, 181–184, 186, 195

Krumbhaar, E. B., **V** 309

Kublai Khan, **I** 327, 335

Kuhlman, Kathryn, **VII** 62

Kuhn, Alfred, **III** 330, 336; **IV** 34, 88; **VIII** 230
Kunin, Robert, **VII** 213
Kuno, Yas, **IX** 197
Kuo, Z. Y., **IV** 293

Kurnia, **II** 297

Kurth, G., **VIII** 37

Kyle, Melvin G., **II** 76, 91; **VI** 22; **VII** 173, 174

L

Laban, **II** 288, 320–325; **VI** 193; **VII** 243–246
Labat, Rene, **VI** 200; **VII** 165, 166, 197
LaChapelle, **I** 136; **II** 53; **III** 48; **V** 24
Lack, David, **II** 18; **III** 18, 33, 161, 292, 295; **IV** 49, 75, 156, 264
Lagoa Santa, **I** 135; **II** 51
LaHaye, Tim, **IX** 103
Lamarck, Jean Baptiste, **I** 357; **V** 184, 187; **VIII** 219
Lamb, Charles, **III** 204
Lamb, Harold, **I** 208
Lamech, **II** 133, 311, 312; **V** 34, 39, 41, 42; **VI** 202; **VII** 199, 200, 205, 208, 223
Lammerts, W. E., **I** 339, 361; **IV** 72, 84; **V** 27, 28; **VIII** 163
Lamont, Daniel, **III** 40; **VIII** 171
Lamsa, George M., **I** 265; **VII** 76
Lamson, Mary Swift, **II** 266
Lancaster, C. S., **I** 341; **IV** 194, 252, 314
Lancaster, J. B., **II** 253
Lancaster, Ray, **V** 136
Landau, Leo Dadvidoch, **V** 120
Lang, Andrew, **II** 74; **IV** 111, 120, 129, 138; **V** 250
Langdon, Stephen H., **IV** 113, 114, 138
Lange, J. Peter, **I** 65, 80, 116, 278, 279; **III** 113; **V** 41; **VI** 194

Langer, Susanne, **I** 241, 277, 288–290, 292, 297, 298; **II** 86, 260, 261, 270; **III** 116, 248, 261; **IV** 35, 36, 294, 320; **VIII** 93, 133, 139; **IX** 234, 235
Langhorne, John and William, **I** 299
Lango, **II** 288, 290; **III** 138
Lani, Maria, **VII** 85–89
Lansing, Albert, **V** 23, 27
Lantian Man, **II** 50
Lao-tse, **V** 254
Lapham, L. W., **III** 332; **VIII** 77
Lapham, Macy H., **I** 162, 163, 258
Laplace, P. S. de, **VIII** 79
LaQuina Woman, **I** 136; **II** 52
Larned, J. N., **I** 92
Lartet, Edouard, **IV** 265
Lasker, Gabriel W., **I** 221; **IV** 239
Lashley, Karl S., **III** 261; **IV** 226
Laughlin, William S., **I** 137; **II** 53; **VIII** 244, 245
Lavoisier, A. L., **VIII** 73, 82
Lawden, D. F., **III** 258, 325; **VIII** 85, 86, 142
Lawrence, Sir Thomas, **VI** 29
Layard, A. H., **I** 110, 111; **II** 77; **V** 252
Lazarus, **III** 144, 304; **IV** 108; **V** 123, 352, 392; **VI** 34; **VII** 43, 45; **VIII** 87
Leach, E. A., **I** 10, 300
Leake, Chauncey D., **I** 353; **III** 272; **VIII** 73, 138

Leakey, L. S. B., **I** 203; **II** 15, 20, 23; **IV** 226

Lebzelter, Viktor, **I** 126, 127; **II** 43, 175, 222; **IV** 67; **VI** 230

Lee, Douglas H. K., **III** 120; **IV** 258

Legge, James, **IX** 86

Leibnitz, **VIII** 55, 172

Leith, T. H., **II** 24, 25

Lemaitre, Abbe, **VIII** 20

Lenneberg, Eric L., **II** 251, 263, 267; **IV** 269, 273, 284, 285

Lenormant, Francois, **II** 77; **V** 51, 98, 100; **VI** 79; **VII** 165, 207; **IX** 83, 84, 90, 91, 96

Leonard, Jonathan N., **I** 324

Leonardo da Vinci. *See* Vinci.

Le Riche, Philip J., **IV** 103; **IX** 63

Leupold, H. C., **I** 66, 80

Lever, Jan, **II** 236

Levi-Strauss, Claude, **I** 158, 165, 175, 258, 287, 300, 326; **II** 156, 287; **III** 208

Levy-Bruhl, Lucien, **I** 287, 313; **II** 67, 251, 258, 259; **III** 85; **IX** 176, 177

Lewis, A. S., **VII** 257

Lewis, Aubrey, **I** 10

Lewis, C. S., **I** 249; **III** 338; **IV** 210; **IX** 188

Lewis, D., **IV** 72; **VIII** 60

Lewis, Gilbert, **I** 183

Lewis, Oscar, **II** 109

Lewis, R. B. W., **III** 204, 295

Lewis, Taylor, **I** 65

Ley, Willey, **I** 104, 210

Liddell, H., **V** 257, 324

Liddon, H. P., **V** 249

Lieberman, P. H., **IV** 275

Liebig, Baron Justus von, **II** 236

Limbaugh, Conrad, **IV** 196, 197

Lincoln, Abraham, **III** 187; **V** 393

Lindegren, Carl C., **II** 75; **V** 79

Lindsey, Arthur Ward, **VIII** 226, 228

Ling, Wang, **I** 213

Lings, Martin, **III** 36

Linnaeus, Karl, **II** 130; **IV** 215; **VII** 212

Linne, Sigvad, **I** 186

Linton, Ralph, **I** 35, 131, 169, 176, 202, 278, 280, 284, 299, 306, 335; **II** 48, 151, 212, 222; **III** 60, 117; **IV** 67, 166, 291, 295, 296; **VIII** 161

Lippman, Harold E., **IV** 97

Livingstone, David, **I** 329, 330; **II** 63, 259, 275, 305; **VI** 215; **VII** 160, 170, 172; **IX** 84, 231

Livy, Titus, **V** 307; **VII** 257

Lloyd, J., **I** 80, 90, 95

Lloyd, Seton, **II** 99

Loewenstein, Prince John, **II** 119

Loftus, W. K., **IX** 24

Long, William J., **III** 71; **IX** 125

Lorch, I. J., **VIII** 75

Lorenz, Konrad, **I** 243, 356; **III** 25; **IV** 229, 293, 301

Lorrain, Claude, **IV** 316

Lot, **II** 314–317; **III** 178, 208; **VII** 151, 156, 159–161, 173–176, 240, 242

Lovejoy, Arthur O., **II** 228; **IV** 48, 65, 213, 325; **V** 396; **VIII** 84, 134, 141

Lovell, A. C. B., **VIII** 20

Lowdermilk, W. C., **IX** 119

Lowe, C. van Riet, **II** 121

Lowe, William G., **IX** 22, 25

Lowie, Robert, **I** 34, 175, 176; **II** 73, 175, 289; **IV** 305; **V** 49; **VI** 188; **VII** 156, 242

Lowrie, Walter, **III** 69, 335

Loyola, Ignatius, **I** 262; **III** 219

Lubbock, Sir John, **I** 170; **II** 123, 189, 190, 275, 289, 305, 307

Lucan, **V** 312

Ludwig, Carl, **I** 353; **III** 272; **VIII** 73, 138

Luke, **I** 16–18, 260; **III** 225, 228–231; **V** 209, 246, 325; **VII** 73, 79, 99–104, 252–259, 262–269; **IX** 216

Luria, A. R., **III** 245

Luther, Martin, **I** 16, 155; **III** 290; **VI** 141; **VIII** 121, 174

Lydekker, Richard, **IV** 98
Lyell, Charles, **II** 32, 61, 127, 146, 250; **IV** 16, 88–90, 98, 266; **V** 127; **VII** 158

M

Maatman, Russell W., **VIII** 38
Macalister, Alexander, **IV** 249, 250
Macaulay, Lord T. B., **III** 245
MacBride, E. W., **VIII** 243
McBride, Glen, **IV** 185
Maccabee, Simon, **VII** 134
McCaul, I. A., **VI** 92
McCay, Clive, **V** 23, 27
McCowan, T. D., **II** 50
McCrady, Edward, **III** 182, 183, 260, 335; **IV** 120; **V** 386, 387; **VI** 113; **VIII** 23; **IX** 75, 92
MacCurdy, George Grant, **I** 136; **II** 52, 120; **IX** 113
McDougall, William, **III** 143
Mace, David R., **V** 263
McGaugh, James L., **III** 253, 254
Macgowan, Kenneth, **I** 136, 141, 166; **II** 52–55, 115, 133, 175, 188; **V** 26; **VI** 184; **IX** 55
McGregor, J. H., **II** 233
Machen, J. Gresham, **V** 78; **VIII** 195
McIlwraith, T. F., **I** 187; **II** 290, 294, 295, 298, 299; **V** 48, 349
MacIntosh, N. W. G., **II** 15
McIntyre, D. M., **VII** 75
MacIvor, D. Randall, **I** 110, 199, 204, 309
Mack, Edward, **VI** 22
MacKay, Ernest, **II** 95, 96
McLennan, J. F., **II** 65
MacLeod, Robert B., **I** 277
MacMillan, Hugh, **III** 76; **IX** 121
McMillin, Stewart E., **I** 185
Mc Neil, David **IV** 274

MacNicol, Nicol, **IV** 120
Macoffin, Ralph N., **I** 196
Macy, John A., **I** 255
Maine, Sir Henry J. S., **II** 65, 68, 307
Major, David R., **II** 267; **IX** 175
Malbim, M. L., **VI** 212
Maldonatus, Joannes, **V** 311
Malinowski, Bronislau, **II** 67, 293, 300
Mallowan, M. E. L., **I** 114, 115; **II** 92, 101, 104
Malthus, Thomas R., **III** 71; **IV** 192, 254
Mandelbaum David C., **IV** 289
Manetho, **IX** 97
Manoilov, W. W., **IV** 154
Manton, I., **II** 16; **IV** 59, 146
Maori, **II** 176
Marais, Eugene, **IV** 256; **IX** 122
Marcus Aurelius, **III** 274
Margenau, Henry, **VIII** 151
Marinatos, Sp., **II** 121
Marinez, Maria, **II** 151
Maritain, Jacques, **I** 31, 281, 283, 314; **VII** 32; **VIII** 113, 126, 200
Mark, **I** 16, 17, 260; **V** 209, 324, 325; **VI** 205; **VII** 79f., 97–105, 252
Markesbury, W. R., **III** 332; **VIII** 77
Marsh, D. B., **I** 161; **II** 161
Marsh, Frank, **IV** 63
Marsh, Henry, **I** 359
Marshack, Alexander, **II** 251
Marshall Islands, **II** 296

Marston, Sir Charles, **I** 35; **III** 215; **V** 21; **VII** 187–189, 191, 192; **VIII** 207

Martha, **III** 132, 235; **VII** 43

Martin, C. P., **IV** 82

Martin, E., **I** 322

Martin, P. S., **IV** 95, 253

Martin, Samuel, **II** 177

Martin of Tours, Saint, **VIII** 111

Mary (of Bethany), **III** 235; **VII** 43

Mary (the mother of Jesus), **II** 310, 327; **III** 144; **V** 139, 152, 155–157, 189, 191–194, 196, 199, 210, 248, 283, 287, 359, 381; **VII** 39, 103, 259, 262–264, 268

Marx, Karl, **II** 83; **VIII** 171

Mascall, E. L., **I** 222, 341, 344, 362; **III** 85, 316; **V** 399, 400; **VIII** 44, 125, 137

Mason, A. Stuart, **II** 185

Mason, J. Alden, **I** 183, 184

Maspero, Sir G. C. C., **I** 85; **IX** 97

Mather, Cotton, **I** 330

Mather, Kirtley F., **IX** 303

Mathiassen, Therkel, **IV** 319

Matisse, Henri, **VII** 87, 88

Matthew, **I** 16, 260, 265; **V** 209, 324, 325; **VII** 73f., 79f., 97–105, 252–254ff., 260, 268, 269

Matthew, W. D., **I** 126; **II** 43

Matthews, H. L., **IV** 238, 251

Maude, Captain A., **I** 209

Mauer Jaw, **I** 137; **II** 53

Maundrell, H., **V** 304

Mauro, Philip, **V** 38, 70; **VI** 238; **VII** 222

Maximian, Emperor, **V** 303

Maxwell, James Clark, **VI** 17; **VIII** 31

Maya, **I** 178, 179, 181, 182, 334; **II** 116, 251

Mayer, J., **IX** 134

Maypures, **II** 157

Mayr, Ernst, **I** 133; **IV** 59, 67, 81, 83, 94; **VIII** 91, 92, 235

Mead, Albert H., **VIII** 113

Mead, George Herbert, **II** 255; **III** 105, 140, 141; **IV** 276

Mead, Margaret, **I** 68; **III** 145, 147, 148; **IV** 294

Medawar, Sir Peter B., **I** 355; **II** 24, 25; **III** 23, 24; **IV** 192, 200, 202, 302, 313, 314; **V** 134, 135, 177, 178; **VIII** 25, 77, 91, 145, 148, 245, 246

Medes, **I** 82, 87, 91, 92

Medici, Catherine de, **VI** 223

Medici, Lorenzo, **VII** 93–95

Meek, T. J., **I** 189, 190, 197; **II** 90, 91, 94; **IV** 114; **V** 64; **VI** 179, 213

Melchizedek, **III** 104; **VII** 168–170

Mello, J. M., **II** 151

Melvin, Bruce L., **IV** 321

Menander, **VII** 124

Mendelssohn, Kurt A. G., **I** 285

Mendelssohn, Moses, **VII** 87

Mentone Cave, **II** 54

Menzies, J. M., **IV** 122

Mercellinus, Ammianus, **I** 87

Meredith, George, **IX** 255

Methuselah, **V** 34, 35, 41, 167

Mezeray, Francois de, **V** 312

Merivale, Herman, **II** 140

Metcalfe, C. R., **IV** 55

Metchnikoff, Eli, **V** 16, 22

Michaelis, P., **VIII** 229, 230

Michelangelo, **V** 168, 175; **VI** 33; **VII** 93–95, **IX** 252

Michelet, Jules, **VIII** 114

Michelson, A. A., **VI** 16–18

Michie, Donald, **V** 186, 187; **VIII** 234

Miholic, Stanko, **I** 202

Mikolaski, Samuel J., **III** 268

Mill, J. Stuart, **I** 272, 288; **IV** 298

Miller, Francis R., **I** 211

Miller, Hugh, **I** 345, 346; **II** 157; **III** 57; **IV** 50, 51, 65; **VI** 29, 107; **VIII** 43; **IX** 38, 39, 63

Miller, Stanley L., **VIII** 73, 135

Millet, Jean-Francois, **VIII** 174

Mills, Wesley, **IV** 268

Milne, E. A., **VI** 20, 41
Milton, Lord, **II** 125
Minos, **II** 32, 37, 120, 135
Mirandola, Pico della, **V** 160
Mirsky, A. E., **V** 185; **VIII** 70
Mitchell, Sir P. Chalmers, **VIII** 72
Mitchell, Sir Thomas, **I** 172
Mitford, Nancy, **VII** 157
Mixter, Russell L., **I** 339; **IV** 58; **VIII** 20, 163
M'lefaat, **II** 86; **V** 61, 66
Moberly, Sir Walter, **VIII** 213
Moffat, Robert, **IX** 84
Mohawk, **I** 78
Mohenjo Daru, **I** 197, 328, 336; **II** 95, 96
Moloney, F. A., **IX** 24, 63
Monod, Jacques, **III** 323; **VIII** 65, 66, 71, 84, 93, 97, 98, 180
Monsma, John C., **I** 350; **III** 346; **IV** 40, 56
Montagna, W., **VIII** 148
Montagu, Ashley, **I** 136; **II** 35, 52, 120, 216; **III** 23, 340; **IV** 178, 184, 214–216, 225, 266; **VIII** 140
Montaigne, Michel, **VII** 87
Monte Circeo, Cave, **II** 232
Montgolfier, Joseph E. **I** 211
Montgomery, John Warwick, **IX** 103
Moodie, R. L., **I** 183
Moody, D. L., **III** 223
Moog, Florence, **V** 124, 133
Moore, A. R., **VIII** 74
Moore, John A., **VIII** 235
Moore, John N., **IV** 201
Moore, R., **II** 157
Mora, Peter T., **IV** 34, 222
More, Thomas, **VIII** 42
Morgan, Jacques de, **I** 10, 196; **II** 71, 72, 90
Morgan, L. H., **IV** 196
Morice, A. G., **II** 296
Morison, Robert S., **VIII** 181
Morley, Edward W., **VI** 16–18
Morris, Henry, **V** 70; **IX** 62

Morris, John D., **IX** 103
Morton, Dudley, J., **IV** 233
Moscow, **I** 91, 97
Moses, **II** 79, 265, 276, 277, 310; **III** 96, 111, 187, 215, 220, 221, 223; **IV** 33; **V** 29, 37, 228, 232, 244, 248, 280, 393; **VI** 32, 33, 40, 52, 58, 148, 165; **VII** 49, 148, 150, 177, 181–186, 192, 194, 238, 282, 297; **VIII** 194, 195; **IX** 20, 189
Mossman, H. W., **V** 112
Mott, Frances J., **III** 74
Mottram, V. H., **II** 219; **III** 140; **V** 89
Mount Carmel. *See* Carmel, Mount.
Movius, Hallam L., **II** 17, 33, 72, 101
Mowrer, O. H., **III** 270
Muller, H. J., **V** 17, 125, 128, 176
Muller, Max **IV** 119, 120, 128, 138; **VI** 179–182, 184, 191; **IX** 74
Multhauf, Robert, **I** 286
Mumford, Lewis, **I** 333; **VIII** 146, 149, 188
Munitz, Milton K., **VIII** 153
Munro, Iverach, **VI** 92
Munro, J. A. R., **I** 116
Murdock, George Peter, **I** 168, 170, 179; **II** 54, 119, 122, 155, 156, 291, 298, 299, 301, 303, 306; **III** 138, 207, 208, 340; **V** 349; **VI** 224–226; **VII** 201; **VIII** 106, 176; **IX** 132, 176
Murphy, James C., **V** 34
Murray, Andrew, **IX** 157
Murray, H. A., **III** 146, 209
Murray, J. O. F., **V** 343
Murray, K. C., **I** 103; **VI** 200; **VII** 197
Mussett, Frances, **II** 243
Mussolini, Benito, **III** 340
Muti Ali, **II** 290, 301
Myers, Beatrice, **I** 273
Myers, J. L., **II** 93; **VI** 188
Myers, W. M., **I** 168
Mylonas, George, **I** 198; **V** 349

N

Naaman, **VI** 131

Nabataeans, **I** 165

Nabonidus, **VII** 152

Nahmanides, **V** 180

Nahor, **II** 314–316, 320; **VII** 155, 240, 242, 243

Naomi, **II** 327

Napoleon, **III** 33, 160, 187, 206, 226; **V** 70, 142, 373, 393

Naskapi, **I** 63; **II** 169, 300; **VII** 201

Nathan, **III** 342

Nathaniel, **I** 68

Naville, Edouard, **I** 265; **VI** 194; **VII** 210, 211; **IX** 85

Neander, Augustus, **VI** 104

Neanderthal Man, **I** 130, 131, 133–135; **II** 27, 45–51, 114, 164, 166, 181, 185, 195–198, 200, 208, 217, 219, 221, 230–236; **III** 49; **V** 58

Neatby, T. Miller, **VII** 180, 188

Nebuchadnezzar, **II** 166; **III** 93, 125, 176, 274; **VI** 125, 131, 133, 136, 138; **VII** 60, 124–126; **IX** 18, 19

Necho, Pharaoh, **II** 76; **V** 49; **VI** 131, 136, 138; **IX** 148

Needham, Joseph (biologist), **VIII** 64, 72

Needham, Joseph (historian), **I** 36, 104, 187, 203, 206–208, 211, 213, 215, 286–288, 305, 321, 325, 328; **II** 104; **VI** 218; **VII** 31; **VIII** 119

Nefertiti, **I** 262

Nelsen, Olin, **V** 113, 139, 183

Nelson, Byron C., **IV** 103; **IX** 62, 75, 76, 91, 96

Nemeskeri, J., **IX** 113

Neptune, **I** 82

Nero, **III** 184; **V** 345; **VI** 131, 137

Nestor, King, **II** 76

Neugebauer, O., **I** 190, 191

Neve, J. L., **III** 171, 290

Newberry, P. E., **I** 201

Newburgh, L. H., **I** 158; **II** 159

Newcomen, Thomas, **II** 148

Newell, Norman D., **IV** 92–94

Newman, Jacob, **V** 180, 397

Newman, James R., **I** 34, 192, 293, 294

Newman, M. T., **II** 234

Newman, Richard, **V** 198

Newman, Robert C., **VIII** 26

Newton, Isaac, **II** 136; **VI** 123; **VIII** 157, 172

Ney, E. P., **V** 47

Niagara Falls, **II** 132

Nicholson, Irene, **I** 331, 334, 335; **II** 109

Nicodemus, **III** 139; **VII** 38, 39

Niebuhr, H. R., **II** 107

Nieburg, H. L., **VIII** 145

Niehoff, A. H., **I** 254; **III** 28

Nietzsche, Friedrich H., **I** 64; **III** 275; **VIII** 151, 180

Nilsson, Heribert, **IV** 57

Nimrod, **I** 57, 102, 103, 108, 113–115; **II** 98; **VI** 82, 200; **VII** 197, 198, 200, 218, 286

Nineveh, **I** 83, 108, 110; **II** 92; **III** 97, 111, 125, 131, 192, 274; **VI** 158, 164, 229; **VII** 60, 151, 200

Noah, **I** 12, 25–27, 46, 47, 55, 59, 105, 116, 118, 119, 139, 140, 144, 145, 148, 149, 155, 247, 251, 255, 258, 259, 260, 337, 338, 366; **II** 30, 56, 80, 81, 134, 138, 313; **III** 47; **IV** 115; **V** 24, 25, 27–29, 33, 35, 37, 39–42, 50, 54, 82, 99, 102,

103; **VI** 60, 66, 110, 176, 193–195, 197, 198, 233, 239; **VII** 97, 105, 149, 150, 195, 201–204, 230-233, 239, 296; **IX** 13, 14, 26, 32–35, 40, 44, 54, 71, 76, 80, 82, 89, 91, 92, 103, 122

Nordenskiold, Baron E., **I** 166, 176, 178, 186; **IV** 100

Novikoff, Alex, **III** 122; **IV** 281

O

Oakley, Kenneth P., **II** 14, 16, 23, 101, 110, 165; **IV** 242, 264
Obercassel, **I** 129, 135; **II** 44, 51, 223
Oberg, Kalervo, **V** 373
Oehlkers, F., **VIII** 230
Ojibway, **I** 78
Okeanos, **I** 81
Oken, Lorenz, **IV** 209, 325
Oldoway Skull (Olduvai), **I** 136; **II** 15, 20, 50, 52
Olshausen, Herman, **V** 329; **VI** 99
O'Neill, Ana Maria, **IV** 213
Onkelos, **V** 71; **VI** 108
Oparin, A. I., **IV** 51

Oppert, Jules, **VI** 79
O'Rahilly, R., **IV** 275
Origen, **V** 303, 327; **VI** 97, 109, 192; **VII** 74; **VIII** 108
Orr, James, **I** 58, 80; **II** 140, 192; **III** 101; **IV** 320; **V** 79; **VIII** 200
Orwell, George, **VII** 115; **VIII** 95
Osborn, Henry F., **I** 123; **II** 40, 229, 230; **IV** 73, 93; **IX** 53
Osthoff, R. C., **VIII** 169
Ouspensky, P. D., **III** 17, 159
Ovid, **VII** 176; **IX** 95–97
Owen, Sir Richard, **I** 360; **III** 57; **IV** 87

PQ

Pachacutec, **I** 30, 278
Packer, J. I., **V** 78
Pallas, **IV** 98, 103
Pallottino, M., **I** 198, 309
Pannekoek, A., **V** 72, 73
Panton, D. M., **VI** 209
Pape, William H., **IX** 106
Papias, **VII** 74
Papin, Denis, **II** 148
Parker, Franke, **VII** 204
Parker, W. K., **IV** 201
Parkinson, James, **IV** 87
Parkman, Francis, **III** 203
Parrot, Andrée, **VII** 202; **IX** 102

Parry, E. St. John, **I** 109
Parsons, F. G., **IV** 233
Pasteur, Louis, **VIII** 135
Paterson, H. Sinclair, **IX** 75, 92, 96
Pattee, H. H., **III** 262
Patten, Bradley M., **V** 112
Patten, Donald W., **VI** 228
Patterson, J. T., **I** 362; **IV** 74; **V** 127
Paul, **I** 17, 37, 253, 265, 304; **II** 331; **III** 179, 199, 200, 223, 225ff., 293, 347; **VI** 43, 45, 52, 158, 164, 166, 205, 206; **VII** 14, 15, 22, 23, 28, 34, 51–54, 120, 153; **VIII** 195, 196; **IX** 190

Paul, Leslie, **I** 219; **III** 85; **VIII** 52, 113, 127, 179; **IX** 154, 188

Pauli, W., **IV** 59

Pausanias, **IX** 95

Pavlov, A., **II** 241

Peachey, Paul, **III** 18

Peake, Harold, **I** 86

Pearl, Raymond, **II** 13, 255; **III** 336; **IV** 176, 215, 216, 298, 306; **V** 45, 91, 134; **VIII** 161, 162; **IX** 55, 125, 138, 146, 155

Pearse, A. S., **V** 89, 139

Pearson, Karl, **I** 346

Peattie, Donald C., **I** 187

Pedersen, J., **I** 277

Peet, T. Eric, **VII** 211

Pegis, Aton, **VIII** 109

Peking Man, **I** 125, 134; **II** 50, 51, 180, 181, 208, 236; **V** 59

Pelasgians, **I** 111, 115

Peleg, **I** 57, 76, 78, 115–117; **VII** 218

Pember, G. H., **IX** 120

Pendlebury, J. D. S., **I** 121, 198; **II** 32, 37, 121

Penfield, E. G., **VIII** 67, 137

Penfield, Wilder, **II** 240, 242–245, 261, 262, 269, 320, 329; **IV** 227, 286; **V** 213

Penn, Granville, **IV** 95, 96

Pericles, **VII** 18, 20, 21

Perry, W. J., **I** 36, 106, 122, 196, 197, 305; **II** 37, 79, 90, 104, 117, 122

Perseus King of Kittim, **I** 95

Persson, Axel, **I** 201; **IV** 124

Perthes, Boucher, de **II** 32

Peterson, Roger Tory, **VIII** 160

Peter, **I** 18, 22, 253; **III** 96, 111, 179, 215; **V** 315, 338, 358; **VI** 31, 127, 137, 138, 153, 154, 158, 205; **VII** 34, 45, 48–52

Peter the Great, **III** 226

Peter (the wild boy of Hanover), **II** 261

Petra, **I** 165, 208

Petrie, Sir William, **VIII** 129

Petrie, Sir Flinders, **I** 194, 311; **II** 89, 137; **IV** 117; **V** 63; **VII** 183

Petrucci, Daniele, **VIII** 71

Pfeiffer, John, **III** 72; **IV** 23; **VIII** 125, 241; **IX** 124

Pfluger, Edouard, **VIII** 66

Pharaoh of the Exodus, **VI** 134, 148, 149

Pharoh of the Oppression, **VII** 185

Philip (apostle), **I** 22, 24, 229; **VII** 28

Philip V of Spain, **V** 308

Philip of Macedon, **VII** 125, 257

Philipp, Frank, **IX** 251

Phillips, Wendell, **I** 138; **II** 56; **III** 201

Philo, Judaeus, **V** 246

Phoenicians, **I** 94, 95

Picasso, Pablo, **II** 164

Pickering, Sir George White, **V** 166

Pieters, Albertus, **III** 20, 281, 292; **VII** 96

Piercy, W. C., **I** 80

Piggott, Stuart, **I** 72, 152; **II** 78, 86; **V** 48; **VI** 202; **VII** 200

Pilate, **I** 22, 23, 265; **III** 81, 218; **V** 305, 315, 318, 319, 325, 338, 345; **VI** 100, 131, 137; **VII** 20

Pilbeam, David, **IV** 224, 282

Piltdown Man, **I** 125; **II** 195, 199; **V** 58

Pinches, T. G., **I** 80, 111, 112; **IV** 116; **V** 96; **VI** 186; **VII** 164–169

Pindar, **VII** 23; **IX** 95, 97

Pinnock, Clark H., **IV** 173

Pithecanthropus, **I** 132; **II** 27, 48, 50, 52, 135, 196, 204–206, 209, 218, 221, 235, 236, 238; **V** 58

Pius XII, Pope, **VIII** 162

Planck, Max, **VIII** 140, 210

Plato, **I** 287; **II** 267; **III** 187; **V** 393, 397; **VII** 22–25, 87; **VIII** 160, 161, 180; **IX** 83, 97

Platt, Rutherford, **IV** 40

Pliny, **I** 88, 117; **V** 307; **VII** 19

Plutarch, **I** 82, 299; **V** 109; **IX** 251

Polano, H., **VI** 211

Polanyi, Michael, **III** 262; **VIII** 79

Pollock, David, **II** 114

Polo, Marco, **I** 90, 205, 206, 322, 325–327, 333–336; **III** 214; **VII** 72

Polybius, **VII** 28

Polyhistor, Alexander, **V** 51

Pompadour, Madame Jeanne de, **VII** 157

Pompey, **VII** 107

Ponnamperuma, Cyril, **III** 258, 325; **VIII** 85, 139, 142

Popham, Robert, **I** 176

Portmann, A., **I** 132; **II** 49, 184, 194, 204, 219; **IV** 160

Postgate, Raymond, **III** 16

Poulton, E. B., **V** 178

Powell, T., **V** 97

Pratt, Fletcher, **I** 210

Predmost Skull, **I** 136; **II** 52

Premack, David, **II** 262; **IV** 269, 274–276, 286

Preston, Ann, **IX** 261

Preston, Theodore, **V** 71

Prestwich, Joseph, **IV** 103; **IX** 63

Price, Derek J. DeSolla, **I** 213, 320

Price, George McCready, **IV** 201; **IX** 61, 62

Price, George R., **III** 264

Price, Weston, **IV** 310

Prichard, James C., **V** 12, 20, 21, 263; **VI** 212; **IX** 69

Pritchard, James B., **IX** 76

Prometheus, **I** 81

Proskauer, Curt, **I** 186, 334

Prosser, C. L., **IV** 154; **VIII** 228

Ptah-Hotep, **I** 30, 278; 294

Ptolemy, **I** 84, 103, 117, 206; **II** 301; **V** 72; **VII** 28

Pushkin, V. N., **III** 334

Putnam, Patrick, **IV** 266

Pycraft, W. P., **II** 184, 213

Pygmies, **I** 131, 139, 199; **II** 47, 56, 74, 105, 119, 216

Pyke, Magnus, **VIII** 73

Pyrrho, **VII** 24

Pythagoras, **III** 106

Queen of Sheba, **I** 20, 21; **IX** 19

R

Rachel, **II** 319, 321, 323–325; **VII** 244

Radcliffe-Brown, A. R., **II** 105; **III** 108

Rader, Melvin, **II** 66; **VIII** 130, 171, 177

Radin, Paul, **I** 31, 314; **IV** 130

Radl, E., **VIII** 169

Rae, J., **IV** 264

Raglan, Lord, **I** 36, 47, 169, 297, 305, 306; **II** 73, 104, 116, 149; **III** 84

Rahman, **I** 20

Rainey, Froelich G., **II** 121

Ramm, Bernard, **I** 359; **IV** 47; **V** 82; **VII** 149

Ramon-y-Cajal, Santiago, **III** 257, 328

Ramsay, Sir William, **I** 76

Ramses II, **I** 96; **VII** 169

Ramses III, **VII** 169

Randall, John, **II** 75; **III** 82, 143; **V** 79; **VIII** 110, 112, 113, 115, 117, 121, 122, 160

Ras Sharma, **II** 91

Rassam, Hormuzd, **I** 21; **II** 274

Rasmussen, Knud, **II** 111
Rasmussen, T., **III** 329; **IV** 227
Rastall, R. H., **II** 26
Rawlinson, George, **I** 80, 86, 92, 93, 96, 97, 99, 110, 198, 309; **II** 77, 78, 123; **IV** 117, 138; **V** 50; **VI** 112
Read, Grantly Dick, **I** 173; **IX** 138, 139, 210
Reavely, S. D., **I** 192
Rebekah, **II** 320–323; **VII** 243–246
Reclus, Elie, **I** 272, 293; **IV** 264; **V** 123; **VI** 226; **IX** 173
Reddie, James, **II** 122, 131; **IV** 58
Redfield, Robert, **I** 134
Red Lady of Paviland, The, **II** 53
Reed, Charles A., **II** 34
Rehwinkel, Alfred, **V** 26; **IX** 62, 97, 102
Reinhard, Franz Volkmar, **III** 291
Reinhard, H. J., **III** 63
Reisfeld, R. A., **IV** 302
Reisner, G. A., **II** 89
Renan, Joseph E., **I** 292; **V** 339
Renckens, Henricus, **VI** 235
Renouf, P. LePage, **I** 292, 324; **IV** 116
Rensch, B., **III** 323, 324; **IV** 226; **VIII** 83, 84
Resen, **I** 108, 110, 112
Reuter, E. B., **I** 312
Reynard, Grant, **IX** 241
Rhodesian Man, **I** 125, 136; **II** 42, 52, 197, 205; **III** 48; **V** 24
Richards, A. I., **II** 126
Richardson, L. R., **IV** 203–205
Richter, Curt P., **IV** 308
Richter, Ludwig, **VII** 85
Ridderbos, N. H., **V** 78
Riphath, **I** 88
Ritland, R. M., **IV** 203; **VI** 209
Rivers, W. H. R., **II** 118, 122; **VI** 226
Robinson, J. H., **VIII** 111

Robinson, J.T., **II** 13, 14, 17, 21, 28, 201; **IV** 223
Robinson, W. Childs, **V** 249
Rockefeller, John D., **IV** 178
Roemer, Ole, **VI** 14, 16
Rogers, Spencer L., **III** 167
Rolland, R., **VII** 33
Romanes, George J., **III** 330, 331, 346; **IV** 71, 199
Rome, **I** 84, 198; **III** 231; **VII** 123, 207, 226
Romer, Alfred, **I** 131, 134, 136; **II** 48, 50, 52, 198, 223, 241; **IV** 58, 152, 153
Romulus and Remus, **VII** 207
Roosevelt, Franklin D., **VII** 118
Rose, H. J., **VI** 201; **VII** 199, 226
Rosenstiel, Annette, **II** 63
Rosenzweig, Irene, **IV** 124
Rosenzweig, Mark R., **IV** 226
Ross, John, **IV** 121
Rostovtzeff, Michael, **I** 294
Rotherham, J. B., **IV** 107
Rothman, Stephen, **III** 120; **IV** 260, 261; **V** 311, 312
Rouault, Georges, **VII** 87, 89
Rouge, M. de, **IV** 116
Roughgarden, Jonathan, **IV** 61
Rouse, Martin L., **I** 80, 87, 88, 109; **VI** 195
Rousseau, Jean Jacques, **III** 21, 28, 35; **VII** 96
Roux, Wilhelm, **III** 332
Row, C. A., **V** 339
Rowe, Prebendary, **IV** 113, 119
Rowell, J. B., **V** 249
Rozin, Paul, **IV** 309
Ruark, Robert C., **III** 68
Rubenstein, Irwin, **III** 250
Rubenstein, Robert, **V** 198
Rule, W. H., **IV** 138
Rusch, Wilbert H., **IV** 264
Ruskin, John, **III** 28; **VIII** 189
Russell, Bertrand, **I** 223; **III** 33, 198, 322; **VIII** 33, 97, 106, 126, 127, 139, 140, 211

Russell, Claire and W. M. S., **IV** 190

Russell, E. S., **I** 356

Russia, **I** 86, 90, 91, 99

Ryan, Francis, **IV** 72

Ryle, Herbert, **VI** 102

S

Saba, **I** 20, 103
Sabatier, P., **VIII** 111
Sagan, Carl, **VIII** 36, 37
Salk, J. E., **V** 184
Samoans, **II** 299, 306; **III** 207
Sampey, John R., **VIII** 124
Samson, **III** 224; **V** 104; **VI** 151
Sapir, Edward, **I** 270; **II** 260, 265; **IV** 289; **VIII** 118; **IX** 174
Sarah, **I** 15; **II** 314, 315, 317–322; **VII** 98, 151, 153, 154ff., 171–173, 196, 239–241, 243
Sargent, S. S., **III** 146
Sargon, **I** 20; **VII** 282
Sarton, George, **I** 172, 190, 191, 202, 207, 304; **II** 79; **V** 72, 73
Satan, **II** 309, 310; **III** 33, 78, 96, 101, 111, 161, 197, 218, 227, 308; **V** 147, 148, 157, 207, 247; **VI** 48, 127, 129, 160, 206, 239; **VII** 227, 289, 290, 300; **VIII** 89
Satyaurata, **I** 35, 81
Sauer, Erich, **III** 183, 341; **V** 84, 146, 182, 387; **VI** 109, 110
Saul, King, **I** 26, 146, 147; **II** 314; **VI** 45; **VII** 232
Savery, Thomas, **II** 148
Savory, Theodore H., **VIII** 64, 66, 72
Saville, Marshall H., **I** 182
Sayce, A. H., **I** 76, 80, 85, 90, 91, 93, 94, 152, 159, 160; **II** 86, 88; **V** 53, 62; **VI** 186, 198; **VII** 164, 167, 169, 170
Scarborough, H., **V** 212; **VIII** 67
Schafer, Edward H., **I** 283, 284, 332; **IV** 123, 124

Schaller, George B., **III** 73
Schapera, I., **II** 296
Scheer, Bradley T., **V** 141
Schenck, J., **V** 311
Schindewolf, Otto H., **IV** 92, 94
Schlegel, Freidrich, **VII** 87
Schleidt, Wolfgang, **IV** 277
Schlemmer, Andre, **IV** 36; **VIII** 132; **IX** 150, 163
Schliemann, Heinrich, **II** 120; **V** 13, 48
Schmidt, Helmut, **III** 264
Schmidt, Wilhelm, **II** 74; **IV** 111, 125–128
Schneider, Joseph, **VIII** 187
Schneirla, T. C., **IV** 293
Schoff, Thomas J. M., **IV** 61
Schofield, Alfred T., **III** 167, 330; **V** 340
Schonland, S., **V** 178
Schoon, Frithjof, **II** 164
Schrader, Eberhard, **I** 80; **VI** 79, 80; **VII** 163, 165, 166
Schreider, F., **V** 141
Schrodinger, Erwin, **VIII** 128
Schulberg, Lucille, **I** 280, 282, 296
Schultz, Adolph H., **I** 128; **II** 21, 222, 223; **IV** 217, 228, 243; **V** 394
Schultz, F. W., **I** 89
Schweig, Bruno, **I** 204
Schweitzer, George K., **VIII** 20, 32
Sciama, Dennis W., **VIII** 21, 26, 36
Scott, D. H., **IV** 56
Scott, J. P., **III** 24; **IV** 189
Scott, Sir Lindsay, **II** 120
Scott, Sir Walter, **V** 299; **IX** 144, 145

Scythians, **I** 82, 85, 90, 106
Seager, Richard B., **I** 198
Seba, **I** 20, 102
Sechenov, I. M., **VIII** 138
Seeds, Nicholas, **III** 332; **VIII** 77
Segraves, Kelly L., **IX** 103
Seifriz, William, **III** 260, 328
Selby, Colin H., **I** 128; **II** 223
Selby, Harry, **III** 68
Seligman, C. G., **I** 312
Sellier, Charles E., Jr., **IX** 103
Selwyn, E. G., **VI** 209
Selye, Hans, **V** 134, 178, 309
Seneca, **I** 78; **VII** 19
Sennacherib, **I** 72, 152; **VII** 123, 163
Sergi, Sergio, **I** 134; **II** 232; **IV** 168, 238
Seth, **V** 34, 38, 41, 167; **VII** 221–222, 227
Shakespeare, William, **I** 276; **II** 152, 190, 251; **III** 149, 239; **IV** 267; **V** 85; **VI** 23, 53, 120; **VII** 21; **VIII** 147, 159, 223; **IX** 143
Shalmanezer, **VII** 123, 282
Shankland, R. S., **VI** 16, 17
Shapiro, Harry L., **I** 311; **II** 68, 69, 73, 211
Shapley, Harlow, **IV** 32; **VIII** 27, 73, 79, 83
Sharma, **I** 35, 81
Sharr, Francis, **IX** 149
Shaw, George Bernard, **II** 225; **III** 16
Shea, William H., **IX** 63, 103
Sheldon, W. H., **III** 145, 149; **V** 393; **VIII** 81
Shelley, W. B., **V** 310
Shem, **I** 12, 14, 16, 18, 21–23, 25–29, 35, 36, 38, 43, 45–49, 69, 71, 75, 81, 101, 102, 113, 120, 140, 145, 150, 155, 215, 216, 247, 248, 251––253, 255, 257, 259–261, 263, 264, 266, 275, 276, 295, 304, 310, 313, 317, 337, 338, 366; **II** 35, 56, 98, 134, 138–140; **IV** 115; **V** 28,

29; **VII** 97, 224, 230, 231, 233, 234, 237
Shepard, W., **II** 149
Shepheard, H., **V** 367
Sherrington, Sir Charles, **III** 182, 257, 262, 328, 333; **IV** 31, 37, 38, 210; **V** 178, 195, 212, 386; **VIII** 67, 84, 86
Shiffrin, Richard M., **III** 238
Shipley, A. E., **V** 178
Shipton, Ursula, **VII** 112–114
Shishak, **VI** 135
Short, Rendle, **II** 214; **IV** 149, 155, 166; **V** 342; **VII** 194; **IX** 47, 48
Shoshone Indians, **I** 329; **II** 70
Shull, A. Franklin, **II** 215; **IV** 55, 105; **VI** 230, 231
Shute, Evan, **II** 18; **IV** 152
Sialk, **I** 188, 193; **II** 81, 86, 97–100, 102; **V** 65, 66
Siculus, Diodorus, **VII** 126
Sidon, **I** 67, 76, 77, 108, 112; **VII** 121
Siemens, David F., **VIII** 157
Siemens, William, **I** 322
Sigerist, Henry, **I** 328, 330
Silliman, Benjamin, **IV** 95
Simey, T. S., **VIII** 211
Simon of Cyrene, **I** 15, 23, 24
Simons, Elwyn L., **II** 15, 16
Simons, Maj. David G., **VI** 23
Simpich, Frederick, **II** 76
Simpson, G. Gaylord, **I** 220, 223, 353–355, 358; **II** 21, 25, 26, 236, 241–243, 251, 253; **III** 10, 18, 33, 50, 161; **IV** 23, 24, 31, 37, 38, 42, 51, 52, 58–60, 62, 70, 71, 73, 94, 139, 142, 152, 153, 157, 172, 173, 175, 207, 214, 254, 276; **VIII** 36, 37, 60, 61, 91, 106, 125, 127, 128, 144, 145, 159, 164, 215
Simpson, P. Carnegie, **III** 280, 281; **VII** 96
Sin, **I** 103, 105–107
Sinclair, John C., **I** 361; **IV** 72, 84; **V** 27, 28

Singer, Charles, **I** 202, 203; **II** 14, 120, 165
Singh, J. A. L., **II** 200, 260; **III** 212
Sinnott, Edmund W., **I** 220, 221; **III** 324; **VIII** 149, 176, 212
Siple, Paul A., **IX** 197
Sitter, W. de, **V** 72
Skinner, John A., **I** 80–83, 93; **VI** 81, 82, 97, 197; **VII** 166, 296; **IX** 85
Skuhl, **I** 134; **II** 50, 135, 223
Skutch, Alexander F., **III** 68; **IV** 247; **IX** 126
Slade, Adolphus, **V** 304
Slaughter, W. H., **IV** 253
Slipher, V. M., **VIII** 18
Slocum, Stephen E., **V** 134, 178
Slusher, Harold S., **IV** 201
Smith, Adam, **VIII** 129; **IX** 136, 137
Smith, Alexander, **II** 124
Smith, Edwin W., **I** 199
Smith, G. Elliott, **I** 19; **II** 121, 148, 230
Smith, George, **VII** 163, 164; **IX** 96
Smith, Hedderly, **VI** 209
Smith, H. P., **VII** 71
Smith, J. Pye, **I** 88
Smith, Maynard, **V** 28; **VII** 237; **VIII** 234
Smith, Merlin Grant, **III** 346
Smith, R. Payne, **I** 97; **V** 50
Smith, W. S., **VI** 211
Smythies, J. R., **III** 319; **IV** 179; **VIII** 14, 23, 56
Snaith, Norman H., **I** 80
Soal, S. G., **VIII** 208
Socrates, **I** 198; **II** 79; **V** 150; **VII** 22–24, 28, 87; **VIII** 180
Sodom, **I** 76–78; **III** 178; **V** 232; **VII** 162, 170, 173–176
Soffer, Louis J., **II** 185
Solandt, O., **I** 158, 159; **II** 159
Sollas, W. J., **II** 119
Solo Man, **I** 136; **II** 52

Solomon, **I** 30, 79, 147; **V** 28, 182, 183; **VI** 45, 58, 61, 141, 152; **VII** 123, 134, 181, 182, 237, 260, 265; **IX** 19, 20
Sonneborn, T. M., **I** 357; **VIII** 235
Sonoran Desert Indians, **I** 158, 162f., 258
Sophocles, **I** 307; **V** 55, 307, 324
Sorokin, Pitirim, **VIII** 128, 129
Spearing, H. G., **I** 197; **II** 94; **V** 65
Speck, Frank, **II** 300
Speer, Robert, **II** 185, 219
Speiser, E. A., **I** 114, 115
Spencer, Herbert, **II** 65, 74; **III** 15, 319, 340; **IV** 110, 126, 178; **VIII** 25, 131
Spengler, Oswald, **II** 83; **VI** 55; **VIII** 128, 129
Sperry, Roger W., **III** 255
Spurgeon, C. H., **VI** 156
Spurrell, G. J., **I** 80, 91
Stagner, R., **III** 149
Stebbins, G. Ledyard, **IV** 62, 175
Stein, Sir Aurel, **I** 212
Stein, Donald G., **III** 252
Steinen, Karl von den, **II** 258
Steiner, George, **III** 18
Steinheim finds, **II** 195
Steinman, Gary, **IV** 31; **VIII** 82
Stephen, V **I** 43; **VII** 14, 38, 45, 46, 50, 51, 60; **IX** 231
Steppat, Leo, **II** 234
Steptoe, P. C., **V** 196; **VIII** 72
Stern, D. J., **II** 166; **IV** 289
Stern, Curt, **III** 146; **IV** 307
Stern, H. J., **I** 212
Stevens, S. S., **III** 238
Steward, Julian H., **IV** 244
Stewart, Desmond, **I** 307
Stewart, Ileen, **I** 293
Stewart, T. D., **I** 134; **II** 50, 197, 234
Stirling, A. M. W., **II** 191
Stirling, Matthew, **I** 166; **II** 120
Stock, John, **V** 249
Stone, Irving, **V** 175
Stone, W. S., **I** 362; **IV** 74; **V** 127

Strabo, **I** 20, 82, 86–89, 96; **II** 76; **VII** 173; **IX** 95

Strauss, W. L., Jr., **II** 14; **IV** 242

Street, Philip, **IV** 156, 264

Stroud, William, **V** 303–309, 311, 327

Stuart, Duncan, **IX** 120

Studdart-Kennedy, **III** 186

Stubbs, Peter, **VIII** 26

Suetonius, **VII** 19, 30

Suidas, **V** 55, 72

Suleiman the Magnificient, **VII** 136

Sulivan, Admiral Sir James, **II** 140, 191

Sullivan, Anne M., **II** 263, 264; **III** 206

Sullivan, J. W. N., **I** 223; **V** 85, 86; **VI** 17, 19; **VIII** 30, 32, 33, 105, 126

Sumerians. *See* Subject Index.

Sumner, F. B., **I** 329; **II** 216; **IV** 69, 78; **VIII** 160, 226, 227

Sung Dynasty, **I** 321

Sung, Su, **I** 321

Susa, **I** 114, 118, 182, 197; **II** 86, 94, 98; **V** 65; **VII** 163

Swanscombe Man, **II** 135, 185, 195; **V** 67

Swanton, John, **IX** 155

Swanton, W. E., **IV** 69

Swartkranz Man, **II** 50

Swartout, Herbert O., **IV** 290

Swartzendruber, Dale, **IV** 40

Swift, Dean Jonathan, **II** 181

Swiss Lake Dwellers, **II** 121

Swyer, G. I. M., **II** 185

Synderman, George S., **IX** 177

Szczesniak, B., **VIII** 154

Szent-Györgyi von Nagyrapolt, Albert, **IV** 36

T

Tabun, **I** 134; **II** 50, 223

Tacitus, **I** 87, 99; **V** 345; **VII** 19, 30, 173

Takeuchi, H., **II** 17

Talgai Skull, **II** 15

T'ang Dynasty, **I** 213, 282, 312

Tarshish, **I** 93, 94

Tart, Charles T., **VIII** 207

Tartars, **II** 297

Tartessos, **I** 94, 95

Tasmanians, **II** 119, 120, 155, 156

Tax, Sol, **II** 31, 76; **III** 117; **IV** 60

Taylor, A. C., **III** 333; **VIII** 76

Taylor, A. M., **II** 110

Taylor, F. B., **I** 116

Taylor, Griffith, **I** 124, 125, 131, 133, 136, 138; **II** 41, 48, 49, 52; **VI** 213; **VIII** 129; **IX** 51

Taylor, H. O., **I** 224; **V** 162

Taylor, H. S., **VIII** 22, 211

Taylor, Hudson, **VI** 43

Taylor, Isaac, **I** 110

Taylor, John, **III** 185, 344, 350; **V** 161, 165, 389; **VIII** 179; **IX** 230

Taylor, Margaret, **II** 76; **V** 49

Taylor, N. B., **IV** 314

Taylor, Nathaniel, **III** 295

Taylor, Rich, **II** 78

Taylor, Walter P., **IX** 117

Taylor, W. E., **II** 90

Tayyeb, Ali, **II** 290, 301

Teggart, F. J., **II** 65

Teilhard de Chardin, Pierre, **I** 223; **II** 25; **III** 117; **IV** 254; **VIII** 141

Teleki, Gexa, **IX** 122

Telemachus, **II** 76

Tell el Amarna, **I** 93, 333

Tell Halaf, **I** 182, 193, 197; **II** 86, 88, 91, 92, 95, 98, 100; **V** 64, 65, 67

Temple, William, **II** 137; **III** 19, 178, 184; **V** 387; **VI** 217; **VIII** 112; **IX** 136, 155

Tennyson, Alfred, **II** 65; **III** 14, 15, 23, 88, 209; **IV** 126, 181; **VIII** 131, 219

Tennyson, Sir Charles, **III** 209

Tepe Gawra, **I** 83, 114

Tepexpan Man, **II** 232f.

Terah, **II** 314–317; **VII** 151–153, 155, 156, 240–242

Ternifine Man, **II** 50

Tertullian, Quintus, **III** 290; **V** 327; **VI** 89

Teutons, **I** 85, 99

Thales, **I** 192; **V** 73

Thayer, J. H., **V** 329

Theophrastus, **V** 312

Theresa of Konnersreuth, **V** 311; **IX** 217

Thiele, Edwin R., **V** 355; **VI** 47; **VII** 70, 181, 182

Thigpen, Corbett H., **IX** 187

Thomas, **III** 179; **IX** 298

Thomas, George, **VIII** 185

Thomas, H. Hamshaw, **IV** 105

Thomas, James, **I** 59, 61

Thomas, W. L., **IV** 217

Thompson, Campbell, **I** 115

Thompson, D'Arcy, **IV** 58

Thompson, F., **I** 221, 341; **II** 12, 50; **IV** 62, 175, 223

Thompson, F. C., **I** 214

Thompson, Francis, **III** 51

Thompson, H. W., **I** 285

Thompson, John A., **II** 185, 219; **IV** 168

Thompson, J. Radford, **IV** 138

Thompson, Laura, **IV** 323; **IX** 123

Thompson, W. R., **II** 26; **III** 97, 259; **IV** 62, 77, 80; **V** 168; **VIII** 96, 234

Thomson, J. E. H., **VII** 74

T'honga, **II** 295

Thornton, S., **II** 34

Thorpe, William H., **III** 261, 270; **IV** 202, 276; **VIII** 23, 59, 75, 91, 138, 141

Thorwald, Jurgen, **I** 329, 331; **II** 145

Thotmes I, **VII** 182

Thotmes II, **VII** 182

Thotmes III, **VII** 160, 182, 184–187

Thotmes IV, **VII** 186

Thucydides, **V** 55; **VII** 23

Tibareni, **I** 96, 97; **VII** 226

Tiber River, **I** 97; **VII** 198, 226

Tierra del Fuego, **I** 148, 170; **II** 74, 105, 114, 115, 118, 122, 140, 157, 189, 191, 259

Tiglath Pileser, **I** 20; **VII** 282

Tiglath Shalmaneser II, **I** 97

Tillet, Maurice, **II** 217–219

Tinder, Donald, **IX** 63

Tinkle, William, **I** 339; **III** 261; **IV** 72; **VIII** 163; **IX** 160

Tisdale, W River, **I** 97; **VII** 198, 226

Tierra del Fuego, **I** 148, 170; **II** 74, 105, 114, 115, 118, 122, 140, 157, 189, 191, 259

Tiglath Pileser, **I** 20; **VII** 282

Tiglath Shalmaneser II, **I** 97

Tillet, Maurice, **II** 217–219

Tinder, Donald, **IX** 63

Tinkle, William, **I** 339; **III** 261; **IV** 72; **VIII** 163; **IX** 160

Tisdale, W. St. Clair, **VIII** 165

Tissot, S. A. D., **V** 312

Titan, **I** 81

Titcomb, J. H., **I** 81; **IV** 130; **IX** 30, 72, 85, 92, 97

Titus, **VI** 59, 63; **VII** 29, 47, 60, 135, 136

Tobias, P. V., **II** 14; **IV** 282

Toda, **II** 122, 176

Togarmah, **I** 88, 89

Tolstoy, Leo, **III** 183, 239, 345; **V** 387

Tomb, J. W., **II** 261

Toorop, Jan, **II** 235

Torrey, R. A., **V** 347, 348

Tournier, Paul, **III** 85

Townes, Charles H., **VIII** 26
Toynbee, Arnold, **I** 207; **II** 83; **III** 27, 209; **VI** 55; **VIII** 128, 129, 198
Tozzer, Alfred M., **III** 146
Trajan, **I** 97; **VII** 19, 29
Trapnell, Steven, **I** 23
Tregelles, S. P., **VI** 92, 93
Tristram, H. B., **II** 274
Trobrianders, **II** 176, 290–293, 300; **III** 138
Troy, **I** 76; **II** 76, 120, 121; **V** 13, 48
Truman, Harry S., **VII** 118
Trypho the Jew, **I** 20
Tsai, Loh Seng, **IV** 318
Tschopik, H., Jr., **I** 173; **VI** 216
Tswana, **II** 296
Tubal, **I** 90, 96, 97; **II** 312; **VII** 208

Tubal-Cain, **II** 311, 312; **VI** 201, 202; **VII** 198–200, 205, 226, 227
Tung-San, Chang, **I** 289
Turck, Fenton B., **I** 311, 312; **II** 138
Turgenev, Ivan S., **II** 181; **IV** 224
Turi, Johan, **III** 62
Turner, C. E. A., **VIII** 124
Tussaud, Madame, **II** 228
Tutankhamen, **I** 181
Tute, Sir Richard, **III** 53, 322; **VIII** 22, 23
Tylor, Sir Edward B., **I** 184; **II** 33, 65, 67–69, 74, 107, 116, 118, 123, 124, 150; **IV** 127; **VI** 224
Tyre, **I** 76, 77, 89, 93; **VI** 138; **VII** 121ff.
Tyrrhenus, **I** 109

U

Ugarit, **I** 93
Underwood, E. A., **I** 178
Unger, G., **III** 251
Unger, Merrill F., **I** 80; **VII** 147, 194
Unuk, **II** 87; **VI** 199, 200; **VII** 225; **IX** 47
Ur, **I** 105; **II** 92, 93, 314; **VII** 151–153, 163, 202
Urban VIII, Pope, **VIII** 156
Urey, Harold, **VIII** 73, 135

Urquhart, C., **II** 90; **V** 63
Urquhart, John, **I** 316; **VI** 196, 199, 238; **VII** 152, 154, 157, 168, 170, 173, 206, 222, 225; **IX** 30, 75, 76, 84, 86, 89, 91, 96
Uruk, **I** 108, 114; **VI** 199, 200; **VII** 225
Ussher, Bishop James, **VI** 178, 238; **VII** 222

V

Valerius, Maximus, **V** 307
Vallois, Henri V., **II** 67, 113, 197; **III** 48; **IV** 152, 235, 265
Valmin, M. Nathan, **I** 198
van Valen, Leigh **II** 195

Vavilov, N. I., **I** 137, 193; **II** 55; **IX** 52
Veith, Ilza, **I** 284
Velikovsky, Immanuel, **VIII** 207
Vertesszolles Man, **II** 50

Vico, Giovanni Battista, **II** 83; **VI** 55; **VIII** 128, 129
Victor of Amiterna, Bishop, **V** 303
Victor (wild Boy of Aveyron), **II** 200
Victoria, Queen, **II** 229; **VII** 312
Vidler, A. R., **III** 292
Villee, Claude, **V** 23; **IX** 124
Vince, Margaret, **IV** 276
Vincent, B., **I** 83

Vinci, Leonardo da, **I** 262; **II** 66, 136; **V** 168
Virchow, Rudulf, **IV** 145
Virgil, **I** 88; **VII** 30
Visscher, Maurice B., **VIII** 140
Viteles, M. S., **III** 34, 158
Voltaire, **V** 312
Von Bunge, G., **V** 105
Vulcan, **II** 312; **VI** 201, 202; **VII** 198, 199, 226

W

Wabemba, **II** 297
Wace, A. J. B., **I** 198
Waddington, C. H., **I** 362; **III** 258, 324; **IV** 179; **VIII** 60, 78, 246
Wagner, Moritz, **IV** 146
Wakerling, George, **I** 294 Wald, George, **IV** 40, 41
Walker, Fred, **VIII** 172
Walker, G. T., **I** 172
Walker, James B., **I** 259
Walker, Kenneth, **I** 349; **II** 111; **III** 32, 40, 159, 183, 345; **IV** 28; **V** 89, 90, 140, 387; **VIII** 122, 127, 132, 205; **IX** 142, 145
Walker, Norma Ford, **VIII** 150; **IX** 158
Wallace, Alfred Russell, **II** 66, 108; **III** 15; **IV** 58, 73, 89, 90, 96
Wallbank, T. W., **II** 110
Wallis, D. I., **III** 114
Wallis, Wilson D., **II** 16, 68, 69, 183, 184, 201, 208, 210, 223, 234, 245; **IV** 148, 160, 268
Walsh, John, **VIII** 14, 190
Walton, L. B., **I** 346; **IV** 78
Washburn, S. L., **I** 341; **II** 224; **IV** 72, 144, 194, 235, 252, 314; **VI** 185
Watson, C. B. G., **II** 121
Watson, E. L. Grant, **VIII** 208

Watson, James, **VIII** 71
Watson, J. B., **I** 270
Watson, John B. S., **III** 140; **V** 290; **VIII** 137
Watt, James, **II** 148
Watts, Alan, **I** 33, 282
Weaver, Warren, **I** 289
Weed, Rt. Rev. Bishop Edwin G., **III** 167
Wegener, Alfred, **I** 116
Weidenreich, Franz, **I** 131, 133, 135, 136, 138, 311; **II** 14, 28, 48, 49, 51, 52, 138, 180–182, 194, 195, 199, 205–207, 223, 224, 236, 238-240; **III** 49, 121; **IV** 149, 150, 217, 224, 228, 229, 231, 268; **VI** 230
Weinberg, Saul, **I** 198
Weinberger, Pearl, **III** 334
Weinert, Hans, **II** 248; **IV** 271
Weinstein, E. A., **IV** 273
Weismann, Auguste, **I** 362; **IV** 74; **V** 85, 86, 89, 90, 139, 140, 178, 184–187; **VIII** 221–223
Weiss, Paul, **III** 182, 333; **V** 385; **VIII** 56, 65, 76
Weizsacker, Karl F. von, **III** 261, 323; **VIII** 19, 23, 28, 145
Welch, Bishop Herbert, **I** 345

Welldon, Rt. Rev. Bishop J. E. C., **IV** 138

Wells, H. G., **I** 194, 288; **II** 89; **III** 16, 17; **IV** 316; **V** 63, 79; **VIII** 113, 114; **IX** 303

Wendt, Herbert, **I** 171; **II** 64, 118, 247, 248; **VIII** 208; **IX** 161

Went, F. W., **IV** 241; **VIII** 39, 40

Wesley, Charles, **III** 38

Westbeau, Georges H., **IX** 123, 124

Weston, Frank, **VII** 104

Weyer, Edward, **I** 160; **II** 160

Whaley, Gordon W., **VI** 230

Whately, Archbishop Richard, **II** 107; **III** 50; **V** 168

Whatmough, Joshua, **I** 109

Wheeler, John A., **VIII** 43, 44

Wheeler, William M., **IV** 291, 292

Whewell, William, **I** 360, 361; **IV** 88, 89

Whitcomb, J. C., **IX** 62

White, Andrew, **I** 324; **II** 75; **VI** 192; **VII** 212, 213; **VIII** 157

White, C. Langdon, **I** 180

White, Ernest, **III** 21, 32, 160, 164

White, Leslie, **I** 133; **VIII** 129

Whitehead, Alfred North, **I** 297; **III** 323, 324; **VIII** 172

Whitehouse, Owen C., **VI** 79

Whitley, D. G., **IV** 138

Whitman, Walt, **III** 168

Whitney, Garth D., **I** 136; **II** 52

Whittaker, E. T., **VIII** 55, 151, 172

Whittier, John Greenleaf, **IX** 108

Whorf, Benjamin Lee, **I** 267–270, 274, 290; **II** 249; **VI** 22, 191; **IX** 156

Whyte, L. L., **IV** 192

Williams, Charles G., **V** 164

Williams, Howel, **IX** 140

Williams, Jesse, **II** 185, 216; **IV** 168

Williams, John, **II** 191

Williams, Ron, **IV** 121, 122

William the Conqueror, **V** 56; **VI** 53

Wilson, Epiphanius, **I** 31, 283

Wilson, G. E. H., **II** 121

Wilson, H. H., **II** 123

Wilson, J. Tuzo, **VIII** 104

Wilson, Maurice, **II** 16, 23

Wilson, Mercer, **IX** 228

Wilson, Richard D., **I** 80; **VII** 72

Wilson, W. H., **IV** 275

Winckler, Hugo, **V** 72

Winckler, J. R., **V** 47

Wind, J., **IV** 275

Winter, J. J., **I** 309, 310

Wiseman, Donald, **IX** 102

Wiseman, P. J., **I** 192, 194; **II** 89, 93; **IV** 115; **V** 62

Wohler, Friedrich, **VIII** 73

Wolff, Werner, **V** 181

Wolsey, Thomas Cardinal, **VII** 112, 114

Wood, Elsie, N., **V** 184

Wood, Theodore, **III** 67; **IV** 198

Woodford, James, **V** 132

Woods, F. H., **IX** 97

Woodward, Sir Arthur Smith, **II** 213

Woolley, Sir Leonard, **II** 93; **IX** 46

Wooster, Charles B., **VIII** 206

Worcester, Edward S., **II** 148

Wright, Charles, **I** 82

Wright, G. Frederick, **V** 341; **IX** 47

Wright, H. E., Jr., **IV** 95, 253

Wright, J. Stafford, **IX** 250

Wu-Chi, Liu, **I** 32, 283

Wuenschel, Fr. E., **V** 337

Wulsin, Frederick R., **I** 158; **II** 159

Wurtenburger, L., **II** 241

Wyndham, C. H., **IV** 261

Wysong, R. L., **VIII** 60

XYZ

Xanthoudides, Stephanos, **I** 198
Xenophon, **I** 97; **VII** 87

Yahuda, A. S., **VII** 74, 75, 180
Yevele, Henry, **IX** 228
Yonge, K. A., **IV** 229
Yoruba, **I** 103; **VI** 200
Young, Davis A., **IX** 62
Young, Peter, **III** 47

Zahl, Paul, **V** 125, 126, 130
Zangwill, O. L., **IV** 227
Zawarzin, A. A., **IV** 155
Zeitlin, D. J., **V** 119
Zeno, **VII** 19
Zeuner, F. E., **II** 31, 100, 102, 133; **IV** 226
Zeus, **I** 82; **IV** 57
Zillah, **II** 311, 312; **VI** 202; **VII** 199, 200, 205, 209, 226, 227

Zimbabwe, **II** 114
Zimisces, Emperor John, **V** 55
Zimmerman, J. G. von, **V** 308
Zimmerman, Paul A., **IV** 264; **VIII** 161
Zimmern, Sir Alfred, **I** 47; **II** 109, 166; **III** 31; **VIII** 113, 131
Zingg, Robert M., **II** 200, 260; **III** 212
Zinjanthropus, **II** 15, 16, 20, 23, 238; **III** 124
Zinner, E., **VIII** 153
Zinsser, H., **IX** 113
Zirkle, Conway, **VIII** 124
Zozimus, Pope, **V** 182
Zuckerman, Sir Solly, **II** 20–22, 198; **III** 25; **IV** 150, 223, 225, 228, 235, 236, 242, 303, 304; **IX** 122
Zulu, **II** 251
Zuni, **II** 151
Zwemer, Samuel, **IV** 111, 120, 129, 130, 138; **IX** 264
Zwingli, Ulrich, **III** 292

Scripture Index

Genesis

1:1—**I** 367; **IV** 16; **V** 230, 231; **VI** 12, 78ff., 123; **VII** 305; **VIII** 12, 248
1:1, 2—**VII** 280; **IX** 18
1:1, 2, 3—**VI** 96
1:1, 2, 3, 4—**VII** 285
1:1-31—**VI** 116
1:1, 3, 5, 6, 8, 9, 10, 14, 20, 22, 24, 26—**II** 268
1:2—**IV** 16f., 107; **VI** 86ff., 127; **VII** 283, 286, 287, 292, 298, 302, 303, 314; **VIII** 248
1:2-5—**VII** 291
1:3—**VII** 292
1:3ff.—**VI** 103, 114
1:3, 4, 5—**VI** 90
1:3, 5—**VII** 305
1:3-31—**IV** 17
1:3, 6, 9, 14, 20, 26,—**VI** 116
1:5—**VII** 288, 294
1:5, 8—**V** 354
1:6—**V** 26
1:6-8—**VII** 300
1:7—**V** 26; **VII** 283
1:9-13—**VII** 301
1:11—**IV** 105, 108; **VII** 303; **VIII** 247
1:11, 12—**III** 130
1:12, 29—**VI** 90

1:14—**VII** 305
1:14-19—**VII** 304
1:16—**III** 104; **VI** 117; **VII** 305
1:20—**V** 270; **VII** 300; **VIII** 247
1:20-23—**VII** 306
1:20, 21, 24—**V** 197
1:21—**I** 367; **V** 270
1:21, 24—**VII** 307
1:24—**V** 270
1:24, 25—**VII** 309
1:26—**III** 101, 103, 107, 108, 111; **IV** 212; **V** 221, 222, 390; **VI** 30; **VIII** 247
1:26, 27—**V** 142, 143; **VII** 312, 313
1:26-31—**VII** 311
1:27—**I** 368; **III** 103; **V** 219
1:28—**V** 166; **VI** 110; **VII** 313; **IX** 122
1:30—**V** 270; **IX** 124
2:1-3—**VIII** 54, 62
2:1-4—**VII** 315
2:4—**II** 276; **VI** 115, 116; **VII** 297
2:5—**II** 269; **III** 303; **V** 149; **VI** 235; **IX** 15, 186
2:7—**III** 90; **V** 173, 193, 194, 262, 263, 266; **VI** 84, 95; **IX** 214
2:7-9—**V** 143
2:8—**IV** 39; **V** 219; **VIII** 249
2:8-17—**III** 289
2:9—**V** 83
2:11—**VI** 104
2:15—**VIII** 61; **IX** 115

2:15-17—V 81
2:15-25—V 143
2:16, 17—V 381
2:17—V 180, 182
2:18—II 269; V 149; VI 235
2:18-23—II 269
2:19—II 269; V 197, 270; IX 38, 184, 185
2:19-23—IX 183
2:20—II 269; V 149; VI 235
2:21, 22—V 391
2:23—V 360
2:24—II 276, 277, 288, 308
2:25—V 103
2:26—IV 21
3—V 102
3:1—VII 286
3:1-9—V 81, 82
3:1-24—III 289; V 143, 144
3:6—V 88, 99, 149
3:7—IV 243; V 150
3:8—V 103, 219; IX 182
3:9—V 219
3:10—V 219; VII 274
3:12—V 150
3:14—VI 229; IX 125
3:15—II 309; III 177; V 247
3:16-19—IX 113
3:17—IX 115
3:18—IX 120
3:19—IX 8, 213, 214
3:20—II 269; VI 235; VII 274, 275, 286; IX 185
3:21—V 82, 103
3:22—V 84, 151, 219, 221, 222, 382; VII 312; IX 114
3:24—V 84, 151, 179, 219, 382; IX 114
4—IV 322; VI 193, 198; VII 205
4:1—VII 274
4:1, 2—II 308, 309, 311; V 247; VII 227
4:1, 16-24—VII 223
4:2—IX 185
4:15—I 108
4:17—I 108; II 87; VII 205, 224, 225; IX 47
4:17-22—II 139
4:19—I 108; VI 104; VII 226
4:19, 22, 23—II 311
4:20—VII 286
4:21—VII 286
4:22—II 99; VI 201; VII 198, 226
4:23—II 312; VI 201; VII 199, 226
4:26—II 310; V 247
5—V 37, 39, 40, 70; VII 203, 204
5:1—II 277
5:3—III 109, 124; V 390; VII 313
5:3-5—V 145
5:4—V 92; VI 233
5:5—V 50, 179; VII 296
5:6ff.—VII 223
5:6-32—VII 229
6:7-8—IX 16, 79
6-9—VII 202
6:1ff.—VI 127
6:1-2—V 157
6:2—VI 211
6:3—V 29, 71; VII 238; IX 35
6:4—II 311; VII 228; IX 89
6:4, 5, 6, 11, 12—IX 15
6:11-13—IX 16
6:12—IX 18
7:1—IX 58
7:11—VII 289
7:11, 12—IX 25
7:16—IX 32
7:19, 20—IX 22
7:21—IX 18
8:1-4—IX 99
8:4—IX 22, 24, 48, 104
8:5—IX 22, 24
8:6-11—IX 40
8:7—IX 24
8:10, 11—VI 66
8:11—IX 104
8:14—IX 25
8:16—IX 58
8:21—III 298
9:1—VI 110

9:3ff.—**V** 24
9:4—**V** 273
9:18—**VII** 97
9:20—**I** 25; **V** 102; **VI** 60; **IX** 49
9:20-25—**II** 313
9:20-27—**I** 140, 144, 148
9:22—**I** 144, 145
9:23—**I** 145; **V** 103
9:24-27—**I** 25, 338
9:25—**I** 145
9:25-27—**VII** 230
9:25-28—**II** 56
9:26, 27—**I** 260
9:27—**I** 99; **II** 36, 140; **VII** 233
9:27-29—**I** 338
10—**I** 11, 12, 13, 16, 53, 55, 57, 59,
    61, 63, 65, 66, 69, 71, 96, 101, 105,
    110, 112, 114, 115, 117, 118, 140,
    141, 260; **II** 57; **VI** 193, 194; **VII**
    201, 203, 218, 224, 229, 234
10:1—**VII** 98
10:1-5—**I** 100
10:2-5—**VI** 196
10:4—**VI** 197
10:5—**I** 17; **VII** 165
10:6—**I** 67, 79
10:6-20—**I** 78
10:7—**I** 118
10:9—**VII** 286
10:9-12—**VII** 200
10:10—**VI** 82
10:12—**I** 108
10:15—**I** 94; **VII** 229
10:15-19—**I** 63, 67
10:22—**I** 79
10:25—**I** 115
10:28—**I** 85, 118
10:30—**I** 117
10:32—**I** 12, 53; **VII** 201
11—**V** 37; **VII** 202
11:1—**VI** 176, 212
11:1, 2—**VII** 197; **IX** 45
11:1-5—**IX** 154
11:1-9—**I** 140
11:2—**I** 120; **IX** 101

11:3—**IX** 45
11:4—**II** 87; **VII** 196, 207, 225; **IX**
    21
11:5—**VI** 214
11:7—**V** 221; **VII** 196, 312
11:8—**VI** 212; **IX** 73
11:9—**I** 27
11:10-29—**VII** 234
11:11-22—**II** 18
11:25-27—**VII** 154
11:25-29—**VII** 239, 240
11:25-31—**II** 314
11:29—**I** 15
11:29, 31—**VII** 156, 242
11:31—**VII** 151
12:1—**VII** 151
12:1, 5, 9-13—**II** 314, 315
12:15—**VII** 154
13—**VII** 159
13:2, 6—**VII** 160
13:10—**III** 208; **VII** 173
13:15—**III** 285
14—**VII** 161f., 194
14:1—**VII** 165
14:9—**VII** 162
14:10—**VII** 174
15:2-4—**II** 317, 318
16:1-3—**II** 318
16:2-4—**VII** 171
16:3—**I** 15
16:6-9—**II** 319
17:8—**III** 285
17:12—**III** 297
18—**V** 244
18:17—**III** 93; **VI** 164
18:21—**VI** 214
19:1—**IX** 214
19:26—**VI** 90; **VII** 286
20—**VII** 154
20:1-12—**II** 315
20:1-18—**IX** 279
21:2, 8-14—**II** 318, 319
21:14—**II** 319
24—**VII** 240
24:2—**II** 318

24:2ff.—II 319, 320
24:15-24—VII 243
24:50—II 322; VII 244
24:51—II 320
24:53—II 322; VII 244
25:1—I 15
25:8—III 303; V 265, 266, 321, 323
25:14—I 117
25:17—III 303; V 265, 266, 323
25:25—VI 145
25:26—V 279
27—VI 145
28:1, 2—II 323
29:1, 4-6, 9-28—II 323, 324
29:5—VII 246
29:12—II 321; VII 244
29:14—V 360
29:20—II 325
30:1, 5—II 319
30:1-8—VII 172
30:6—II 319
30:7, 8—II 319
30:22-24—VII 172
31:19, 34—VI 87
31:47—VI 193
32:24—V 237
32:28—V 237
32:30—V 237, 244
33:4—II 330
35:18—V 272, 323
35:29—III 303; V 265, 266, 323
37—VII 177, 178
37:2ff.—VI 145
37:2, 27, 28—VI 145
38:2-30—II 325, 326
38:6-10—VII 49
38:11—II 327
38:26—II 327
39:1, 2—VII 179
39:11—VII 179
40:19—VII 179
40:22—VII 179
41:15—VII 282
41:43—VII 180
41:57—IX 19

45:5, 7, 8—VI 146
45:14—II 330
48:15, 16—V 237
49:3—VI 82
49:11—V 108
49:33—III 303; V 266, 323
50:4—VII 180
50:20—VI 147

Exodus

1:5—VII 185
1:11—VII 210
2:5-10—III 220
2:9—IX 280
2:15—VII 185
2:16, 17—III 221
3:13, 14—VI 40
3:18—VII 183
4:2f.—VI 32
4:2-4—IV 33
4:10—III 221
4:11—VI 147, 159
5:7-18—VII 210
5:23-25—VII 213
6:2, 3—II 310; V 248
7:10—VI 32
7:17ff.—VII 212, 213
8:10—VI 134
9:16—VI 149
10:5-15—IX 18
10:13-15—IX 16
10:20—VI 134
10:21f.—VII 288
11:2, 3—VII 181
13:20—VII 210
14:15—III 235; IX 277
15:35—VII 213
17:2-7—V 235
20:5—I 145, 146; VI 169
20:11—VI 116, 117; VII 297
21:12, 13—V 232
21:22—V 263
21:28—IX 17

23:18—**V** 109
23:28-30—**III** 214
23:29—**VI** 150; **IX** 123
24:9ff.—**V** 228
24:10, 11—**V** 244
32:14—**VI** 157
32:33—**VII** 258
33:11—**V** 244
33:17—**IX** 189
33:19—**VI** 147
33:20—**V** 95
34:25—**V** 109

Leviticus

1:1—**VII** 284
10:9, 10—**V** 109
17:11—**V** 273
18, 19—**I** 144
18:9—**VI** 220
18:17—**II** 327

Numbers

6:3-6—**V** 103, 104
11:31ff.—**VII** 213, 214
12:1—**VII** 185
12:3—**III** 221; **IX** 20
12:7, 8—**V** 244
13:23, 24—**VI** 61
16:22—**III** 303; **V** 195, 264, 266
16:28-33—**VII** 49
19:11, 12—**V** 349
21:2, 3, 34—**V** 324
21:6, 7—**V** 235
22:21—**III** 96
22:28—**VI** 143, 147
22:30—**III** 223
23:9—**VI** 58
23:19ff.—**VI** 164
23:26—**VI** 164
26:20—**II** 327

30:3—**V** 272
32:13—**VII** 60

Deuteronomy

1:8, 21, 27—**V** 324
1:28—**IX** 21
2:24, 30, 31, 33, 36—**V** 324
2:25—**IX** 19
4:35—**VI** 129
4:35, 39—**VI** 125
5:9—**VI** 169
6:16—**VI** 171
7:21—**III** 213
7:22—**II** 134; **III** 213, 214; **VI** 138
7:23—**III** 213
8:7—**VII** 289
8:15—**III** 223
8:15, 16—**VI** 149
9:1—**IX** 21
9:10—**V** 232
9:14—**VII** 258
10:16—**VII** 286
11:12—**VI** 82
13:1—**VI** 146
13:1-3—**VI** 161
17:6—**VII** 40
22:10—**III** 347
22:11—**IX** 213
25:19—**VII** 258
29:20—**VII** 258
30:20—**III** 177
32:4—**VI** 84
32:10—**VI** 92
32:11—**VII** 292
32:14—**V** 108
32:39-41—**VI** 147
33:21—**VI** 82
33:27—**V** 219

Joshua

3:15—**III** 223; **VI** 149; **VII** 192

4:24—**IX** 20
5:13-6:2—**V** 244
6:10—**VII** 190
7:1—**II** 327
10:8, 12, 19, 30, 32, 35—**V** 324
10:13—**VI** 212
11:20—**VI** 149

Judges

1:1—**VII** 284
2:1—**V** 237
2:20-23—**VI** 150
2:21-23—**III** 216
2:22—**VI** 138
3:8—**VI** 46
3:14—**VI** 46
4:2, 3—**VI** 46
6, 7—**IX** 185
6:1—**VI** 46
6:10, 13, 15, 22, 24, 25, 30, 31—**VI** 91
6:12—**VII** 274
6:13, 15, 22—**VII** 274
6:27—**III** 222; **VI** 91; **VII** 274
7:1, 2, 3, 12, 13, 14—**VI** 91
7:2, 12—**VII** 274
7:14—**VII** 274
9:1-57—**VI** 46
10:7, 8—**VI** 46
11:39—**VI** 90, **VII** 286
13—**V** 104, 105
13:1—**VI** 46
13:18—**III** 139
13:21, 22—**V** 244
14:4—**VI** 152
16:17—**V** 104
20:23—**VI** 150
20:20-27—**VI** 147
20:35—**VI** 151
21:15—**VI** 151

Ruth

1:12, 13—**II** 327

I Samuel

9:2—**III** 199
9:15—**VI** 87
10:6-9—**VII** 48
12:6—**VII** 297
15:21—**VI** 82
17:50-58—**I** 146; **II** 313; **VII** 232
17:55—**I** 26, 147
17:58—**I** 147
25:13—**III** 234
25:21—**VI** 87
28:3—**VI** 87; **VII** 286
29:11—**IX** 18
30:16—**IX** 18
30:24—**III** 234

II Samuel

2—**VII** 297
2:18—**III** 105; **VI** 116
5:1, 19—**V** 360
5:5—**VI** 47
5:8—**VII** 132
7:14—**VI** 138
7:14, 15—**III** 217
10:6—**VII** 71
10:18—**VII** 70
11:1-27—**III** 184; **V** 388
11:2-12:15—**III** 32
12:13—**III** 342; **V** 360
12:23—**III** 297
13:1—**II** 328
13:2—**II** 328
13:4—**II** 328
13:13—**II** 328
17:14—**VI** 137
18:18—**VI** 87
24:1—**VI** 172

24:3, 15—**VI** 172
24:16—**VI** 157
24:24—**VII** 71

I Kings

2:11—**VI** 47
2:36f.—**V** 182
5:17—**III** 176, 191
6:1—**VI** 45, 46; **VII** 181
6:7—**III** 176, 191
8:18—**III** 193; **V** 315
10:24—**IX** 19, 20
11:9-12—**I** 147
11:42—**VII** 182
12:24—**III** 195
12:31—**III** 104; **VI** 116; **VII** 297
13:24-28—**III** 96
14:31—**VII** 260, 261
15:2—**VII** 260, 261
15:8—**VII** 260
15:8, 11—**VII** 261
17:4—**III** 96; **VI** 143
17:6—**III** 223
17:14—**VI** 33
17:21—**III** 90
17:21, 22—**V** 272
17:22—**V** 281
18:10—**IX** 18
18:19—**IX** 231
21—**VII** 255
21:1-22:37—**III** 32
21:1-29—**III** 184; **V** 388
22:19—**V** 244
22:23—**VI** 128, 129

II Kings

1:7—**VIII** 87
4:34, 35—**III** 90
4:43—**VI** 33
5:1—**VI** 143
6:17—**VI** 127, 129

10:2, 10—**I** 20
14:27—**VII** 258
17:3—**VI** 90; **VII** 287
22:12, 14—**III** 105; **VI** 116
25:27-30—**VII** 266

I Chronicles

1:1-4—**V** 38
1:7—**I** 96
2:31—**VII** 263
3:11—**VII** 255
3:15—**VII** 254
3:16—**VII** 254
3:17—**VII** 254, 266
3:19—**VII** 266
4:35—**III** 105; **VI** 116; **VII** 297
5:22—**VI** 143
6:2—**V** 37
11:11—**VII** 70
11:20, 21—**VII** 260
14:17—**IX** 19, 20
17:10-14—**V** 283
17:16—**V** 233
17:21—**V** 233
19:18—**VII** 70
21:25—**VII** 71
28:3—**VI** 164

II Chronicles

3:1—**V** 244
6:8—**VI** 164
7:14—**IX** 188
9:21—**I** 94
10:15—**VI** 152
11:3, 4—**VI** 152
12:7-9—**VI** 135
13:2—**VII** 261
20:7—**III** 93
20:36—**I** 94
24:15—**V** 29
28:9—**IX** 21

35:20-24—**VI** 136
35:22—**IX** 148
36:15-21—**VI** 62
36:23—**VI** 136; **IX** 19, 20

Nehemiah

7:5—**VII** 266
9:6—**I** 149

Job

1:6—**VI** 203
1:10—**III** 197; **IX** 152
1:12—**VI** 128, 129
2:9—**III** 101
2:10—**VI** 170; **IX** 163
3:11—**V** 265, 323
3:23—**III** 197; **IX** 152
5:17, 18—**III** 218
8:7—**VI** 82
10:18—**III** 303; **V** 265, 323
11:7—**VII** 34
12:23—**VI** 134, 143
13:15—**VII** 59; **VIII** 108
13:19—**V** 323
14:1, 5, 6—**VI** 140
14:4—**III** 302; **V** 190
14:5—**VI** 117
14:6—**VI** 174
14:10—**V** 323
23:3, 4—**VIII** 198
23:13—**VI** 124
25:4—**III** 302; **V** 190
27:3—**III** 303; **V** 266
27:3, 4—**V** 262
28:14—**VII** 289
32:8—**III** 90, 94
34:14, 15—**III** 303, **V** 195, 265, 266
38:4-7—**I** 367
38:7—**I** 230; **V** 289
38:9—**VII** 305
40:19—**VI** 82

42:12—**VI** 82; **VII** 280
42:16—**VII** 239

Psalms

2:2—**V** 224
2:3—**V** 224
8:3—**VI** 83; **VII** 283
8:4—**I** 226; **IV** 209; **VIII** 144
9:5—**VII** 258
17:13—**VI** 147
17:13, 14—**III** 217; **VI** 138
17:15—**III** 105; **VII** 313
18:28—**VII** 288
18:30—**VIII** 55
19:1—**VIII** 12
22:27, 28—**VI** 133, 134, 143
22:31—**VI** 144
23:4—**III** 213, 217
24:1—**IX** 16
32:1—**III** 298, 310
32:8, 9—**III** 94
33:6—**VI** 123
33:9—**IX** 181
33:11—**VI** 124
34:8—**V** 101
36:6—**VI** 93; **VII** 289, 291
37:3, 6—**IV** 245
37:5—**IX** 258
39:10—**VI** 83; **VII** 283
45:6—**V** 231
45:7—**V** 231
46:10—**III** 133
47:6-8—**VI** 134, 143, 147
47:7—**III** 95
49:7—**V** 192
49:20—**III** 91
50:3, 5—**VII** 11
51:5—**III** 300, 310; **V** 191
51:7—**VI** 47
51:11—**IX** 248
51:12—**VI** 47
53:1, 2—**III** 91
55:6—**III** 133, 205

62:11—**VI** 124
65:4—**VI** 147, 157
69:10—**V** 272
69:20—**V** 313
69:28—**VII** 258
73:13—**VIII** 189
75:6—**III** 219
75:6, 7—**VI** 134, 143
76:10—**VI** 138, 147, 174
77:15—**VI** 83; **VII** 283
78:49—**VI** 128, 129, 146
80:8—**VI** 61
80:8-19—**VI** 60
80:10—**VII** 291
90:4—**VII** 296
90:10—**V** 191
94:8—**III** 91
95:6-10—**V** 238
102—**V** 234
102:18—**I** 268
102:24—**V** 231
102:25—**V** 231; **VII** 281
103:7—**VI** 165
103:12—**III** 305
103:19—**VI** 125, 129
104:2—**V** 103
104:9—**VI** 117
104:29, 30—**VI** 103
105:16, 17—**VI** 147
105:25—**VI** 147
106:7—**III** 241
107:25-29—**VI** 143
107:26—**IX** 21
110:1—**V** 224; **VII** 263
114:3, 4—**VII** 191
114:8—**III** 223
115:3—**VI** 129, 146
118:26, 27—**V** 224
119:9, 25, 73, 81—**III** 284
119:73—**VII** 71
119:73-80—**VII** 71
119:91—**VI** 137, 143; **IX** 191
127:3—**VIII** 80
135:6—**VI** 125, 129
139:14—**IX** 193

139:14-16—**IV** 46
139:14-17—**I** 365; **IV** 9
139:15, 16—**III** 176
147:4—**IX** 183
148:2, 5—**I** 367
148:7, 8—**VI** 143; **IX** 140

Proverbs

3:6—**IX** 258
4:7—**VI** 82
6:30—**V** 272
8:22—**VII** 281
8:23—**VI** 81, 83
8:31—**III** 126
10:3—**V** 272
12:10—**V** 273
14:34—**VI** 64
16:1—**VI** 140
16:9—**VI** 140, 143
16:19—**VI** 143
19:21—**VI** 140, 143
20:24—**VI** 141, 146
21:1—**VI** 134, 143
21:30—**VI** 146, 161
23:32—**V** 75
25:5—**V** 272
26:28—**VI** 84
27:7—**V** 272
28:25—**V** 272
30:2, 3—**III** 91

Ecclesiastes

2:7—**V** 194
3:14—**VI** 67
3:19-21—**V** 266
3:21—**IV** 212, 245; **V** 198; **VIII** 80
7:8—**VII** 281
7:13—**VI** 146, 161
7:29—**IV** 245
8:8—**III** 303; **V** 195, 263, 264, 266, 325, 378

11:1—**IX** 84
12:1—**V** 222
12:7—**III** 303; **V** 195, 264, 266; **VIII** 80, 81

Song of Solomon

1:1—**I** 149
1:5—**I** 20; **IX** 242

Isaiah

1:9—**VII** 286
1:26—**VI** 81; **VII** 281
5:1-7—**VI** 60, 61
5:4-7—**VII** 312
5:14—**V** 272
6—**V** 289; **VI** 31
6:3—**I** 230
6:5—**V** 234
6:8—**V** 222, 238; **VII** 312
6:9—**V** 238
6:10—**V** 234
7:14—**V** 191; **VII** 142
7:16—**III** 297
7:20—**III** 217; **VI** 138, 143
7:24—**VII** 287
9:2—**VII** 288
9:6—**I** 232; **V** 194, 282, 283
9:8—**VI** 205; **IX** 190
10:5—**III** 217; **VI** 147, 165
10:5-12—**III** 131, 192
10:5-18—**VI** 163
10:12—**VI** 164
10:26—**VI** 138
11:6—**IX** 124
11:7—**V** 24, 69
11:9—**IX** 162
11:69—**V** 95
14:24, 27—**VI** 124
17:1—**VII** 287
23:1—**I** 94
23:7, 12—**VII** 121

23:8—**VII** 123
24:10—**VI** 92; **VII** 287
26:12—**VI** 147, 159
28:21—**VI** 145
30:7—**III** 133
34:8—**VI** 93
34:11—**VI** 92, 93; **VII** 287
34:13, 14—**IX** 120
35:1—**IX** 121
35:4—**II** 310; **V** 248
35:4, 5—**V** 236
35:4-6—**VII** 37
35:5, 6—**V** 317
36:16—**V** 69
37:3—**IX** 280
40:9—**VII** 103
40:31—**III** 132
41:23—**VI** 147, 149; **VII** 120
41:29—**VI** 92
42:1—**VII** 103
43:13—**VI** 141, 143, 146
43:21—**VIII** 199
43:25—**III** 239
44:8, 28—**VI** 135, 143, 147
45:1, 5, 6—**VI** 135
45:4—**VI** 205; **IX** 191
45:7—**VI** 128, 129, 170; **IX** 163
45:11—**IX** 191
45:12—**I** 368
45:18—**I** 364; **IV** 23, 25, 106; **VI** 84, 92, 95; **VII** 287, 298; **VIII** 39, 247
45:19—**VI** 96; **VII** 287
46:9, 10—**VI** 136
46:10—**VI** 82
48:16, 17—**V** 240, 243
49:4—**VI** 92
49:12—**I** 107
49:15—**IV** 294
49:22—**V** 242
50:4-9—**V** 242
52:14—**V** 298, 338
53—**VII** 37
53:6—**V** 330
53:7—**V** 320, 325, 378
53:8—**VII** 37

53:8, 11—**IX** 140
53:12—**V** 284
54:16—**VI** 128, 129; **IX** 163
55:2—**V** 272
56:8—**V** 242
58:10—**V** 272
59:1, 2—**VIII** 199
59:2—**III** 288, 297; **IX** 281
61:1—**V** 242
61:1, 2—**VII** 312; **V** 241
63:8-10—**V** 238
65:20—**V** 69, 133, 141
65:22—**V** 69
65:24—**VI** 40; **IX** 260
65:25—**V** 24, 69, 95; **VII** 314; **IX** 124, 125, 162
66:8—**VI** 144

Jeremiah

1:5-8—**III** 223
1:6, 7—**VI** 159
4:23—**VI** 91-93; **VII** 287
4:25—**VII** 286
7:11—**VII** 286
10:23—**VI** 141, 143
11:16—**VI** 66
12:21—**VII** 286
13:23—**I** 102
17:9—**III** 17, 36; **IX** 286
17:10—**III** 192; **VI** 160
17:13—**IX** 189
18—**VI** 95
18:7-10—**VI** 143
21:14—**III** 192
22:30—**VII** 266
23:9—**VII** 292
24:7—**VI** 147, 157
25:9—**VI** 136
26:1—**VI** 80, 82
26:18—**VII** 287
27:1—**VI** 80
27:1-11—**VII** 124
27:6, 7—**VI** 136, 143, 146

28:1—**VI** 80
29:2—**VII** 265
30:7—**VI** 205; **IX** 191
31:29—**I** 146; **VI** 169
31:30—**I** 146
31:34—**III** 239
31:38-40—**VII** 129, 137
31:39—**VII** 139
33:11—**V** 400
34:1—**IX** 18
37:15—**III** 104; **VII** 297
41:7—**VII** 194
43:10—**VI** 136
46:6, 7—**VI** 138
47:6, 7—**III** 217
49:34—**VI** 80
50:20—**VI** 147
50:40—**V** 233
51:27—**I** 85; **IX** 104

Lamentations

1:19—**V** 323
3:25—**V** 400
3:33—**IX** 112
3:37—**VI** 131, 143
3:38—**VI** 170
3:37-38—**IX** 163
4:21—**V** 102
5:21—**VI** 147, 158

Ezekiel

1:1—**VII** 284
1:10—**VII** 103
4:14—**V** 272
11:19—**VI** 147, 157
19:10-14—**VI** 62, 63
26:3-5, 12, 14—**VII** 122, 123
26-28:19—**VII** 124
27—**I** 77; **VII** 124
27:7—**I** 93
27:14—**I** 89

29:18-20—**VI** 138, 139; **VII** 124
32:26—**I** 96
37:5—**III** 303; **V** 195, 266
38:2, 3—**I** 96
38:6—**I** 89
44:2—**VII** 129
44:18—**IX** 213, 214
47:9—**V** 271

Daniel

2:20, 21—**VI** 134, 143
2:37, 38—**IX** 19
2:47—**I** 149
4:11—**IX** 21
4:16—**III** 93
4:17—**I** 149; **VI** 143; **VII** 233
4:17, 24-26—**VI** 133
4:34, 35—**VI** 125, 129, 143
4:34-36—**III** 93
4:34-37—**VIII** 198
5:19—**IX** 19
5:21—**VI** 133, 143
5:23—**VI** 136
6:22—**III** 96
6:25—**IX** 20
7—**VII** 37
7:13—**VII** 40
7:22—**VIII** 41
8:14—**VI** 101; **VII** 294
9:17—**V** 233; **IX** 265
9:24-27—**VII** 36
10:13—**VI** 128
10:21—**VI** 203
11:30—**I** 95
11:36—**VI** 143
11:41—**VI** 82
12:4—**VII** 109

Hosea

6:2—**V** 350
9:10—**VI** 63, 82

9:17—**VI** 63
10:1—**VI** 63
12:3-5—**V** 242
12:4, 5—**V** 237

Joel

2:18-32—**VI** 71
2:28—**VII** 48
3:4-8—**VII** 123

Amos

1:9, 10—**VII** 123
3:6—**VI** 116, 170; **VII** 283; **IX** 163
4:11—**V** 232
6:1—**VI** 82
9:1—**V** 244

Jonah

1:17—**III** 96; **VI** 143; **VII** 193
2:4—**VII** 60
3:3—**VII** 287, 292
3:8—**VI** 229
4:3—**III** 131
4:11—**III** 97, 111; **VI** 158; **IX** 17

Micah

3:12—**VII** 129
6:8—**III** 198

Nahum

1:3—**IX** 141
1:7—**V** 400

Habakkuk

1:12—**III** 217
1:13—**VIII** 199
2:5—**V** 272
2:15—**V** 102

Zephaniah

1:7—**V** 233
1:8—**V** 233
3:17—**III** 177

Zechariah

4:11-14—**VI** 69
6:12—**VII** 103
9:9—**VII** 103
12:1—**III** 303; **V** 194, 195, 262, 266
12:4—**V** 236
12:10—**V** 235
14:6, 7—**VII** 294
14:10—**VII** 129

Malachi

2:10—**V** 391; **VII** 40
3:1—**V** 235, 237
3:10—**VI** 171; **IX** 275

Apocrypha

I Esdras
4:21—**V** 323

The Wisdom of Solomon
2:23—**V** 164

I Maccabees
1:1—**I** 95
8:5—**I** 95

II Maccabees
2:29—**VI** 118
7:28—**IV** 9

Matthew

1:7—**VII** 260, 261
1:7, 8—**VII** 216
1:8—**VII** 255, 259
1:11—**VII** 254
1:12—**VII** 254, 265
1:13—**VII** 266
1:17—**VII** 254, 269
1:20—**II** 309; **V** 247; **VII** 228
1:21—**III** 304; **V** 235; **VII** 264
1:25—**II** 329
2—**I** 20
2:2—**VIII** 198
3:3—**V** 235
3:11—**VII** 106
3:17—**VIII** 186
4:24—**III** 166
5:13—**II** 141; **III** 184
5:18—**VII** 71
5:28—**V** 315
6:25-34—**III** 95, 111
6:30—**IX** 116
7:11—**VII** 106
7:16—**III** 132, 192
7:20-23—**III** 193
7:21-23—**VI** 171, 172
7:22, 23—**III** 35
8:27—**VI** 132, 147
8:30, 31—**III** 111
9:1-8—**VII** 102
9:4—**VII** 106
9:9, 10—**VII** 99
9:15—**VII** 106
9:16, 17—**VII** 106
10:9—**VII** 102
10:29—**VII** 59
10:42—**VI** 174
11:2ff.—**VII** 37
11:3—**V** 317; **VII** 82

11:4-6—**V** 317
11:11—**VII** 106
11:14—**III** 139
11:19—**VII** 82
11:25—**V** 224; **VI** 161
11:30—**VII** 265
12:14-16—**VII** 42
12:31—**III** 312; **IX** 21
12:36—**III** 247
12:40—**V** 353, 357
12:42—**IX** 19
12:43—**VI** 127; **VII** 229
12:44, 45—**III** 129, 190
13:11—**VI** 147
13:35—**VI** 41
13:44-46—**VII** 101
13:55—**VII** 265
14:2—**IX** 174
14:38—**V** 269
15:18, 19—**III** 43
15:21-31—**VII** 126
15:28—**VII** 79, 81
15:32—**IX** 246
16:14—**IX** 174
16:19—**IX** 147
16:21—**V** 357
16:22—**III** 101
16:24—**III** 190
17:1-9—**V** 163
17:5—**VIII** 186
17:9—**V** 164
17:23—**V** 357
17:24-27—**VII** 102
17:27—**III** 96; **IX** 148
18:3—**V** 159
18:7—**VI** 162
18:8—**VII** 81
18:23-34—**VII** 102
19:26—**VII** 80
20:1-16—**V** 355
20:19—**V** 357; **VII** 73, 80
21:2—**VII** 80
21:5—**III** 96
21:9—**V** 224; **VII** 75
21:12-17—**VII** 45

21:16—**VI** 84
21:18-20—**VI** 70; **VII** 45
21:20—**VI** 71, 132, 143, 147
21:33-43—**VI** 63
21:43—**I** 17; **VI** 64; **VII** 233
22:7—**III** 218; **VI** 143, 147
22:15-22—**III** 108
22:20—**VII** 313
22:21—**IX** 148
24:2—**VII** 135
24:6—**IX** 154
24:6, 7—**VIII** 182
24:14—**I** 366; **IX** 19
24:21—**VI** 98
24:32—**VI** 71
24:39—**II** 311; **VII** 228
25:30—**VI** 165, 168
25:34—**VI** 41
26:20—**IX** 246
26:29—**V** 163
26:37—**V** 284
26:38—**V** 199
26:41—**V** 266
26:53—**VI** 127, 129
26:55—**VII** 80
26:61—**V** 318
26:62—**V** 318
27:3, 5—**VI** 157
27:4—**V** 319
27:19—**V** 219
27:24—**V** 319
27:25—**I** 22; **VII** 98
27:26—**I** 22; **VII** 98
27:37—**VII** 79
27:45—**VI** 48
27:46—**III** 307, 311; **V** 359
27:50—**III** 303; **V** 195, 264, 266, 321-324, 326, 327
27:51—**VII** 61
27:62-66—**V** 338
27:63—**V** 357
27:64—**V** 319, 357; **VI** 64; **VII** 38
28:1—**V** 353, 354
28:9—**V** 343, 360
28:12, 13—**V** 350

28:18—**VI** 129
28:18, 19—**VI** 125
28:19—**V** 223, 226

Mark

1:3—**V** 235
1:7—**VII** 106
1:13—**III** 96; **VI** 132, 143, 147
1:20—**VII** 100
1:27—**VI** 129, 146
2:3-12—**VIII** 89
2:5—**VII** 106
2:8—**VII** 106
2:14f.—**VII** 99
2:18—**VII** 106
2:19—**VII** 106
2:21, 22—**VII** 106
3:28—**IX** 21
4:24—**VII** 106
4:25—**VII** 106
5:9—**IX** 186
5:19, 20—**V** 228; **VII** 81
5:21-24—**V** 350
5:35—**V** 123; **VII** 42
5:35-43—**V** 350
5:41—**VII** 73, 81
5:43—**V** 351
6:3—**VII** 265
6:30—**IX** 246
7:21-23—**III** 33, 161, 301, 311, 345
7:24-31—**VII** 126
7:29—**VII** 79, 81
7:37—**VI** 131
8:31—**V** 357
9:19—**VII** 106
9:24—**VII** 101
9:31—**V** 357
9:35—**VII** 101
9:43—**VII** 81
10:6—**VI** 98, 99
10:14—**III** 97
10:34—**V** 357
10:44—**I** 17

11:2—**VII** 80
12:12—**V** 231
13:7—**IX** 154
13:19—**VI** 98, 99
13:32—**VII** 101
13:34—**VI** 147, 159
14:3—**V** 207
14:37—**V** 313
14:38—**III** 301
14:41, 42—**V** 378
14:49—**VII** 80
14:53-65—**V** 317
15:21—**I** 260
15:25—**V** 357
15:26—**VII** 79
15:33—**VI** 48
15:37—**V** 264, 321-324
15:38—**V** 322
15:39—**V** 323, 324
15:44—**V** 345, 380
15:44, 45—**V** 305
16:1, 2—**V** 353
16:9-12—**V** 361
16:15—**III** 86; **IX** 17
16:17, 18—**VII** 48
16:20—**VII** 101

Luke

1:27—**III** 302
1:32—**VII** 263
1:35—**III** 139, 169, 292; **V** 156, 196, 283, 287; **IX** 116
1:38—**VII** 313
1:41—**III** 144
1:43—**V** 230, 287
1:44—**V** 277
2:1—**IX** 20
2:8, 9—**III** 234
2:10, 11—**VII** 102
2:25-38—**VII** 36
2:40—**III** 169
2:41-50—**VII** 44
3—**V** 37

3:4—**V** 235
3:6—**VII** 102
3:15—**VII** 35, 36
3:17—**VII** 266
3:23—**VII** 269
3:27—**VII** 266
3:27, 28—**VII** 265
3:38—**III** 109
4:13—**V** 398
4:18, 19, 21—**V** 241
5:20—**VII** 106
5:22—**VII** 106
5:24—**VII** 41
5:29—**VII** 99
5:33—**VII** 106
5:36-39—**VII** 106
6:40—**VI** 84
6:48, 49—**VI** 98
7:11-15—**V** 123
7:11-17—**V** 350
7:11-18—**VII** 42
7:19-22—**V** 236
7:20—**VII** 82
7:28—**VII** 106
7:29—**IX** 7
7:34—**VII** 82
7:37—**V** 345
8:18—**VII** 106
8:31—**VII** 290
8:39—**V** 229; **VII** 81
8:54—**V** 265; **VII** 81
8:55—**III** 303; **V** 195, 265, 266
9:22—**V** 357
9:32, 35—**III** 169
9:33—**III** 215
9:41—**VII** 106
9:54—**IX** 260
10:8f.—**VI** 194
11:1—**IX** 260
11:13—**VII** 106
11:27—**I** 26, 147; **II** 314; **VII** 232
11:50—**VI** 41
11:52—**VIII** 199
12:6, 7—**V** 400
12:41—**V** 231

12:56—**VII** 120
13:6—**VI** 71
13:6-9—**VII** 44
13:32—**V** 357
14:29—**VI** 98
15—**VI** 168
15:11, 12, 31—**II** 329
15:20—**II** 330
15:25-28—**II** 330
15:29—**VI** 169
15:30—**VI** 151
15:31—**VI** 169
16:8—**I** 46
17:10—**III** 193; **VI** 165
17:15—**V** 230
17:16—**V** 229, 230; **VII** 82
17:21—**III** 94
18:9—**V** 231
18:16—**III** 55, 111
18:25—**VII** 76
18:27—**VII** 81
18:32—**VII** 80
18:33—**V** 357
18:35—**VII** 73
19:7—**IX** 246
19:13, 17, 24—**VII** 76
19:14—**VII** 46, 51
19:30—**VII** 80
19:38—**VII** 75
20:19—**V** 231
20:27, 28—**VII** 241
20:27-38—**II** 316; **VII** 155
21:3—**III** 224
21:9—**IX** 154
21:24—**I** 17, 260; **VII** 142, 165
21:28—**IV** 245; **IX** 190
21:29, 30—**VI** 71
22:28—**V** 398
22:31, 32—**III** 96, 111
22:42—**V** 380
22:43—**IX** 216
22:44—**IX** 213, 215, 216
22:50, 51—**VI** 31
22:51—**IV** 33
22:53—**VII** 80

22:56, 57—**V** 340
23:26—**I** 22; **VII** 98
23:34—**VII** 38
23:38—**VII** 79
23:41—**V** 319
23:43—**VI** 43
23:44—**VI** 26, 48
23:46—**V** 264, 321-324, 327
23:47—**V** 319
24—**V** 340-342
24:1—**V** 353
24:7—**V** 357
24:21—**V** 345, 357
24:28-31—**VI** 35
24:30—**IX** 246
24:30, 31—**V** 163
24:30f.—**V** 338
24:31—**V** 299
24:36-45—**VI** 35
24:39—**III** 327; **V** 358, 360
24:42—**IX** 297
24:42, 43—**V** 163
24:43—**VI** 35
24:45—**III** 90, 94
24:46—**V** 357
24:52—**V** 344; **VII** 47

John

1:1—**V** 194, 231, 283; **VI** 83, 123; **IX** 182
1:1-3—**V** 230
1:2—**V** 283
1:3—**I** 367; **III** 272; **V** 231; **VI** 123
1:7—**IX** 21
1:10—**V** 219
1:11—**IX** 190
1:11-13—**VI** 147, 159
1:12—**III** 110; **IX** 191; **VII** 313
1:12, 13—**III** 109
1:13—**VI** 157
1:14—**I** 232, 238; **V** 117, 194, 246, 383; **VI** 123; **IX** 182
1:18—**V** 218, 228, 244, 364

1:21—**VII** 37
1:29—**III** 163, 298, 305, 310; **V** 317
1:32—**VII** 292
1:47—**VI** 205
1:48—**VI** 70
1:49—**IX** 191
2:1—**IX** 246
2:1ff.—**VII** 39
2:1-11—**VIII** 87
2:3ff.—**VI** 132
2:4—**VII** 39
2:13-16—**VII** 44
2:19—**V** 318, 357
3:2—**VII** 39
3:3—**III** 46, 55, 95, 111, 303, 311; **IV** 137; **V** 162, 195, 266
3:3, 7—**VIII** 96
3:5-7—**III** 55
3:7—**III** 95, 170, 303; **V** 195, 266
3:8—**V** 268
3:13—**VI** 41, 44, 48
3:16—**I** 232; **III** 126; **V** 284, 400
3:30—**III** 130, 191
4:46-53—**V** 123, 350
4:47—**VII** 42
4:53—**V** 351
5:14—**VIII** 89
5:17—**VI** 124; **VII** 40; **VIII** 54, 58, 88
5:17-38—**VII** 39
5:18—**VII** 40
5:19—**VII** 40
5:20—**VII** 40
5:24—**VII** 143
5:25—**VI** 42
5:25, 26—**VII** 40
5:27—**VII** 40
5:28—**III** 306
5:29—**III** 306
5:43—**V** 224
5:47—**V** 244
6:4—**VII** 45
6:9, 13—**VI** 33
6:21—**VI** 44
6:42—**VII** 264

7:43—**VII** 38
8:1-11—**IX** 189
8:2—**IX** 21
8:7—**III** 302
8:21—**III** 300
8:46—**V** 159, 319; **III** 212
8:58—**VI** 39
9—**IX** 112
9:1ff.—**I** 146
9:1-3—**VI** 170
9:16—**VII** 38
9:34—**III** 300
10:16—**V** 242
10:17, 18—**V** 315, 378
10:18—**V** 302, 313, 322, 325, 379
10:19—**VII** 38
10:22-26—**VII** 41
10:28—**VI** 147, 159
10:29—**V** 242
10:30—**III** 323
11—**V** 123, 351; **VII** 43; **VIII** 87
11:5—**V** 351
11:6, 17, 32—**V** 352
11:20—**III** 235
11:25, 26—**VI** 43
11:39—**III** 144; **VI** 34
11:49-51—**VI** 140, 143; **VII** 46
11:51—**VI** 164; **IX** 148
11:53, 54—**VII** 42
12:2—**IX** 246
12:15—**VII** 43
12:19—**V** 352
12:21—**I** 18; **VII** 98
12:27—**V** 199, 284
12:32—**IX** 21
12:37—**V** 234
12:39—**VI** 146, 161
12:40—**VI** 161
12:40, 41—**V** 234
12:42—**VII** 38
13:10—**III** 307
13:19—**VI** 136; **VII** 120
14:1—**VIII** 199
14:3—**VI** 42
14:6—**III** 100, 125, 177; **IV** 315; **V**
95; **VIII** 199; **IX** 264
14:9—**I** 229; **IV** 209
14:12—**IV** 210; **V** 389
14:16—**V** 239
14:17—**IX** 248
14:18-21—**III** 177
14:19—**V** 335
14:19, 20—**V** 363, 364
14:28—**III** 323; **V** 199, 284
14:30—**III** 302, 310
15:1—**V** 101; **VI** 61
15:3—**V** 334
15:15—**III** 93; **VI** 164, 174; **VII**
101; **IX** 191
15:16—**III** 235; **VI** 147, 159; **IX** 191
15:19—**III** 344, 346
15:22—**III** 312
16:8, 9—**III** 312
17:24—**VI** 41, 98
18:38—**V** 318; **VII** 20
19:10—**VI** 137
19:11—**III** 312; **VI** 137, 143
19:16—**V** 320, 325, 379
19:19—**VII** 79
19:25—**V** 340
19:28—**V** 330
19:30—**V** 264, 314, 320, 321, 322,
324, 379; **VI** 49
19:34—**V** 306, 345
19:35—**V** 345
19:37—**V** 235
20:1—**V** 353
20:1-10—**V** 357
20:2—**V** 345
20:4-6—**V** 338
20:11-18—**V** 357, 358
20:22—**III** 90, 94
20:23—**IX** 147
20:27—**V** 299, 346; **VI** 35
20:27, 28—**V** 343
20:28—**V** 230; **VII** 82
21:3—**III** 179; **V** 345
21:4-13—**VI** 34
21:9—**IX** 246, 297

Acts

1:21, 22—**V** 347
2—**VI** 211
2:5—**I** 22; **IX** 20
2:9-11—**I** 22
2:11, 12—**VII** 48
2:14—**VII** 48
2:17—**VII** 48
2:17f.—**VI** 71
2:22—**I** 22; **VII** 98
2:23—**I** 233; **III** 92, 193; **V** 315, 379; **VI** 144, 153
2:32—**V** 347
2:34—**VI** 44
2:36—**VII** 48
2:41—**VII** 74
2:46—**VII** 45
3:1—**VII** 45
3:2—**IX** 229
3:17—**VII** 38
4:10—**V** 347
4:13—**V** 340
4:26—**V** 224
4:27—**I** 23; **V** 283
4:27f.—**VI** 153
4:27, 28—**III** 92; **VI** 144
4:28—**III** 193
5:3, 4—**V** 225; **VI** 67
5:5, 10—**III** 303; **V** 195, 264, 266, 320, 323
5:11—**VII** 49
5:12-16—**VII** 48
5:13—**VI** 156
5:19, 20—**VII** 51
5:28—**I** 22; **V** 340
5:31—**VI** 147
5:34-39—**VII** 38
5:40-42—**IX** 147
5:42—**VII** 45
6:2—**VI** 57
7:4, 5—**VI** 88
7:22—**III** 220; **VII** 184
7:25—**III** 221; **VII** 185
7:45—**V** 235

7:51—**VI** 154
7:56—**VI** 43; **VII** 46
7:59—**III** 303; **V** 195, 264, 266
7:60—**III** 312; **V** 264
8:28—**VII** 28
8:35—**I** 22; **VII** 99
9—**VI** 205; **IX** 190
9:5—**III** 226
9:15—**III** 180
10—**VII** 99
10:1-4—**IX** 264
10:4—**III** 125; **VIII** 198
10:9, 10—**III** 179
10:34—**I** 22
10:34, 35—**III** 100
10:35—**III** 125
10:38—**VII** 45
10:40—**V** 357
10:43—**III** 305
10:44-46—**VII** 52
10:48—**V** 223, 226
11:18—**VI** 147, 156
11:28—**IX** 19
12:6—**III** 179
12:6-10—**VII** 51
12:20-25—**VII** 49
12:23—**V** 323
13:1—**I** 23; **VII** 98
13:2—**VI** 205; **IX** 190
13:5—**VII** 100
13:6f.—**VII** 52
13:6-8—**I** 19
13:9—**III** 180; **VI** 205; **IX** 190
13:17-22—**VI** 45
13:28—**VII** 44
13:34-39—**V** 327
13:36—**VI** 147, 174
13:37-39—**V** 335
13:46—**VII** 53
13:48—**VI** 147
13:50—**IX** 252
14:9—**VII** 53
14:12—**VII** 53
15:21—**IX** 19
16:7, 8—**III** 229

16:10—III 229
16:14—VI 147, 156
16:16-18—VII 52
16:18—III 229
16:25ff.—VII 51, 52
16:26—VI 98
16:30—III 229
17:2, 3—VII 53
17:18—V 347
17:23—I 265; VII 20, 34
17:24-26—I 116
17:24-28—I 51
17:26—I 319; IV 254; V 201, 204, 391; VI 235; IX 154, 156
17:28—VIII 87
18:4—VII 53
18:6—VII 233
18:27—VI 147, 158
19:10—IX 20
19:11, 12—VII 52
19:27—IX 20
20:5—III 229
20:6—III 229
20:9-12—VII 52
20:10—III 90
20:28—V 230
22:14—VI 173
23:2-5—IX 148
23:4, 5—III 234
23:10—III 229
25:18—VII 293
26:6-8—V 334
27—III 229
27:3—III 230
28:3-6—VII 52
28:8, 9—VII 52
28:16—III 230
28:25—VII 50
28:25, 26—V 238
28:28—VII 50

Romans

1:3, 4—VII 263

1:8—IX 20
1:18—V 256, 257
1:18-23—VI 117
1:20—V 400; VIII 80
1:21—III 110
1:22-25—III 103
1:23-25—IV 326
1:25—VI 114
1:28—V 396; VII 152
2:4—VI 147, 156
3:3—III 313
3:4—VI 168
3:6—VI 172
3:7—VI 172
3:8—VI 172
3:10-12—III 38
3:20—III 312
3:21—III 31
3:23—III 293
3:26—III 281
5:5—V 225
5:7—VI 166
5:12—III 12, 185, 287, 290, 294, 310; V 19, 88, 130, 142, 164, 183, 190, 382, 389; IX 113
5:12-14—V 144, 145, 152
5:14—III 293; VI 238
5:19—III 287, 294
6:1—III 312
6:5—III 130
6:6—III 313
6:12—III 129, 190, 308
6:14—IX 188
6:23—V 376; VI 147, 159
7:7—III 312
7:8—III 301, 308, 311
7:13—III 310
7:18—III 37
7:18-20—III 37
7:18-24—III 299
7:20—III 308
7:22—III 177; V 207, 269, 365
7:23—III 300, 310, 313; V 269; IX 114
7:24—III 307, 343

8:1—**III** 178, 280, 305
8:3—**III** 290, 299, 301, 305, 310; **V** 117, 191, 383
8:11—**III** 299; **V** 162
8:13—**VII** 54
8:15—**III** 110, 125
8:16—**III** 125
8:20—**VI** 169
8:20-22—**IX** 17
8:21-22—**III** 86
8:22—**VI** 98
8:25—**I** 239
8:26—**III** 130, 191
8:28—**III** 195, 235; **IX** 163, 271
8:29—**III** 109; **V** 200, 390; **VI** 147; **VII** 313
8:36—**III** 233
9:11-13—**VI** 144
9:13—**VI** 145
9:17—**VI** 134, 149
9:19—**VI** 141, 142, 171
9:21—**III** 175, 348; **VI** 146, 155, 156
9:21, 22—**VI** 138, 146
9:22—**VI** 162
10:9—**V** 335
10:21—**V** 231
11:5—**VI** 147
11:17-27—**VI** 66, 67
11:19—**VI** 154
11:25—**VII** 50
11:26—**VI** 205; **IX** 191
11:32—**VI** 146, 161
11:33—**I** 368; **V** 155, 211
11:33-36—**VI** 154
11:34—**V** 211
11:36—**V** 211
12:1—**I** 253; **III** 313
12:2—**III** 17, 39, 46, 95, 274; **V** 169; **VIII** 196
12:4—**III** 348
12:5—**III** 348
13—**IX** 147
13:1, 2—**VI** 139
13:1-6—**VI** 143
13:1-7—**IX** 143

13:3—**VI** 139
13:4—**IX** 146
13:7—**VI** 140; **IX** 148
13:14—**III** 129, 190, 308
14:14, 15—**VII** 55
14:15—**VI** 68
15:4—**VI** 152
15:13—**III** 176; **V** 207
15:15—**VI** 147, 159
15:18, 19—**VII** 53
15:20—**VI** 98
16:8—**VII** 194

I Corinthians

1:4—**VI** 147, 159
1:10—**V** 191; **VI** 84
1:12—**VI** 205
1:21—**I** 265; **VII** 18, 34; **VIII** 196
1:23—**V** 334
1:26—**IV** 133
2:2—**III** 233
2:3—**III** 233
2:4—**III** 223
2:8—**VII** 38
2:11—**VIII** 199
2:16—**III** 272
3:5, 6—**VI** 147, 158
3:9—**III** 176, 349
3:10-12—**VI** 98
3:12-15—**VI** 68
4:5—**VI** 167
4:7—**VI** 146, 155, 156
4:10—**III** 233
5:1-5—**VII** 55
5:5—**V** 266; **VI** 68
5:10—**III** 347
6:15—**III** 348
6:20—**V** 195, 266
7:31—**V** 168
8:10—**VII** 55
8:11—**VI** 68; **VII** 55
9:1—**III** 131, 192; **VI** 160
9:5—**VI** 205

9:16-17—**III** 132, 193; **VI** 164
10:9—**V** 235
10:13—**III** 130, 191
10:17—**III** 348
11:15—**V** 103
11:19—**VI** 146, 161; **IX** 149
11:29-30—**VI** 68; **VII** 54
11:32—**VI** 67
12:1-11—**VII** 53
12:4-11—**VI** 147, 159
12:12—**III** 338, 348
12:18—**III** 174, 224; **VI** 147, 159
12:22, 24—**III** 224
12:27—**III** 348
13:2—**III** 29
13:3—**III** 132, 193; **VI** 171
14:18—**VII** 52
14:20—**III** 94
14:33—**VI** 84, 95
15:1, 3, 4—**V** 349
15:3—**III** 313
15:5—**VI** 205
15:6—**V** 298, 343
15:10—**III** 233
15:14, 15, 17—**V** 347
15:19—**VIII** 214
15:21—**V** 145
15:22—**III** 183, 293, 304, 310, 341;
    V 145, 206, 387, 393
15:23—**III** 304
15:24, 28—**I** 368
15:32—**III** 227
15:42—**III** 306
15:44—**III** 306
15:45—**III** 109, 305, 338
15:50—**V** 361
15:51—**V** 163, 399; **IX** 116
15:54—**V** 169, 274

II Corinthians

1:3-5—**III** 230
1:8-10—**III** 230
2:4—**III** 233

2:12—**III** 230
3:17—**V** 225
4:4—**V** 390
4:6—**VI** 96, 114; **VII** 293, 298
4:7—**III** 176, 233; **V** 207
4:7-5:10—**III** 230
4:8-10—**III** 233
4:9—**VI** 99
4:11—**III** 233
4:17—**III** 200
5:4—**III** 233, 299
5:5—**III** 176, 191
5:8—**VI** 42
5:17—**I** 368; **III** 170; **V** 208, 364; **IX** 188
5:17-21—**III** 46
5:21—**III** 281, 302, 305, 310; **V** 319, 328, 329, 377
6:14—**III** 347
7:1—**V** 195, 266
8:12—**III** 193
9:7—**IX** 267
10:2—**III** 233
10:10—**III** 199, 223, 232; **VI** 147, 159
11:6, 7—**III** 232
11:16-19—**III** 233
11:25—**IV** 108; **VI** 102; **VII** 294
12:7—**III** 225-228
12:7-9—**III** 230; **VI** 147
12:9, 10—**III** 128, 189
12:11—**III** 233
12:12—**VII** 53
12:16—**III** 232
13:5—**III** 177; **V** 207
13:8—**VI** 52
13:9—**V** 191
13:11—**VI** 84

Galatians

1:4—**III** 313
1:11-17—**III** 228
1:16—**III** 177; **V** 361

2:6—**III** 233
2:11-13—**III** 179
2:20—**III** 130, 177, 191; **V** 206, 330, 364
3:13—**V** 318, 320, 334
3:16—**III** 177, 285; **V** 191, 208, 252, 365
4:1, 4, 5—**II** 330
4:4—**V** 199, 283; **VII** 18, 34
4:5—**IX** 188
4:6—**III** 110, 125
4:12—**III** 233
4:13—**III** 227, 233
4:14—**III** 226, 227
4:15—**III** 234
4:19—**III** 131, 177, 233
4:20—**III** 233
4:29—**II** 319
5:9-11—**III** 131
5:16—**III** 308
5:17—**III** 226
5:19—**III** 292
5:22, 23—**III** 131, 192; **VI** 160, 173
5:24—**III** 308
5:25, 26—**III** 226
6:11—**III** 234

Ephesians

1:4—**VI** 41
1:5—**VIII** 186
1:9—**III** 93
1:11—**VI** 124, 125, 129
1:23—**III** 346, 349
2:3—**III** 308
2:8—**VI** 147, 159
2:10—**I** 368; **III** 131, 175, 191, 192; **VI** 147, 159, 171, 173
2:14—**VII** 53
2:15, 16—**III** 349
2:19-22—**III** 349
2:20—**VI** 98
2:20-22—**III** 176, 191
3:6—**III** 349

3:7—**VI** 147, 159
3:8—**III** 233
3:9—**V** 231
3:17-19—**III** 177
3:19—**III** 176; **V** 207
3:21—**I** 149 (fn. 4)
4:7—**VI** 147, 159
4:12—**V** 191
4:12, 13—**III** 349
4:13—**III** 177; **V** 389
4:15—**V** 208
4:16—**III** 176, 349
4:17, 18—**III** 93
4:23—**III** 95, 313; **V** 162; **VIII** 197
4:25—**III** 348
4:30—**V** 238
5:1—**III** 110
5:2—**V** 330
5:9-11—**III** 192
5:16—**VI** 48
5:17—**III** 91
5:23—**III** 349; **V** 162
5:30—**III** 349; **V** 362
6:12—**V** 361
6:13—**III** 133

Philippians

1:6—**III** 131
1:11—**III** 176; **V** 207
1:15-18—**IX** 148
1:16—**VII** 293
1:29—**VI** 147, 158
2:6—**V** 286, 287
2:7—**V** 286, 287
2:8—**V** 152, 287, 325, 379
2:11—**V** 248
2:13—**III** 92, 132, 193; **VI** 174
3:5—**I** 149
3:12—**III** 174
3:21—**I** 239; **III** 299, 306; **V** 161, 163; **VI** 35
4:13—**III** 177; **V** 231; **VI** 125
4:19—**IX** 260

Colossians

1:10—**III** 131, 192; **VI** 160
1:14—**III** 313
1:15—**III** 86; **V** 231, 390; **IX** 17
1:16—**I** 367; **V** 231; **VI** 125
1:16, 17—**VI** 128, 129; **VIII** 12
1:18—**III** 349
1:19—**III** 177; **V** 207
1:21, 22—**I** 238; **V** 162
1:23—**IX** 17, 19
1:24—**III** 349
1:27—**III** 177; **V** 207; **IX** 188
2:9—**III** 176; **V** 207
2:18—**III** 37, 200
3:4—**III** 177; **V** 207
3:5—**III** 129, 190
3:10—**III** 109; **V** 390; **VII** 313; **VIII** 197
3:15—**III** 348
4:14—**III** 231

I Thessalonians

2:3-5—**III** 233
2:4—**VI** 147
3:10—**VI** 84
3:11-13—**V** 225
4:13-17—**VI** 43
5:18—**III** 195

II Thessalonians

2:7-8—**VIII** 95
2:13—**VI** 147, 159
3:5—**V** 225

I Timothy

2:4—**IX** 21
2:5—**V** 232
2:6—**III** 305

2:13, 14—**V** 145
2:14—**V** 190, 382
3:16—**I** 238; **III** 327; **V** 230
5:21—**VI** 127, 129
5:23—**III** 293; **V** 110
6:10—**IX** 21
6:19—**VI** 98

II Timothy

1:4—**I** 253
1:7—**VIII** 197
1:10—**I** 234
2:13—**III** 349
2:19—**VI** 98
2:20—**III** 175
2:21—**III** 129, 190
2:24, 25—**VI** 156
2:25—**VI** 147
3:16—**VII** 70, 269
4:6—**V** 316
4:11—**I** 17; **VII** 100

Titus

1:2—**VI** 147, 159
3:1—**VI** 139; **IX** 148

Philemon

11—**VI** 168
15—**VI** 168

Hebrews

1:1, 2—**VI** 123
1:2—**VII** 283
1:3—**III** 109, 186; **V** 390
1:5—**V** 283, 286, 287
1:5, 6—**V** 199
1:6—**V** 287
1:7—**V** 231

1:8—**V** 230, 231
1:8, 10—**I** 367; **VI** 123
1:8-12—**V** 235
1:10—**V** 230, 231; **VI** 98, 99; **VII** 281
1:10-12—**VIII** 12, 31
1:14—**VI** 127, 129
2:3, 4—**VII** 50
2:4—**VI** 147, 159
2:9—**I** 234; **III** 305, 310; **V** 117, 206
2:10—**V** 163; **IX** 116
2:14—**V** 361; **VI** 128
2:16—**I** 236; **V** 222
3:7-10—**V** 238
3:9, 10—**VI** 165
4:3—**VI** 41
4:8—**V** 235
4:12—**I** 267
4:15—**III** 301, 310; **V** 319
4:15, 16—**III** 130
4:16—**III** 191; **IX** 228
6:1—**VI** 98, 99
7:3—**VII** 168, 169
7:9—**III** 187
7:16—**III** 302; **IV** 326; **V** 191, 302, 325, 376
7:20-22, 28—**VII** 298
7:21—**III** 104
7:27—**V** 316, 320, 378; **VII** 60
7:28—**III** 104, 163
8:10—**I** 368; **III** 112; **VIII** 96
8:10, 11—**III** 94
8:10-12—**III** 239
8:13—**VII** 61
9:3—**I** 149
9:12-24—**V** 360
9:15—**V** 232
9:26—**III** 298, 310; **VI** 41
10:3—**III** 239
10:4—**V** 381
10:4-7—**I** 232; **V** 173, 193, 194
10:5—**III** 169; **V** 10, 163, 191, 359, 381; **VI** 84
10:5-7—**III** 144; **V** 282
10:7—**V** 244, 359

10:10—**I** 238; **V** 162
10:11—**VII** 60
10:19, 20—**V** 162
10:22—**III** 307
10:25—**IX** 250
10:36—**VI** 171
11:1—**VIII** 185
11:3—**III** 53, 323; **IV** 9; **V** 222; **VI** 84; **VII** 283, **VIII** 12, 23
11:6—**III** 125, **VIII** 53, 200; **IX** 262
11:8—**VII** 151
11:10—**VI** 98; **VII** 153
11:11—**VI** 99
11:11, 12—**VII** 173
12:2—**V** 164, 302, 377; **VI** 147, 159
12:6—**III** 218; **VI** 138
12:9—**III** 303; **V** 195, 264, 266; **VI** 68
12:17—**VI** 157
12:23—**III** 303; **V** 195, 266
12:26—**IV** 108
13:21—**VI** 84

James

1:14—**III** 308, 311
2:23—**VI** 164
2:26—**III** 303; **V** 195, 263, 266
3:12—**VI** 70
4:3—**IX** 275
4:13-15—**VI** 141
4:17—**III** 312
5:9—**VII** 49
5:17, 18—**IX** 20
5:19, 20—**VI** 68; **VII** 54

I Peter

1:2—**VI** 147
1:19-21—**VI** 158
1:20—**VI** 41
1:21—**VI** 147
1:23—**III** 177; **V** 208

1:24—**IV** 39
2:5—**III** 176, 191, 349
2:8—**VI** 146, 161
2:9—**III** 350
2:10—**III** 124, 186; **V** 390
2:11—**III** 308
2:17—**VI** 137
2:17, 18—**IX** 148
2:22—**III** 312; **V** 319
2:24—**I** 238; **III** 299, 304, 311; **V** 162
3:20—**IX** 35
4:1—**V** 162
4:2—**III** 308
4:10—**VI** 155
5:10—**VI** 84

II Peter

1:1—**I** 23
1:3, 4—**III** 186
1:4—**III** 110, 177
1:10—**VI** 156
2:1—**VII** 54
2:7, 8—**III** 178
2:12—**III** 91; **VI** 162
2:19—**III** 35, 308
2:22—**II** 124
3:4—**VI** 98, 99
3:4-11—**III** 179
3:5—**VII** 302
3:6—**IV** 17
3:8—**VI** 40
3:9—**VI** 158, 173
3:10—**VIII** 12

I John

1:7—**III** 163, 298, 310
1:8—**III** 298, 307
1:9—**III** 279, 298, 305, 306
1:10—**III** 178
2:2—**III** 313

2:12—**III** 299, 304, 311
2:16—**III** 308
3:1, 2—**III** 109
3:2—**VII** 313
3:5—**III** 302, 310; **V** 319
3:9—**III** 177; **V** 208, 252, 365
3:12—**II** 309; **V** 247; **VII** 228
3:16—**I** 230; **V** 230
3:24—**III** 177; **V** 207, 364
4:4—**III** 177; **V** 207, 365
4:19—**III** 126
5:6—**III** 307
5:11—**III** 177
5:11, 12—**V** 207
5:12—**III** 177; **V** 364
5:16, 17—**VI** 68
5:18—**V** 365
5:20—**III** 93

Jude

4—**VI** 146, 161
6—**VI** 128, 129
9—**III** 96, 111; **VII** 293
14—**VI** 43
23—**IX** 214

Revelation

2:17—**VI** 206; **IX** 188, 189
3:5—**VII** 258
3:7—**IX** 32
3:20—**III** 177; **V** 207, 364; **VII** 143; **IX** 246
4:11—**VIII** 186, 199
9:11—**VI** 94; **VII** 289
11—**VII** 61, 63
11:3-12—**V** 179
11:4—**VI** 69
11:7—**VII** 289
11:15—**V** 224
12:10—**VI** 99
13:8—**I** 233; **IV** 21; **VI** 41

17:8—**VI** 41; **VII** 289
17:17—**VI** 133, 143
19:6—**VI** 122
19:8—**IX** 214
19:16—**I** 149
20:1, 3—**VII** 289
20:10—**VI** 128, 129
20:12—**III** 240, 278
20:13—**VII** 229

20:14—**III** 306
21:1—**VIII** 12, 89
21:1, 5—**I** 368
21:3—**V** 165
21:14-19—**VI** 98
22:2—**III** 289; **V** 83, 151, 179; **VI** 73; **IX** 114
22:5—**V** 169

Index to Hebrew and Greek Words

Regarding the Method of Transliteration of Hebrew and Greek Words

There is considerable difference of opinion among standard biblical reference works which are widely used by the ordinary reader as to the best way to transliterate either Hebrew or Greek words. As a consequence, in quoting from various sources, one finds apparent contradictions. It is too late to uniform them in those aids to biblical research that have long been on the market; and any attempt in the present volumes to achieve strict uniformity can only lead to confusion. One system is used in Young's Concordance, another in Bagster's *Englishman's Hebrew and Chaldee Concordance of the Old Testament* and its companion for the New Testament, and another system in Eerdmans' *Theological Dictionary of the Old Testament* now in process. Such confusion as presently exists seems to be unavoidable but need not seriously mislead the ordinary reader.

Hebrew words (in Hebrew characters)

אֲדָמָה	"soil," "ground"	**IX** 15
אֶחָד	"one," "number one"	**VI** 104
אִישׁ	"man"	**V** 147
אִשָּׁה	"woman"	**V** 147
אֶרֶץ	"land," "earth"	**IX** 15

251

בֹּהוּ	"desolation," "void"	VI 93
בָּרָא	"create," "put final touches to," "polish," "finish"	VI 83; VII 282
גָּוַע	"give" or "give up" (of the spirit)	V 323
דֶּרֶךְ	"road" or "way"	VII 151
הֲוָת	"was" or "became" (Aramaic)	VI 108
הָיָה	"became" (for "was")	V 147; VI 90,91,92
הָיְתָה	"she became"	VII 274
הָרַס	"tear down," "destroy"	VI 117
וּ	"and," "but," etc.	VII 284
חֹשֶׁךְ	"darkness," "pall"	VII 288
יְדוֹן	"remain" (?) LXX	V 71
יוֹם	"day"	VII 294,296
יָצַר	"to fashion"	VI 95
בּוּן	"to set in order"	VI 95
לְ	preposition	VI 90,91,92
לַיְלָה	"nighttime"	VII 288
לָקַח	"take," "seize"	VI 118
מָלֵא	"to fill"	VI 110; VII 314
נָטַשׁ	"to stretch out," "scatter"	VI 118
נָפַל	"fall," "fall upon"	VI 118
נֶפֶשׁ	"soul," "creature"	V 270; VII 307
נָתַץ	"break down," "destroy"	VI 118
עוֹלָם	"age" (of indefinite length)	VI 102; VII 295; IX 35

עָנָה	"a period of time"	V 355
עָשָׂה	"make," "appoint"	VI 95; VII 283,297
עָתַק	"to transfer"	VII 151
פָּנִים	"face(s)" (or any part of the face)	IX 214
פָּרַץ	"demolish," "scatter"	VI 118
צְדִיָא	"was destroyed" (Aramaic)	VI 108
רֵאשָׁנָה	"beginning"	VI 81
רִאשׁוֹן	"beginning," "first"	VI 104
רֵאשִׁית	"first—"	VI 78,81; VII 280
רָחַף	"flutter over," "hover over"	VII 292
שָׁחַת	"break in pieces," "devastate"	VI 118
שָׁפֵל	"fall" or "sink down," "humble"	VI 118
תֵּבֵל	"world"	IX 16
תְּהוֹם	"the deep," "the confusion"	VI 93
תֹּהוּ	"ruin," "without form"	VI 92,95
תֹּהוּ וָבֹהוּ	"a ruin and a desolation" or "without form and void"	VI 92
תְּחִלָּה	"beginning," "commencement"	VI 83

Hebrew words (in transliteration) using the Young's Concordance system of representation

'adhāmāh	"soil," "ground"	**IX** 15
'asah	"make," "appoint"	**VI** 95,116f.; **VII** 283,297,305
bārā	"create," "put final touches to," "polish," "finish"	**VI** 83,116,117; **VII** 282,283,298
bōhu	"desolation," "void"	**VI** 93f.; **VII** 287
chōshek	"darkness," "pall"	**VII** 288
'echād	"one," "number one"	**VI** 104
'Elohim	"God," or "gods"	**VII** 281,292
'eretz	"land," "earth"	**IX** 15
gāva'	"give" or "give up" (of the spirit)	**V** 323
hāras	"to tear down," "destroy"	**VI** 117
hawāth	"was" or "became" (Aramaic)	**VI** 108
hāyāh	"became" (for "was")	**VI** 90f.; **VII** 285,304
'ish	"man"	**V** 147
'ishāh	"woman"	**V** 147
kūn	"set in order"	**VI** 95; **VII** 298
lāmedh	preposition	**VI** 90,91,92
lāqach	"take," "seize"	**VI** 118
lāyelāh	"nighttime"	**VII** 288
māle'	"to fill"	**VI** 110; **VII** 314
min	"kind," "akin to"	**VII** 303
nāphal	"fall," "fall upon"	**VI** 118
nātash	"stretch out," "scatter"	**VI** 118

nāthatz	"break down," "destroy"	**VI** 118
nephesh	"soul," "creature"	**V** 270; **VII** 307
'olam	"age" (of indefinite length)	**VI** 102; **VII** 295; **IX** 35
'onāh	"a period of time"	**V** 355
pāratz	"demolish," "scatter"	**VI** 118
rāchaph	"hover over," "flutter over"	**VII** 292
rēshith	"first—"	**VI** 78,81; **VII** 280,281
rishōnāh	"first"	**VI** 81
rosh	"head of," "beginning," "very first"	**VI** 81,83
sātam	"lurk for," "waylay"	**VI** 118
shāchath	"break in pieces," "devastate"	**VI** 118
shāphēl	"fall" or "sink down," "humble"	**VI** 118
tēbēl	"world"	**IX** 16
techillāh	"beginning," "commencement"	**VI** 81,83
tehōm	"the deep," "the confusion"	**VI** 93,94; **VII** 288,289
tōhu	"ruin," "without form"	**VI** 93,95; **VII** 287,298
tōhu va bōhu	"a ruin and a desolation" or "without form and void"	**VI** 92; **VII** 287
tzadhya'	"cut," "lay waste" (Aramaic)	**VI** 108

waw	"and," "but," etc.	**VI** 87,88,89,91; **VII** 284
yātzar	"to fashion"	**VI** 95; **VII** 298
yōm	"day"	**VI** 101,115; **VII** 294,296

Greek words (in Greek characters)

ἄβυσσος	"abyss"	**VI** 94
ἀκατασκεύαστος -	"unfinished," "unpolished," "rough" (LXX)	**VI** 94
ἀκαταστασίας	"ruin," "chaos"	**VI** 84
ἁμαρτία	as "a condition of sinfulness"	**V** 329
ἀντί	"for," i.e., "instead of"	**V** 164
ἀρχή	"beginning"	**VI** 88,98
ἀφίημι	"to breathe out," i.e., "expire"	**V** 322,323
βάλλω	"throw"	**VI** 99
εἰς τὸν αἰῶνα	"indefinitely"	**V** 71
ἐκπνέω	"to breathe out," "expire"	**V** 322,323
ἐκψύχω	to be "ex-souled"	**V** 320
ἐπιφερω	"to bear upon," "to bring to bear upon"	**VII** 293
θεμέλιος	"foundation"	**VI** 98,99
και	"and," "but," "however," etc.	**VI** 88
καταβαλλω	"cast down," "throw down," and so "to found"	**VI** 99,100
καταβολη	"disruption," or "foundation"	**VI** 100
καταμένω	"remain"	**V** 71
κόσμος	"world," "order," "ornament"	**VI** 84,98,100

κτίζω	"to create," "frame"	**VI** 88
κτίσις	"creation," "creature"	**VI** 98
λόγος	"word," "argument"	**VI** 100
νυχθήμερον	"a night and a day"	**VI** 102
πάντα vs. τὰ πάντα	"anything" vs. "the whole"	**V** 231; **VI** 124,125
παραδίδωμι	"to hand over voluntarily without compulsion"	**V** 322,324,379
ποιέω	"do" or "make"	**V** 328; **VI** 88
πρόσωπον	"face"	**IX** 214 (fn. 2)
πύργος	"tower"	**VI** 199; **VII** 207
ψυχη	"soul"	**V** 271

Greek words in transliteration

'abussos	"abyss"	**VI** 94; **VII** 289
'akataskeuastos	"unfinished," "unpolished," "rough" (LXX)	**VI** 94
'akatastasias	"chaos," "ruin"	**VI** 84
'anamartētos	"without sin," "sinless"	**III** 302
'anēr	"man"	**VI** 204
'aphiēmi	"to breathe out," "expire"	**V** 322
'archē	"beginning"	**VI** 83,98
ballō	"throw"	**VI** 99
chōris	"apart from"	**III** 302,310
cosmos	see under *kosmos*	
'ekpneo	"to breathe out," "expire"	**V** 322, 323
'ekpsuchō	"to be ex-souled"	**V** 320,323
'epipherō	"to bear upon"	**VII** 292

'epithumia	"lust," "concupiscence," "craving," "passion"	III 308
gunē	"woman"	VI 204
'amartia (hamartia)	as "a condition of sinfulness"	V 329
kai	"and," "but," "however," etc.	VI 88,89; VII 284
kataballō	"cast down," "thrown down," and so "to found"	VI 99,117,118
katabolē	"foundation" or "disruption"?	VI 98,99,117,118
katartizō	"to make perfect"	VI 84
kosmos	"world," "order," "ornament"	VI 84,98,100; VII 283
ktisis	"creation"	VI 98
metanoia	"change of mind"	III 313
nuchthēmeron	"a night and a day"	VI 102
panta vs. ta panta	"anything" vs. "the whole," "the universe"	V 231; VI 124,125
paradidōmi	"hand over voluntarily without compulsion"	V 320,322,324,330
pelagos	"the open sea"	I 117
poieō	"do" or "make"	V 328
pros	"with regard to"	V 231 (fn. 1)
psuchē	"soul"	V 271
purgos	"tower"	VI 199; VII 207
tetelestai!	"it is finished!"	V 330